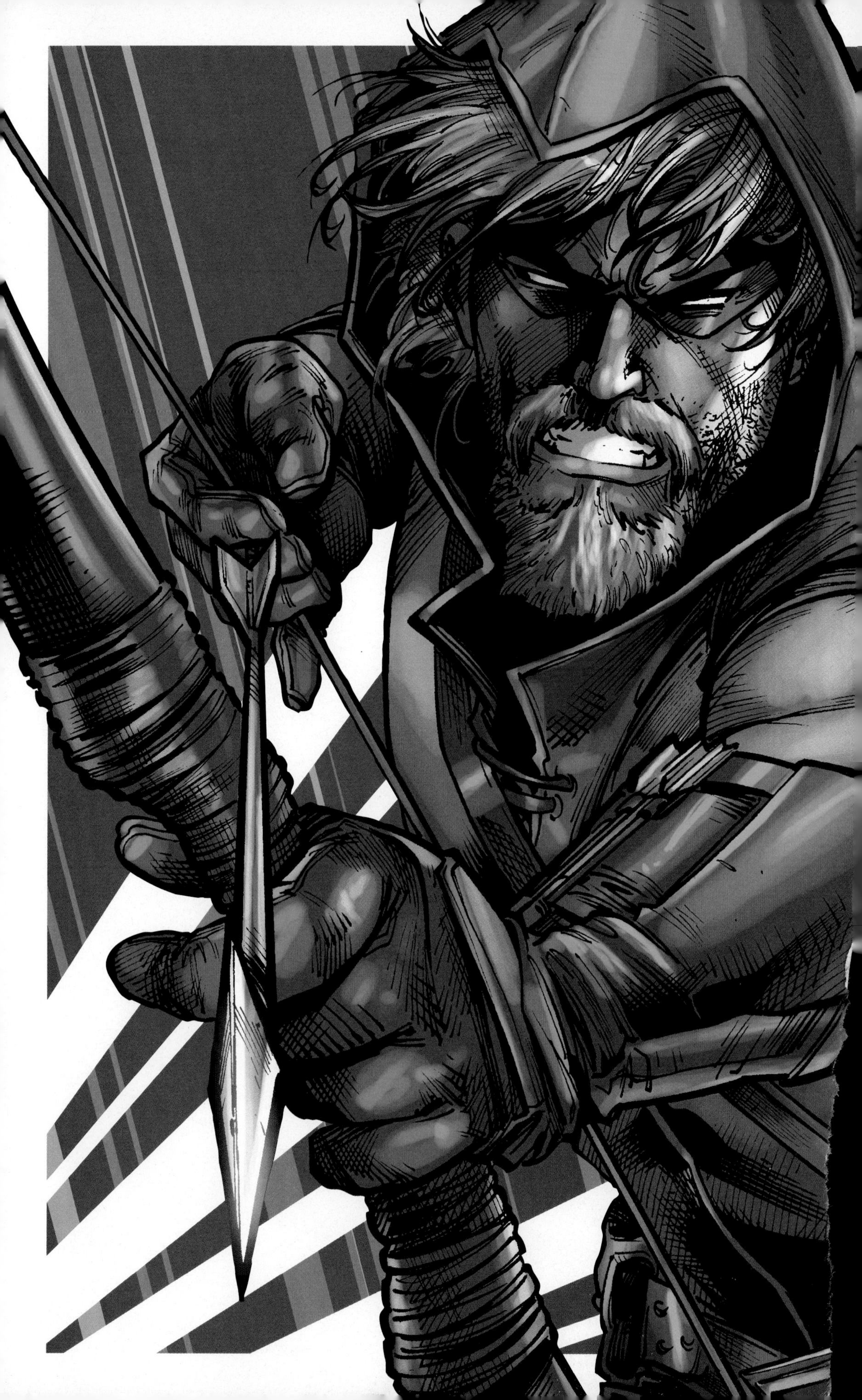

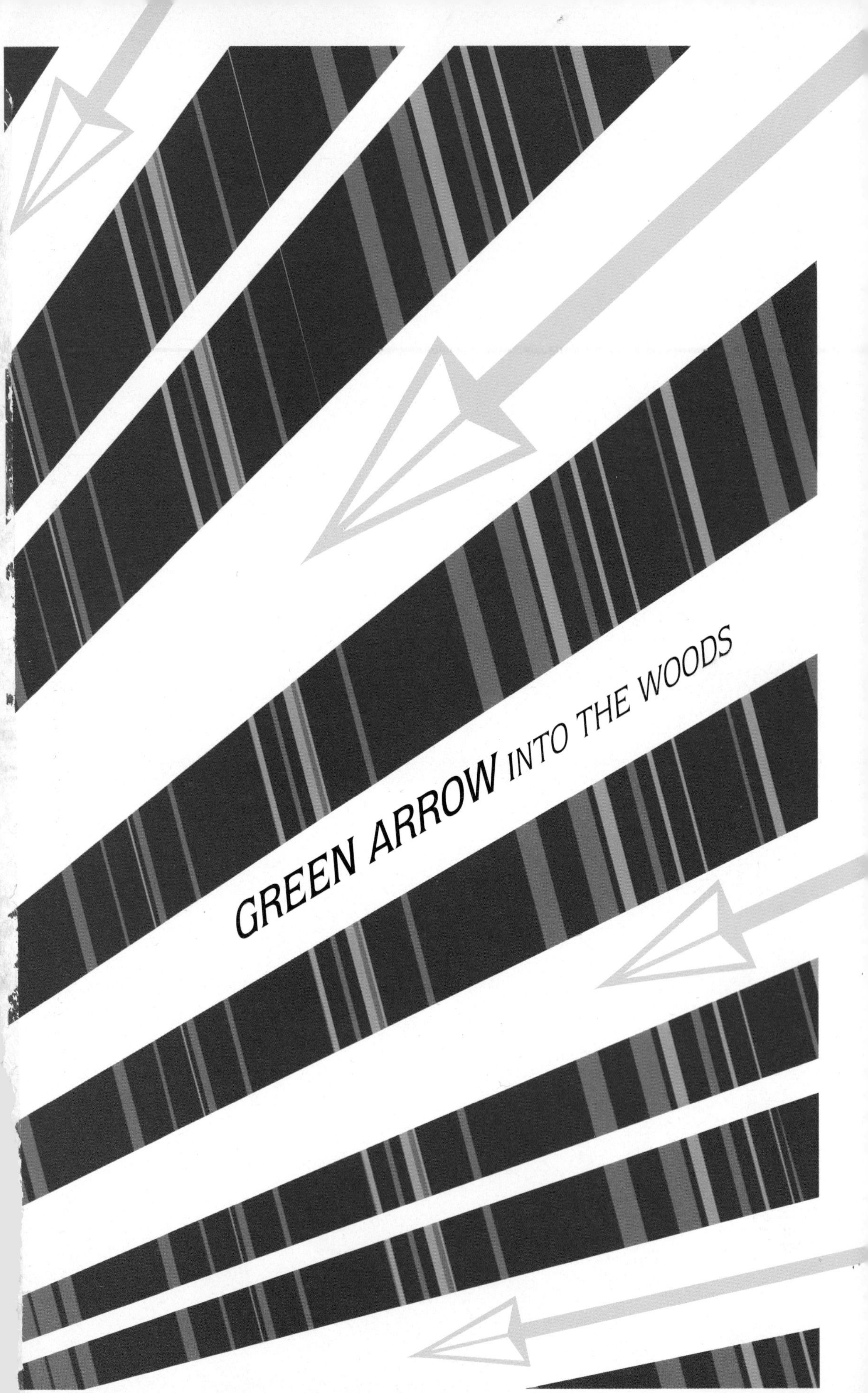
GREEN ARROW INTO THE WOODS

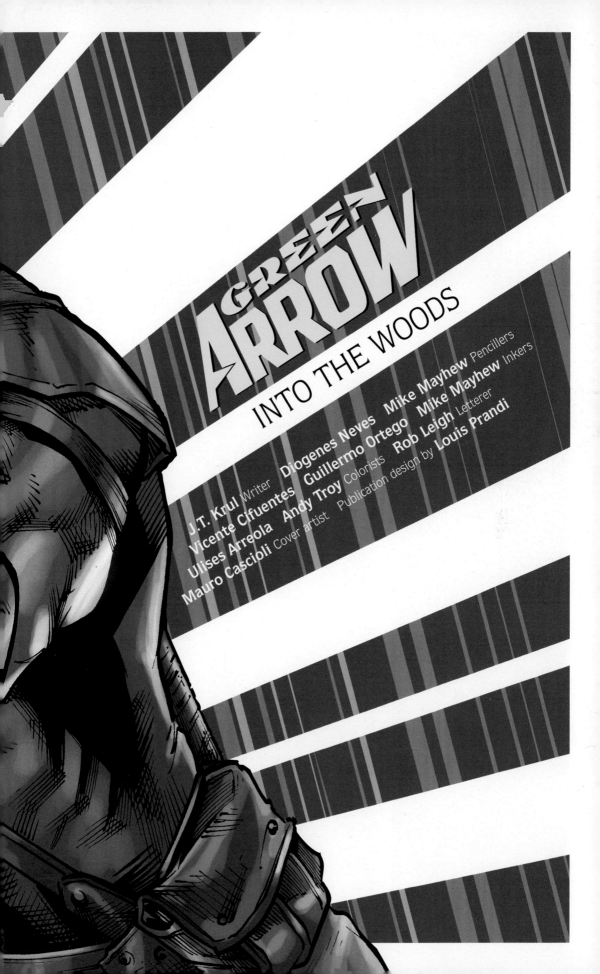

GREEN ARROW

INTO THE WOODS

J.T. Krul Writer   Diogenes Neves   Mike Mayhew Pencillers
Vicente Cifuentes   Guillermo Ortego   Mike Mayhew Inkers
Ulises Arreola   Andy Troy Colorists   Rob Leigh Letterer
Mauro Cascioli Cover artist   Publication design by Louis Prandi

GREEN ARROW: INTO THE WOODS Published by DC Comics. Cover and compilation Copyright © 2011 DC Comics. All Rights Reserved. Originally published in single magazine form in GREEN ARROW 1-7. Copyright © 2010, 2011 DC Comics. All Rights Reserved. All characters, their distinctive likenesses and related elements featured in this publication are trademarks of DC Comics. The stories, characters and incidents featured in this publication are entirely fictional. DC Comics does not read or accept unsolicited submissions of ideas, stories or artwork. DC Comics, 1700 Broadway, New York, NY 10019. A Warner Bros. Entertainment Company. Printed by Quad/Graphics, Versailles, KY, USA. 6/3/11 First printing. ISBN: 978-1-4012-3073-9

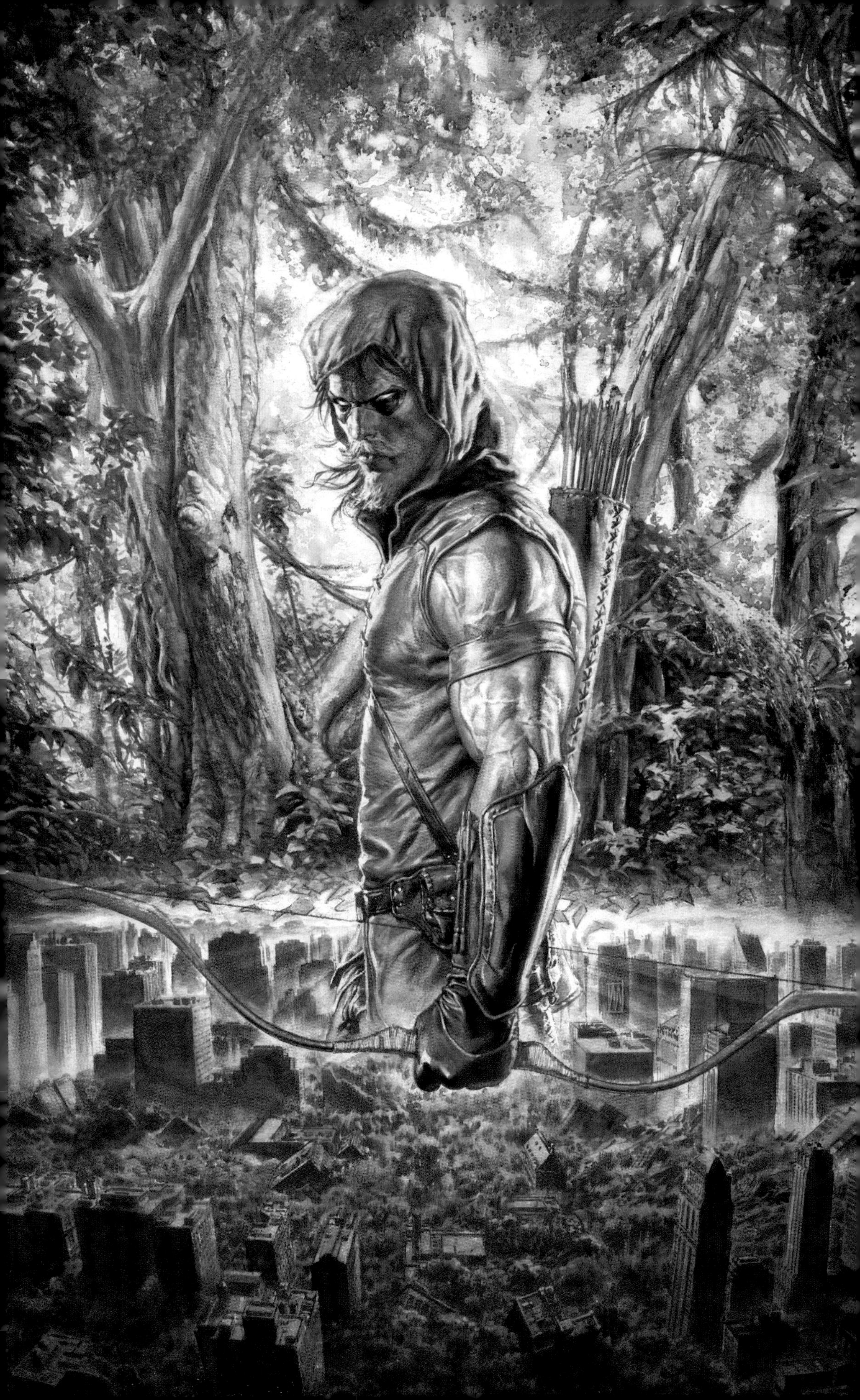

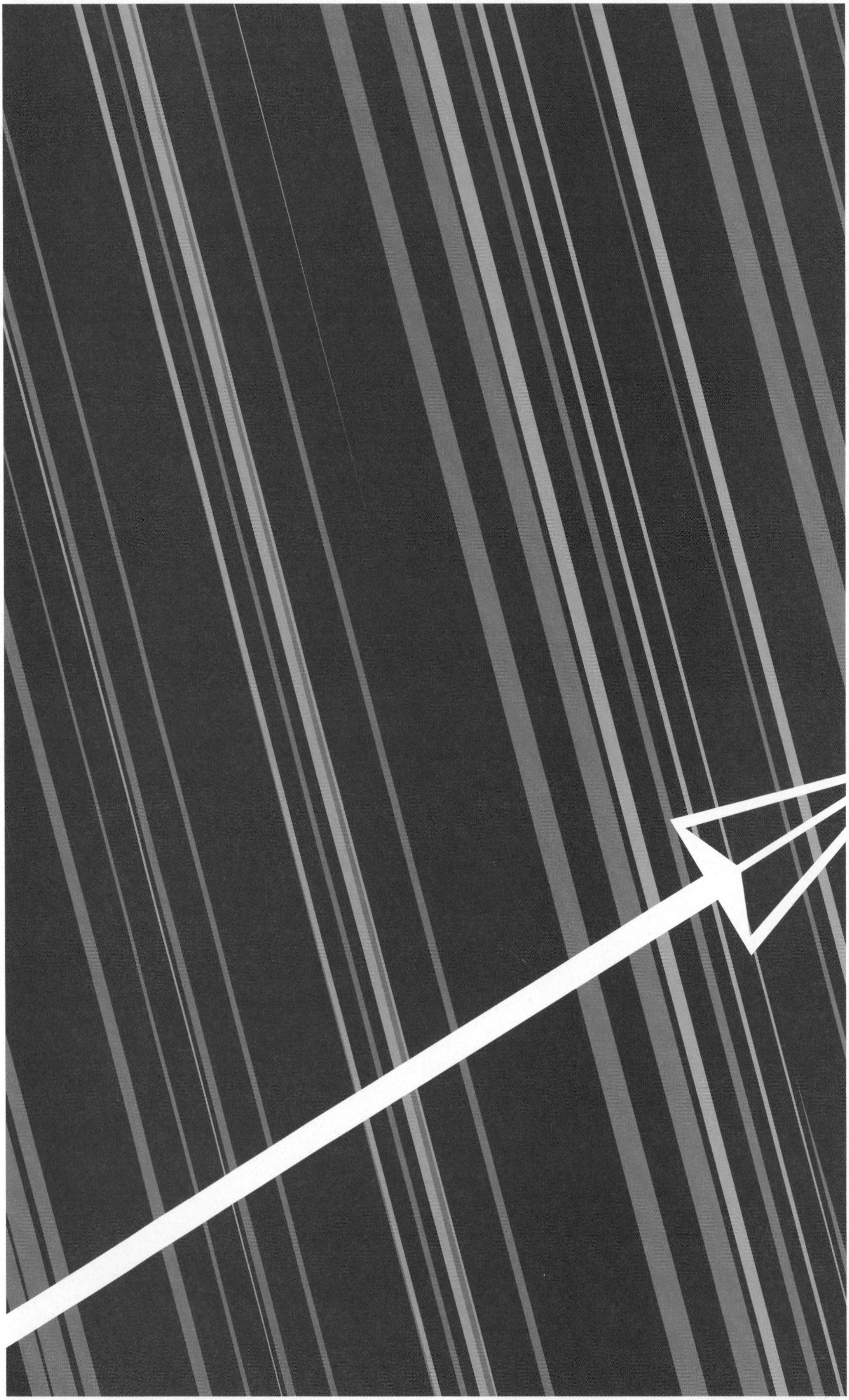

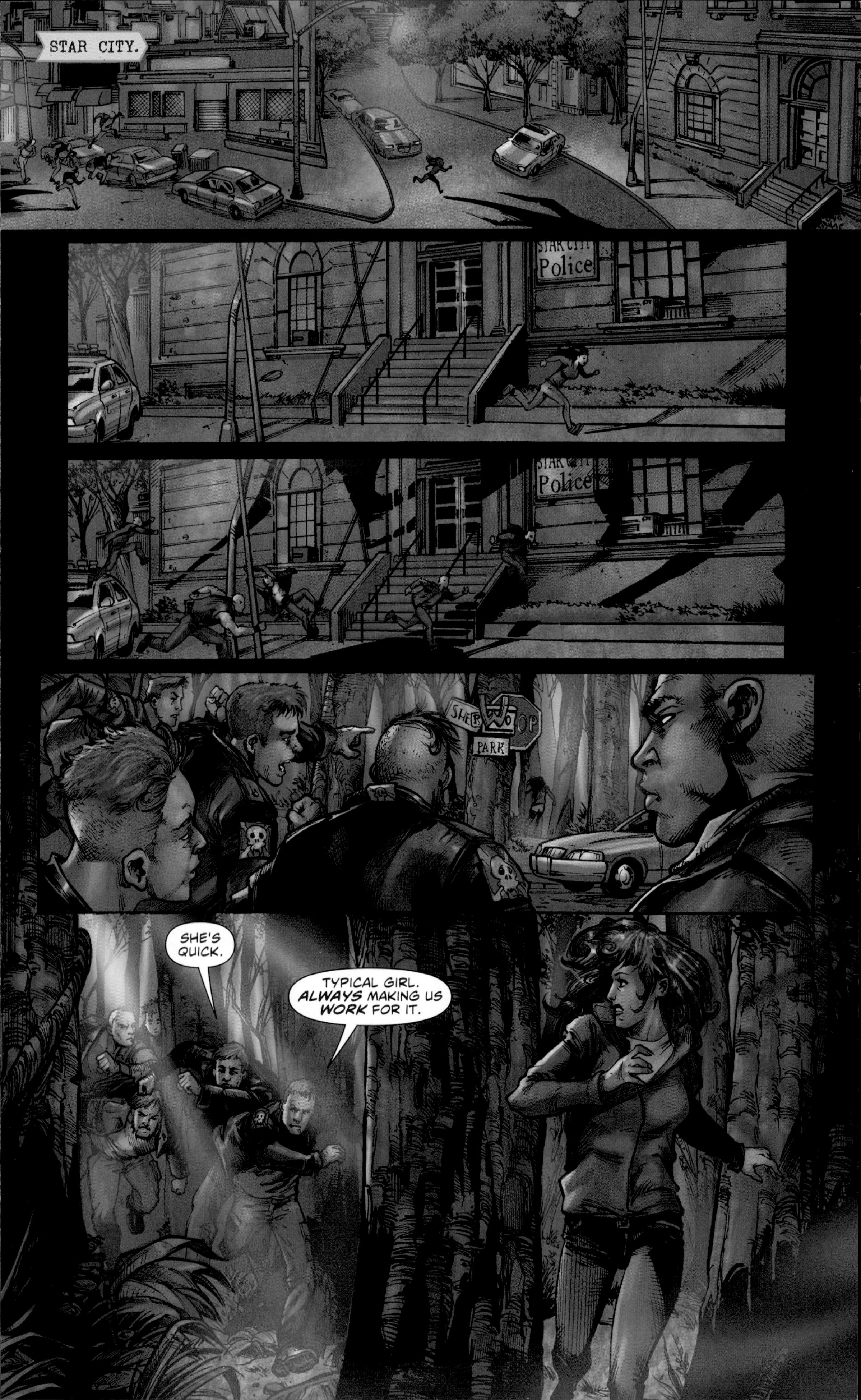
STAR CITY.
STAR CITY Police
STAR CITY Police
PARK
SHE'S QUICK.
TYPICAL GIRL. ALWAYS MAKING US WORK FOR IT.

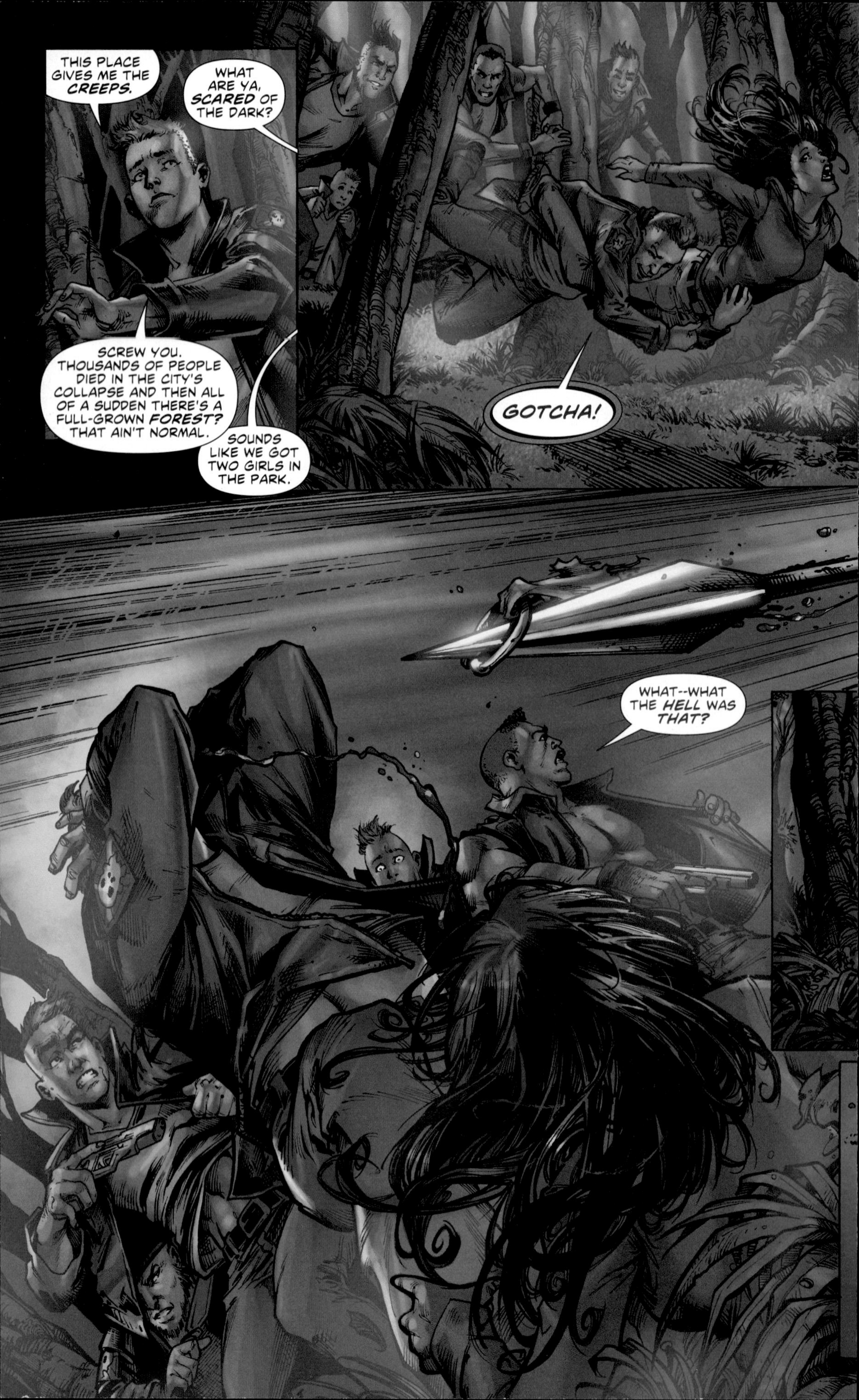
THIS PLACE GIVES ME THE CREEPS.
WHAT ARE YA, SCARED OF THE DARK?
SCREW YOU. THOUSANDS OF PEOPLE DIED IN THE CITY'S COLLAPSE AND THEN ALL OF A SUDDEN THERE'S A FULL-GROWN FOREST? THAT AIN'T NORMAL.
SOUNDS LIKE WE GOT TWO GIRLS IN THE PARK.
GOTCHA!
WHAT--WHAT THE HELL WAS THAT?

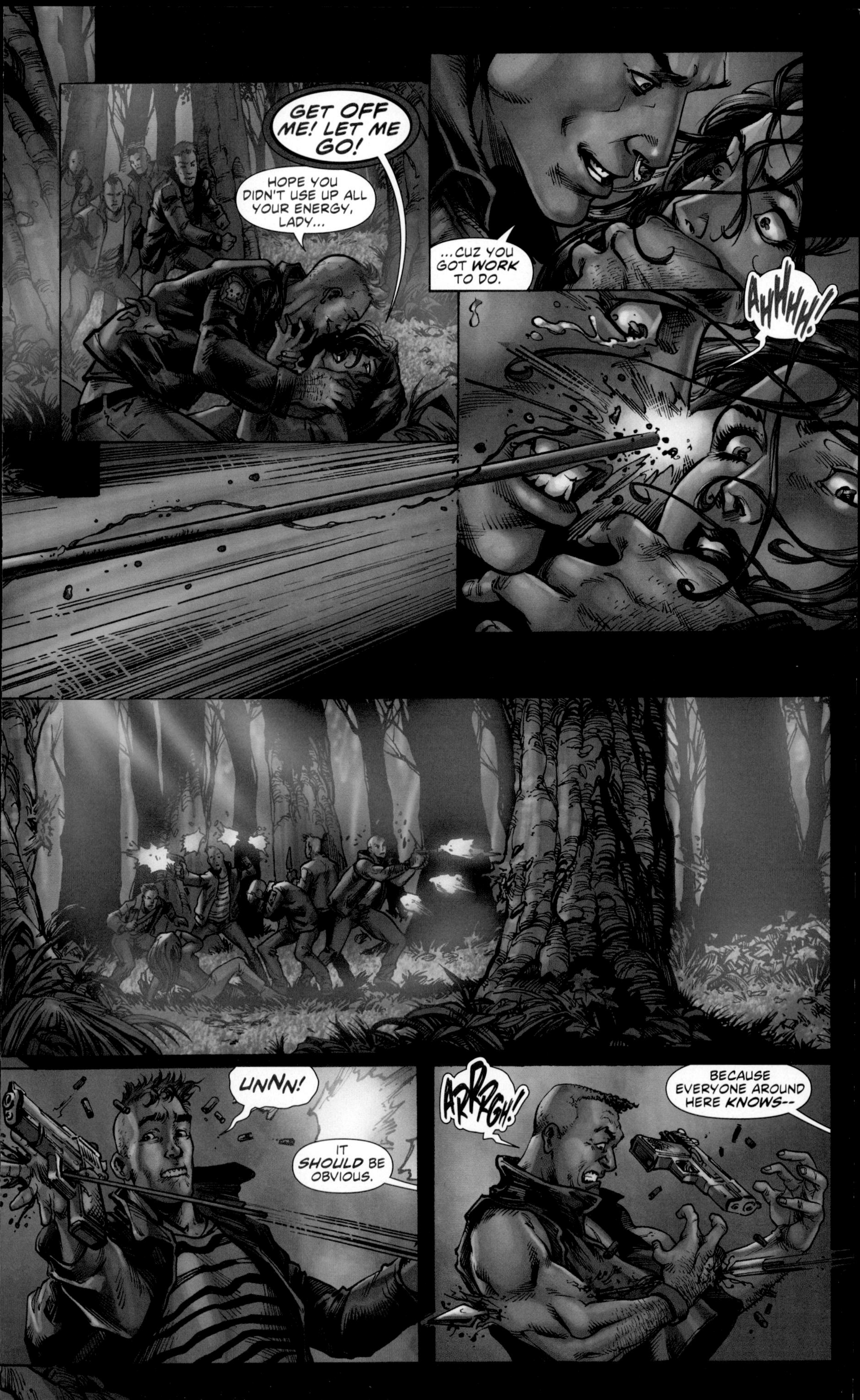
GET OFF ME! LET ME GO!
HOPE YOU DIDN'T USE UP ALL YOUR ENERGY, LADY...
...CUZ YOU GOT WORK TO DO.
AHHHH!
UNNN!
IT SHOULD BE OBVIOUS.
ARRRGH!
BECAUSE EVERYONE AROUND HERE KNOWS--

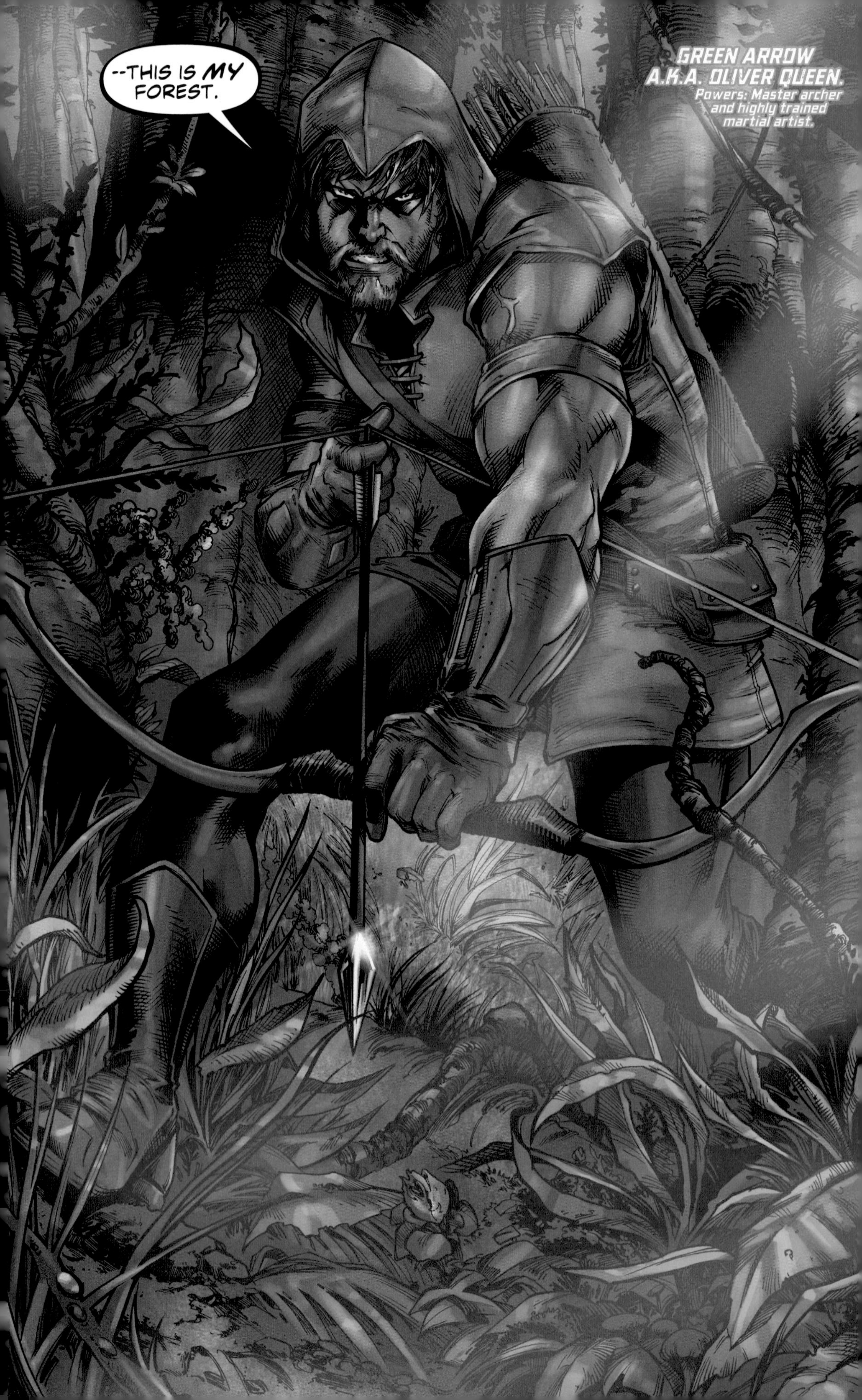
--THIS IS MY FOREST.
GREEN ARROW
A.K.A. OLIVER QUEEN.
Powers: Master archer and highly trained martial artist.

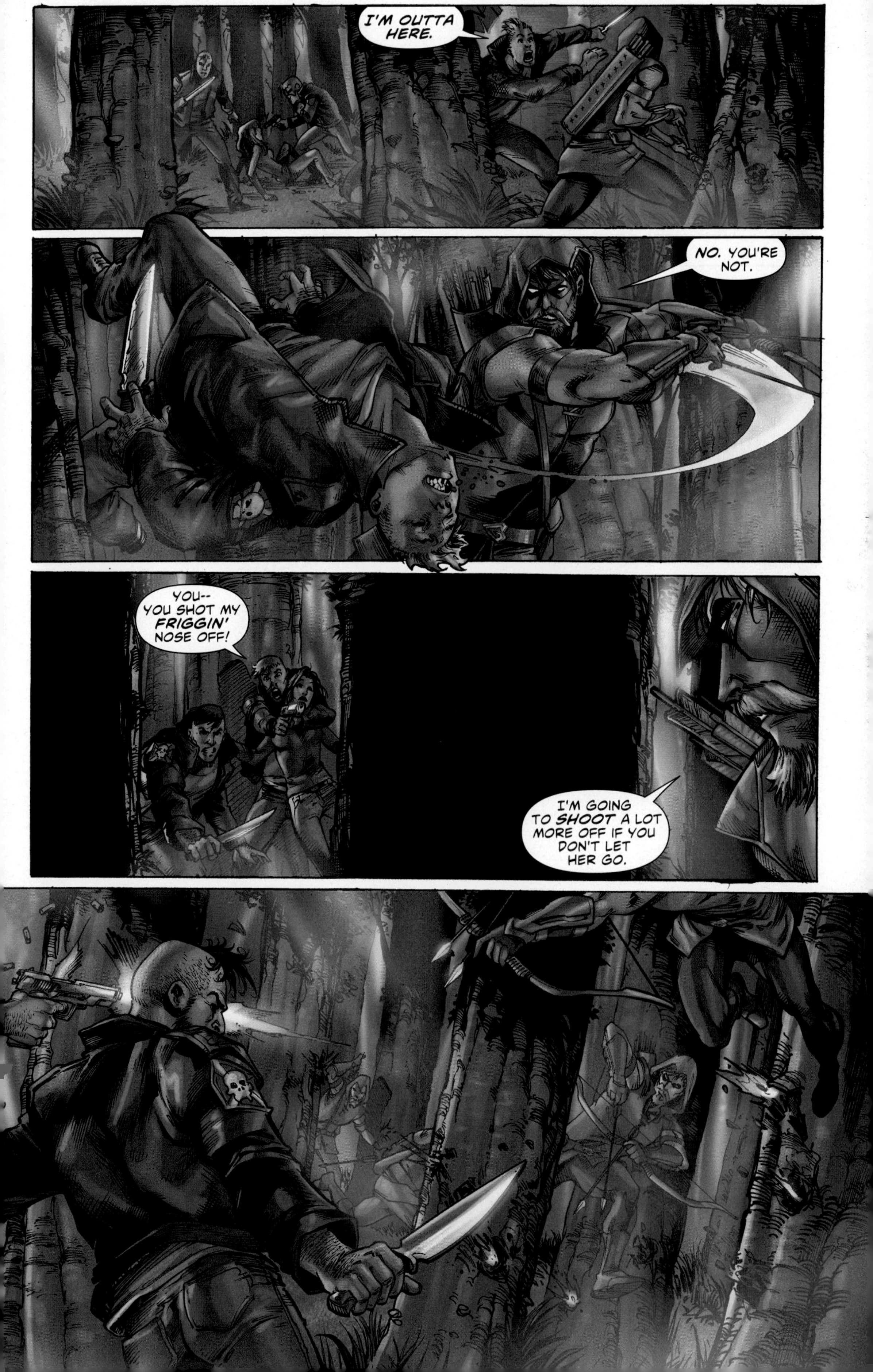
I'M OUTTA HERE.
NO. YOU'RE NOT.
YOU-- YOU SHOT MY FRIGGIN' NOSE OFF!
I'M GOING TO SHOOT A LOT MORE OFF IF YOU DON'T LET HER GO.

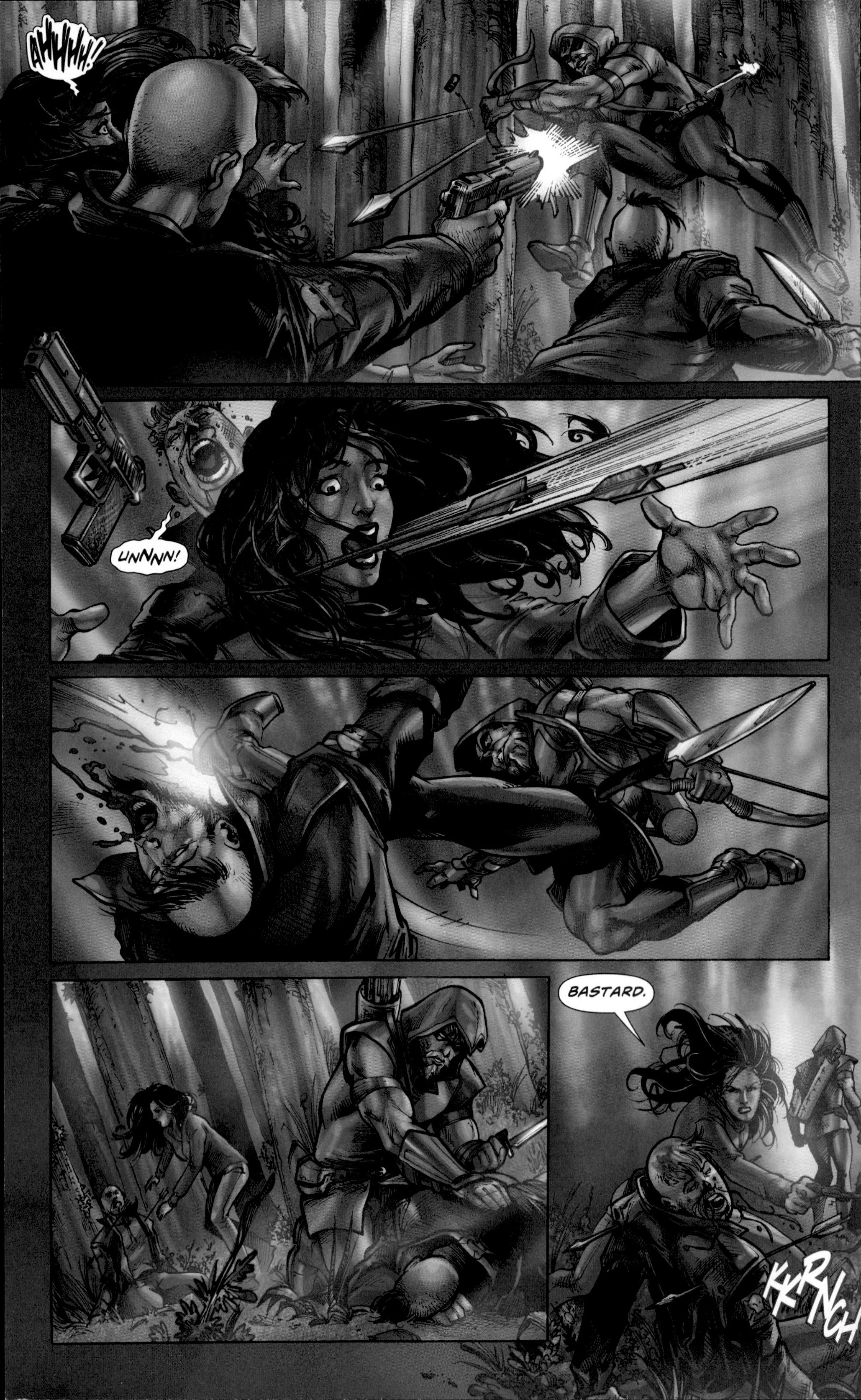
AHHHH!
UNNNN!
BASTARD.
KKRNCH

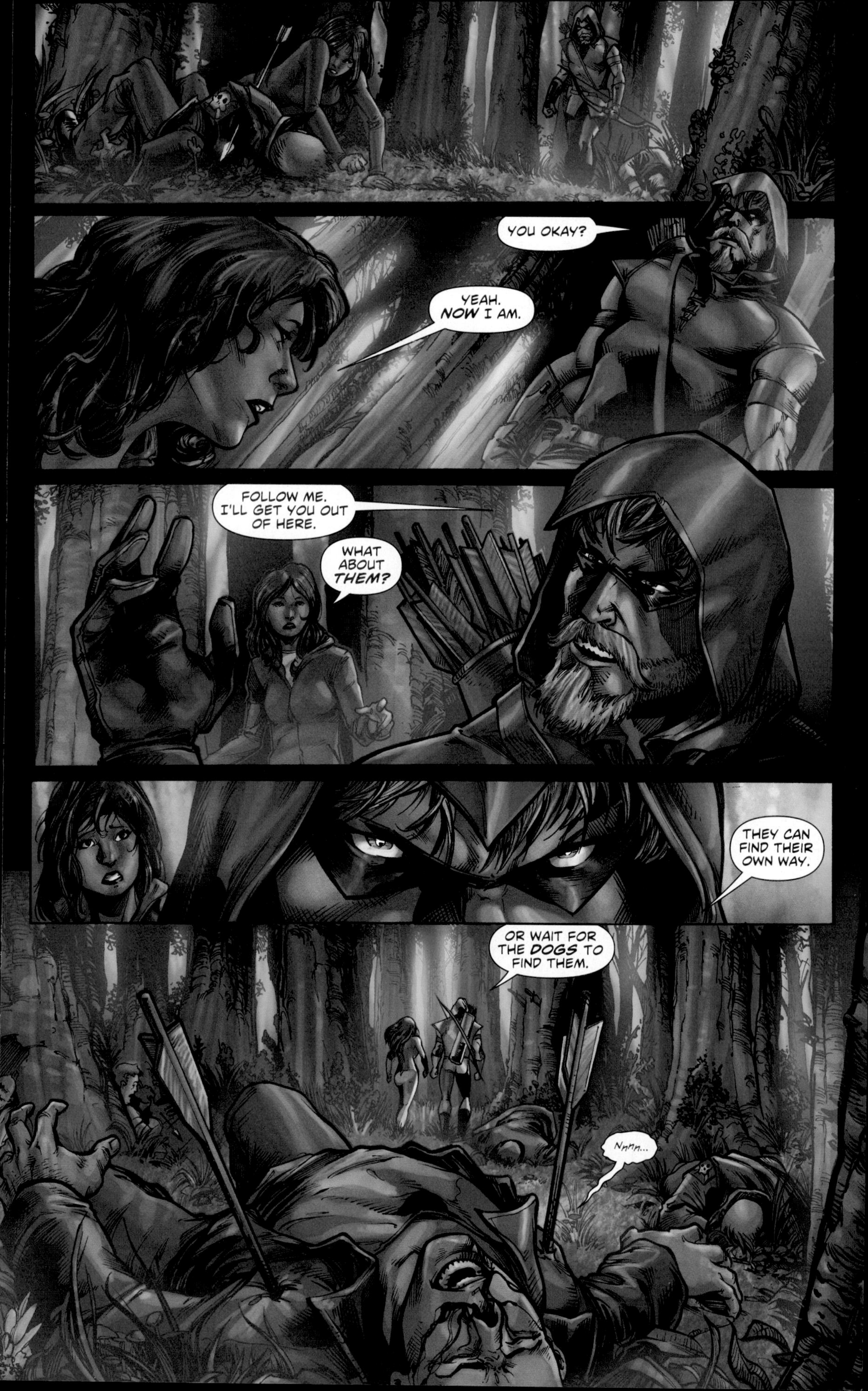
YOU OKAY?
YEAH. NOW I AM.
FOLLOW ME. I'LL GET YOU OUT OF HERE.
WHAT ABOUT THEM?
THEY CAN FIND THEIR OWN WAY.
OR WAIT FOR THE DOGS TO FIND THEM.
Nnnn...

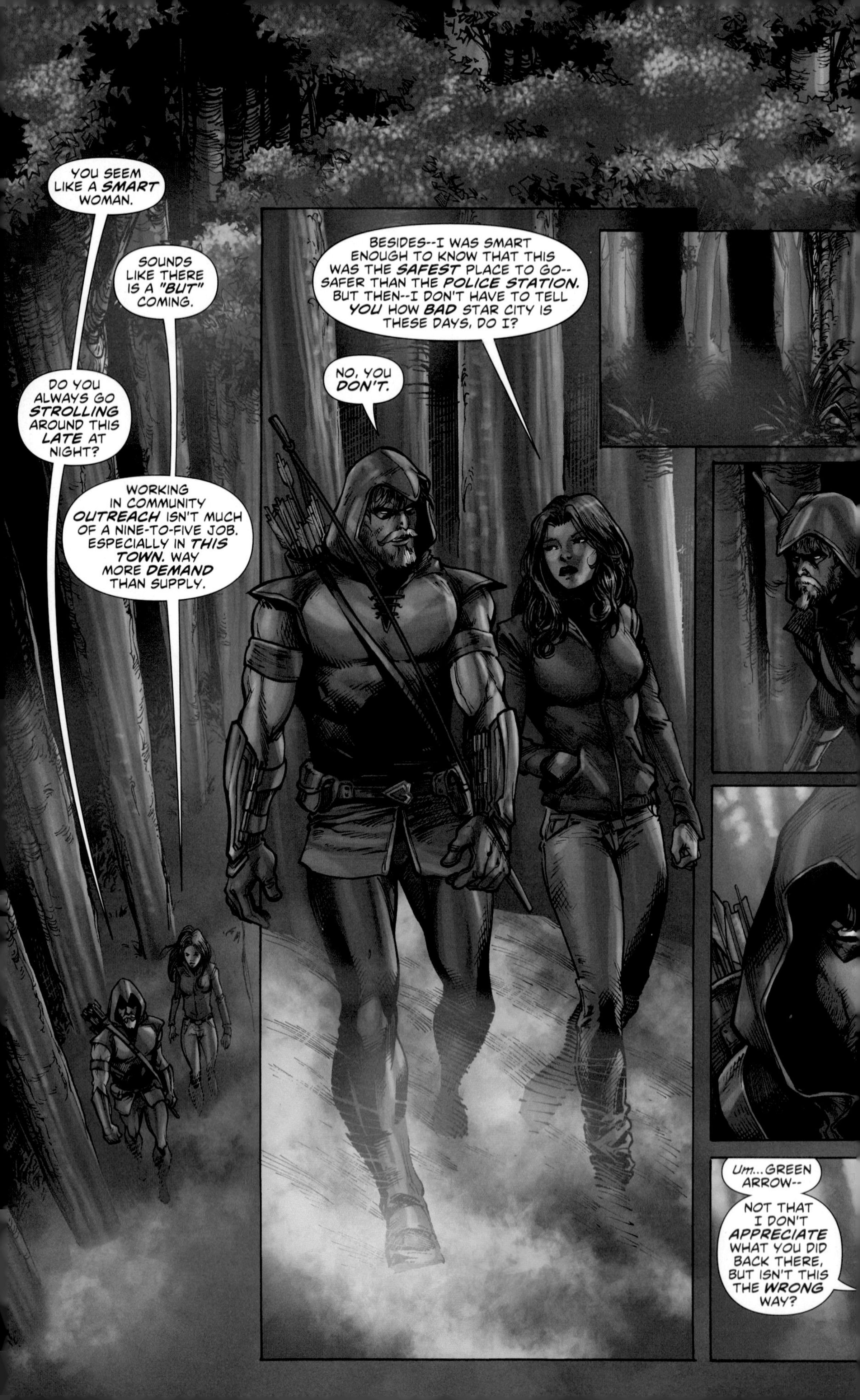
YOU SEEM LIKE A SMART WOMAN.
SOUNDS LIKE THERE IS A "BUT" COMING.
DO YOU ALWAYS GO STROLLING AROUND THIS LATE AT NIGHT?
WORKING IN COMMUNITY OUTREACH ISN'T MUCH OF A NINE-TO-FIVE JOB. ESPECIALLY IN THIS TOWN. WAY MORE DEMAND THAN SUPPLY.
BESIDES--I WAS SMART ENOUGH TO KNOW THAT THIS WAS THE SAFEST PLACE TO GO--SAFER THAN THE POLICE STATION. BUT THEN--I DON'T HAVE TO TELL YOU HOW BAD STAR CITY IS THESE DAYS, DO I?
NO, YOU DON'T.
Um...GREEN ARROW--
NOT THAT I DON'T APPRECIATE WHAT YOU DID BACK THERE, BUT ISN'T THIS THE WRONG WAY?

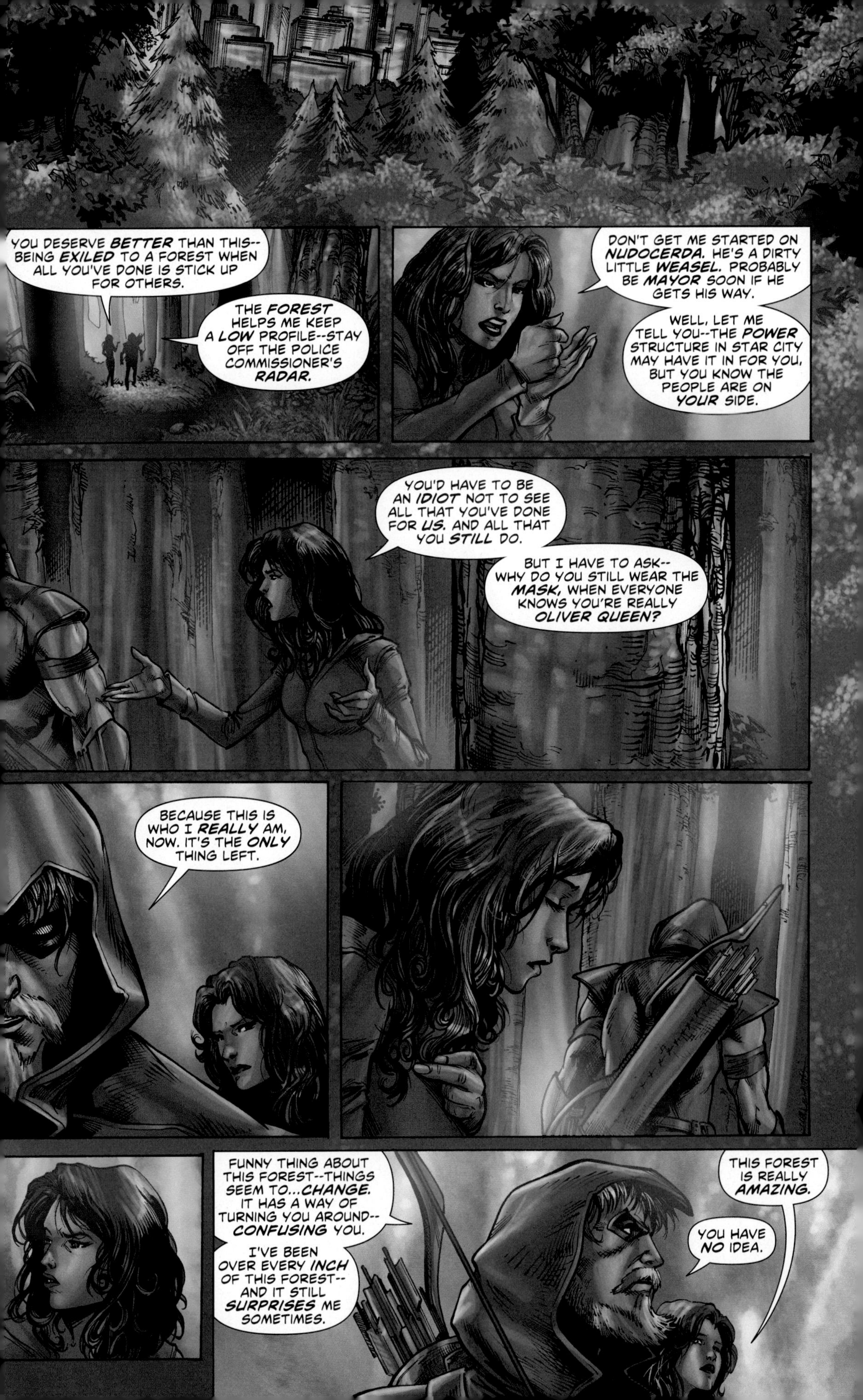

YOU DESERVE BETTER THAN THIS--BEING EXILED TO A FOREST WHEN ALL YOU'VE DONE IS STICK UP FOR OTHERS.
THE FOREST HELPS ME KEEP A LOW PROFILE--STAY OFF THE POLICE COMMISSIONER'S RADAR.
DON'T GET ME STARTED ON NUDOCERDA. HE'S A DIRTY LITTLE WEASEL. PROBABLY BE MAYOR SOON IF HE GETS HIS WAY.
WELL, LET ME TELL YOU--THE POWER STRUCTURE IN STAR CITY MAY HAVE IT IN FOR YOU, BUT YOU KNOW THE PEOPLE ARE ON YOUR SIDE.
YOU'D HAVE TO BE AN IDIOT NOT TO SEE ALL THAT YOU'VE DONE FOR US. AND ALL THAT YOU STILL DO.
BUT I HAVE TO ASK--WHY DO YOU STILL WEAR THE MASK, WHEN EVERYONE KNOWS YOU'RE REALLY OLIVER QUEEN?
BECAUSE THIS IS WHO I REALLY AM, NOW. IT'S THE ONLY THING LEFT.
FUNNY THING ABOUT THIS FOREST--THINGS SEEM TO...CHANGE. IT HAS A WAY OF TURNING YOU AROUND--CONFUSING YOU.
I'VE BEEN OVER EVERY INCH OF THIS FOREST--AND IT STILL SURPRISES ME SOMETIMES.
THIS FOREST IS REALLY AMAZING.
YOU HAVE NO IDEA.

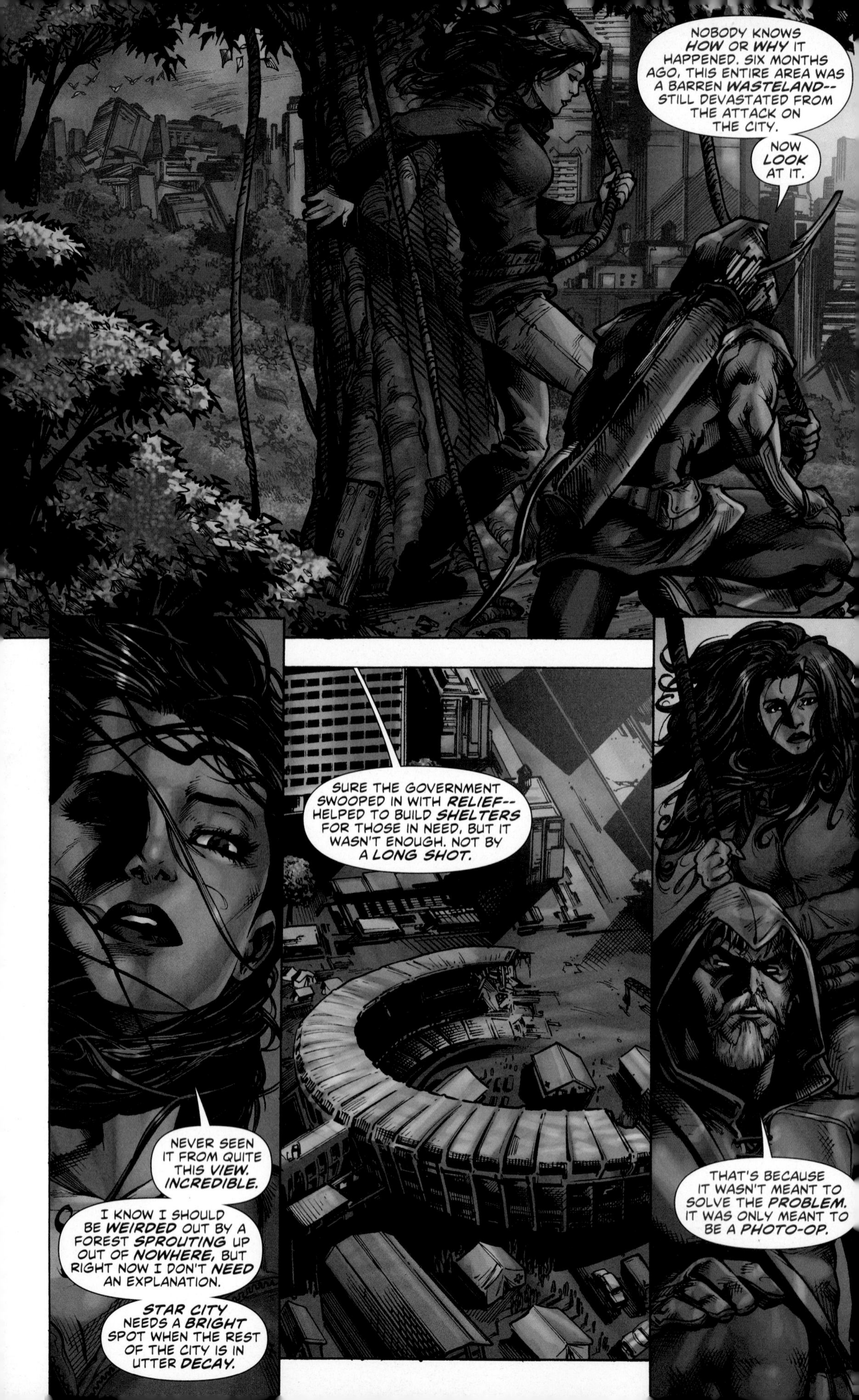
NOBODY KNOWS HOW OR WHY IT HAPPENED. SIX MONTHS AGO, THIS ENTIRE AREA WAS A BARREN WASTELAND-- STILL DEVASTATED FROM THE ATTACK ON THE CITY.
NOW LOOK AT IT.
NEVER SEEN IT FROM QUITE THIS VIEW. INCREDIBLE.
I KNOW I SHOULD BE WEIRDED OUT BY A FOREST SPROUTING UP OUT OF NOWHERE, BUT RIGHT NOW I DON'T NEED AN EXPLANATION.
STAR CITY NEEDS A BRIGHT SPOT WHEN THE REST OF THE CITY IS IN UTTER DECAY.
SURE THE GOVERNMENT SWOOPED IN WITH RELIEF-- HELPED TO BUILD SHELTERS FOR THOSE IN NEED, BUT IT WASN'T ENOUGH. NOT BY A LONG SHOT.
THAT'S BECAUSE IT WASN'T MEANT TO SOLVE THE PROBLEM. IT WAS ONLY MEANT TO BE A PHOTO-OP.

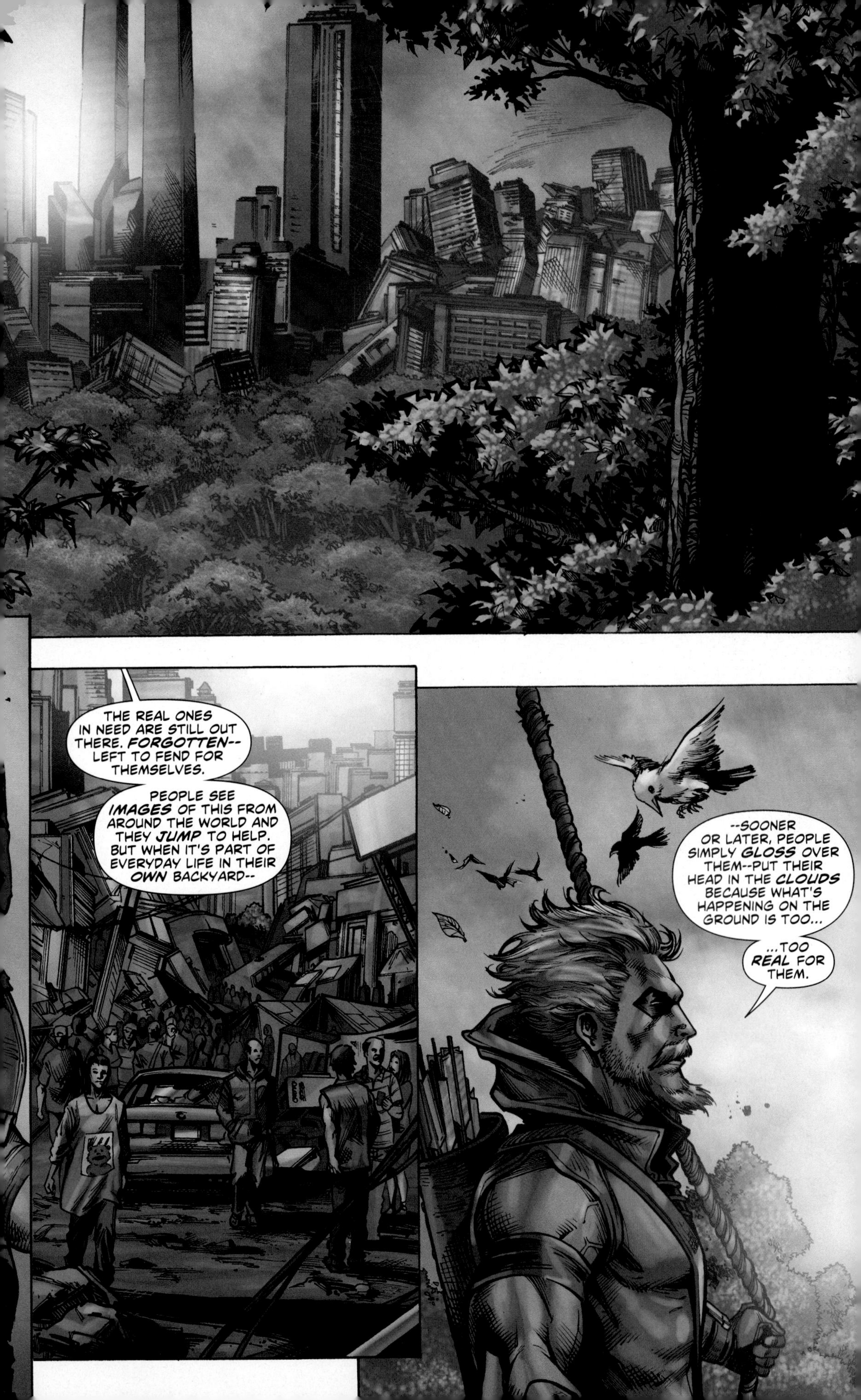
THE REAL ONES IN NEED ARE STILL OUT THERE. FORGOTTEN-- LEFT TO FEND FOR THEMSELVES.
PEOPLE SEE IMAGES OF THIS FROM AROUND THE WORLD AND THEY JUMP TO HELP. BUT WHEN IT'S PART OF EVERYDAY LIFE IN THEIR OWN BACKYARD--
--SOONER OR LATER, PEOPLE SIMPLY GLOSS OVER THEM--PUT THEIR HEAD IN THE CLOUDS BECAUSE WHAT'S HAPPENING ON THE GROUND IS TOO...
...TOO REAL FOR THEM.

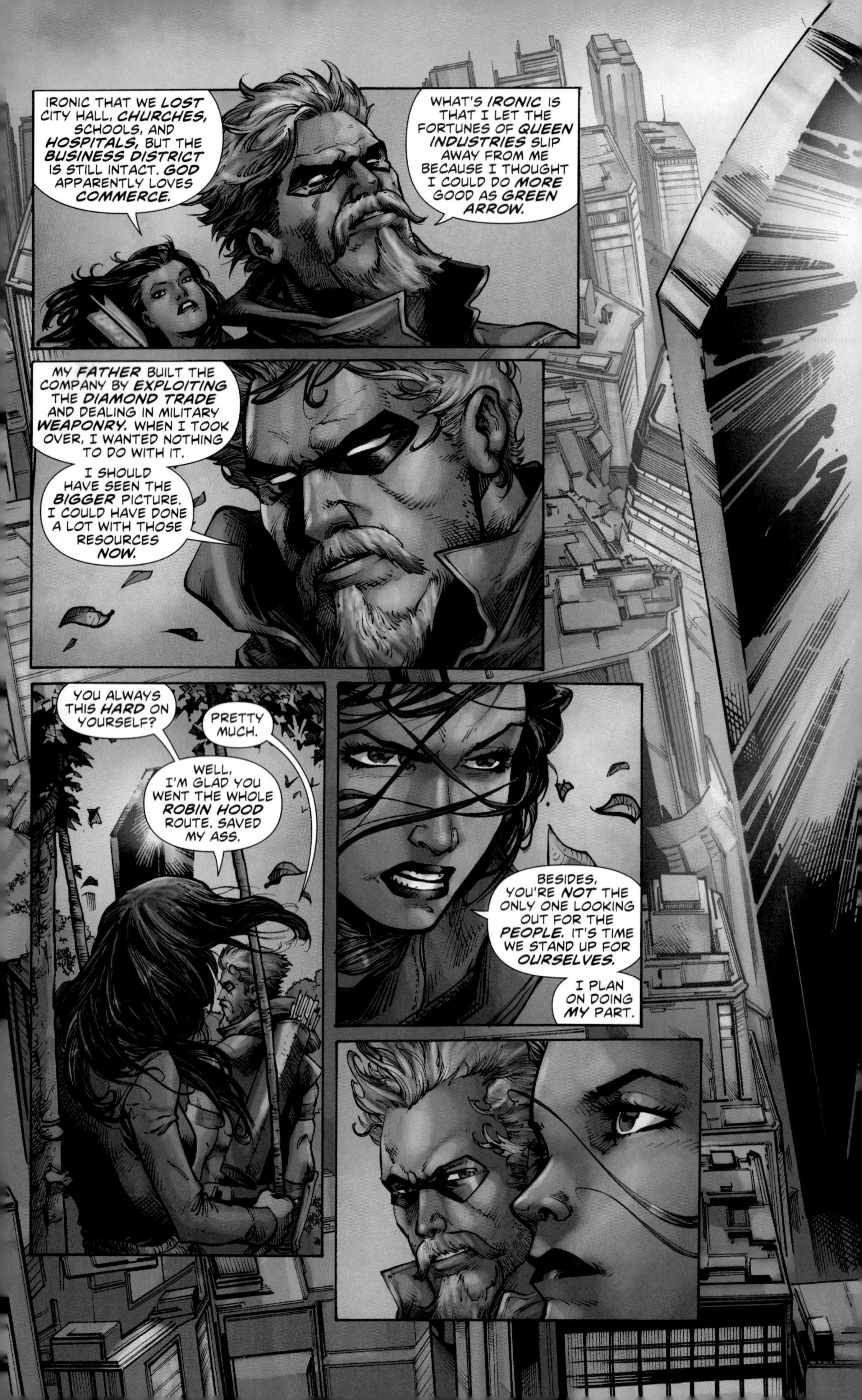
IRONIC THAT WE LOST CITY HALL, CHURCHES, SCHOOLS, AND HOSPITALS, BUT THE BUSINESS DISTRICT IS STILL INTACT. GOD APPARENTLY LOVES COMMERCE.
WHAT'S IRONIC IS THAT I LET THE FORTUNES OF QUEEN INDUSTRIES SLIP AWAY FROM ME BECAUSE I THOUGHT I COULD DO MORE GOOD AS GREEN ARROW.
MY FATHER BUILT THE COMPANY BY EXPLOITING THE DIAMOND TRADE AND DEALING IN MILITARY WEAPONRY. WHEN I TOOK OVER, I WANTED NOTHING TO DO WITH IT.
I SHOULD HAVE SEEN THE BIGGER PICTURE. I COULD HAVE DONE A LOT WITH THOSE RESOURCES NOW.
YOU ALWAYS THIS HARD ON YOURSELF?
PRETTY MUCH.
WELL, I'M GLAD YOU WENT THE WHOLE ROBIN HOOD ROUTE. SAVED MY ASS.
BESIDES, YOU'RE NOT THE ONLY ONE LOOKING OUT FOR THE PEOPLE. IT'S TIME WE STAND UP FOR OURSELVES.
I PLAN ON DOING MY PART.

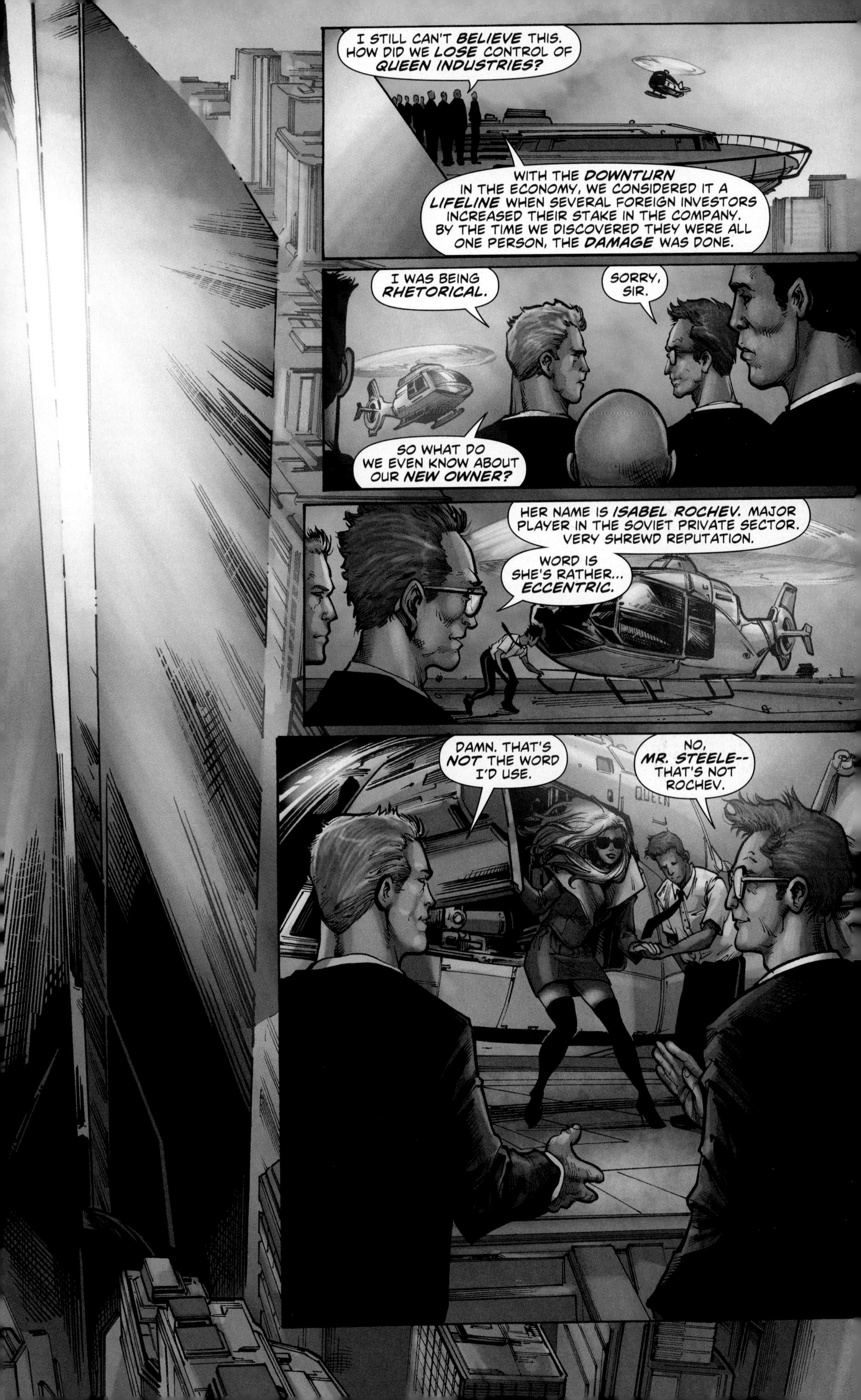
I STILL CAN'T BELIEVE THIS. HOW DID WE LOSE CONTROL OF QUEEN INDUSTRIES?
WITH THE DOWNTURN IN THE ECONOMY, WE CONSIDERED IT A LIFELINE WHEN SEVERAL FOREIGN INVESTORS INCREASED THEIR STAKE IN THE COMPANY. BY THE TIME WE DISCOVERED THEY WERE ALL ONE PERSON, THE DAMAGE WAS DONE.
I WAS BEING RHETORICAL.
SORRY, SIR.
SO WHAT DO WE EVEN KNOW ABOUT OUR NEW OWNER?
HER NAME IS ISABEL ROCHEV. MAJOR PLAYER IN THE SOVIET PRIVATE SECTOR. VERY SHREWD REPUTATION.
WORD IS SHE'S RATHER... ECCENTRIC.
DAMN. THAT'S NOT THE WORD I'D USE.
NO, MR. STEELE-- THAT'S NOT ROCHEV.
QUEEN

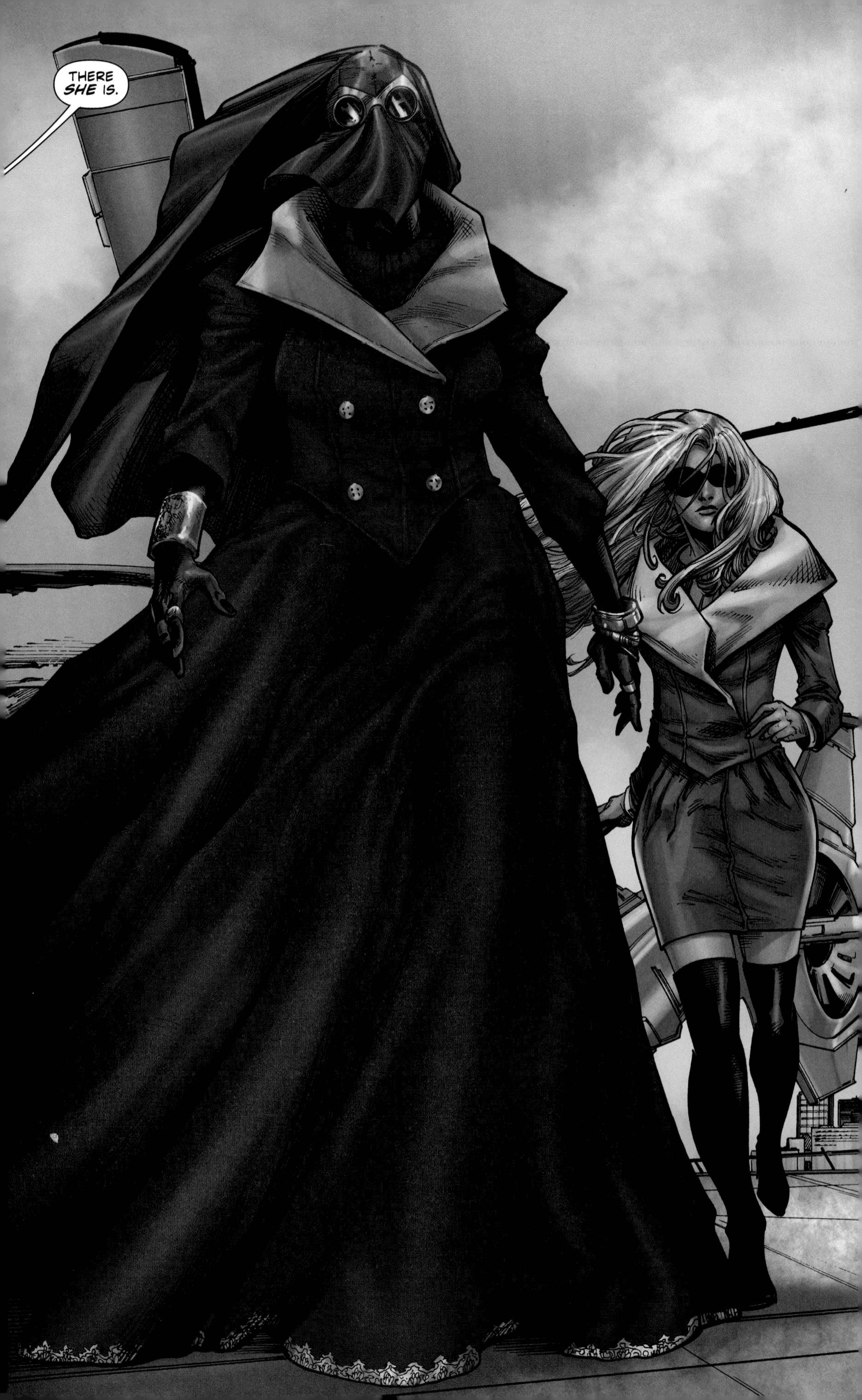
THERE *SHE* IS.

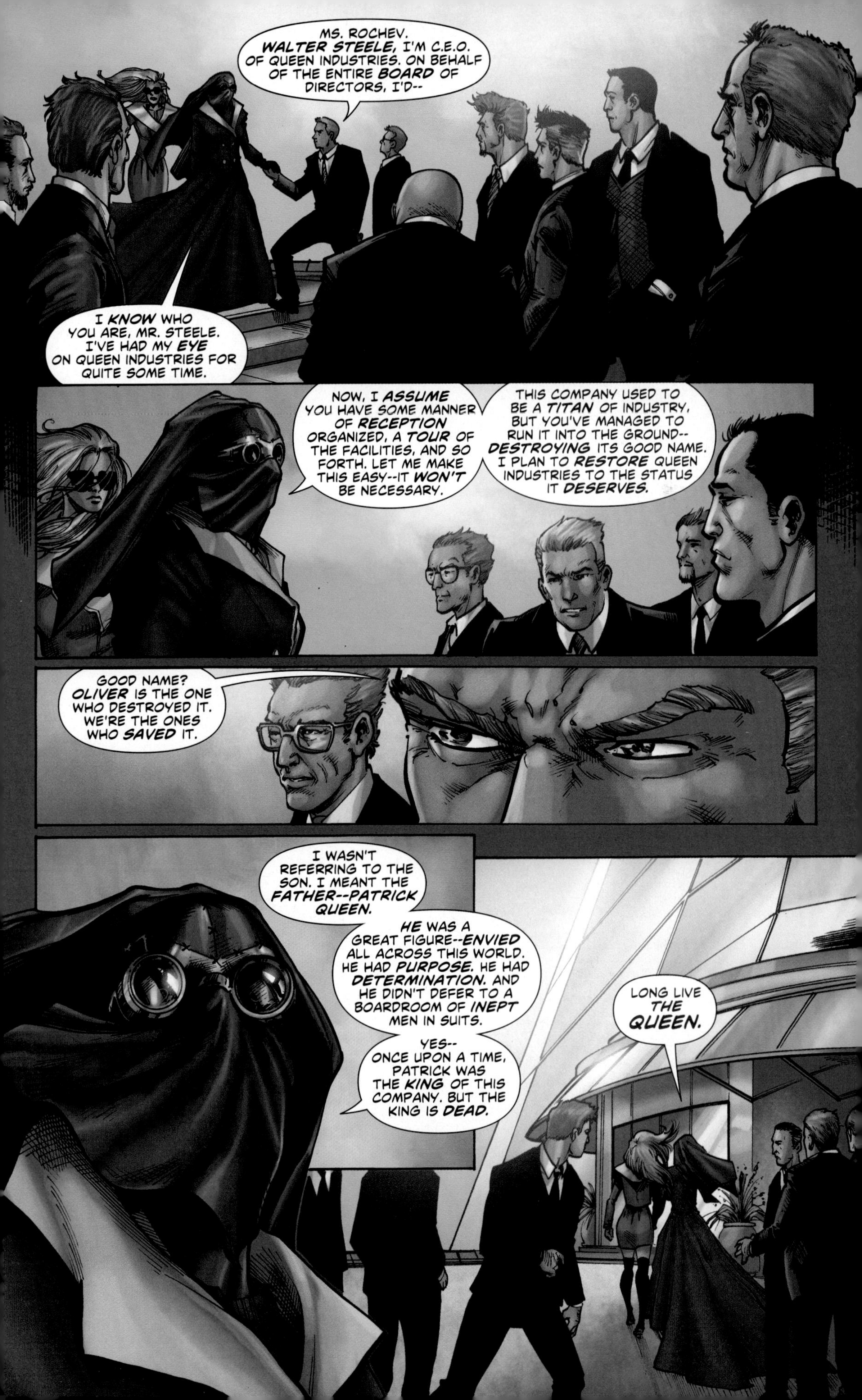
MS. ROCHEV. WALTER STEELE, I'M C.E.O. OF QUEEN INDUSTRIES. ON BEHALF OF THE ENTIRE BOARD OF DIRECTORS, I'D--
I KNOW WHO YOU ARE, MR. STEELE. I'VE HAD MY EYE ON QUEEN INDUSTRIES FOR QUITE SOME TIME.
NOW, I ASSUME YOU HAVE SOME MANNER OF RECEPTION ORGANIZED, A TOUR OF THE FACILITIES, AND SO FORTH. LET ME MAKE THIS EASY--IT WON'T BE NECESSARY.
THIS COMPANY USED TO BE A TITAN OF INDUSTRY, BUT YOU'VE MANAGED TO RUN IT INTO THE GROUND--DESTROYING ITS GOOD NAME. I PLAN TO RESTORE QUEEN INDUSTRIES TO THE STATUS IT DESERVES.
GOOD NAME? OLIVER IS THE ONE WHO DESTROYED IT. WE'RE THE ONES WHO SAVED IT.
I WASN'T REFERRING TO THE SON. I MEANT THE FATHER--PATRICK QUEEN.
HE WAS A GREAT FIGURE--ENVIED ALL ACROSS THIS WORLD. HE HAD PURPOSE. HE HAD DETERMINATION. AND HE DIDN'T DEFER TO A BOARDROOM OF INEPT MEN IN SUITS.
YES-- ONCE UPON A TIME, PATRICK WAS THE KING OF THIS COMPANY. BUT THE KING IS DEAD.
LONG LIVE THE QUEEN.

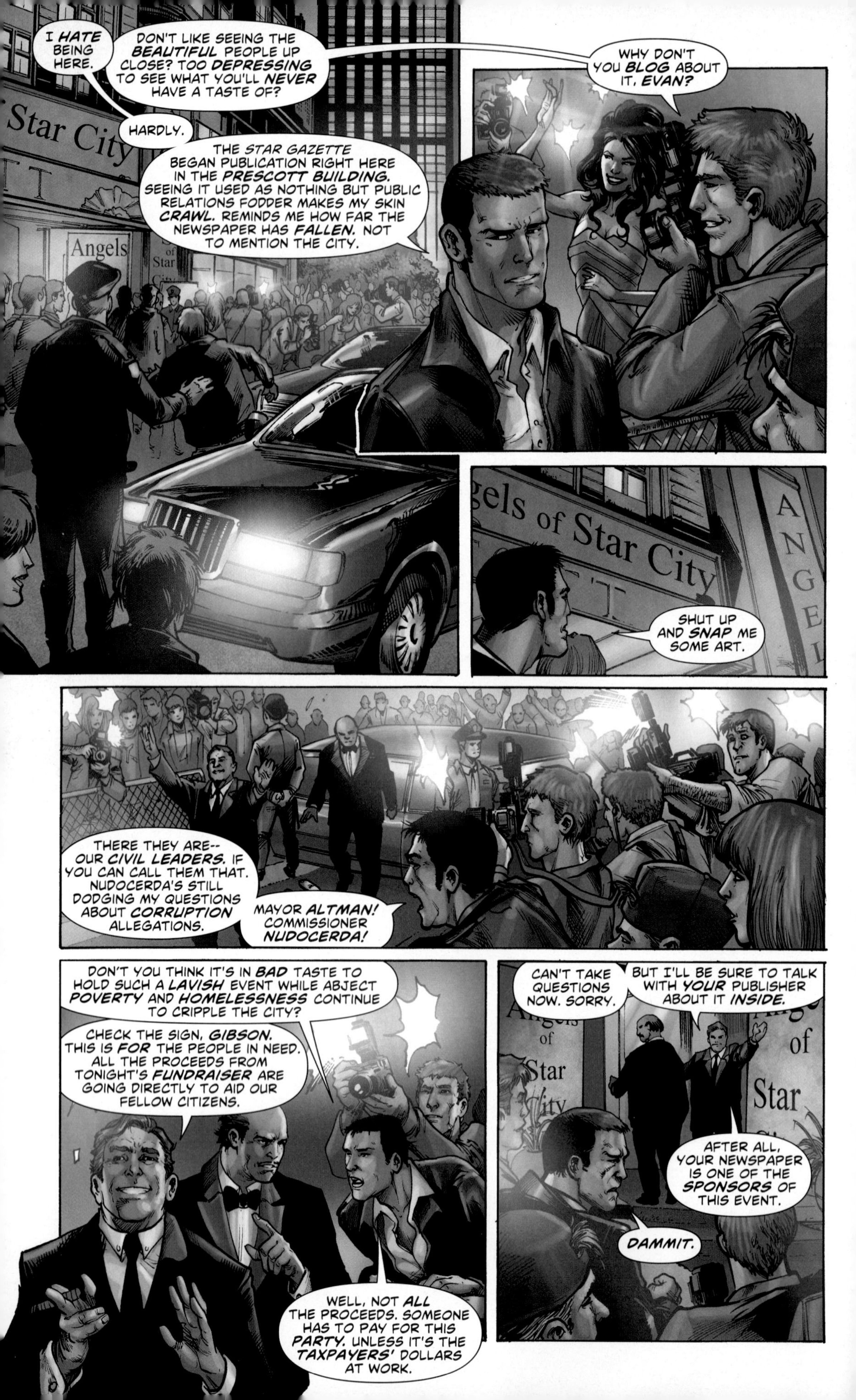

Star City
Angels
of Star City
I HATE BEING HERE.
DON'T LIKE SEEING THE BEAUTIFUL PEOPLE UP CLOSE? TOO DEPRESSING TO SEE WHAT YOU'LL NEVER HAVE A TASTE OF?
HARDLY.
THE STAR GAZETTE BEGAN PUBLICATION RIGHT HERE IN THE PRESCOTT BUILDING. SEEING IT USED AS NOTHING BUT PUBLIC RELATIONS FODDER MAKES MY SKIN CRAWL. REMINDS ME HOW FAR THE NEWSPAPER HAS FALLEN. NOT TO MENTION THE CITY.
WHY DON'T YOU BLOG ABOUT IT, EVAN?
gels of Star City
ANGEL
SHUT UP AND SNAP ME SOME ART.
THERE THEY ARE-- OUR CIVIL LEADERS. IF YOU CAN CALL THEM THAT. NUDOCERDA'S STILL DODGING MY QUESTIONS ABOUT CORRUPTION ALLEGATIONS.
MAYOR ALTMAN! COMMISSIONER NUDOCERDA!
DON'T YOU THINK IT'S IN BAD TASTE TO HOLD SUCH A LAVISH EVENT WHILE ABJECT POVERTY AND HOMELESSNESS CONTINUE TO CRIPPLE THE CITY?
CHECK THE SIGN, GIBSON. THIS IS FOR THE PEOPLE IN NEED. ALL THE PROCEEDS FROM TONIGHT'S FUNDRAISER ARE GOING DIRECTLY TO AID OUR FELLOW CITIZENS.
WELL, NOT ALL THE PROCEEDS. SOMEONE HAS TO PAY FOR THIS PARTY. UNLESS IT'S THE TAXPAYERS' DOLLARS AT WORK.
CAN'T TAKE QUESTIONS NOW. SORRY.
BUT I'LL BE SURE TO TALK WITH YOUR PUBLISHER ABOUT IT INSIDE.
of Star
AFTER ALL, YOUR NEWSPAPER IS ONE OF THE SPONSORS OF THIS EVENT.
DAMMIT.

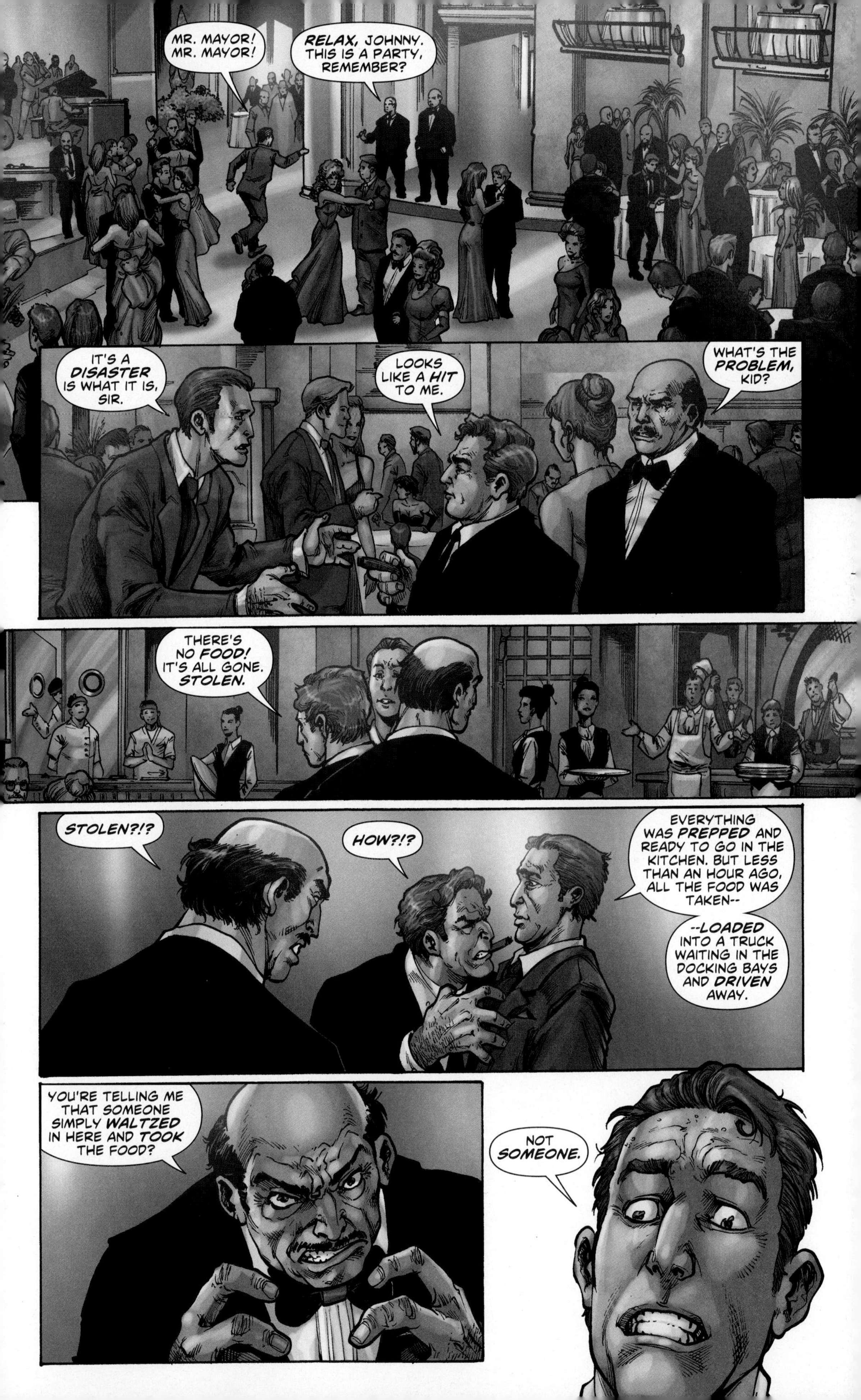
MR. MAYOR! MR. MAYOR!
RELAX, JOHNNY. THIS IS A PARTY, REMEMBER?
IT'S A DISASTER IS WHAT IT IS, SIR.
LOOKS LIKE A HIT TO ME.
WHAT'S THE PROBLEM, KID?
THERE'S NO FOOD! IT'S ALL GONE. STOLEN.
STOLEN?!?
HOW?!?
EVERYTHING WAS PREPPED AND READY TO GO IN THE KITCHEN. BUT LESS THAN AN HOUR AGO, ALL THE FOOD WAS TAKEN--
--LOADED INTO A TRUCK WAITING IN THE DOCKING BAYS AND DRIVEN AWAY.
YOU'RE TELLING ME THAT SOMEONE SIMPLY WALTZED IN HERE AND TOOK THE FOOD?
NOT SOMEONE.

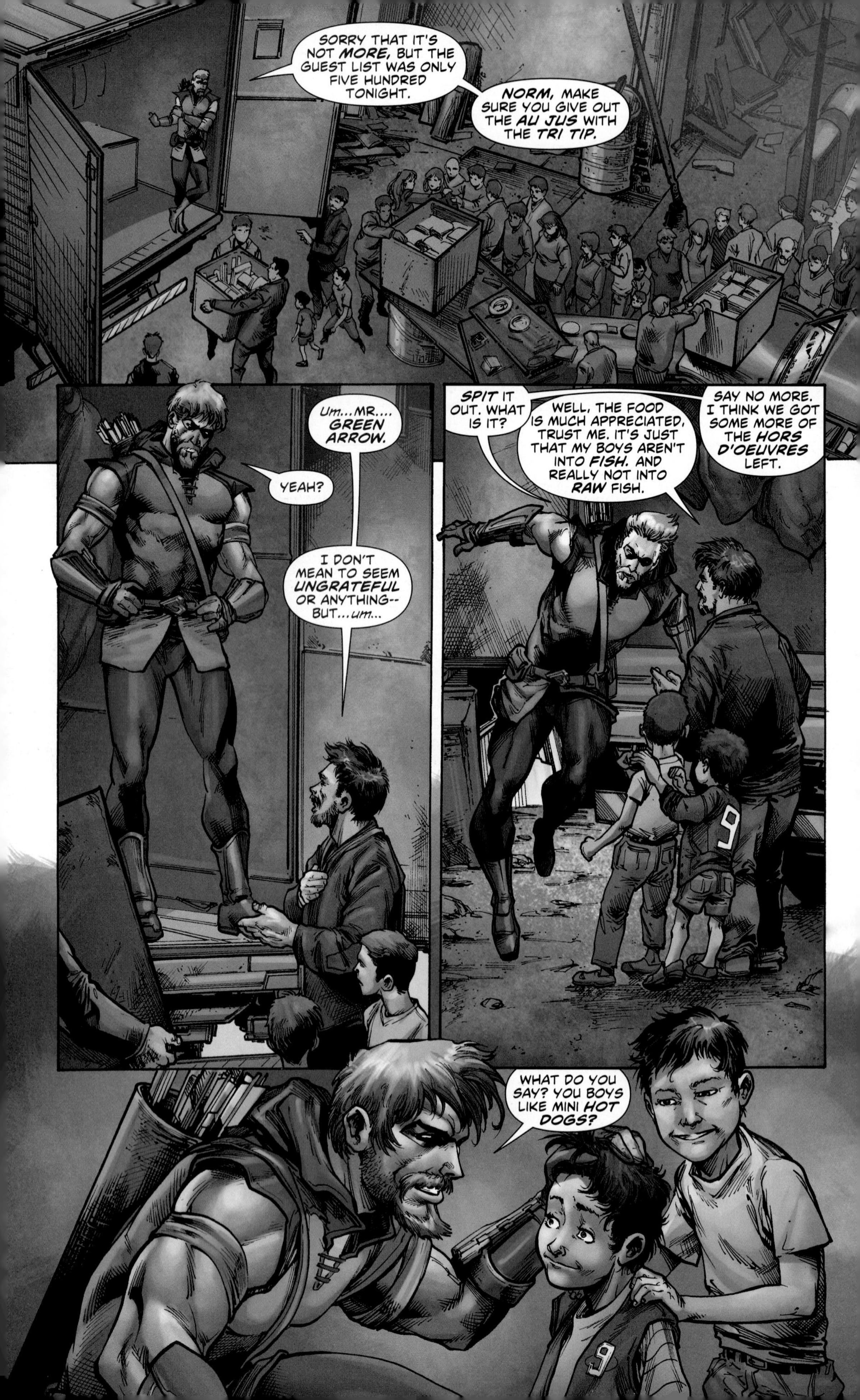
SORRY THAT IT'S NOT MORE, BUT THE GUEST LIST WAS ONLY FIVE HUNDRED TONIGHT.
NORM, MAKE SURE YOU GIVE OUT THE AU JUS WITH THE TRI TIP.
Um...MR.... GREEN ARROW.
YEAH?
I DON'T MEAN TO SEEM UNGRATEFUL OR ANYTHING-- BUT...um...
SPIT IT OUT. WHAT IS IT?
WELL, THE FOOD IS MUCH APPRECIATED, TRUST ME. IT'S JUST THAT MY BOYS AREN'T INTO FISH. AND REALLY NOT INTO RAW FISH.
SAY NO MORE. I THINK WE GOT SOME MORE OF THE HORS D'OEUVRES LEFT.
WHAT DO YOU SAY? YOU BOYS LIKE MINI HOT DOGS?

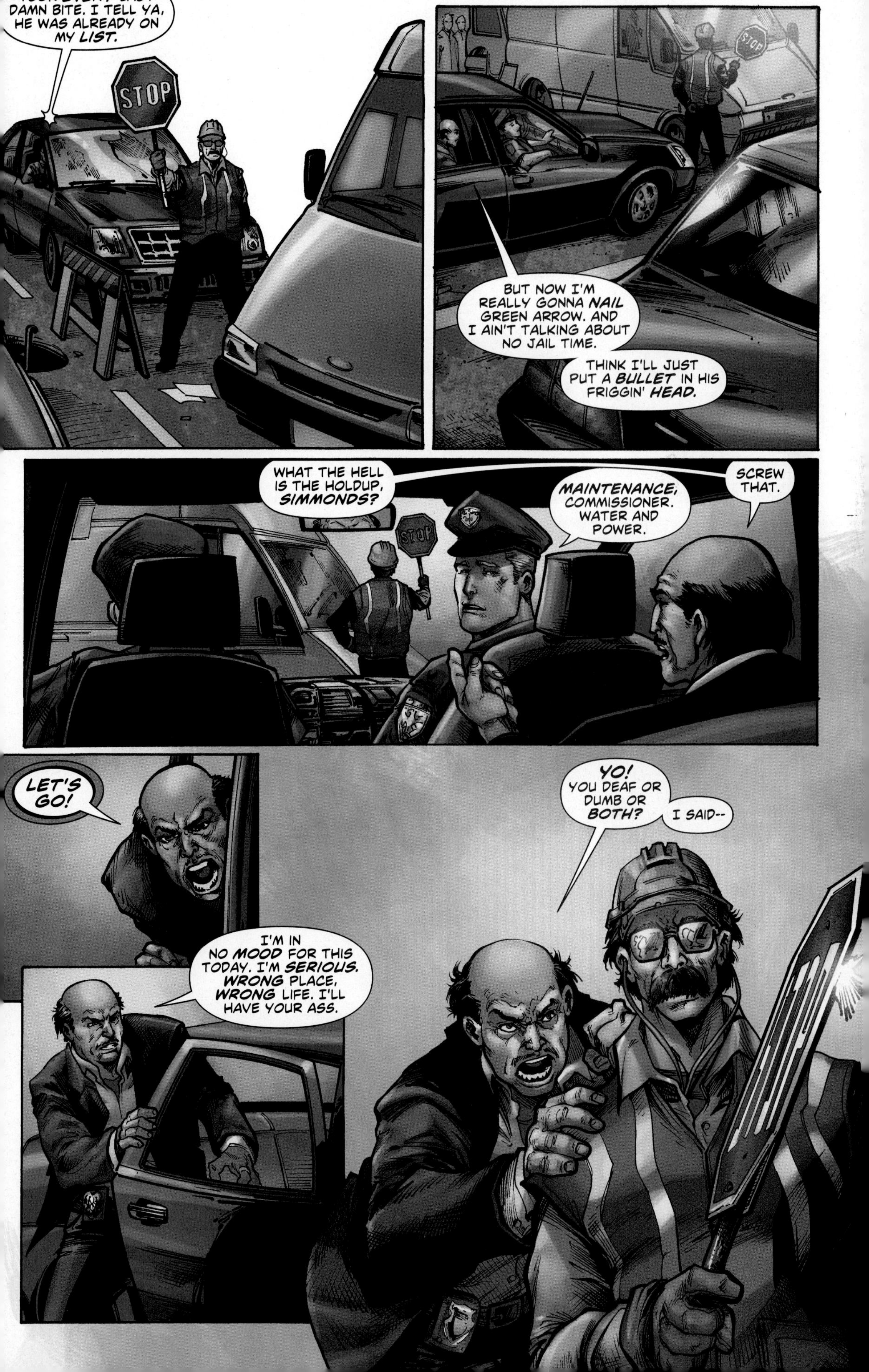
TOOK EVERY LAST DAMN BITE. I TELL YA, HE WAS ALREADY ON MY LIST.
STOP
STOP
BUT NOW I'M REALLY GONNA NAIL GREEN ARROW. AND I AIN'T TALKING ABOUT NO JAIL TIME.
THINK I'LL JUST PUT A BULLET IN HIS FRIGGIN' HEAD.
WHAT THE HELL IS THE HOLDUP, SIMMONDS?
MAINTENANCE, COMMISSIONER. WATER AND POWER.
SCREW THAT.
STOP
LET'S GO!
I'M IN NO MOOD FOR THIS TODAY. I'M SERIOUS. WRONG PLACE, WRONG LIFE. I'LL HAVE YOUR ASS.
YO! YOU DEAF OR DUMB OR BOTH?
I SAID--

Nnnnn.

Y-YOU STABBED ME.

GaAAHhGg!

WHAT ARE YOU DOING?!? *STOP!*

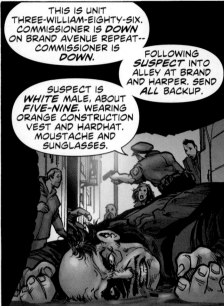

THIS IS UNIT THREE-WILLIAM-EIGHTY-SIX. COMMISSIONER IS *DOWN* ON BRAND AVENUE REPEAT-- COMMISSIONER IS *DOWN.*

FOLLOWING *SUSPECT* INTO ALLEY AT BRAND AND HARPER. SEND *ALL* BACKUP.

SUSPECT IS *WHITE* MALE, ABOUT *FIVE-NINE.* WEARING ORANGE CONSTRUCTION VEST AND HARDHAT. MOUSTACHE AND SUNGLASSES.

SCRATCH THE ORANGE VEST.

WHAT IN THE HELL?

Nnnnnn

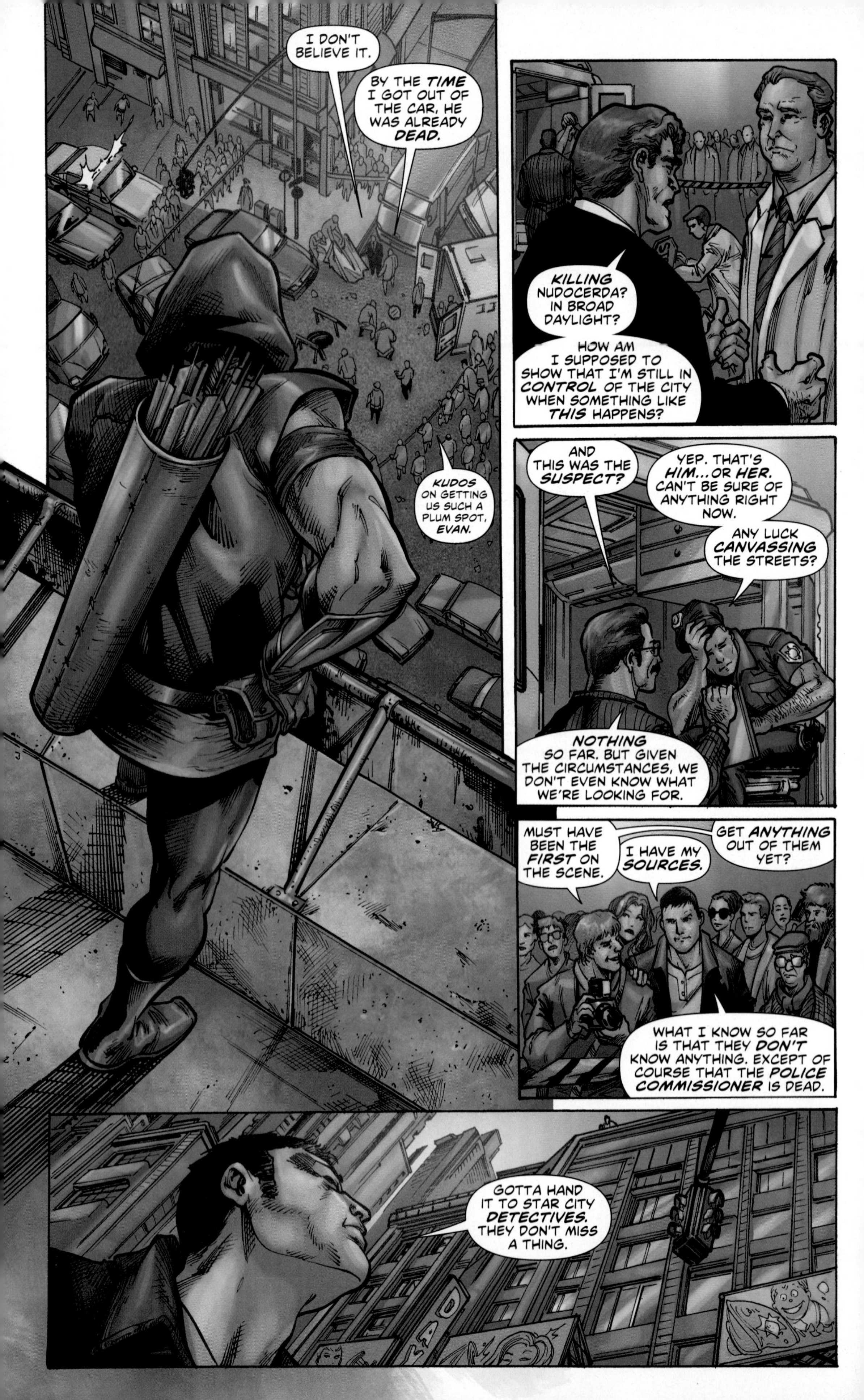
I DON'T BELIEVE IT.
BY THE TIME I GOT OUT OF THE CAR, HE WAS ALREADY DEAD.
KUDOS ON GETTING US SUCH A PLUM SPOT, EVAN.
KILLING NUDOCERDA? IN BROAD DAYLIGHT?
HOW AM I SUPPOSED TO SHOW THAT I'M STILL IN CONTROL OF THE CITY WHEN SOMETHING LIKE THIS HAPPENS?
AND THIS WAS THE SUSPECT?
YEP. THAT'S HIM...OR HER. CAN'T BE SURE OF ANYTHING RIGHT NOW.
ANY LUCK CANVASSING THE STREETS?
NOTHING SO FAR. BUT GIVEN THE CIRCUMSTANCES, WE DON'T EVEN KNOW WHAT WE'RE LOOKING FOR.
MUST HAVE BEEN THE FIRST ON THE SCENE.
I HAVE MY SOURCES.
GET ANYTHING OUT OF THEM YET?
WHAT I KNOW SO FAR IS THAT THEY DON'T KNOW ANYTHING. EXCEPT OF COURSE THAT THE POLICE COMMISSIONER IS DEAD.
GOTTA HAND IT TO STAR CITY DETECTIVES. THEY DON'T MISS A THING.

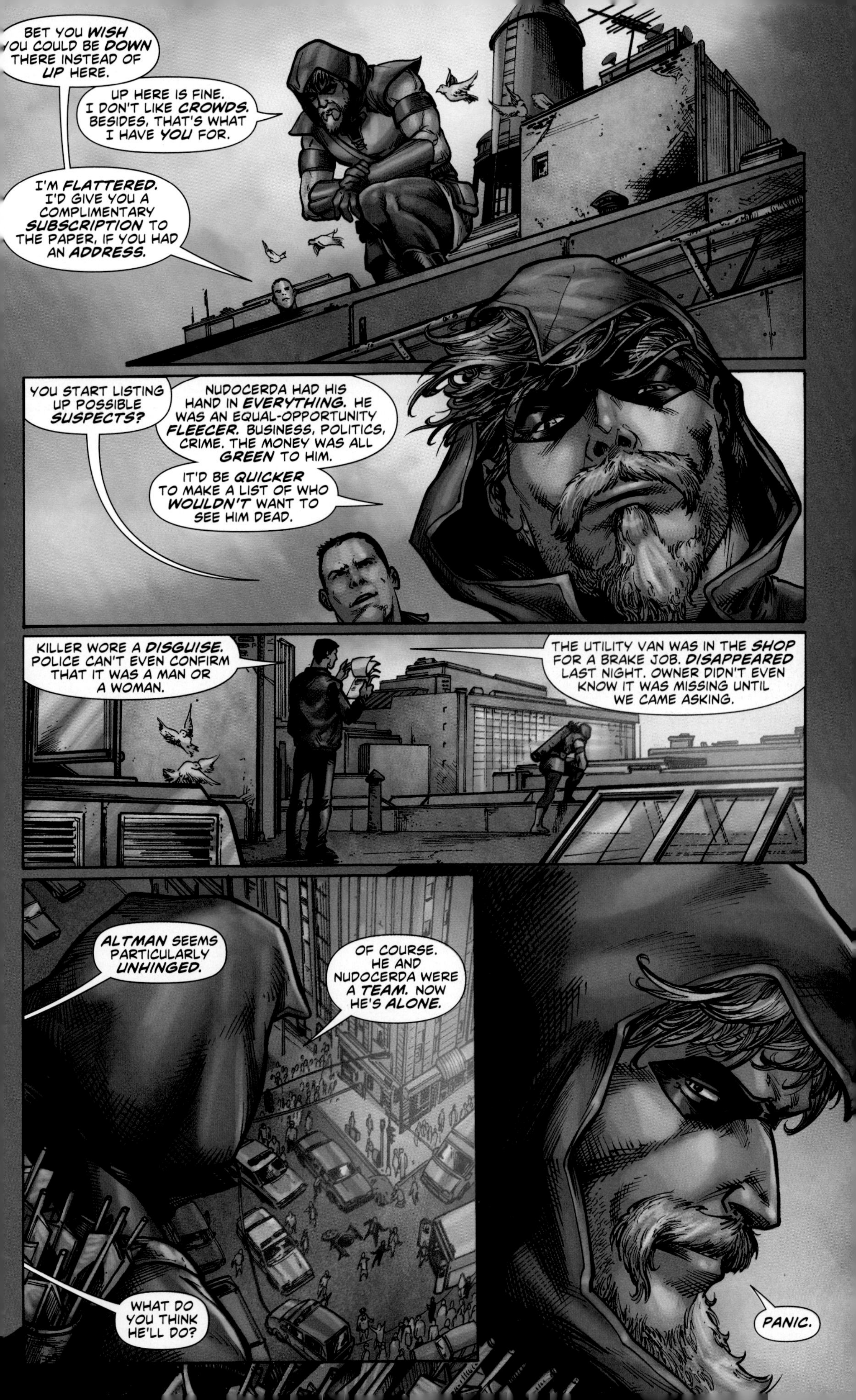
BET YOU *WISH* YOU COULD BE *DOWN* THERE INSTEAD OF *UP* HERE.
UP HERE IS FINE. I DON'T LIKE *CROWDS.* BESIDES, THAT'S WHAT I HAVE *YOU* FOR.
I'M *FLATTERED.* I'D GIVE YOU A COMPLIMENTARY *SUBSCRIPTION* TO THE PAPER, IF YOU HAD AN *ADDRESS.*
YOU START LISTING UP POSSIBLE *SUSPECTS?*
NUDOCERDA HAD HIS HAND IN *EVERYTHING.* HE WAS AN EQUAL-OPPORTUNITY *FLEECER.* BUSINESS, POLITICS, CRIME. THE MONEY WAS ALL *GREEN* TO HIM.
IT'D BE *QUICKER* TO MAKE A LIST OF WHO *WOULDN'T* WANT TO SEE HIM DEAD.
KILLER WORE A *DISGUISE.* POLICE CAN'T EVEN CONFIRM THAT IT WAS A MAN OR A WOMAN.
THE UTILITY VAN WAS IN THE *SHOP* FOR A BRAKE JOB. *DISAPPEARED* LAST NIGHT. OWNER DIDN'T EVEN KNOW IT WAS MISSING UNTIL WE CAME ASKING.
ALTMAN SEEMS PARTICULARLY *UNHINGED.*
OF COURSE. HE AND NUDOCERDA WERE A *TEAM.* NOW HE'S *ALONE.*
WHAT DO YOU THINK HE'LL DO?
PANIC.

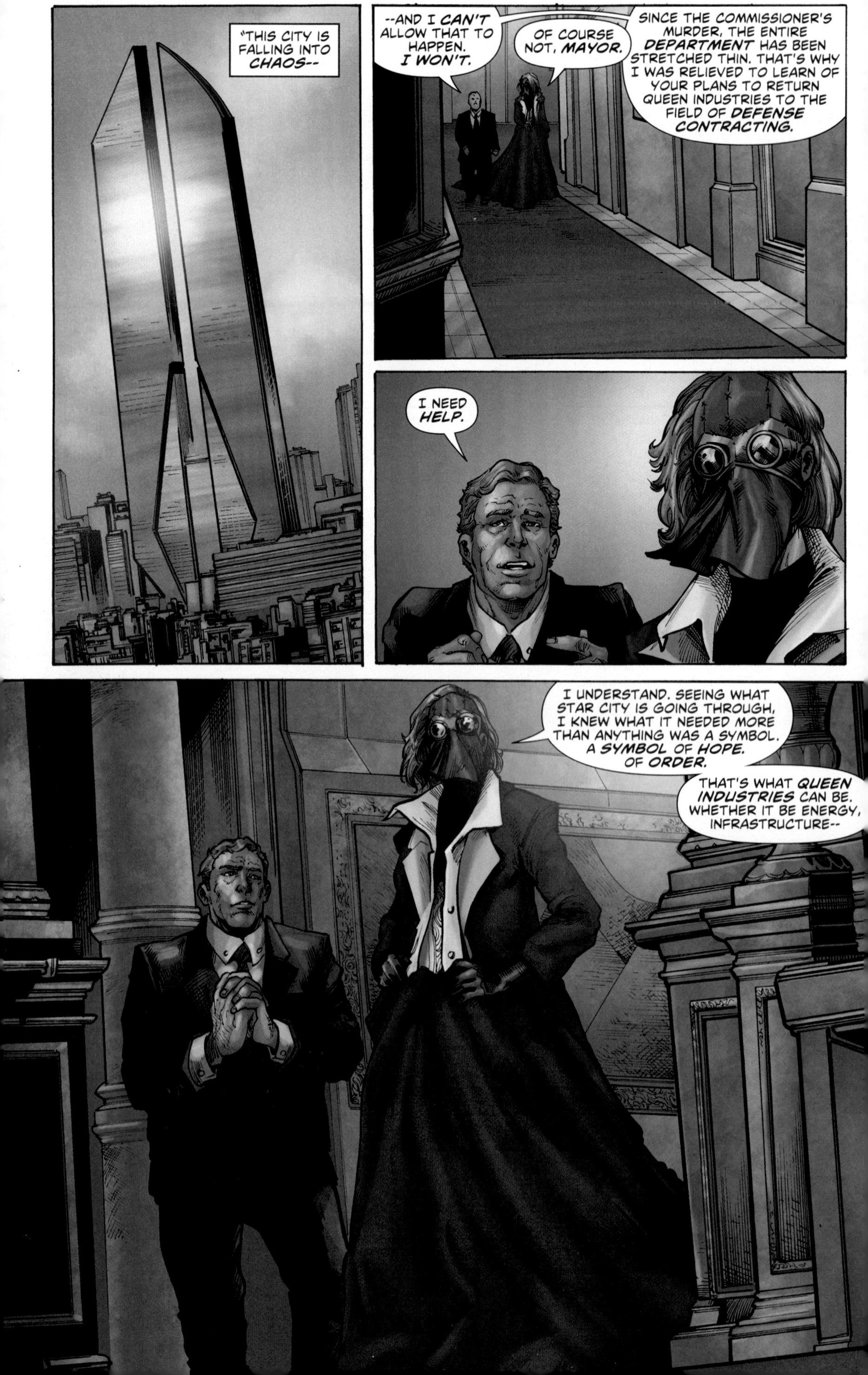
"THIS CITY IS FALLING INTO CHAOS--
--AND I CAN'T ALLOW THAT TO HAPPEN. I WON'T.
OF COURSE NOT, MAYOR.
SINCE THE COMMISSIONER'S MURDER, THE ENTIRE DEPARTMENT HAS BEEN STRETCHED THIN. THAT'S WHY I WAS RELIEVED TO LEARN OF YOUR PLANS TO RETURN QUEEN INDUSTRIES TO THE FIELD OF DEFENSE CONTRACTING.
I NEED HELP.
I UNDERSTAND. SEEING WHAT STAR CITY IS GOING THROUGH, I KNEW WHAT IT NEEDED MORE THAN ANYTHING WAS A SYMBOL. A SYMBOL OF HOPE. OF ORDER.
THAT'S WHAT QUEEN INDUSTRIES CAN BE. WHETHER IT BE ENERGY, INFRASTRUCTURE--

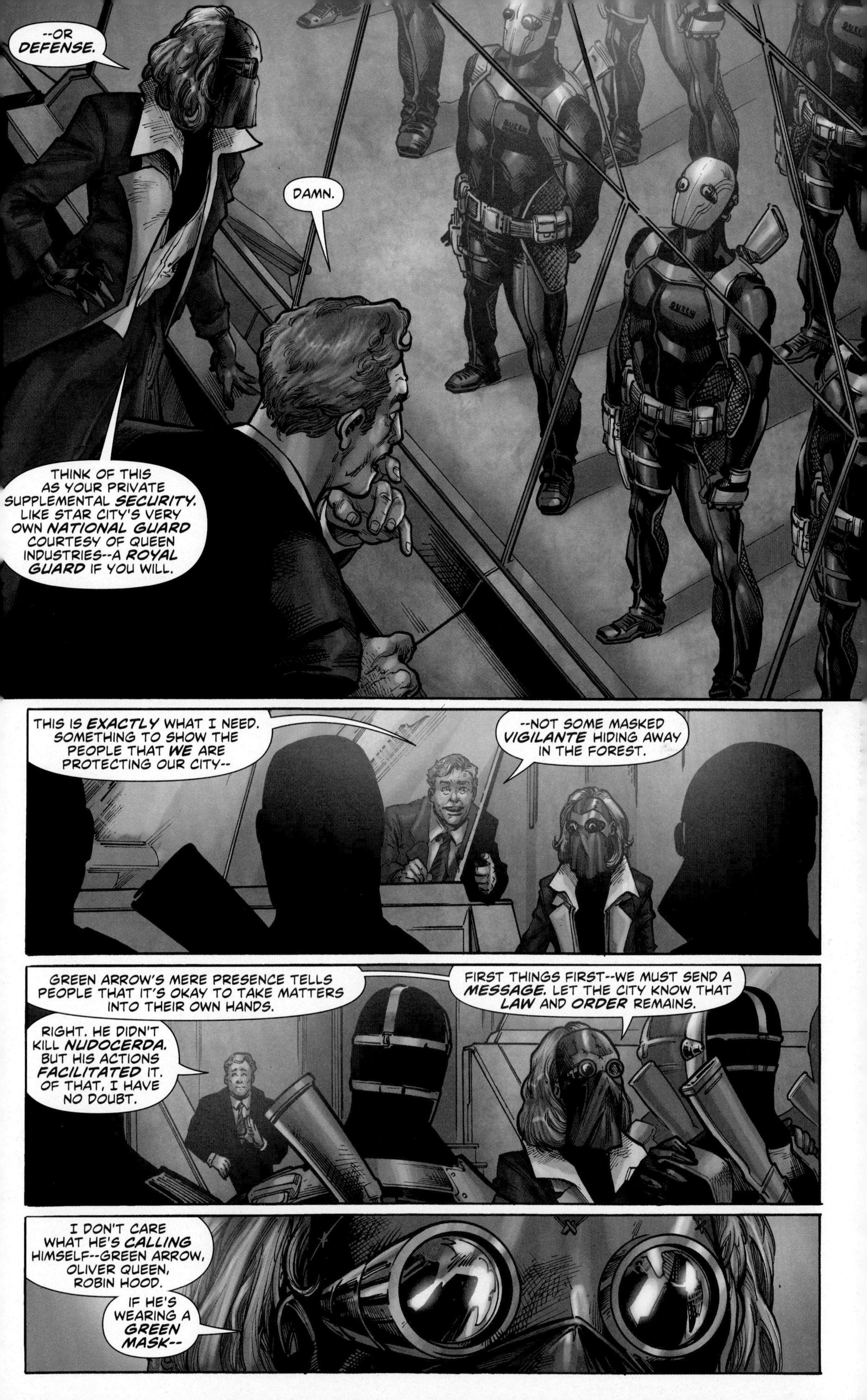
--OR DEFENSE.
DAMN.
THINK OF THIS AS YOUR PRIVATE SUPPLEMENTAL SECURITY. LIKE STAR CITY'S VERY OWN NATIONAL GUARD COURTESY OF QUEEN INDUSTRIES--A ROYAL GUARD IF YOU WILL.
THIS IS EXACTLY WHAT I NEED. SOMETHING TO SHOW THE PEOPLE THAT WE ARE PROTECTING OUR CITY--
--NOT SOME MASKED VIGILANTE HIDING AWAY IN THE FOREST.
GREEN ARROW'S MERE PRESENCE TELLS PEOPLE THAT IT'S OKAY TO TAKE MATTERS INTO THEIR OWN HANDS.
FIRST THINGS FIRST--WE MUST SEND A MESSAGE. LET THE CITY KNOW THAT LAW AND ORDER REMAINS.
RIGHT. HE DIDN'T KILL NUDOCERDA. BUT HIS ACTIONS FACILITATED IT. OF THAT, I HAVE NO DOUBT.
I DON'T CARE WHAT HE'S CALLING HIMSELF--GREEN ARROW, OLIVER QUEEN, ROBIN HOOD.
IF HE'S WEARING A GREEN MASK--

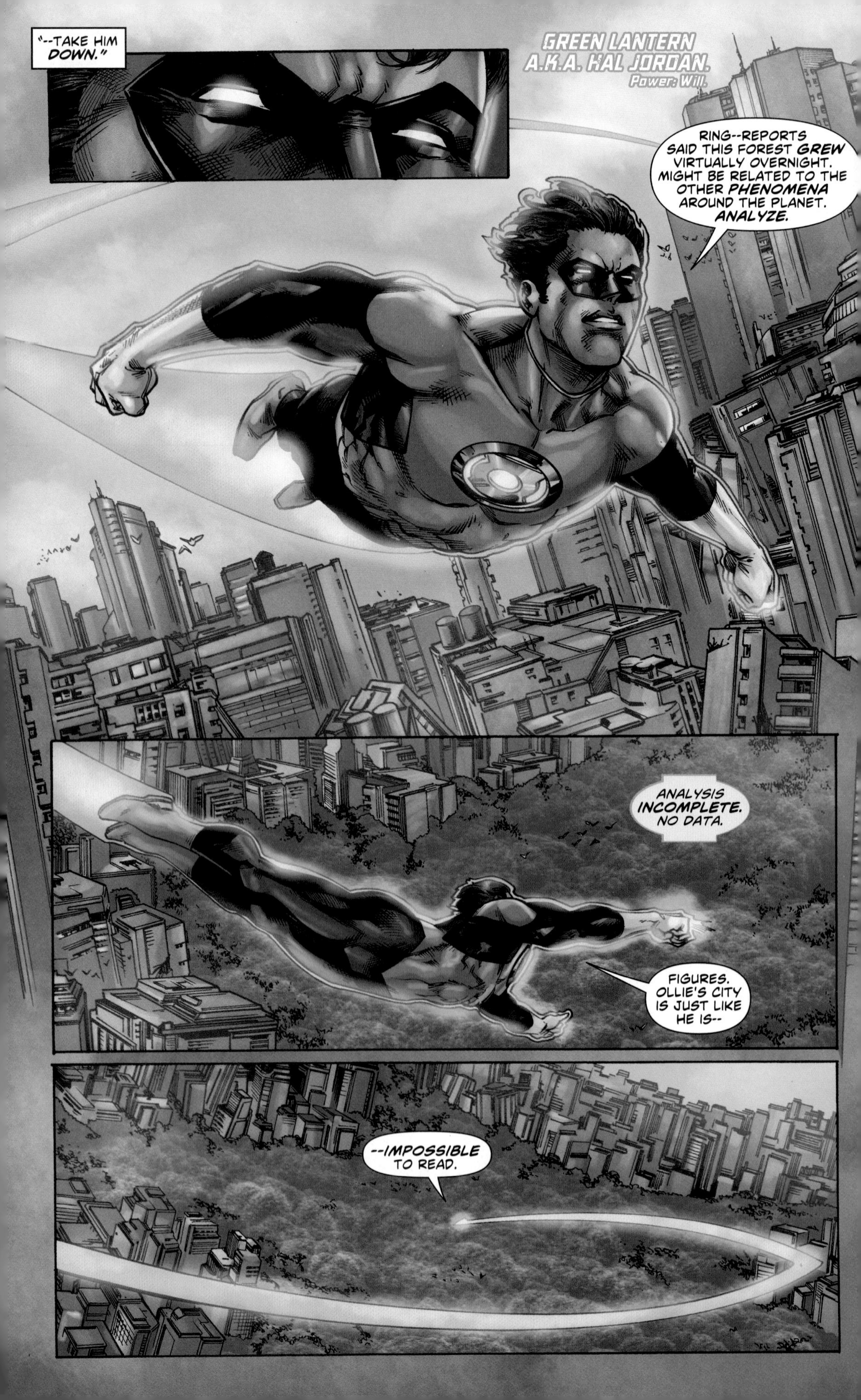
"--TAKE HIM DOWN."
GREEN LANTERN A.K.A. HAL JORDAN.
Power: Will.
RING--REPORTS SAID THIS FOREST GREW VIRTUALLY OVERNIGHT. MIGHT BE RELATED TO THE OTHER PHENOMENA AROUND THE PLANET. ANALYZE.
ANALYSIS INCOMPLETE. NO DATA.
FIGURES. OLLIE'S CITY IS JUST LIKE HE IS--
--IMPOSSIBLE TO READ.

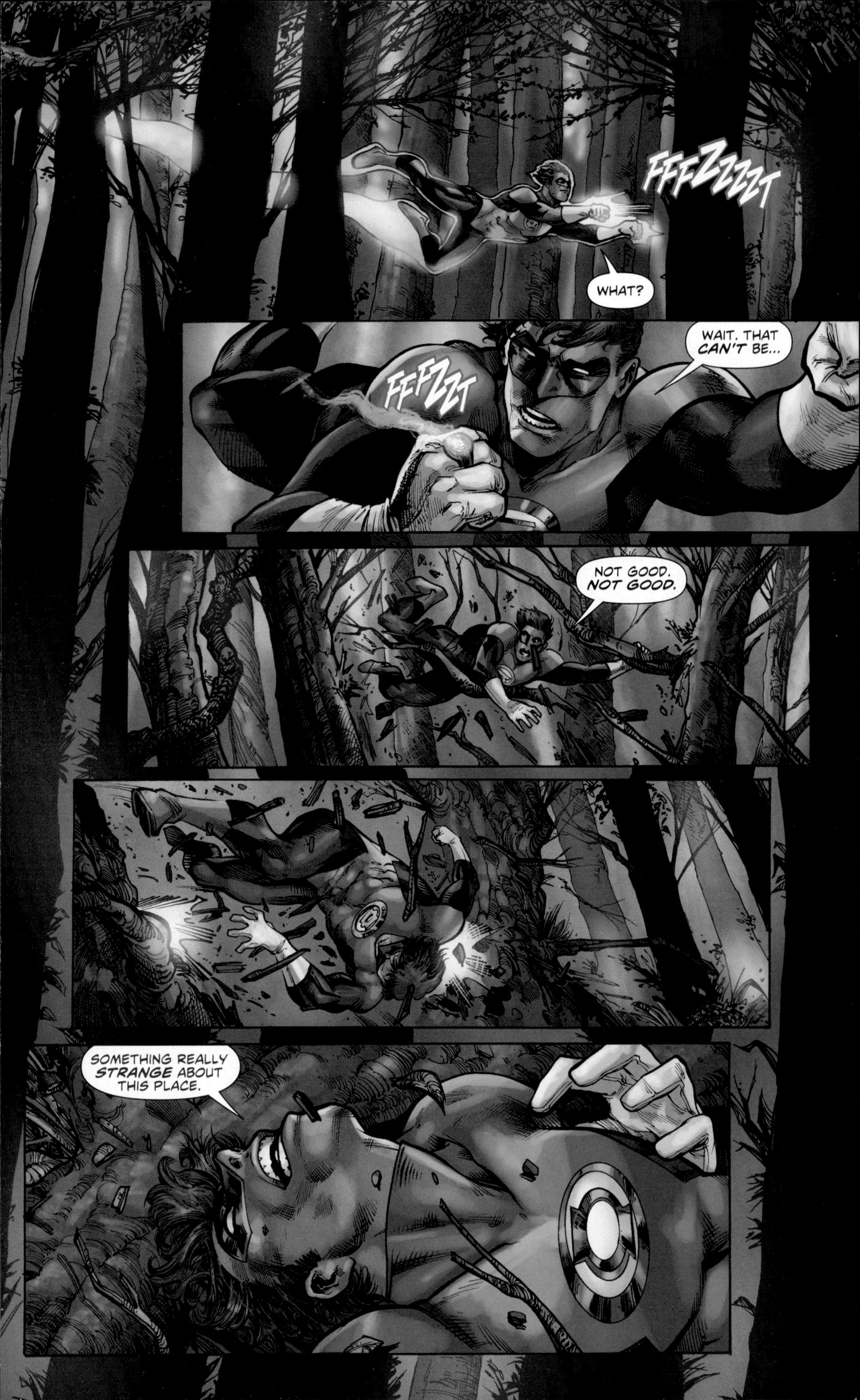
FFFZZZZZT
WHAT?
WAIT. THAT CAN'T BE...
FFFZZZT
NOT GOOD. NOT GOOD.
SOMETHING REALLY STRANGE ABOUT THIS PLACE.

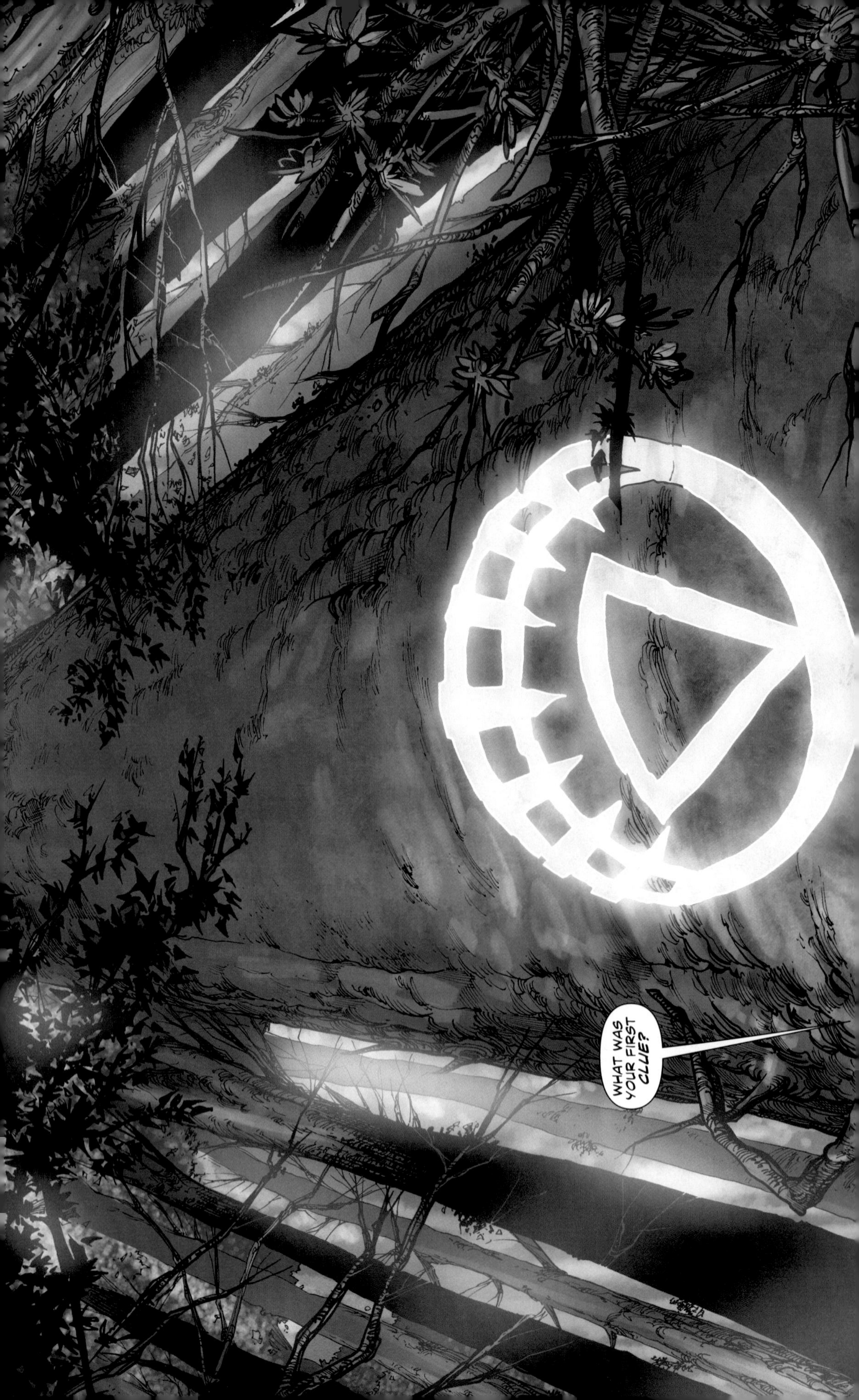
WHAT WAS YOUR FIRST *CLUE?*

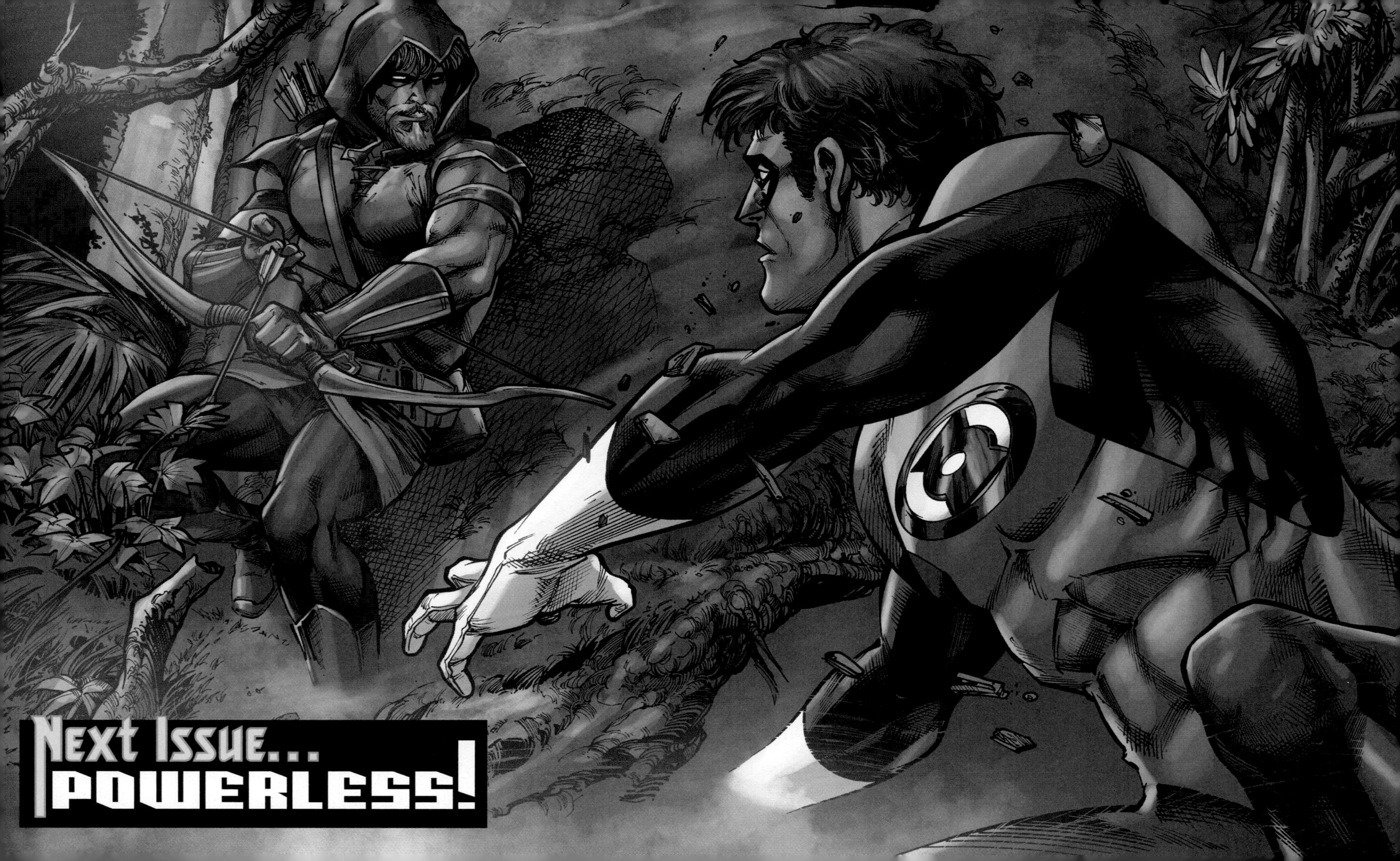
Next Issue...
POWERLESS!

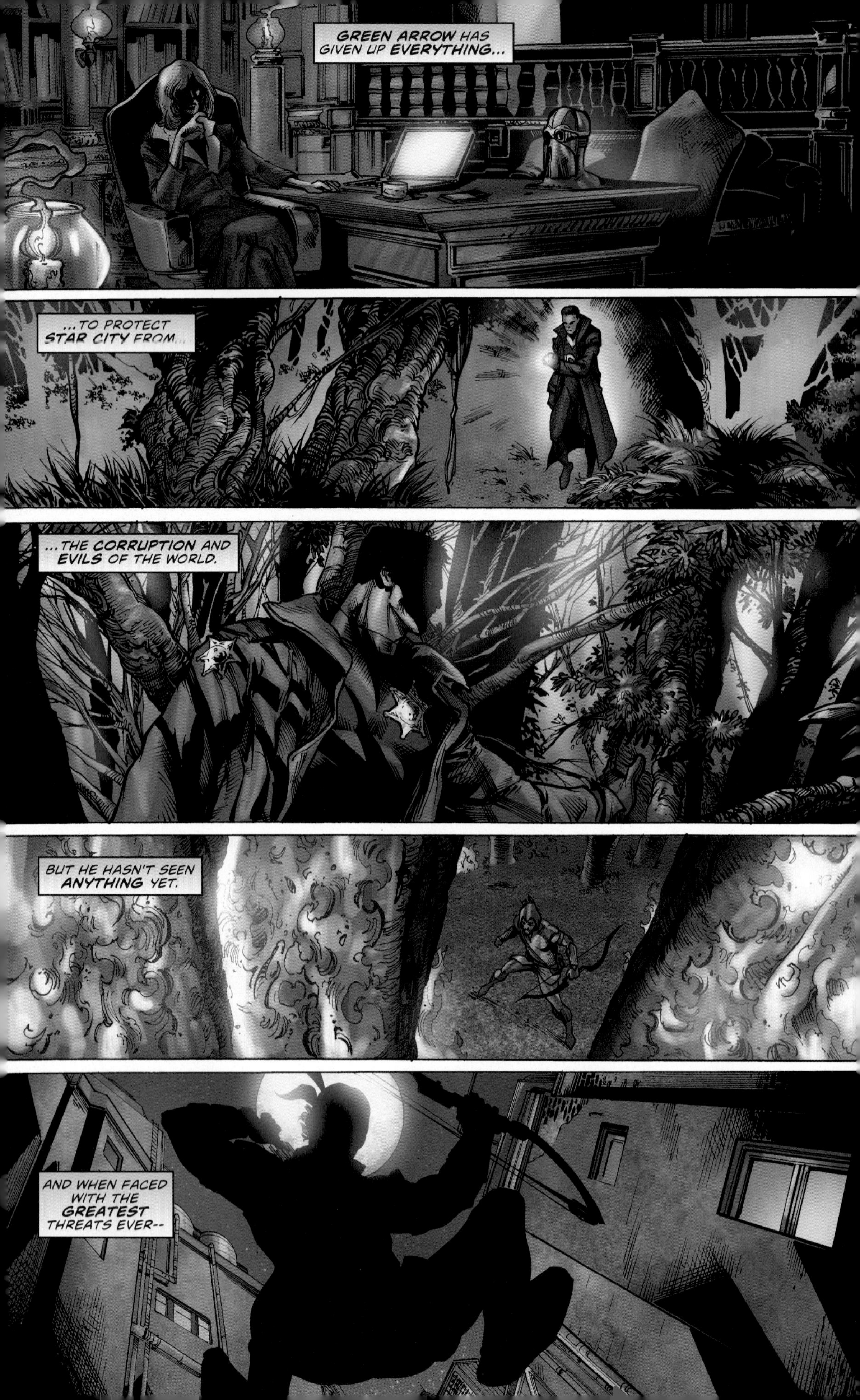
GREEN ARROW HAS GIVEN UP EVERYTHING...
...TO PROTECT STAR CITY FROM...
...THE CORRUPTION AND EVILS OF THE WORLD.
BUT HE HASN'T SEEN ANYTHING YET.
AND WHEN FACED WITH THE GREATEST THREATS EVER--

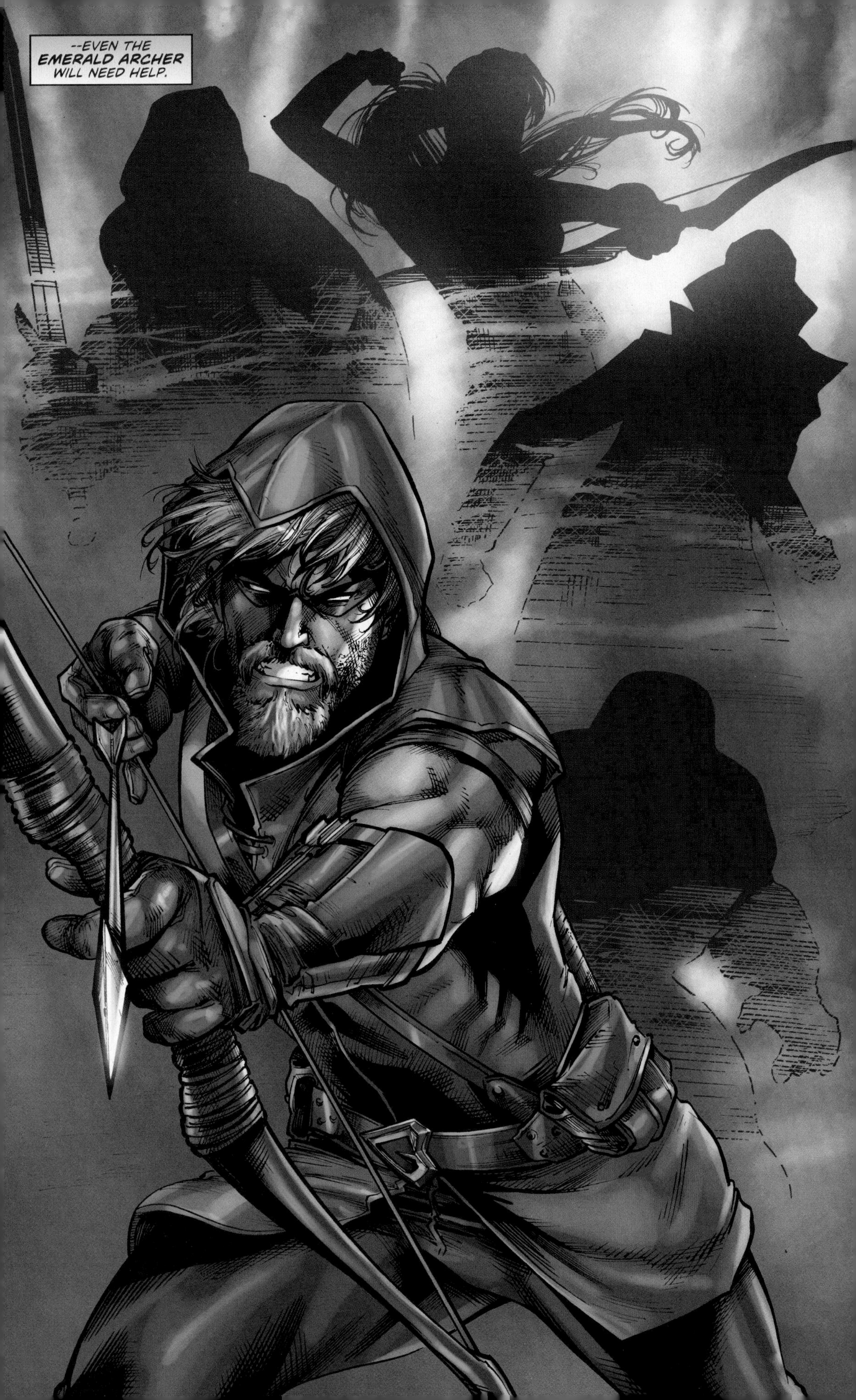
--EVEN THE EMERALD ARCHER WILL NEED HELP.

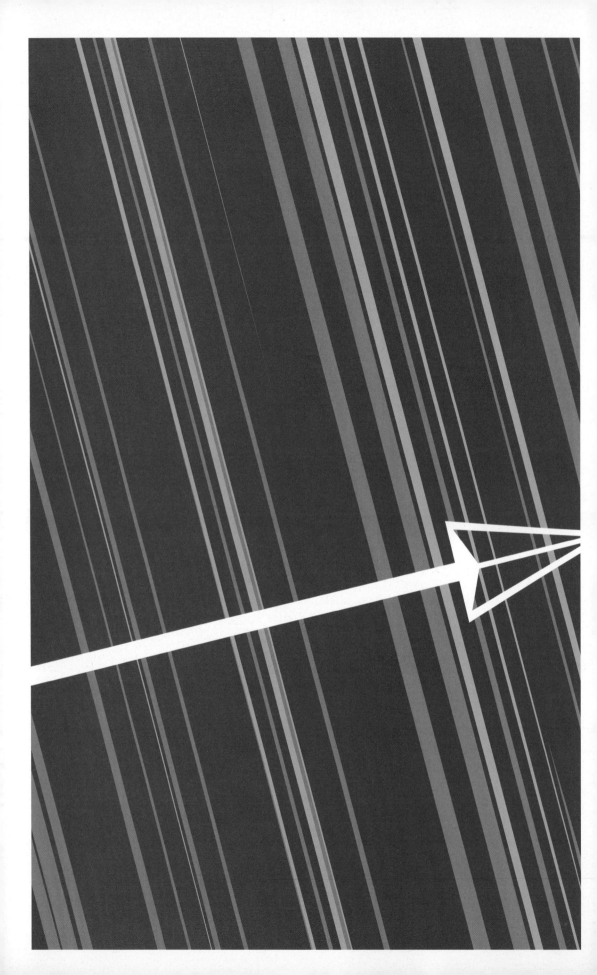

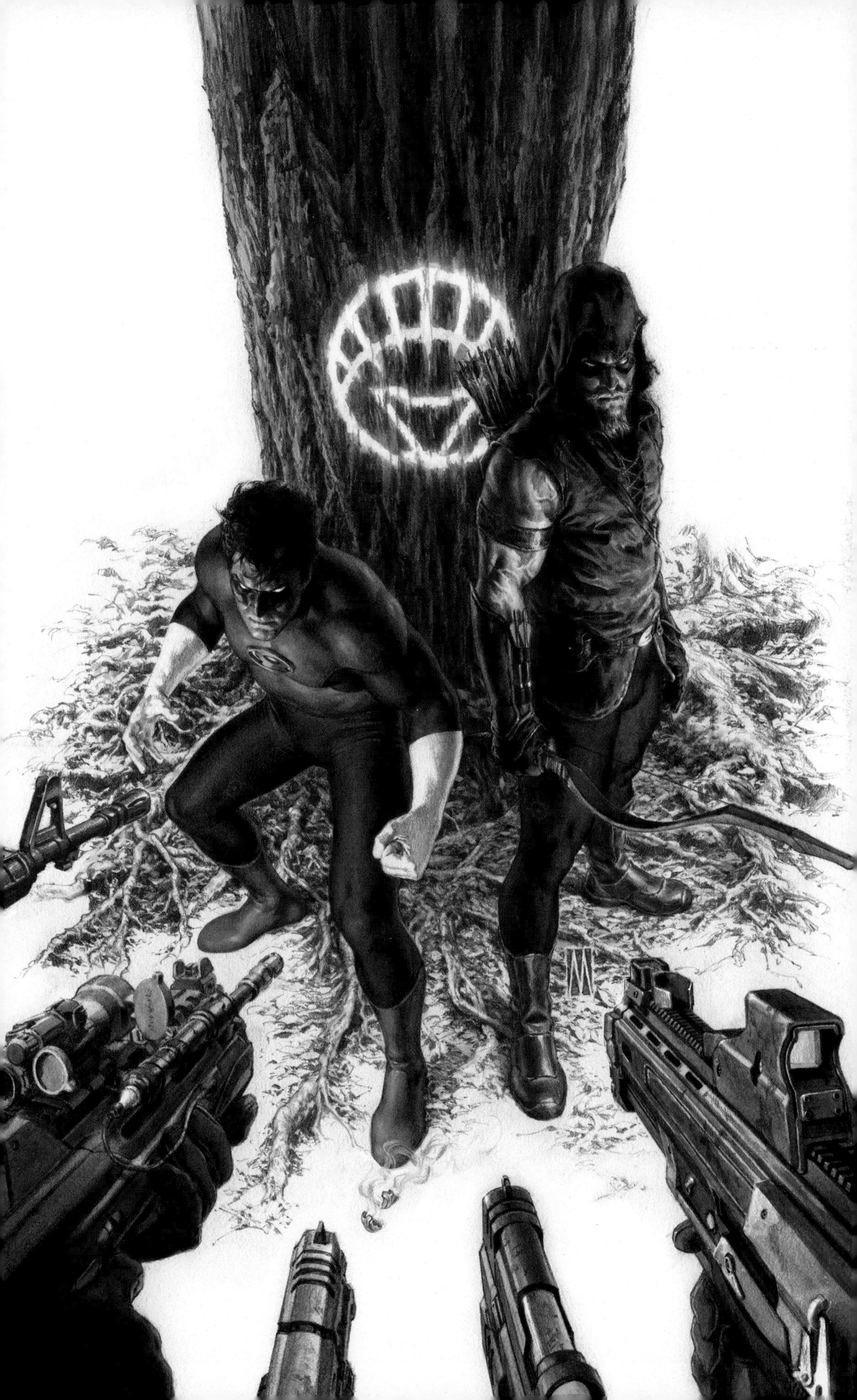

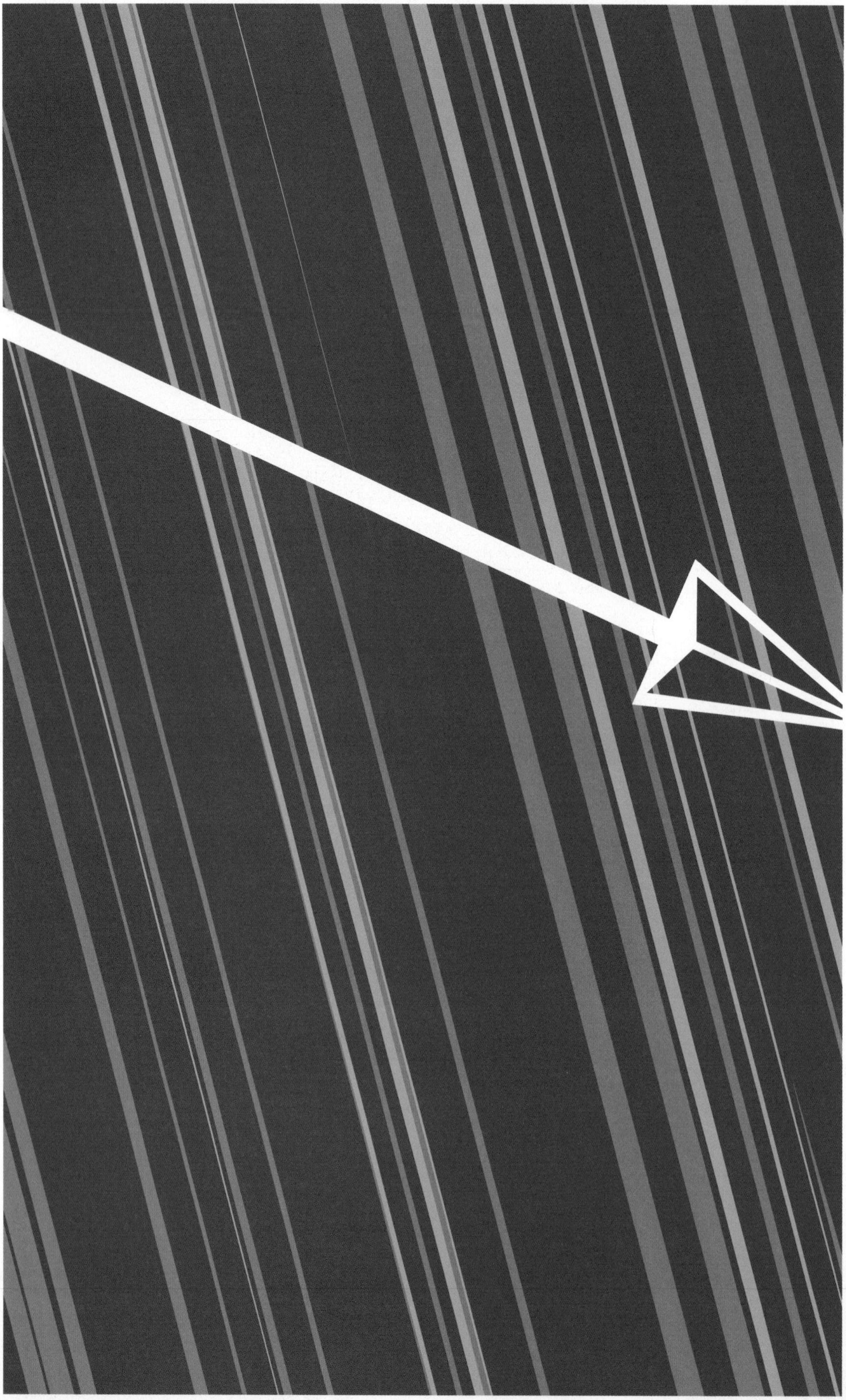

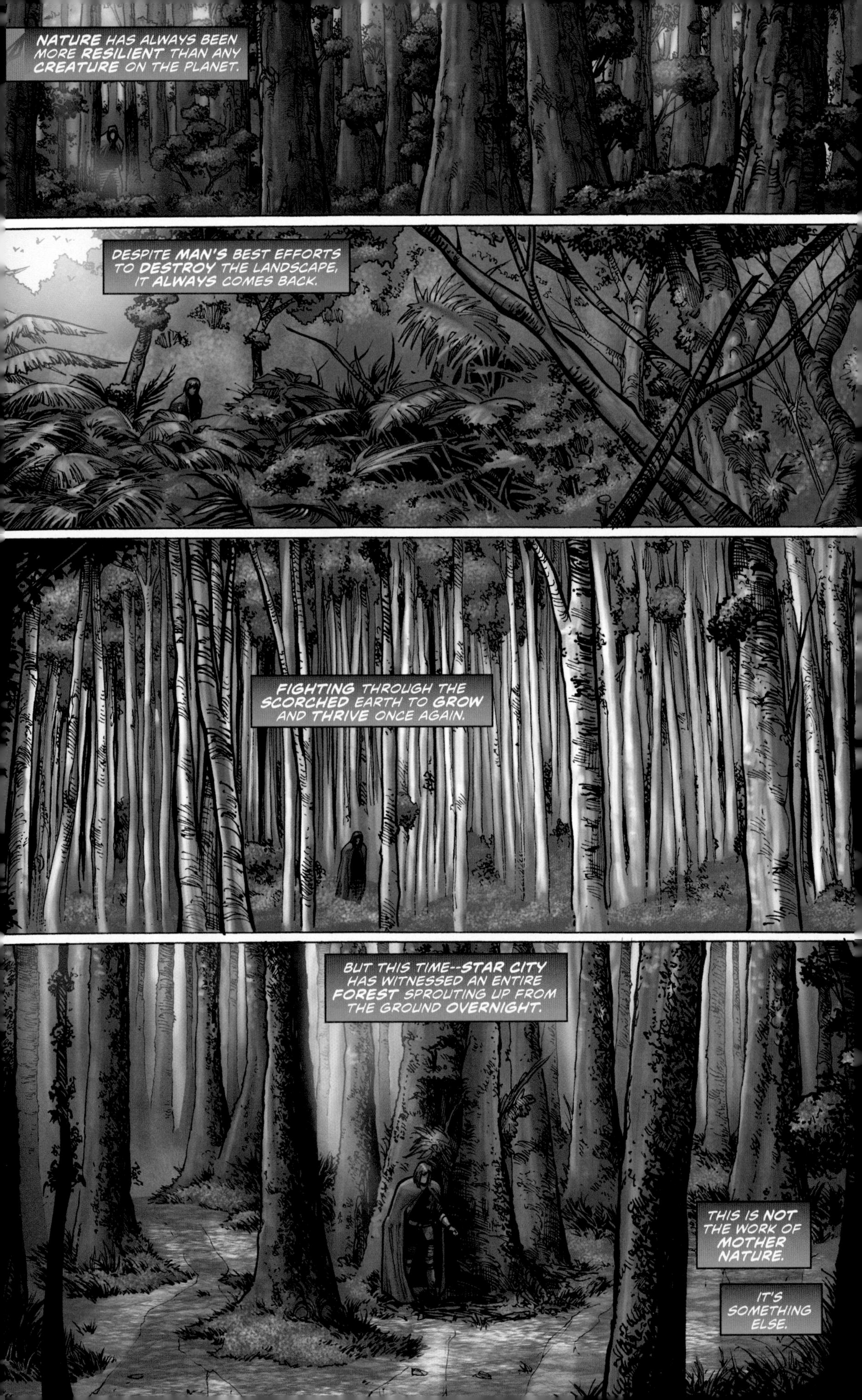
NATURE HAS ALWAYS BEEN MORE RESILIENT THAN ANY CREATURE ON THE PLANET.
DESPITE MAN'S BEST EFFORTS TO DESTROY THE LANDSCAPE, IT ALWAYS COMES BACK.
FIGHTING THROUGH THE SCORCHED EARTH TO GROW AND THRIVE ONCE AGAIN.
BUT THIS TIME--STAR CITY HAS WITNESSED AN ENTIRE FOREST SPROUTING UP FROM THE GROUND OVERNIGHT.
THIS IS NOT THE WORK OF MOTHER NATURE.
IT'S SOMETHING ELSE.

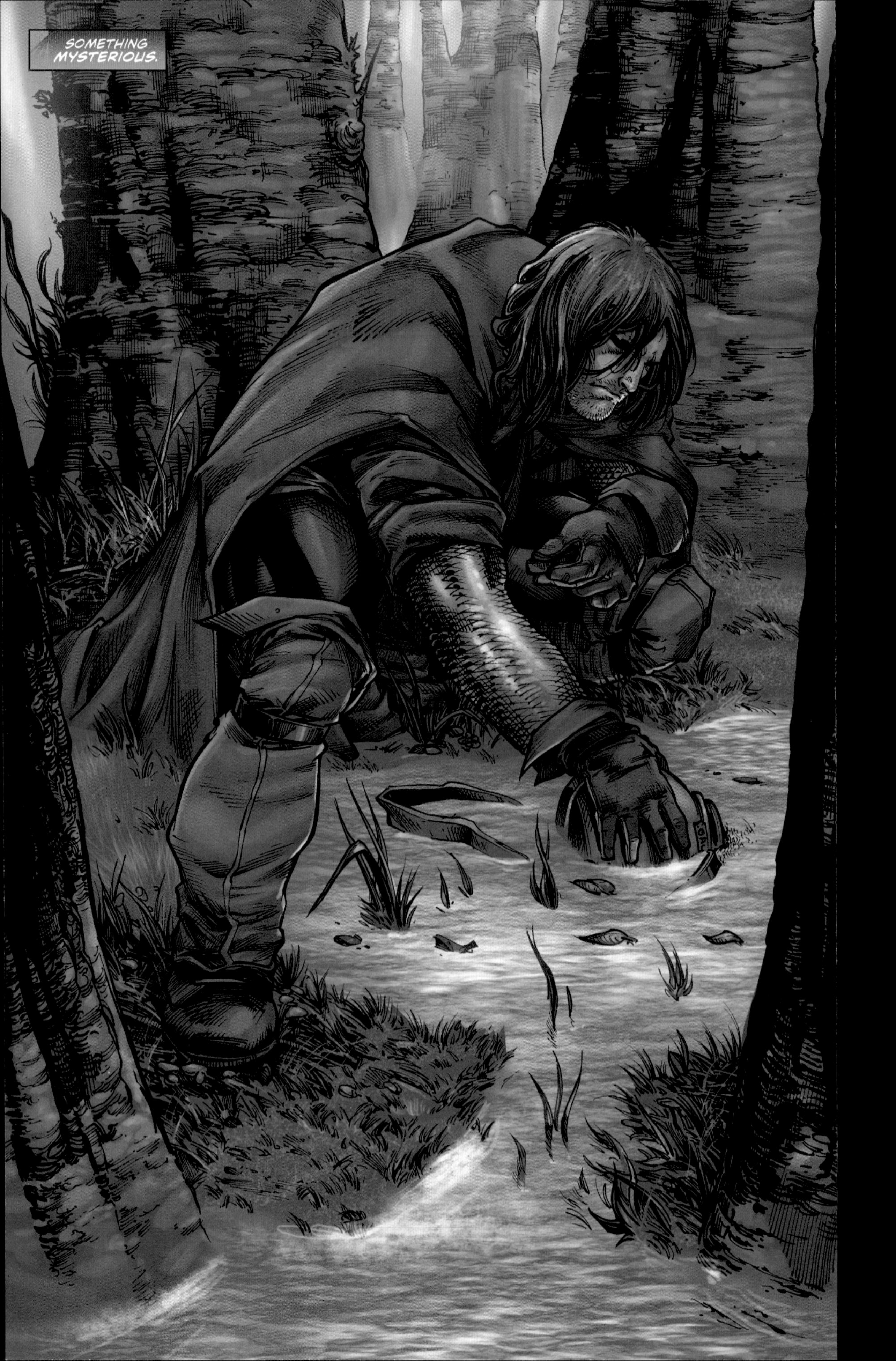
SOMETHING MYSTERIOUS.

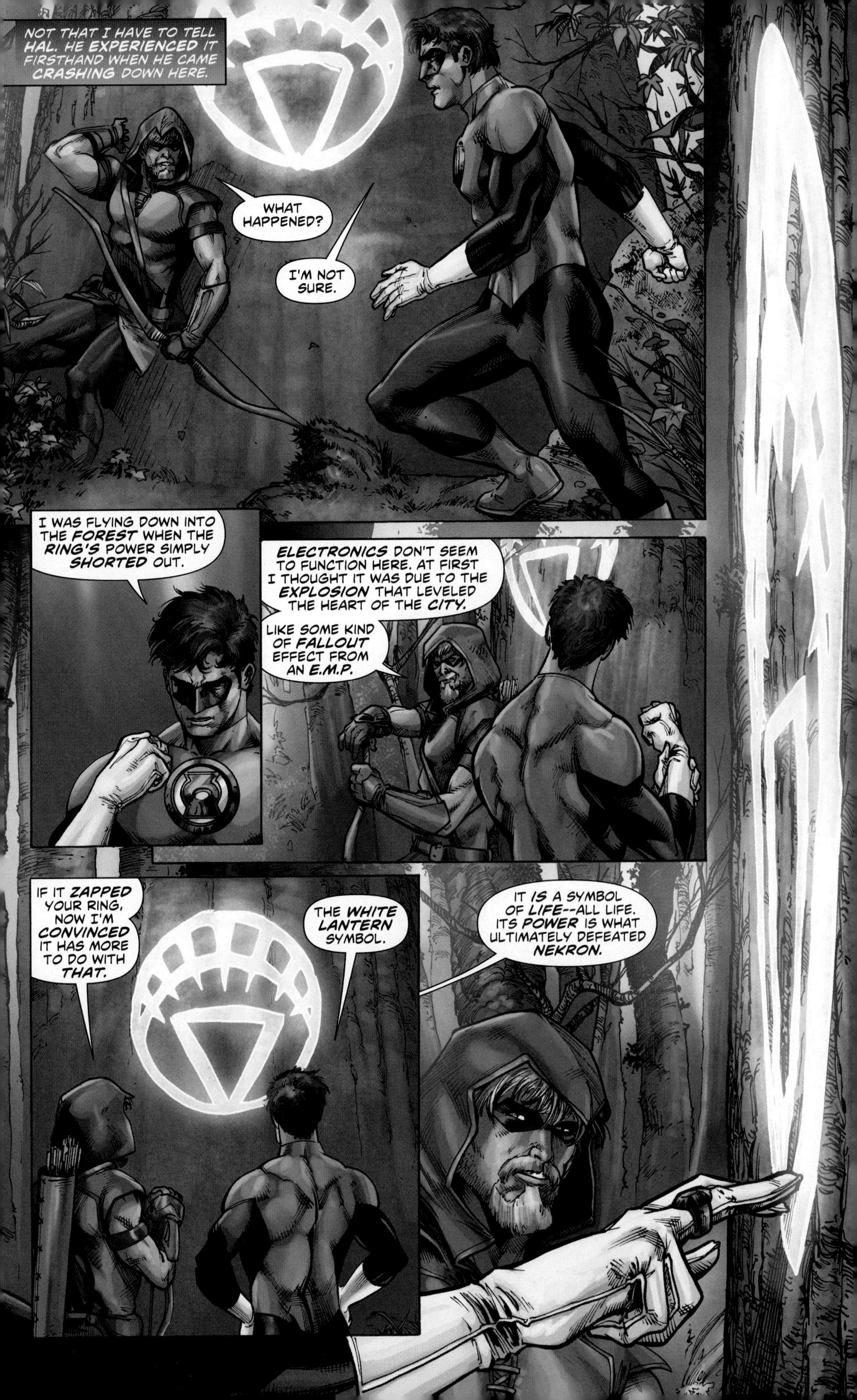
NOT THAT I HAVE TO TELL HAL. HE EXPERIENCED IT FIRSTHAND WHEN HE CAME CRASHING DOWN HERE.
WHAT HAPPENED?
I'M NOT SURE.
I WAS FLYING DOWN INTO THE FOREST WHEN THE RING'S POWER SIMPLY SHORTED OUT.
ELECTRONICS DON'T SEEM TO FUNCTION HERE. AT FIRST I THOUGHT IT WAS DUE TO THE EXPLOSION THAT LEVELED THE HEART OF THE CITY.
LIKE SOME KIND OF FALLOUT EFFECT FROM AN E.M.P.
IF IT ZAPPED YOUR RING, NOW I'M CONVINCED IT HAS MORE TO DO WITH THAT.
THE WHITE LANTERN SYMBOL.
IT IS A SYMBOL OF LIFE--ALL LIFE. ITS POWER IS WHAT ULTIMATELY DEFEATED NEKRON.

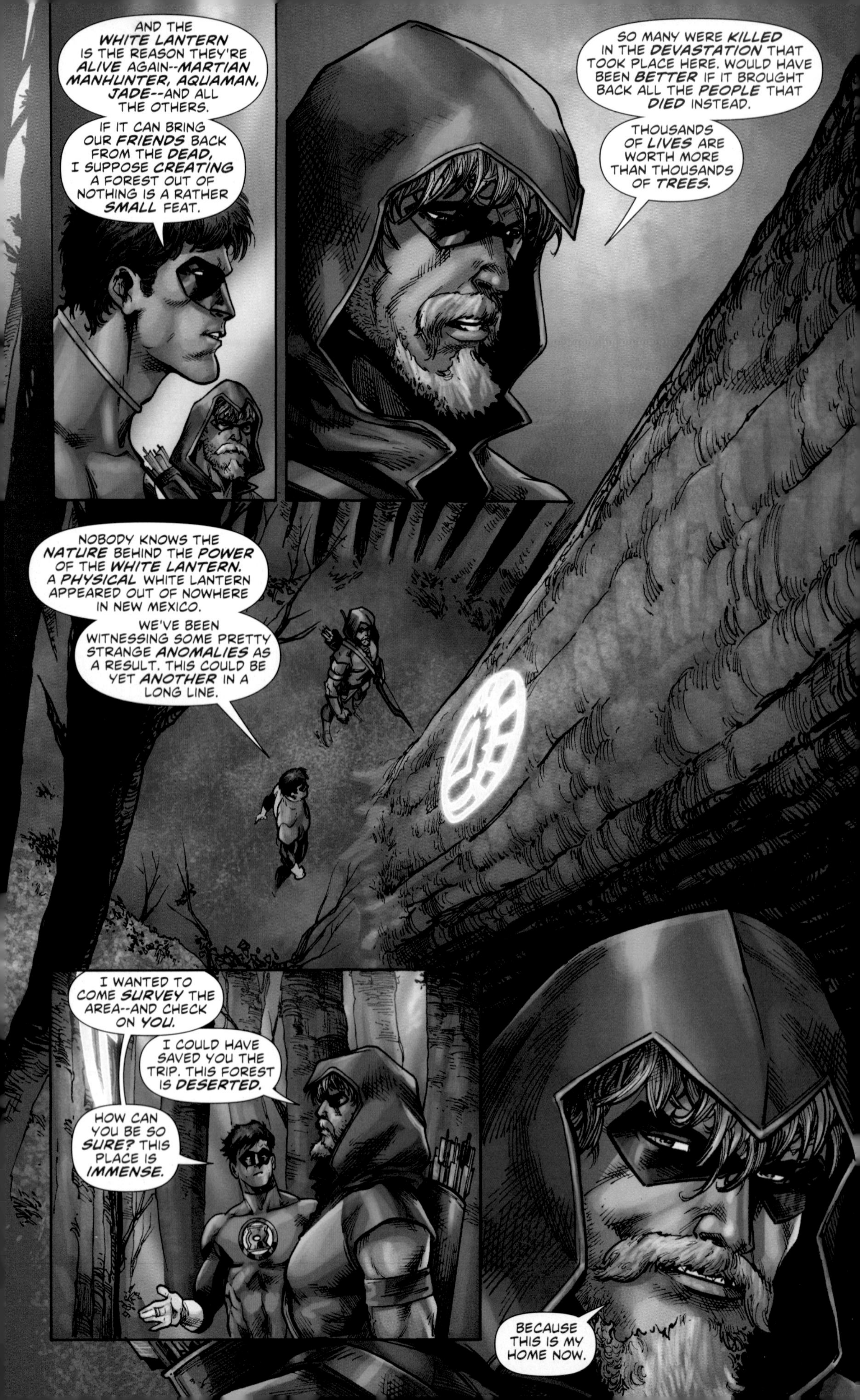
AND THE WHITE LANTERN IS THE REASON THEY'RE ALIVE AGAIN--MARTIAN MANHUNTER, AQUAMAN, JADE--AND ALL THE OTHERS.
IF IT CAN BRING OUR FRIENDS BACK FROM THE DEAD, I SUPPOSE CREATING A FOREST OUT OF NOTHING IS A RATHER SMALL FEAT.
SO MANY WERE KILLED IN THE DEVASTATION THAT TOOK PLACE HERE. WOULD HAVE BEEN BETTER IF IT BROUGHT BACK ALL THE PEOPLE THAT DIED INSTEAD.
THOUSANDS OF LIVES ARE WORTH MORE THAN THOUSANDS OF TREES.
NOBODY KNOWS THE NATURE BEHIND THE POWER OF THE WHITE LANTERN. A PHYSICAL WHITE LANTERN APPEARED OUT OF NOWHERE IN NEW MEXICO.
WE'VE BEEN WITNESSING SOME PRETTY STRANGE ANOMALIES AS A RESULT. THIS COULD BE YET ANOTHER IN A LONG LINE.
I WANTED TO COME SURVEY THE AREA--AND CHECK ON YOU.
I COULD HAVE SAVED YOU THE TRIP. THIS FOREST IS DESERTED.
HOW CAN YOU BE SO SURE? THIS PLACE IS IMMENSE.
BECAUSE THIS IS MY HOME NOW.

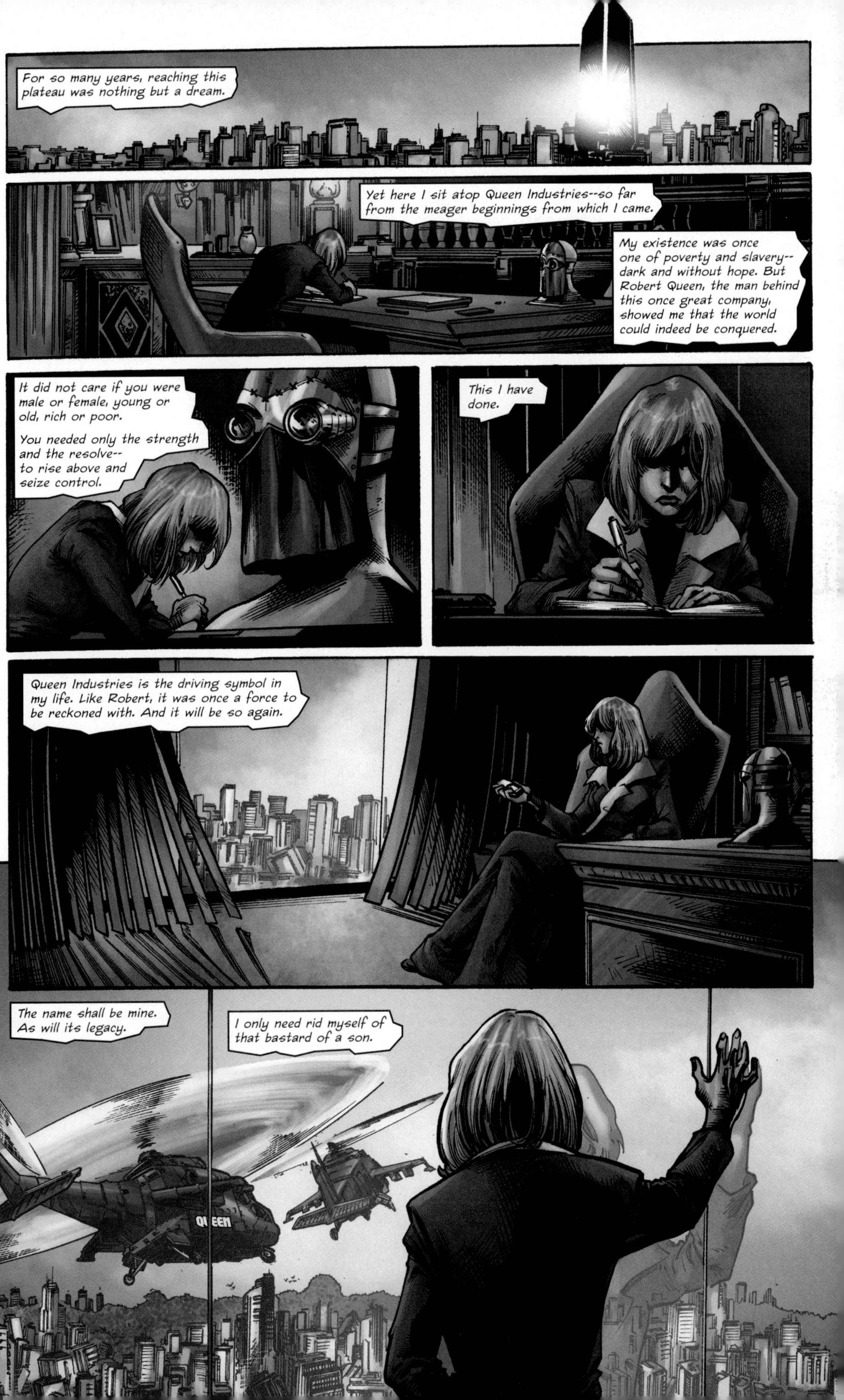
For so many years, reaching this plateau was nothing but a dream.
Yet here I sit atop Queen Industries--so far from the meager beginnings from which I came.
My existence was once one of poverty and slavery--dark and without hope. But Robert Queen, the man behind this once great company, showed me that the world could indeed be conquered.
It did not care if you were male or female, young or old, rich or poor.
You needed only the strength and the resolve--to rise above and seize control.
This I have done.
Queen Industries is the driving symbol in my life. Like Robert, it was once a force to be reckoned with. And it will be so again.
The name shall be mine. As will its legacy.
I only need rid myself of that bastard of a son.
QUEEN

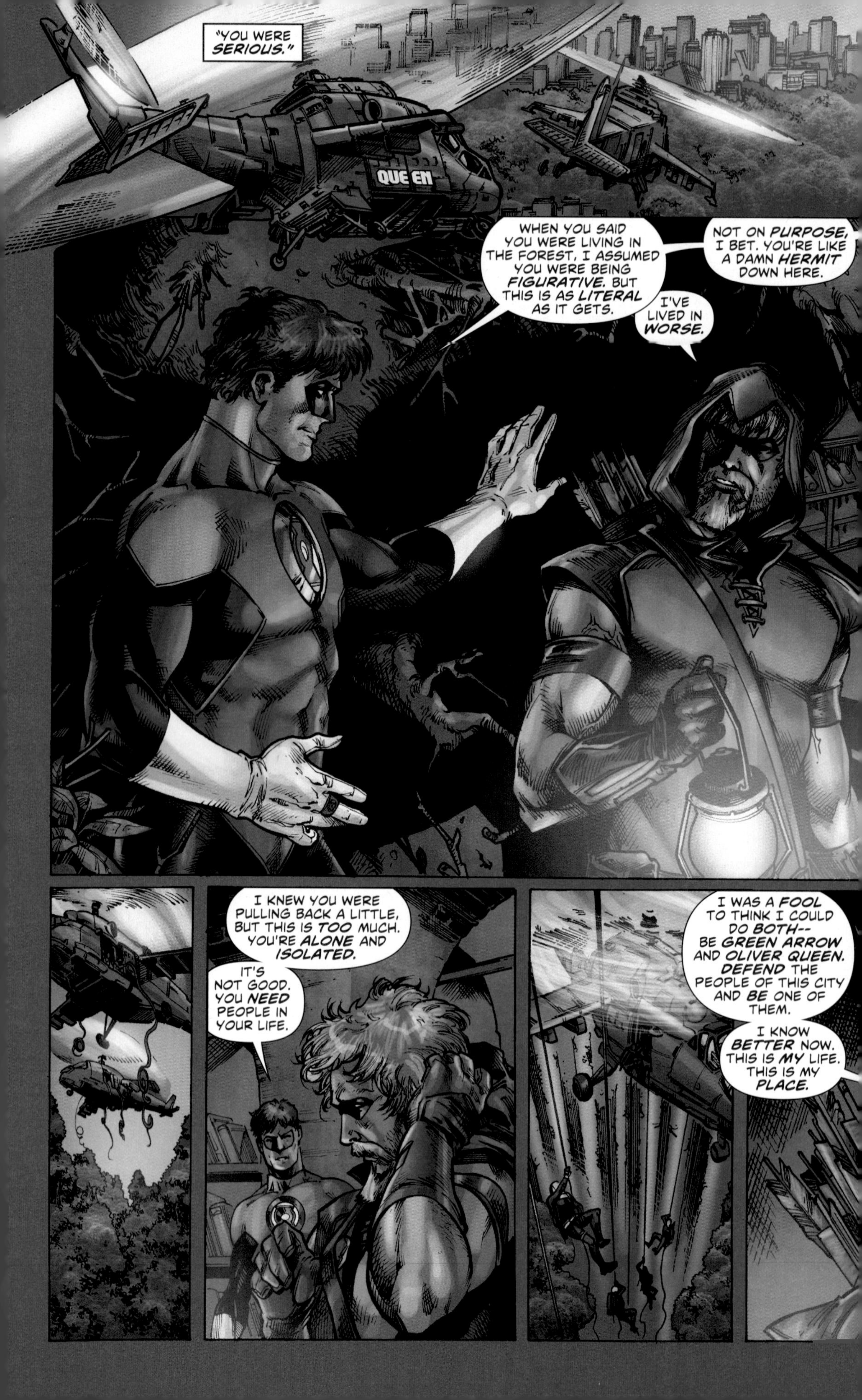
"YOU WERE SERIOUS."
QUE EN
WHEN YOU SAID YOU WERE LIVING IN THE FOREST, I ASSUMED YOU WERE BEING FIGURATIVE. BUT THIS IS AS LITERAL AS IT GETS.
NOT ON PURPOSE, I BET. YOU'RE LIKE A DAMN HERMIT DOWN HERE.
I'VE LIVED IN WORSE.
I KNEW YOU WERE PULLING BACK A LITTLE, BUT THIS IS TOO MUCH. YOU'RE ALONE AND ISOLATED.
IT'S NOT GOOD. YOU NEED PEOPLE IN YOUR LIFE.
I WAS A FOOL TO THINK I COULD DO BOTH-- BE GREEN ARROW AND OLIVER QUEEN. DEFEND THE PEOPLE OF THIS CITY AND BE ONE OF THEM.
I KNOW BETTER NOW. THIS IS MY LIFE. THIS IS MY PLACE.

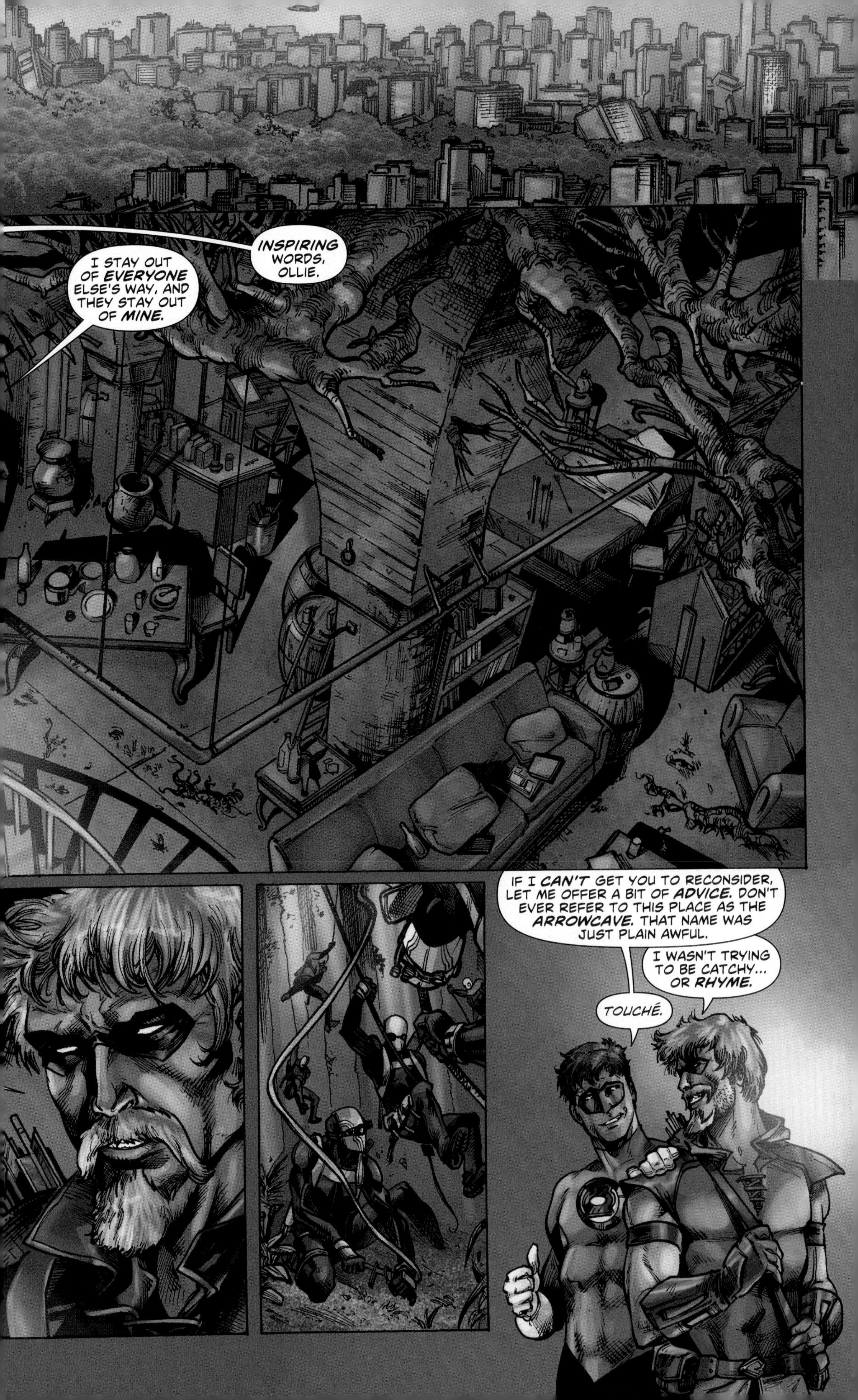
I STAY OUT OF EVERYONE ELSE'S WAY, AND THEY STAY OUT OF MINE.
INSPIRING WORDS, OLLIE.
IF I CAN'T GET YOU TO RECONSIDER, LET ME OFFER A BIT OF ADVICE. DON'T EVER REFER TO THIS PLACE AS THE ARROWCAVE. THAT NAME WAS JUST PLAIN AWFUL.
I WASN'T TRYING TO BE CATCHY... OR RHYME.
TOUCHÉ.

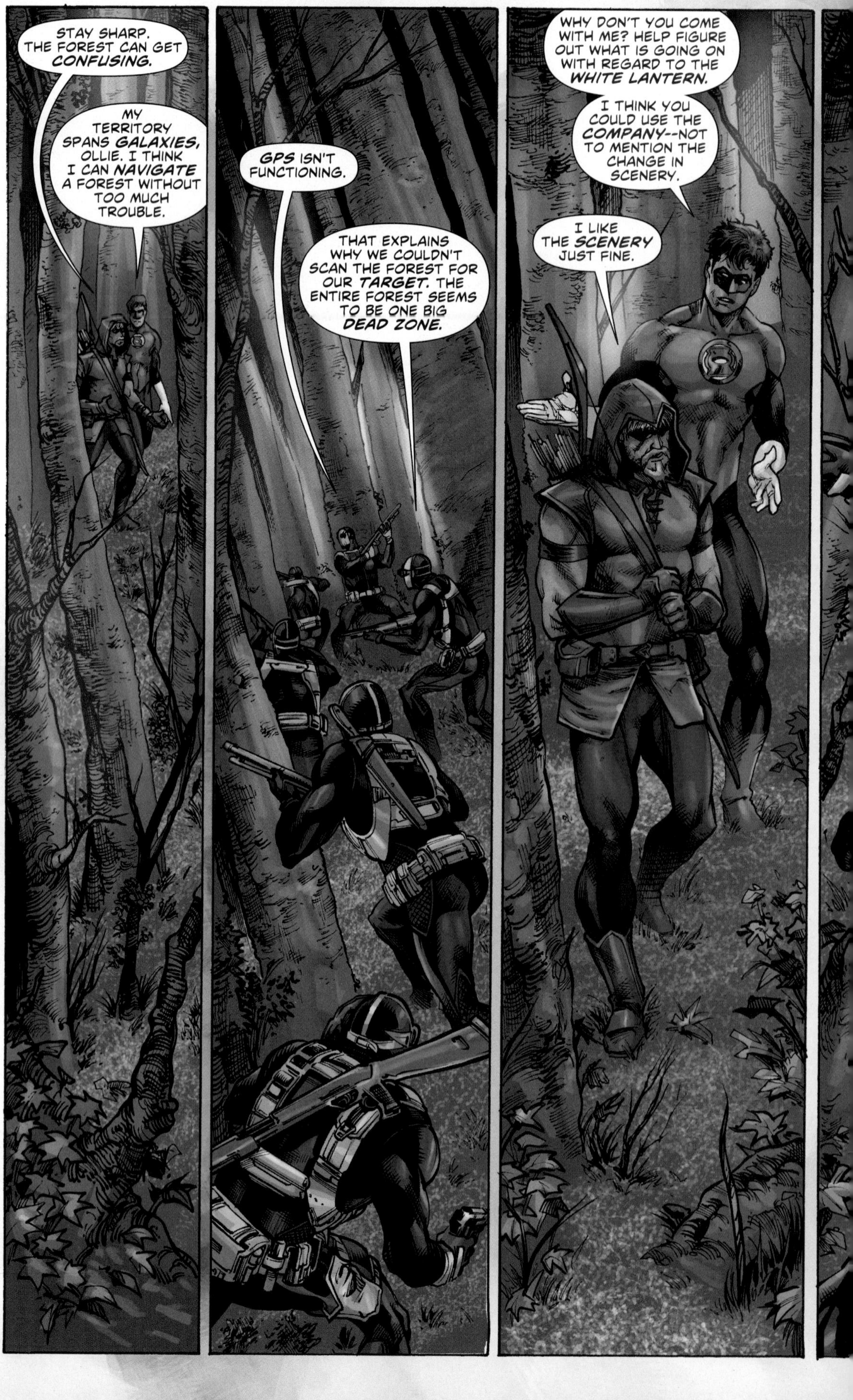
STAY SHARP. THE FOREST CAN GET CONFUSING.
MY TERRITORY SPANS GALAXIES, OLLIE. I THINK I CAN NAVIGATE A FOREST WITHOUT TOO MUCH TROUBLE.
GPS ISN'T FUNCTIONING.
THAT EXPLAINS WHY WE COULDN'T SCAN THE FOREST FOR OUR TARGET. THE ENTIRE FOREST SEEMS TO BE ONE BIG DEAD ZONE.
WHY DON'T YOU COME WITH ME? HELP FIGURE OUT WHAT IS GOING ON WITH REGARD TO THE WHITE LANTERN.
I THINK YOU COULD USE THE COMPANY--NOT TO MENTION THE CHANGE IN SCENERY.
I LIKE THE SCENERY JUST FINE.

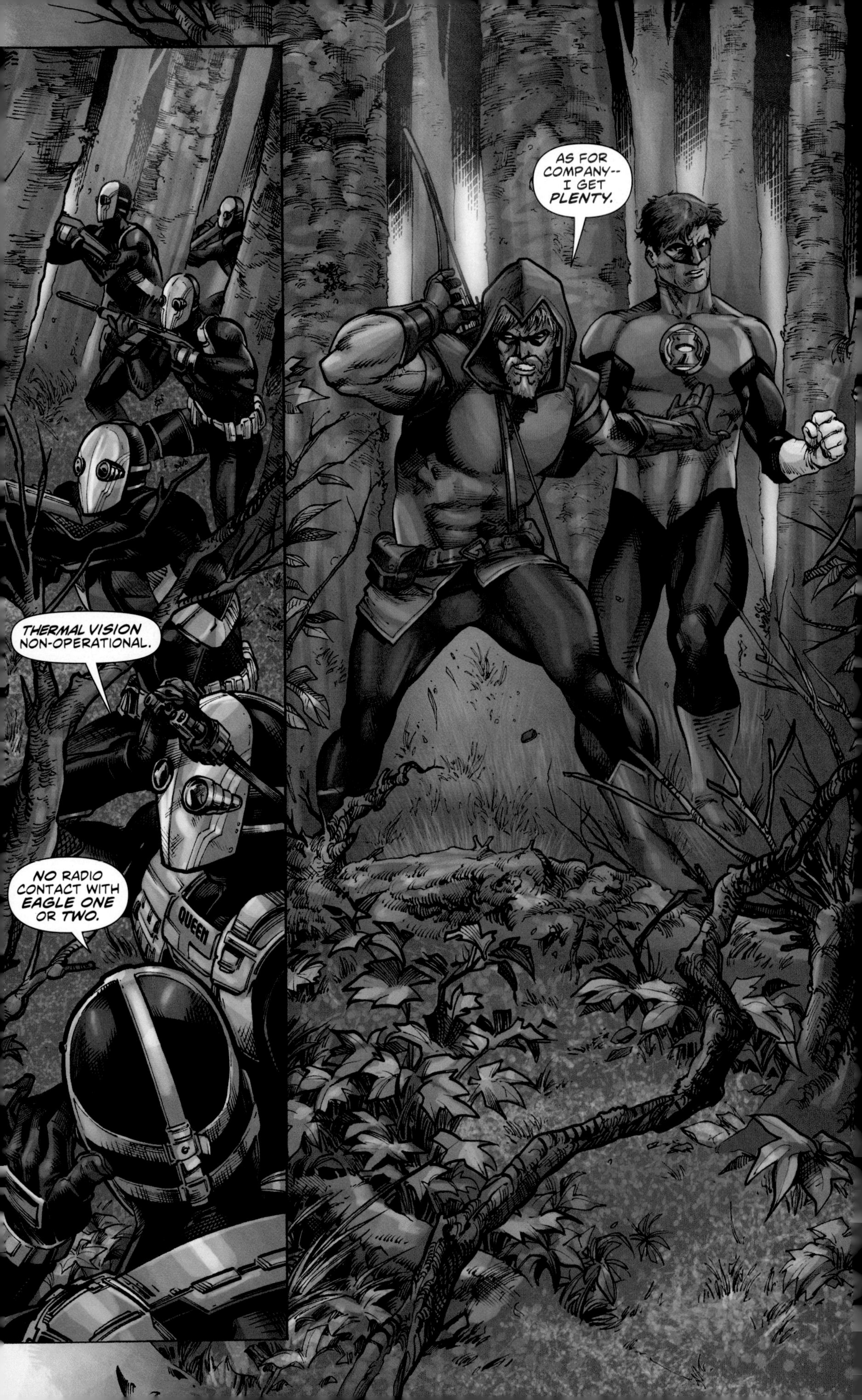
THERMAL VISION NON-OPERATIONAL.
NO RADIO CONTACT WITH EAGLE ONE OR TWO.
QUEEN
AS FOR COMPANY-- I GET PLENTY.

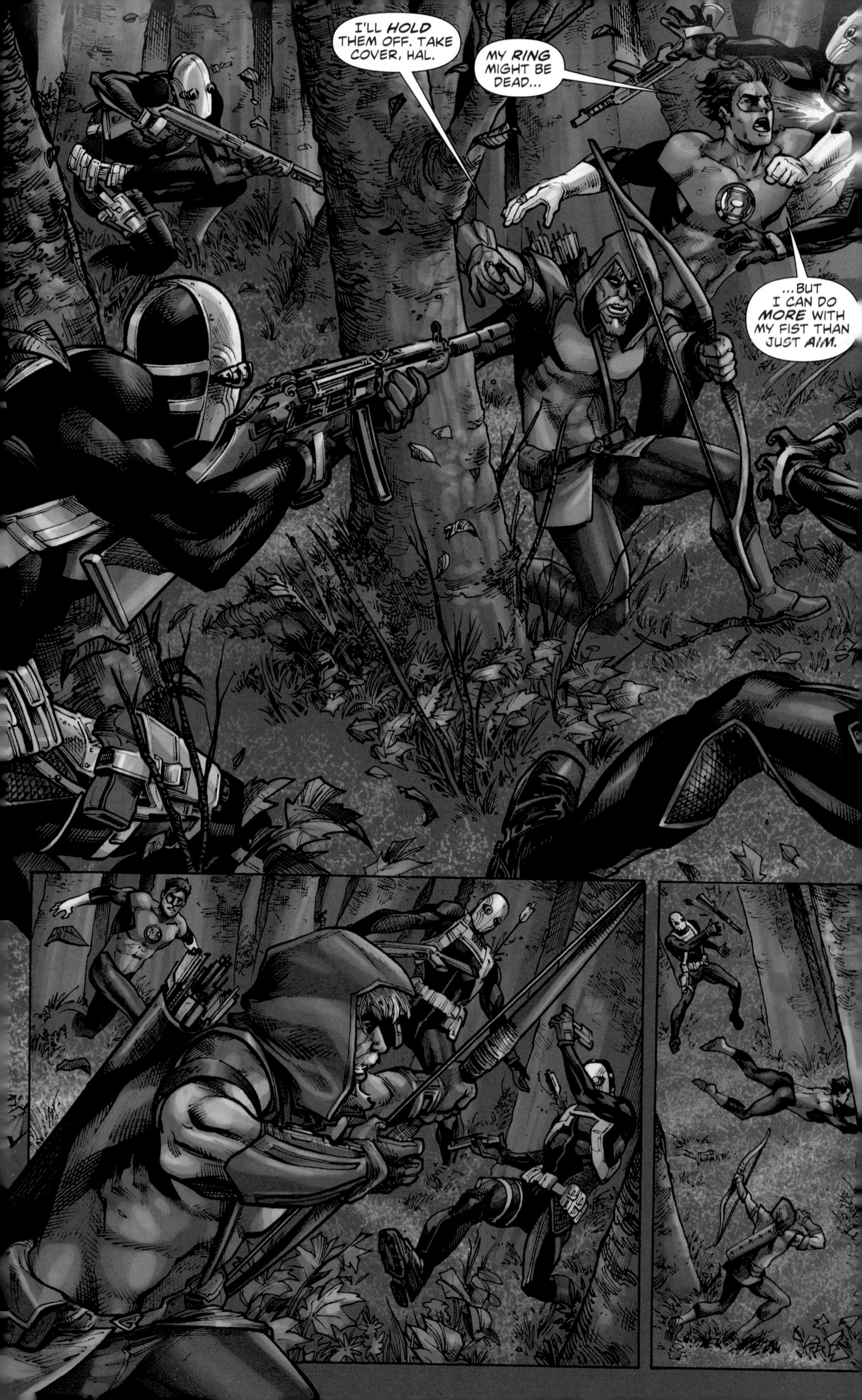

I'LL **HOLD** THEM OFF. TAKE COVER, HAL.
MY **RING** MIGHT BE DEAD...
...BUT I CAN DO **MORE** WITH MY FIST THAN JUST **AIM.**

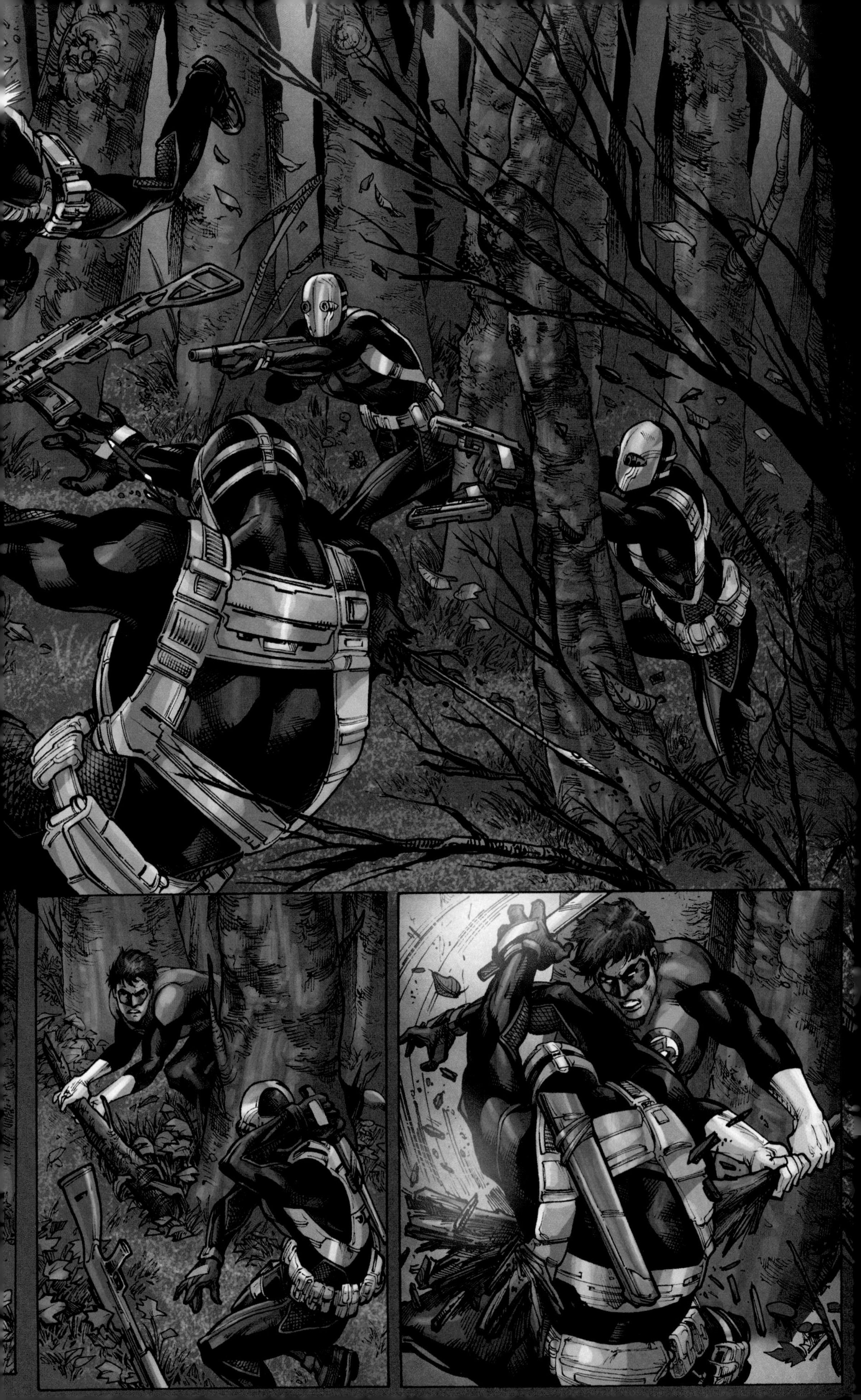

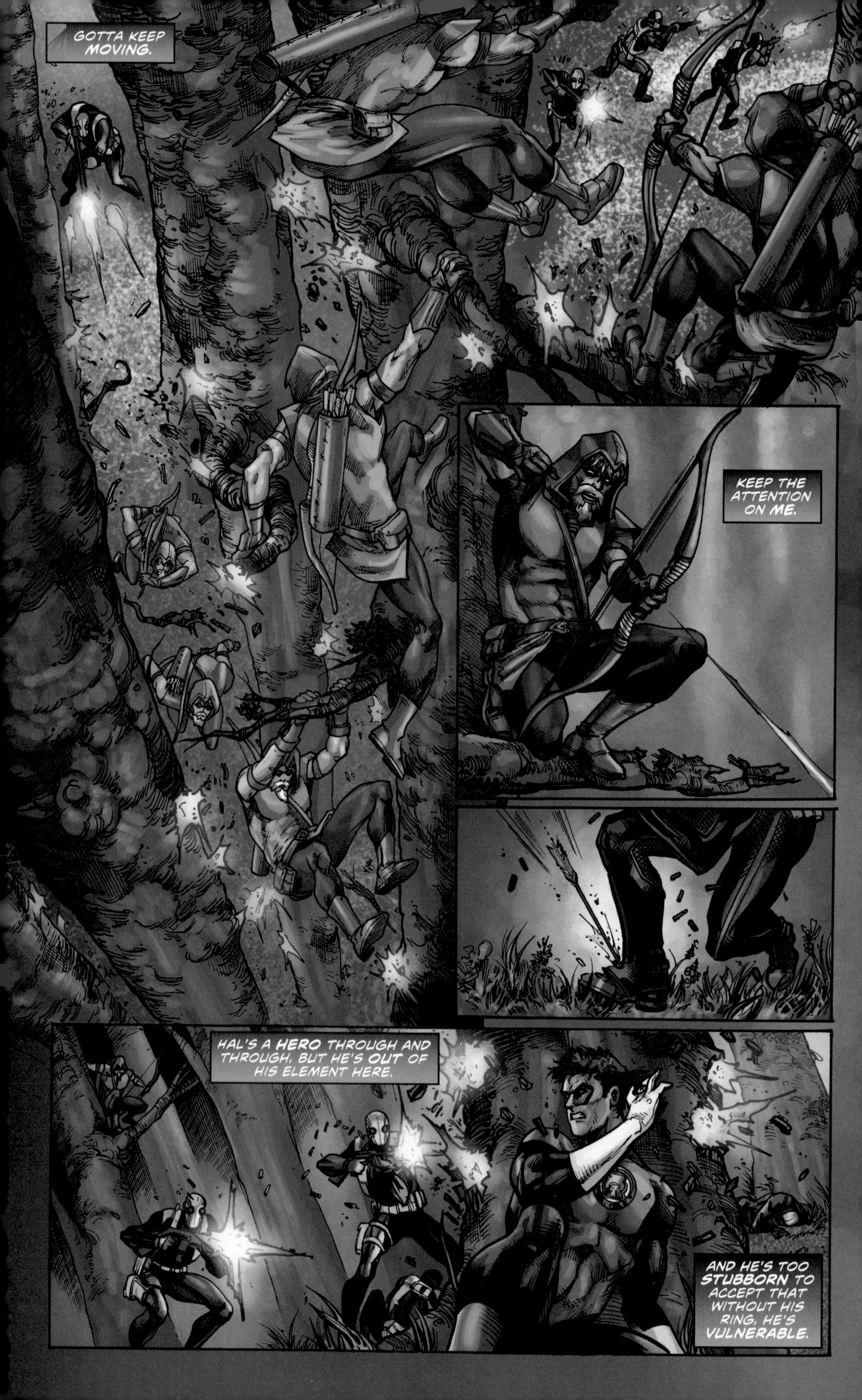
GOTTA KEEP MOVING.
KEEP THE ATTENTION ON ME.
HAL'S A HERO THROUGH AND THROUGH, BUT HE'S OUT OF HIS ELEMENT HERE.
AND HE'S TOO STUBBORN TO ACCEPT THAT WITHOUT HIS RING, HE'S VULNERABLE.

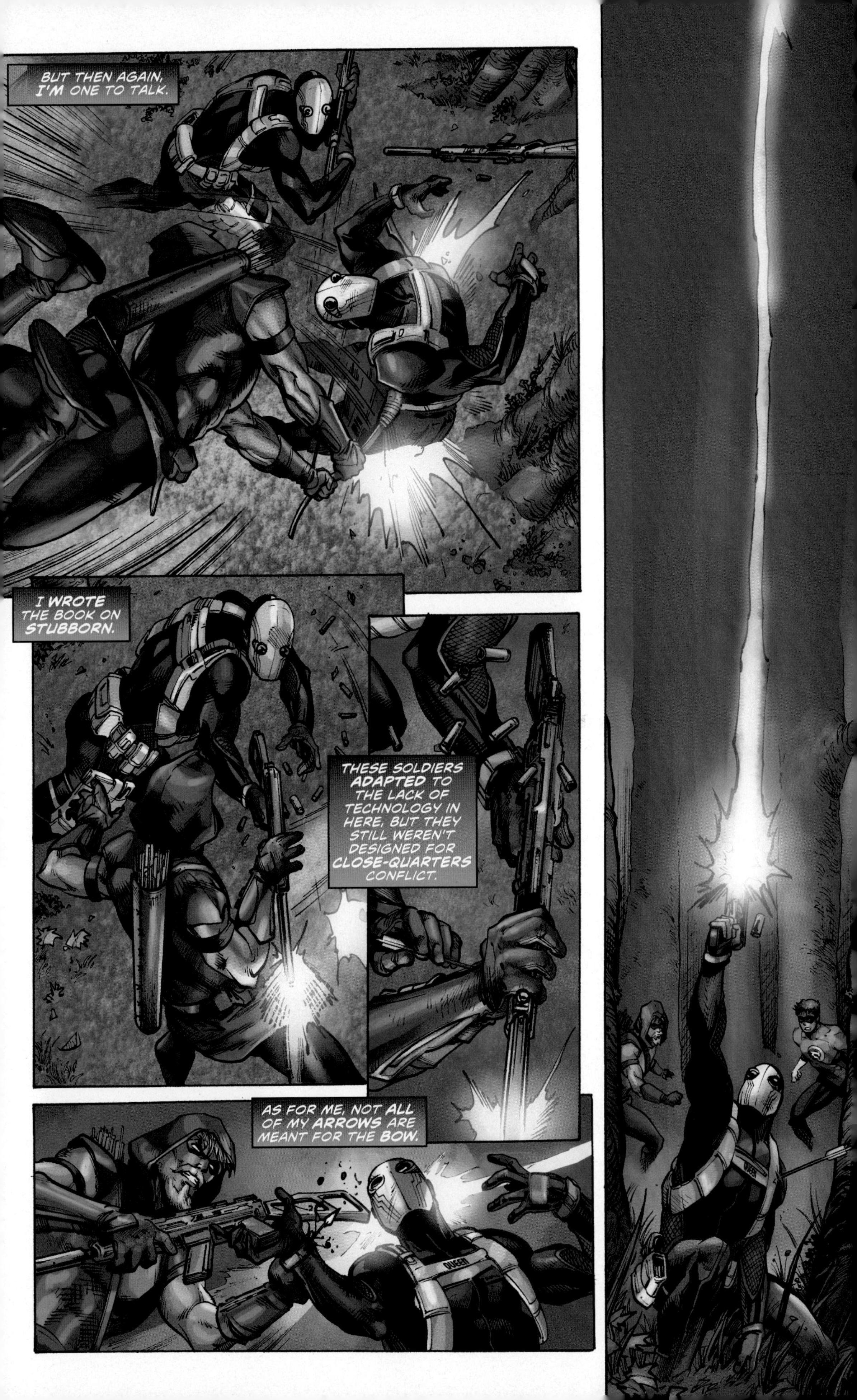
BUT THEN AGAIN, I'M ONE TO TALK.
I WROTE THE BOOK ON STUBBORN.
THESE SOLDIERS ADAPTED TO THE LACK OF TECHNOLOGY IN HERE, BUT THEY STILL WEREN'T DESIGNED FOR CLOSE-QUARTERS CONFLICT.
AS FOR ME, NOT ALL OF MY ARROWS ARE MEANT FOR THE BOW.
QUEEN
QUEEN

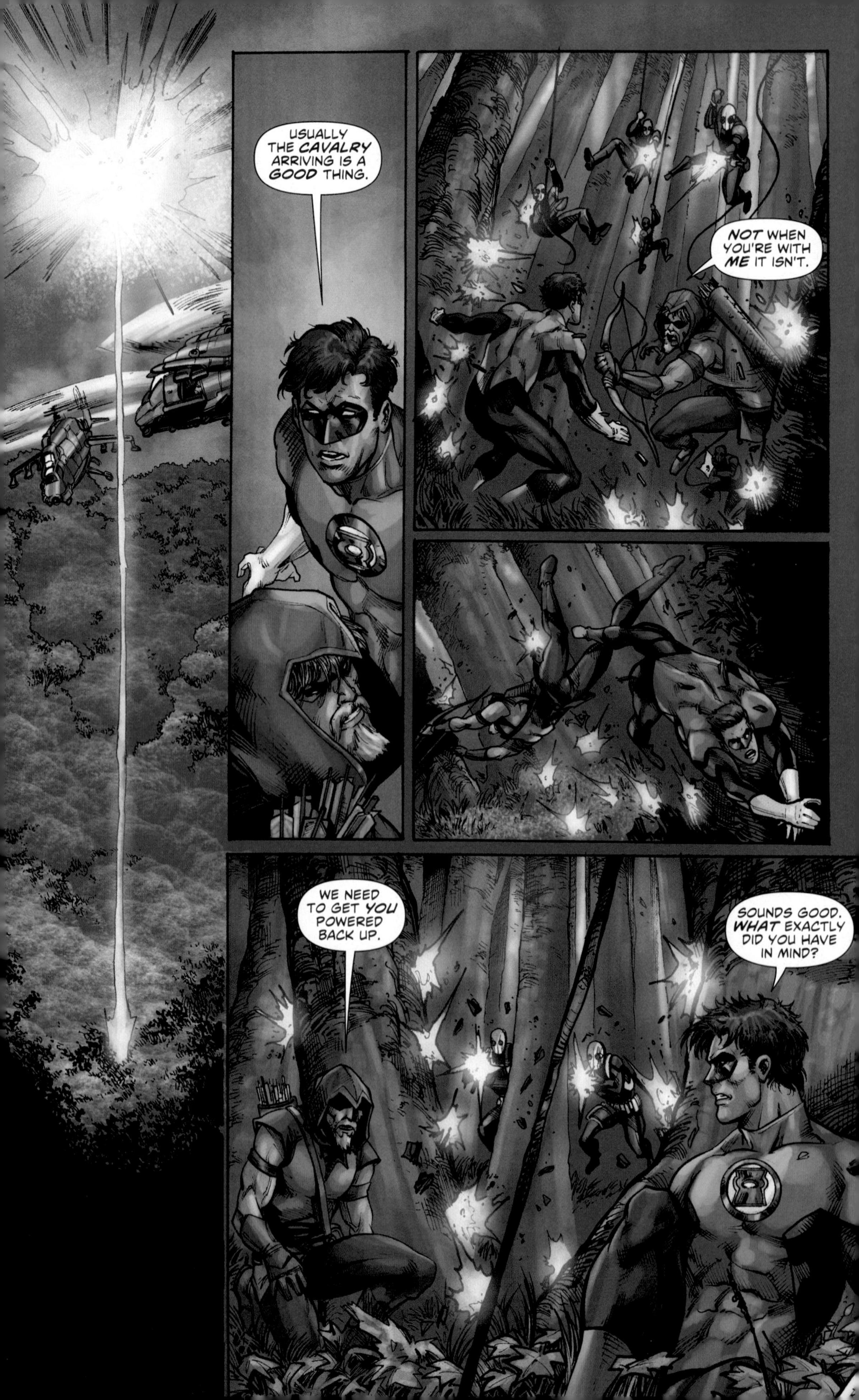
USUALLY THE CAVALRY ARRIVING IS A GOOD THING.
NOT WHEN YOU'RE WITH ME IT ISN'T.
WE NEED TO GET YOU POWERED BACK UP.
SOUNDS GOOD. WHAT EXACTLY DID YOU HAVE IN MIND?

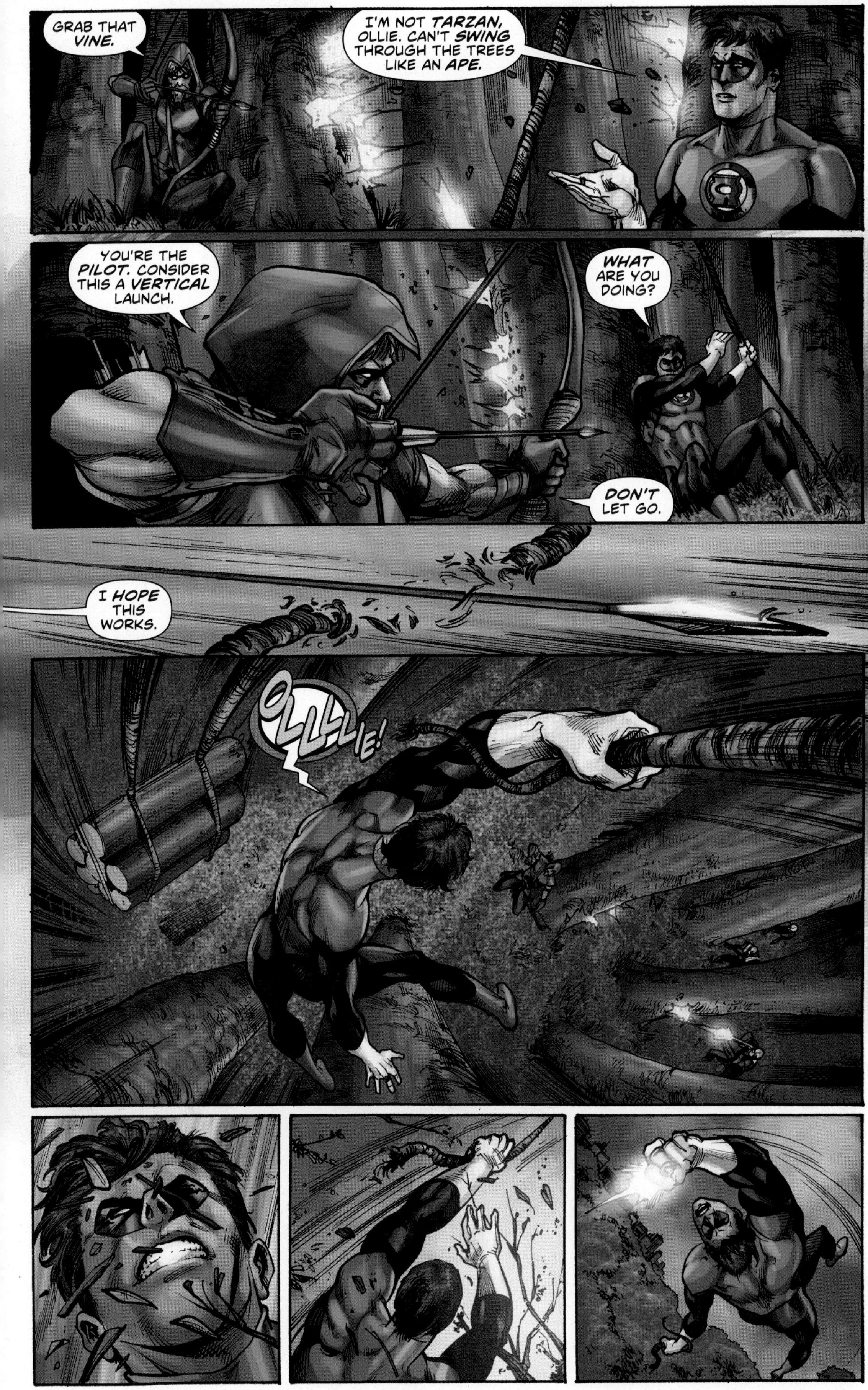
GRAB THAT VINE.
I'M NOT TARZAN, OLLIE. CAN'T SWING THROUGH THE TREES LIKE AN APE.
YOU'RE THE PILOT. CONSIDER THIS A VERTICAL LAUNCH.
WHAT ARE YOU DOING?
DON'T LET GO.
I HOPE THIS WORKS.
OLLLLIE!

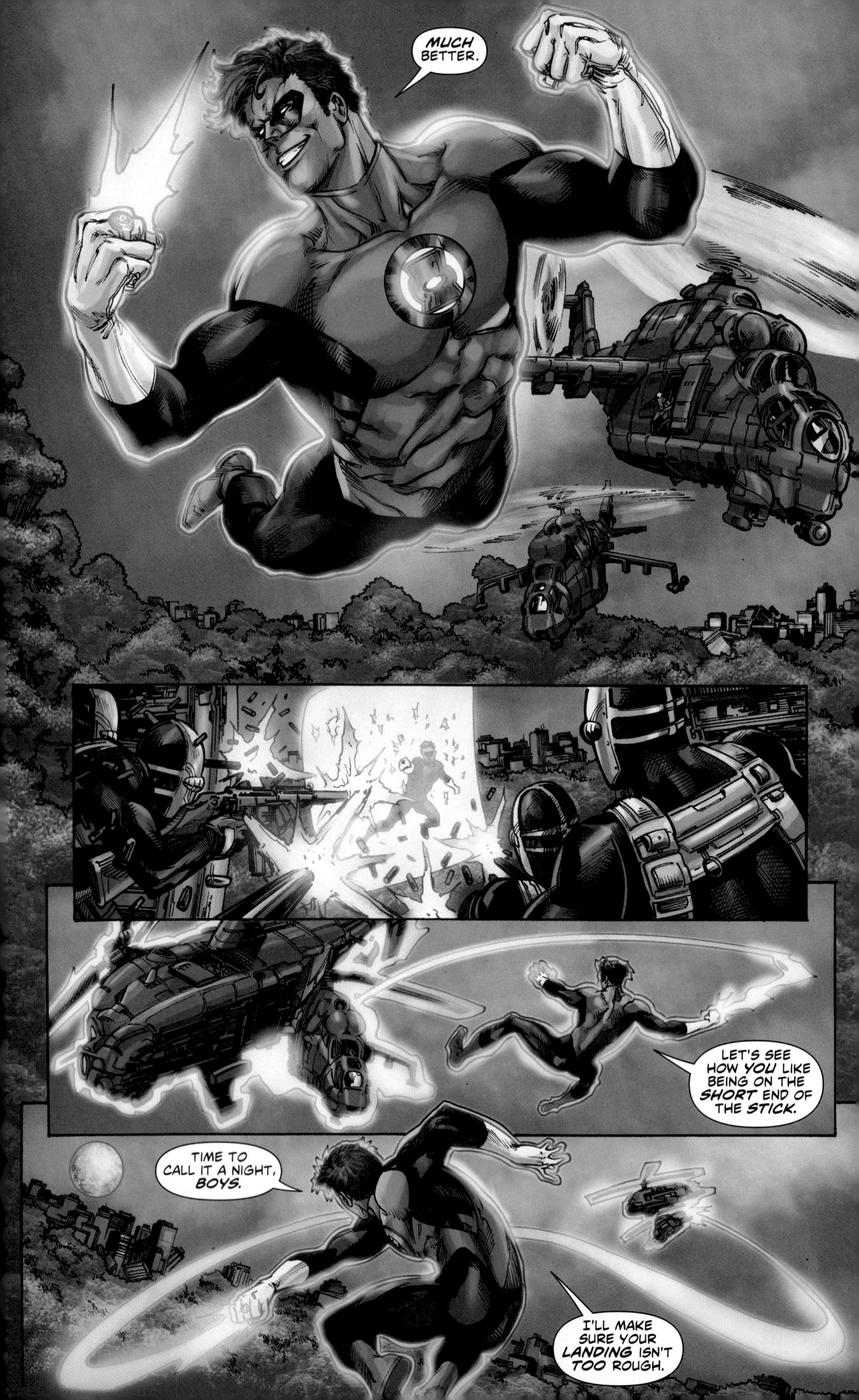
MUCH BETTER.
LET'S SEE HOW YOU LIKE BEING ON THE SHORT END OF THE STICK.
TIME TO CALL IT A NIGHT, BOYS.
I'LL MAKE SURE YOUR LANDING ISN'T TOO ROUGH.

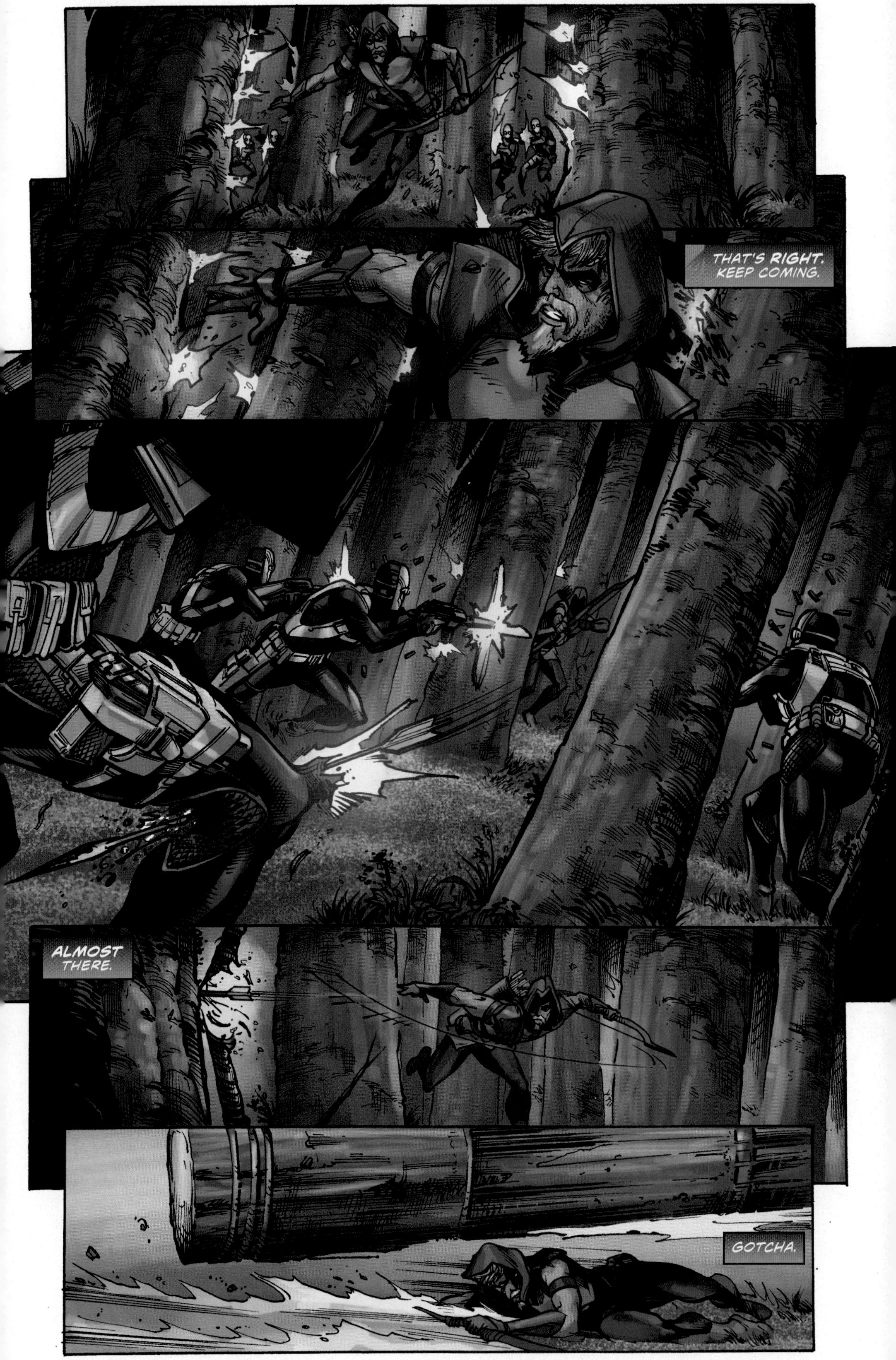
THAT'S RIGHT. KEEP COMING.
ALMOST THERE.
GOTCHA.

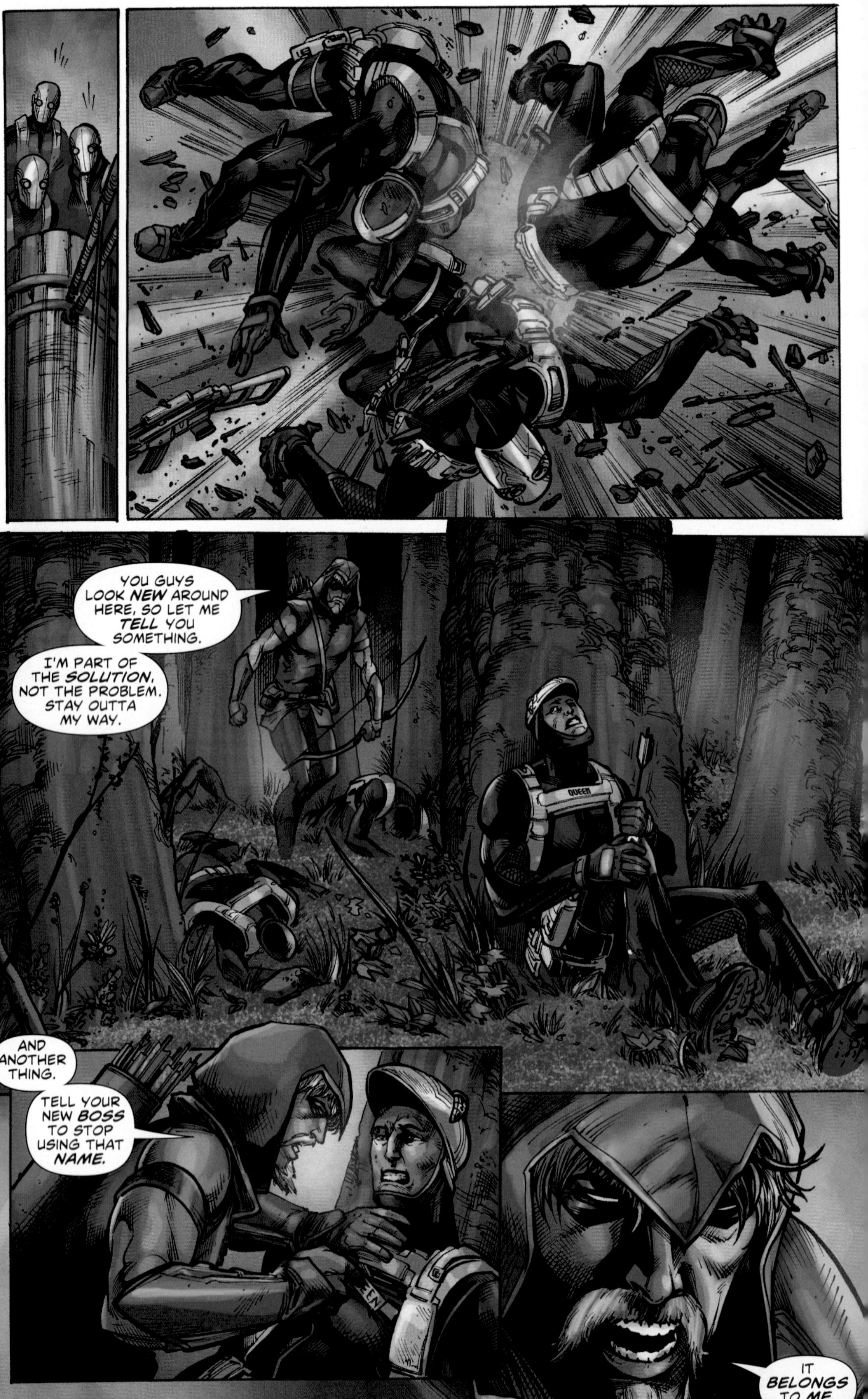
YOU GUYS LOOK NEW AROUND HERE, SO LET ME TELL YOU SOMETHING.
I'M PART OF THE SOLUTION, NOT THE PROBLEM. STAY OUTTA MY WAY.
QUEEN
AND ANOTHER THING.
TELL YOUR NEW BOSS TO STOP USING THAT NAME.
IT BELONGS TO ME.

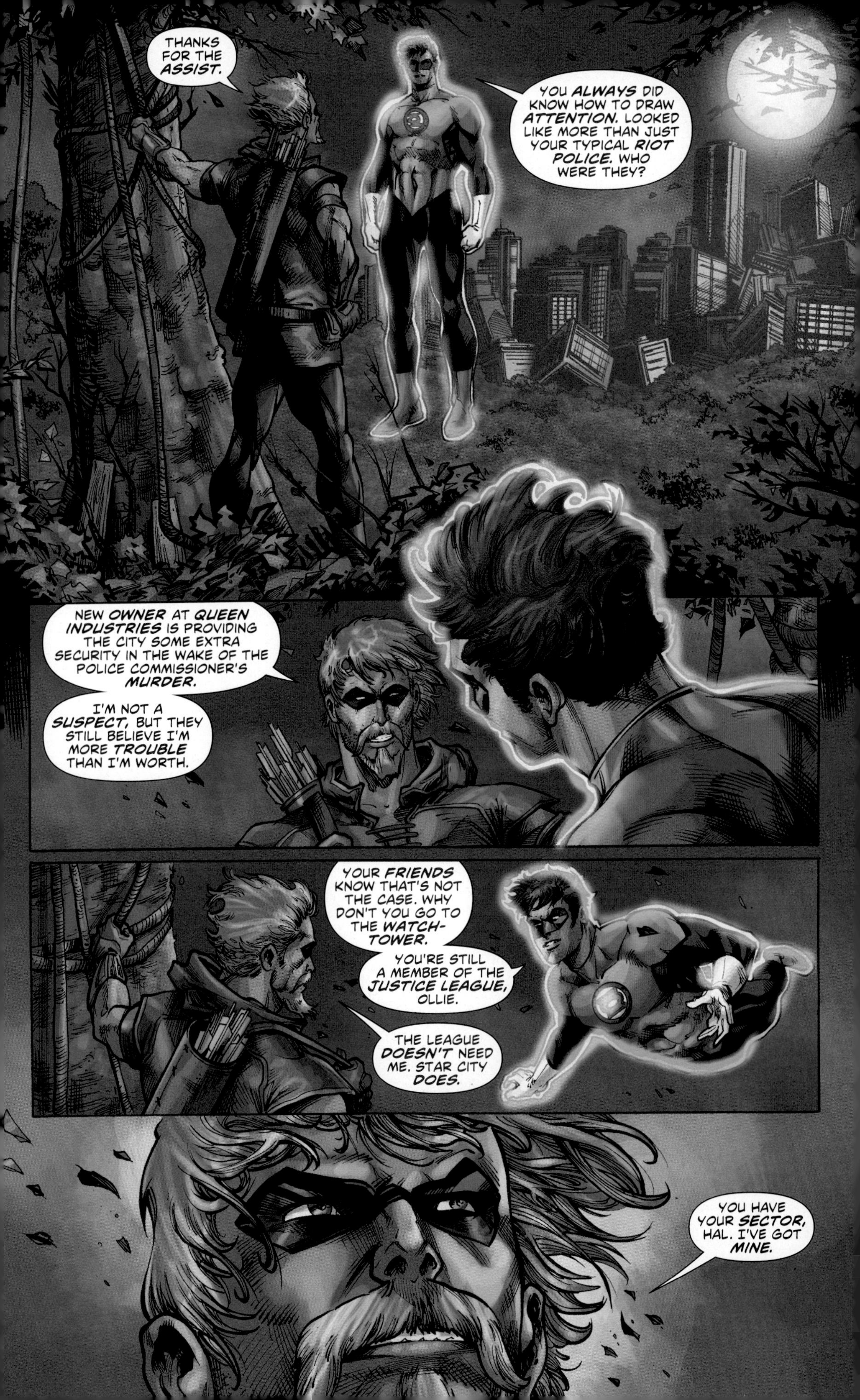
THANKS FOR THE ASSIST.
YOU ALWAYS DID KNOW HOW TO DRAW ATTENTION. LOOKED LIKE MORE THAN JUST YOUR TYPICAL RIOT POLICE. WHO WERE THEY?
NEW OWNER AT QUEEN INDUSTRIES IS PROVIDING THE CITY SOME EXTRA SECURITY IN THE WAKE OF THE POLICE COMMISSIONER'S MURDER.
I'M NOT A SUSPECT, BUT THEY STILL BELIEVE I'M MORE TROUBLE THAN I'M WORTH.
YOUR FRIENDS KNOW THAT'S NOT THE CASE. WHY DON'T YOU GO TO THE WATCH-TOWER.
YOU'RE STILL A MEMBER OF THE JUSTICE LEAGUE, OLLIE.
THE LEAGUE DOESN'T NEED ME. STAR CITY DOES.
YOU HAVE YOUR SECTOR, HAL. I'VE GOT MINE.

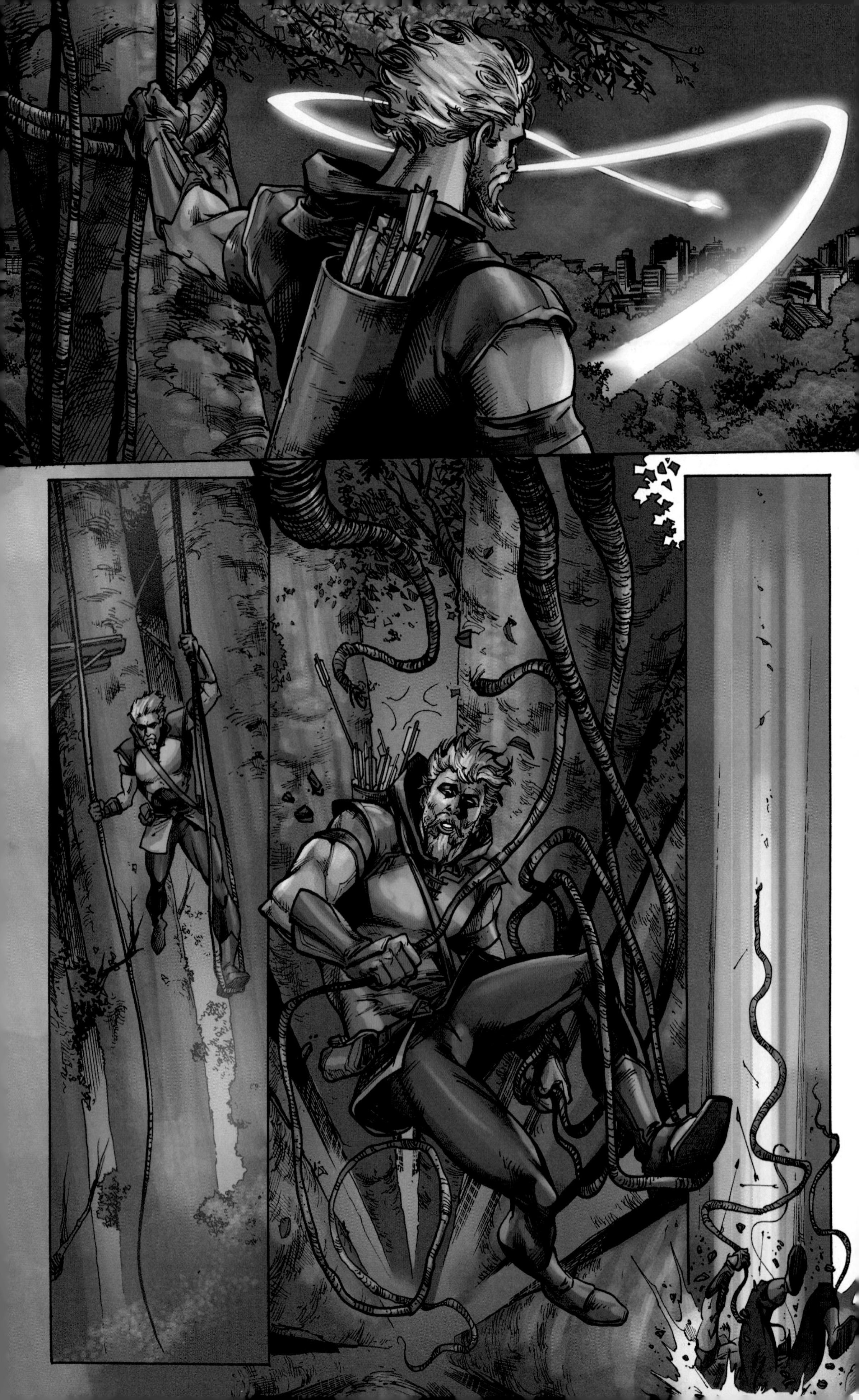

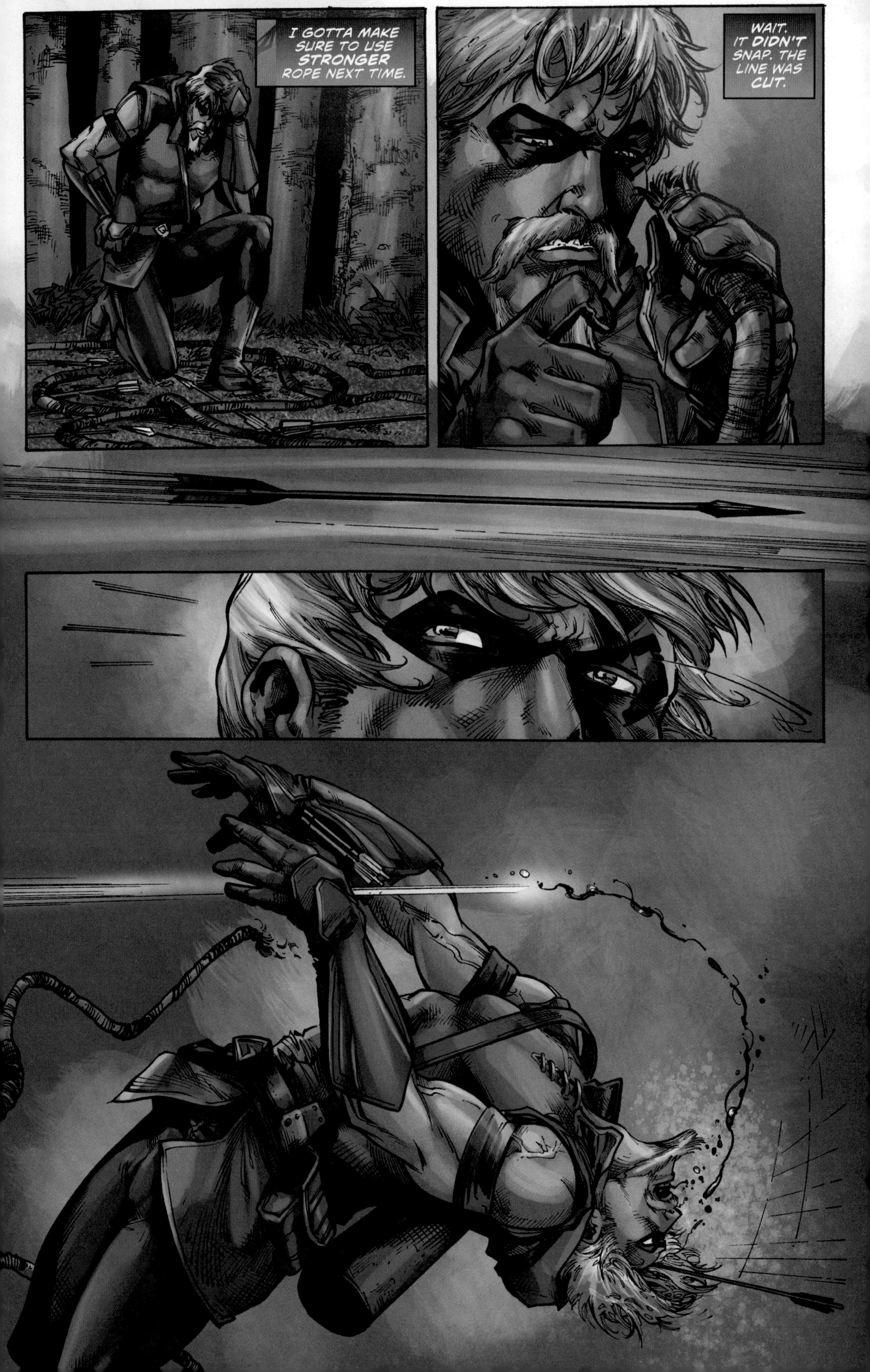
I GOTTA MAKE SURE TO USE STRONGER ROPE NEXT TIME.
WAIT. IT DIDN'T SNAP. THE LINE WAS CUT.

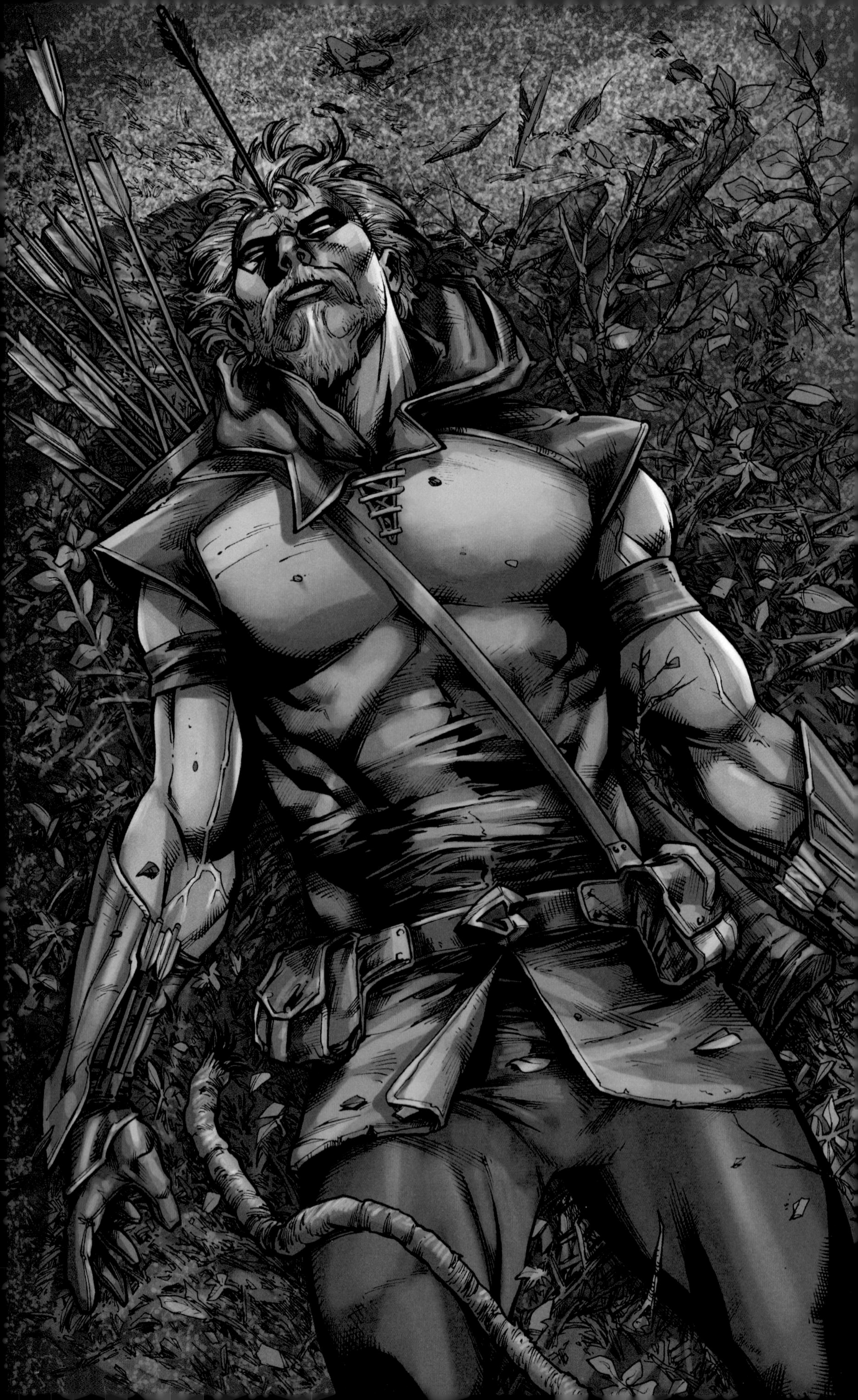

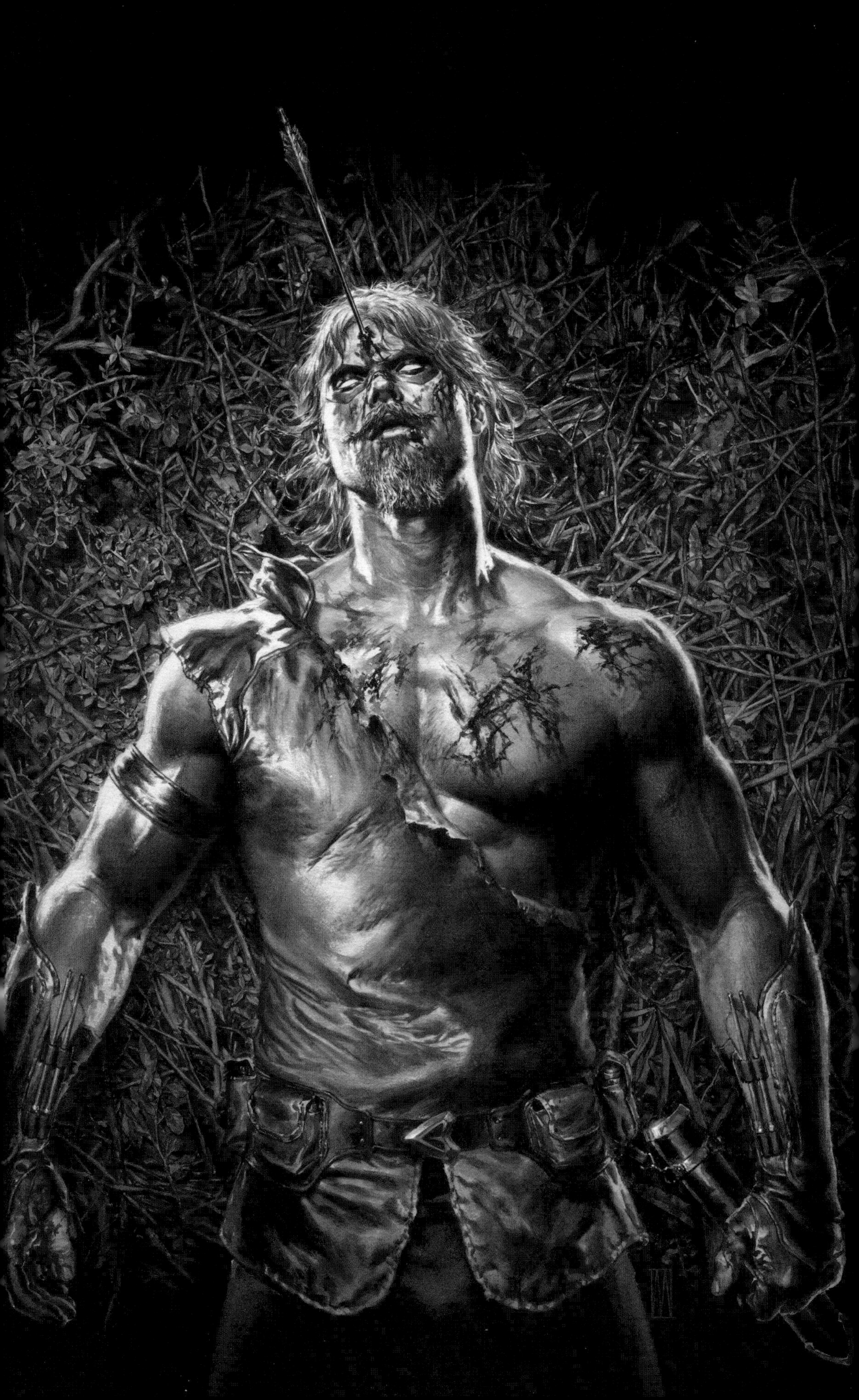

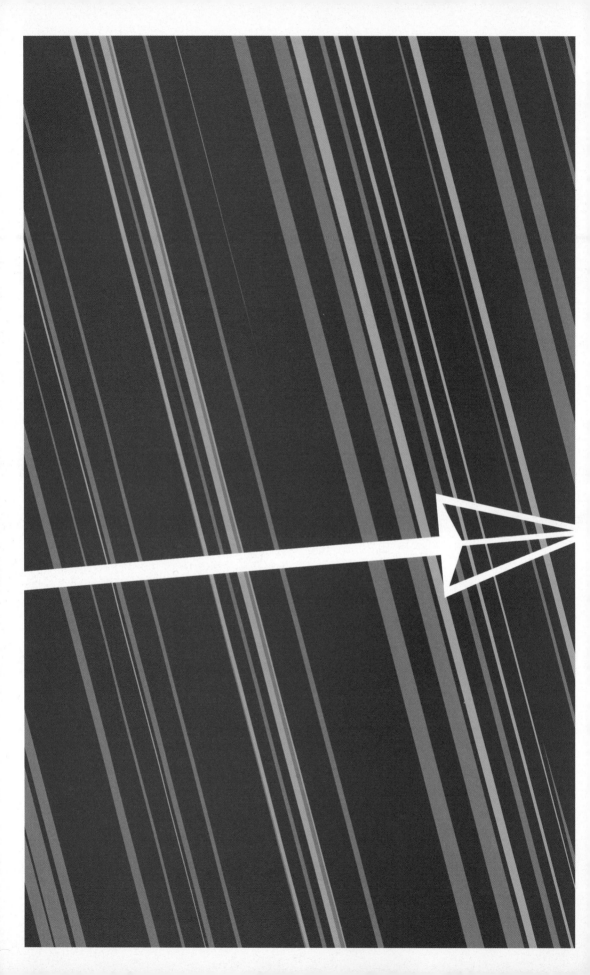

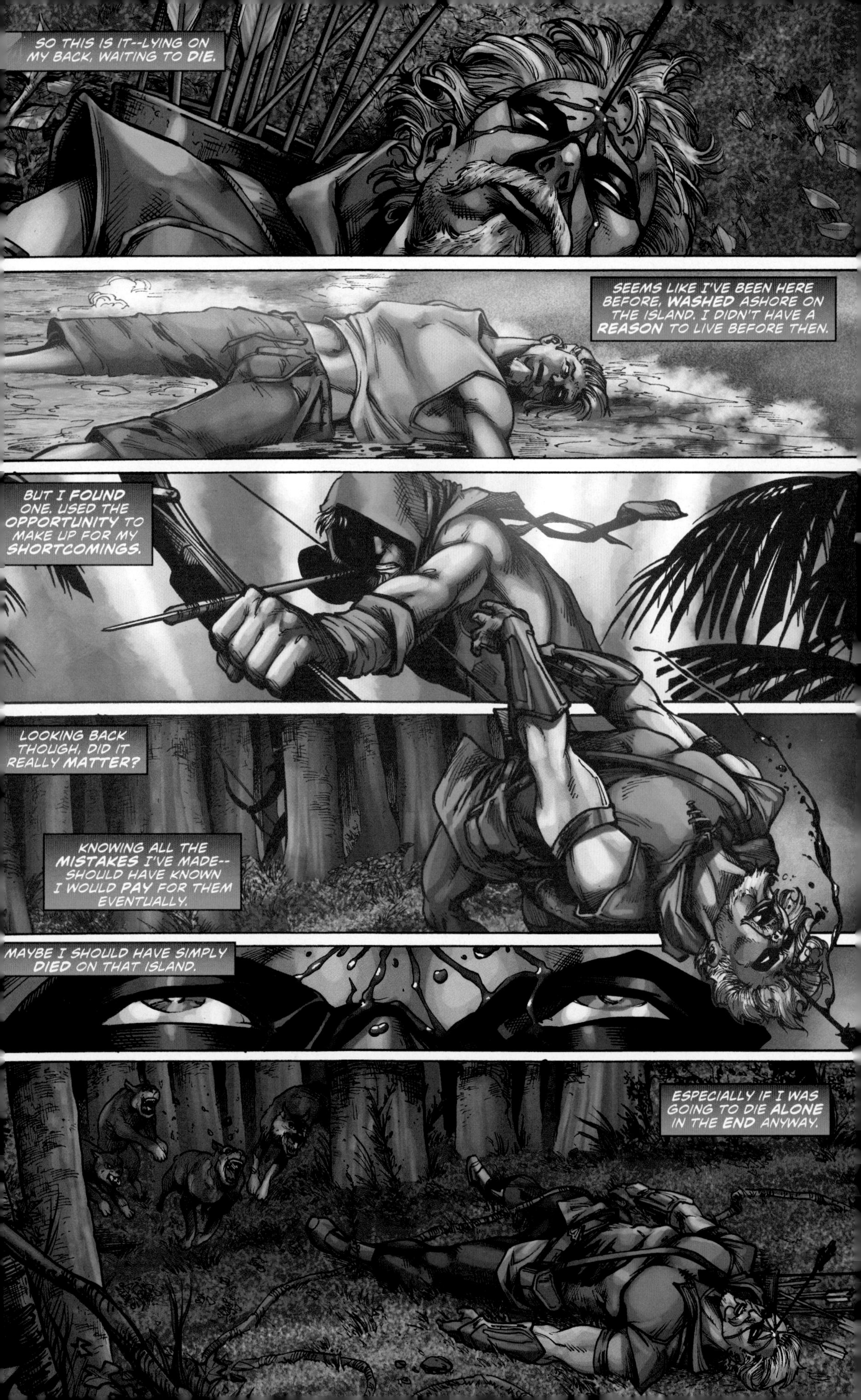
SO THIS IS IT--LYING ON MY BACK, WAITING TO DIE.
SEEMS LIKE I'VE BEEN HERE BEFORE, WASHED ASHORE ON THE ISLAND. I DIDN'T HAVE A REASON TO LIVE BEFORE THEN.
BUT I FOUND ONE. USED THE OPPORTUNITY TO MAKE UP FOR MY SHORTCOMINGS.
LOOKING BACK THOUGH, DID IT REALLY MATTER?
KNOWING ALL THE MISTAKES I'VE MADE--SHOULD HAVE KNOWN I WOULD PAY FOR THEM EVENTUALLY.
MAYBE I SHOULD HAVE SIMPLY DIED ON THAT ISLAND.
ESPECIALLY IF I WAS GOING TO DIE ALONE IN THE END ANYWAY.

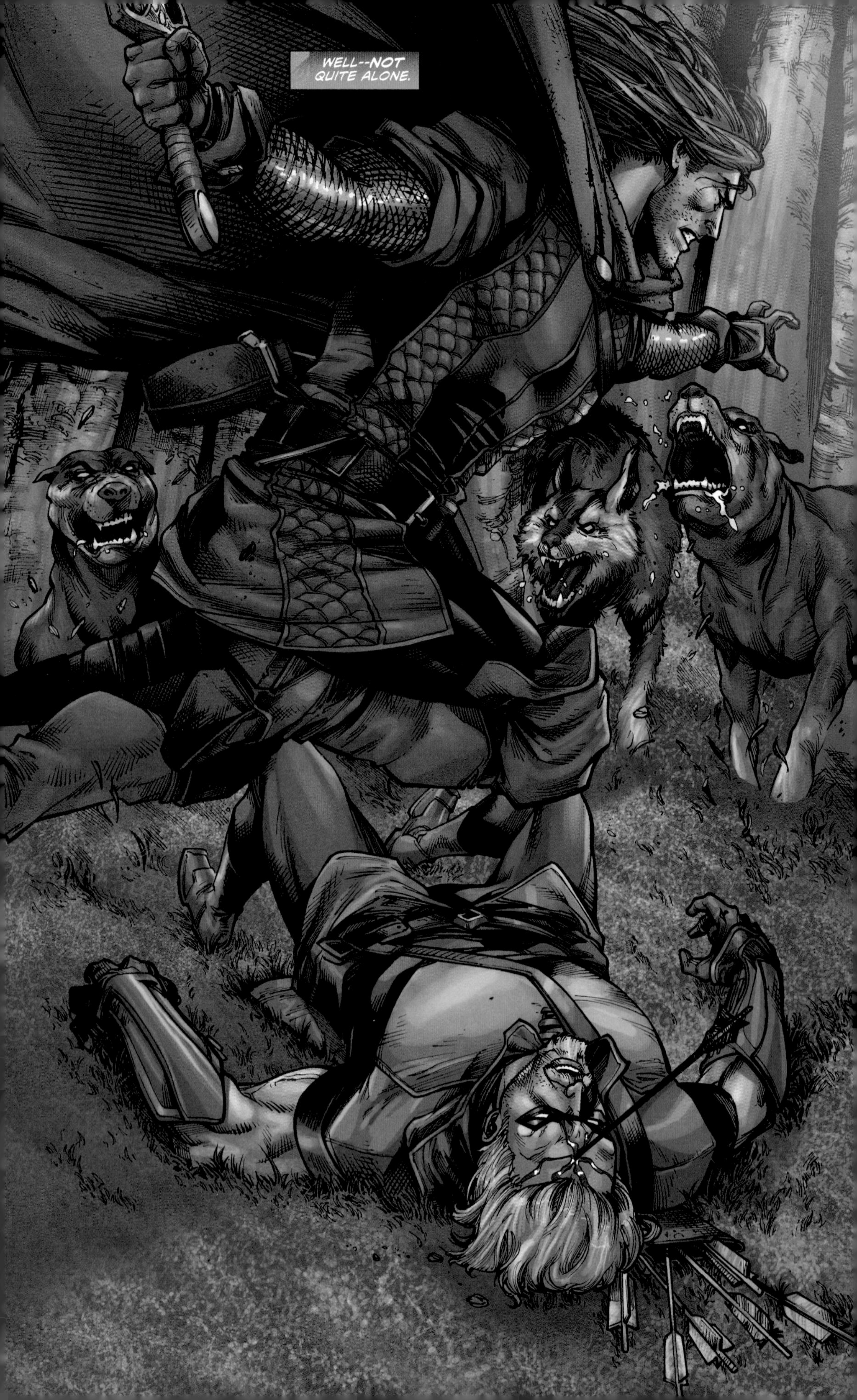
WELL--NOT QUITE ALONE.

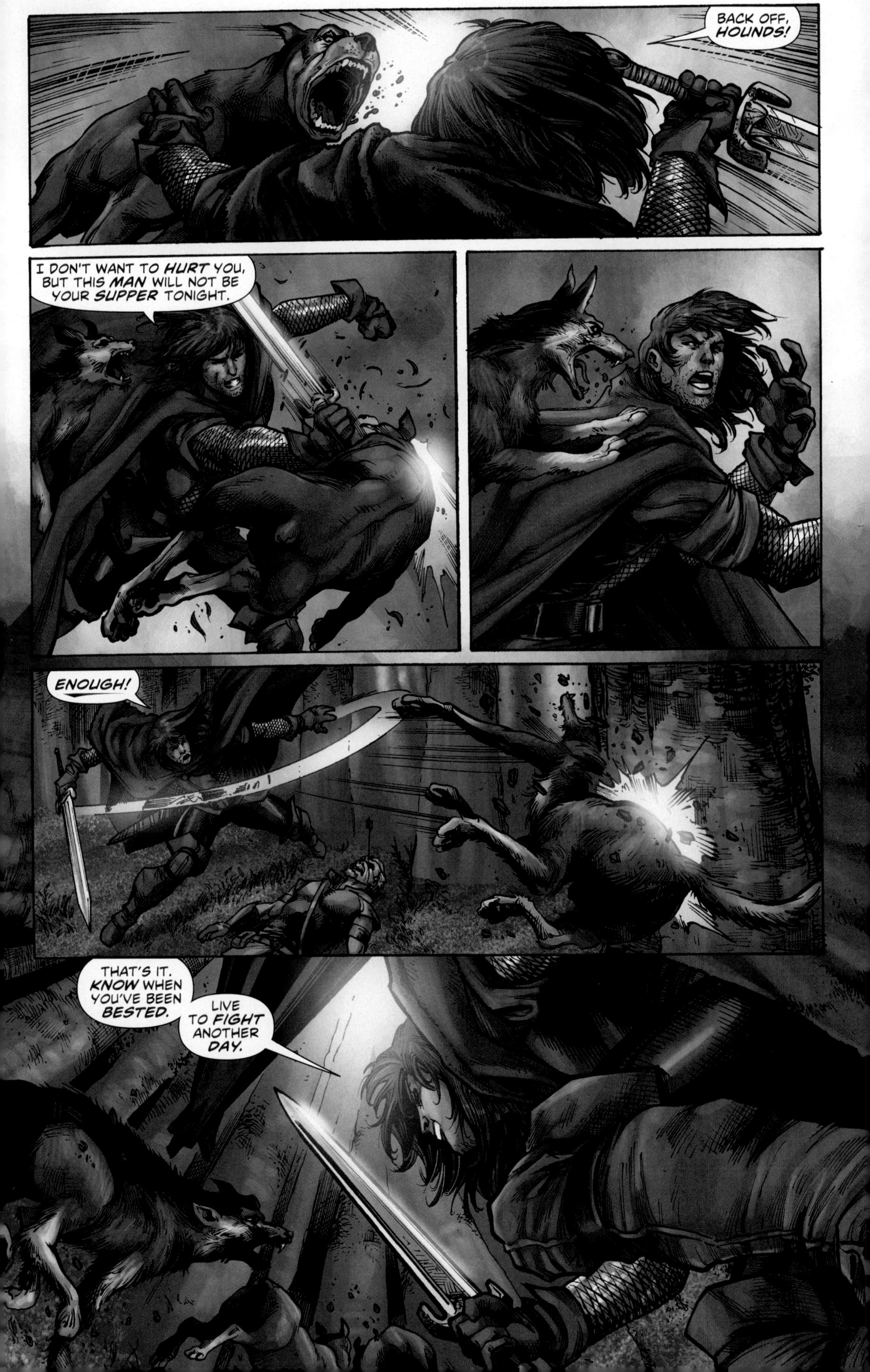
BACK OFF, HOUNDS!
I DON'T WANT TO HURT YOU, BUT THIS MAN WILL NOT BE YOUR SUPPER TONIGHT.
ENOUGH!
THAT'S IT. KNOW WHEN YOU'VE BEEN BESTED.
LIVE TO FIGHT ANOTHER DAY.

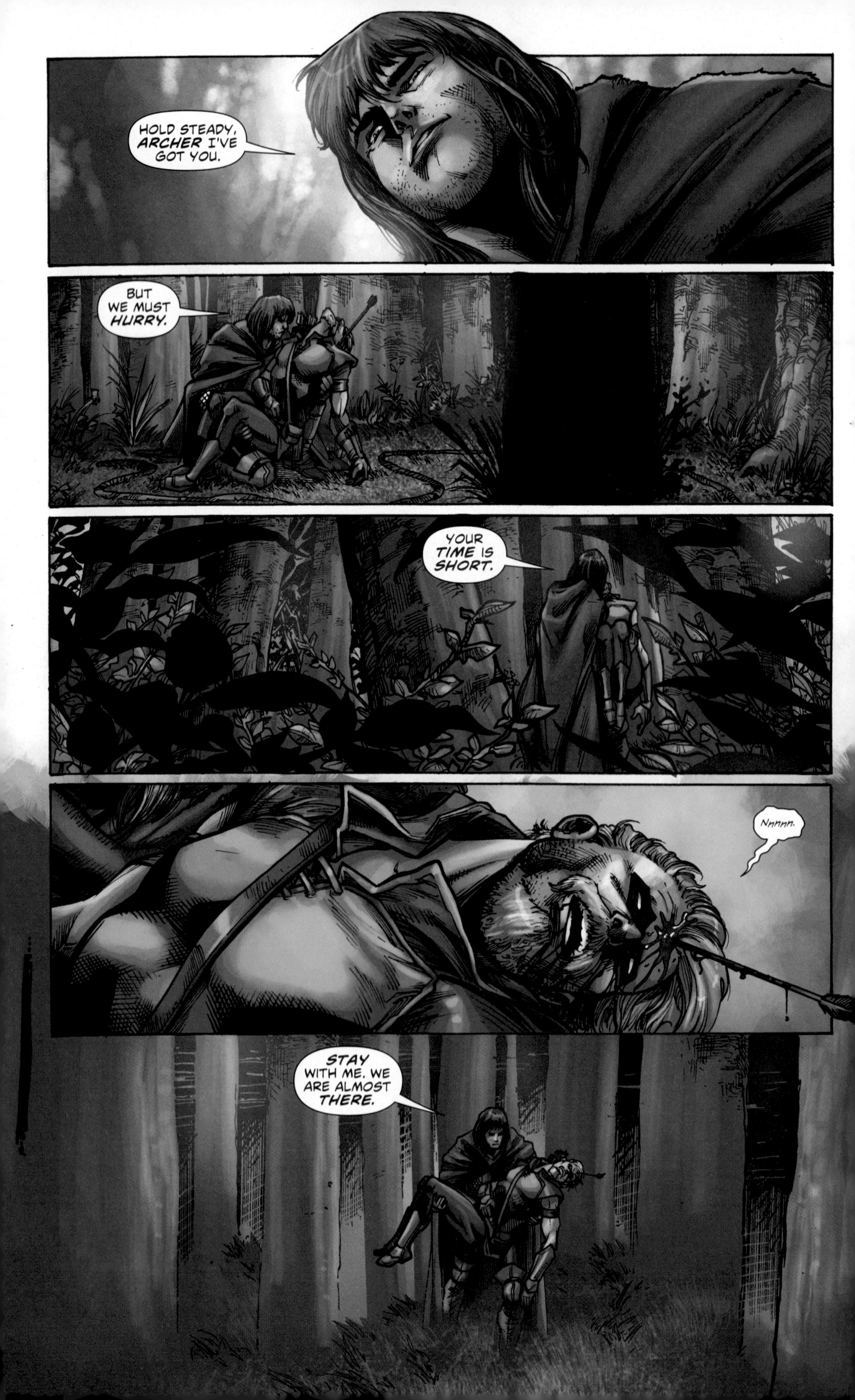
HOLD STEADY, ARCHER I'VE GOT YOU.
BUT WE MUST HURRY.
YOUR TIME IS SHORT.
Nnnnn.
STAY WITH ME. WE ARE ALMOST THERE.

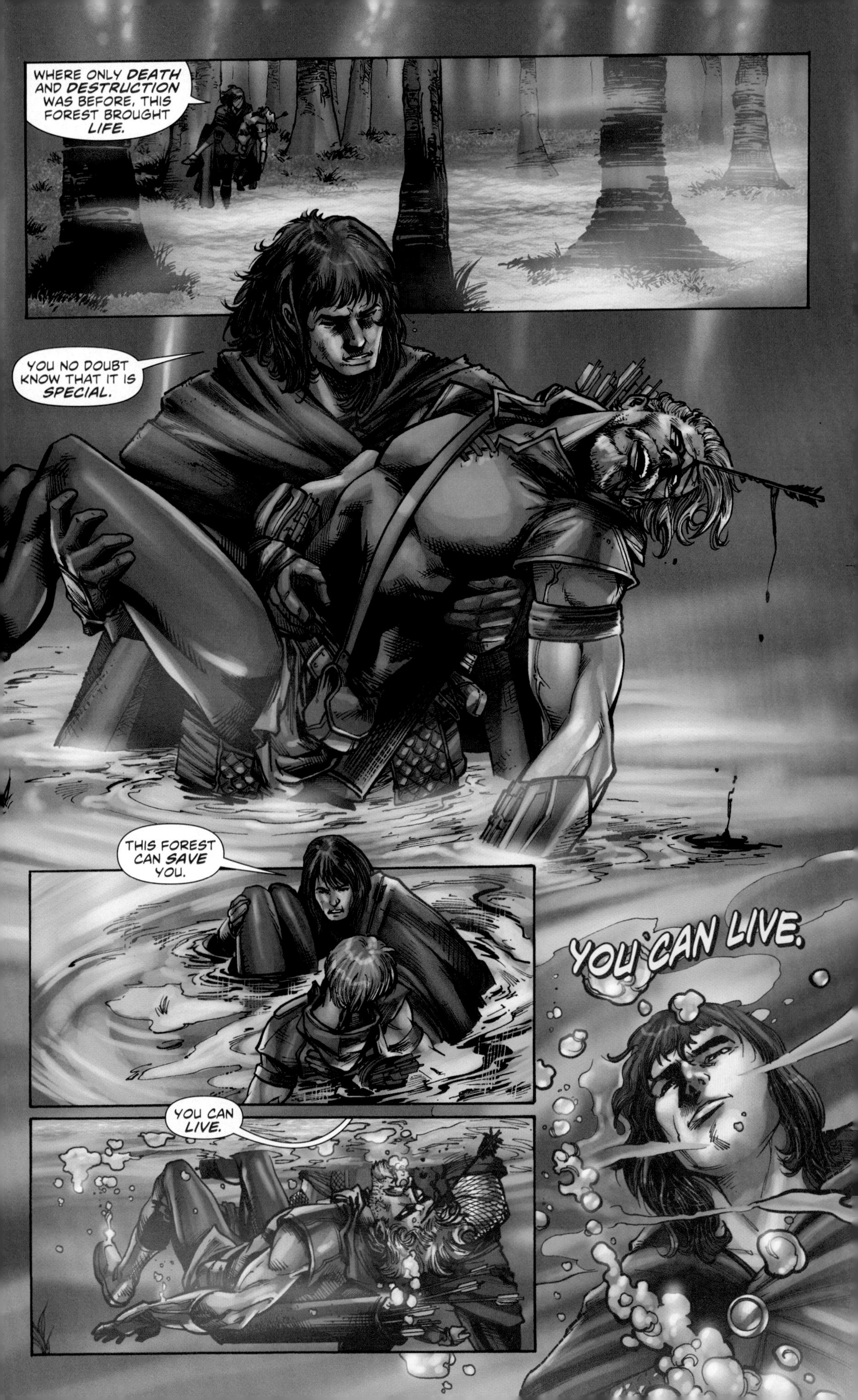
WHERE ONLY DEATH AND DESTRUCTION WAS BEFORE, THIS FOREST BROUGHT LIFE.
YOU NO DOUBT KNOW THAT IT IS SPECIAL.
THIS FOREST CAN SAVE YOU.
YOU CAN LIVE.
YOU CAN LIVE.

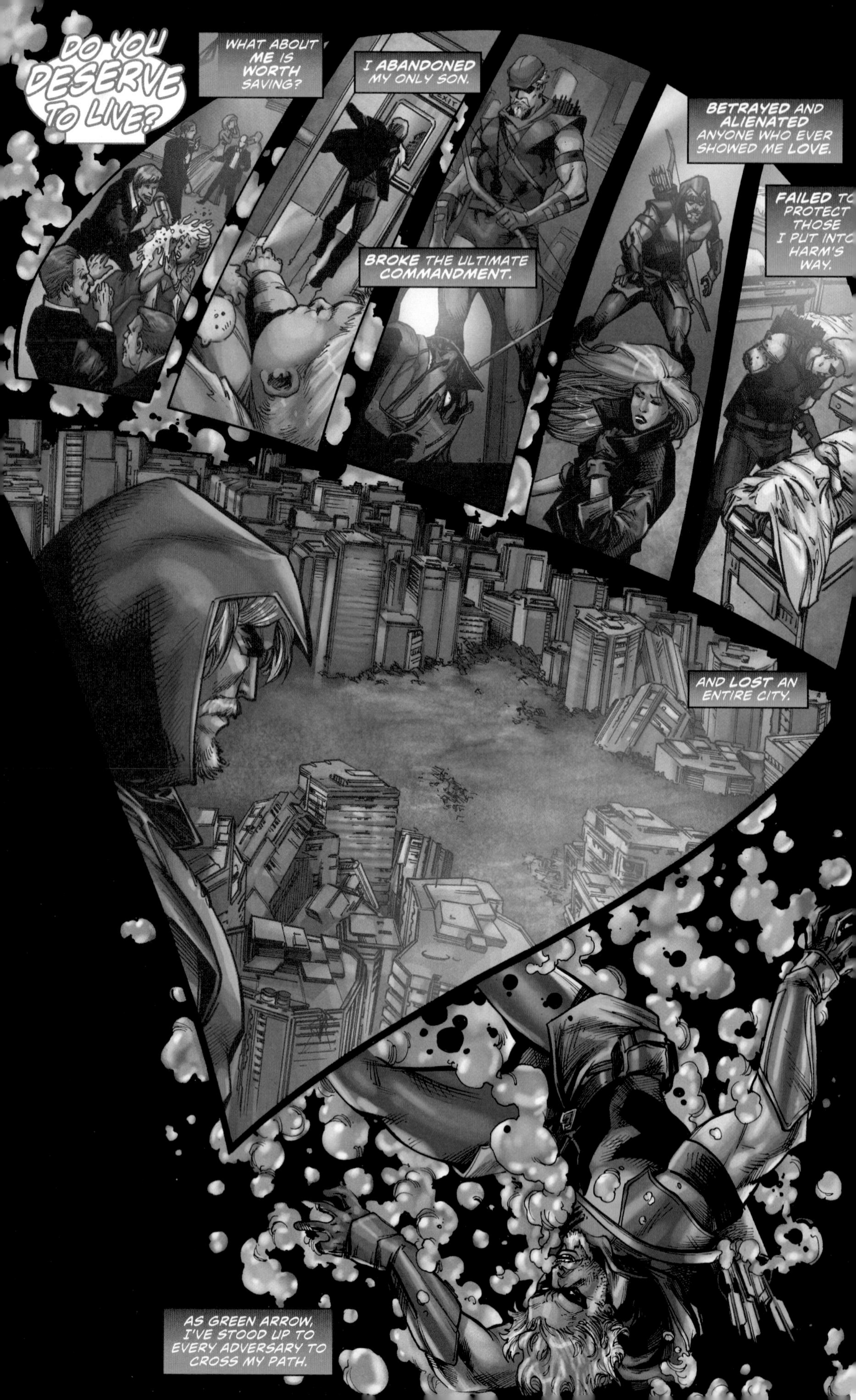
DO YOU DESERVE TO LIVE?
WHAT ABOUT ME IS WORTH SAVING?
I ABANDONED MY ONLY SON.
BROKE THE ULTIMATE COMMANDMENT.
BETRAYED AND ALIENATED ANYONE WHO EVER SHOWED ME LOVE.
FAILED TO PROTECT THOSE I PUT INTO HARM'S WAY.
AND LOST AN ENTIRE CITY.
AS GREEN ARROW, I'VE STOOD UP TO EVERY ADVERSARY TO CROSS MY PATH.

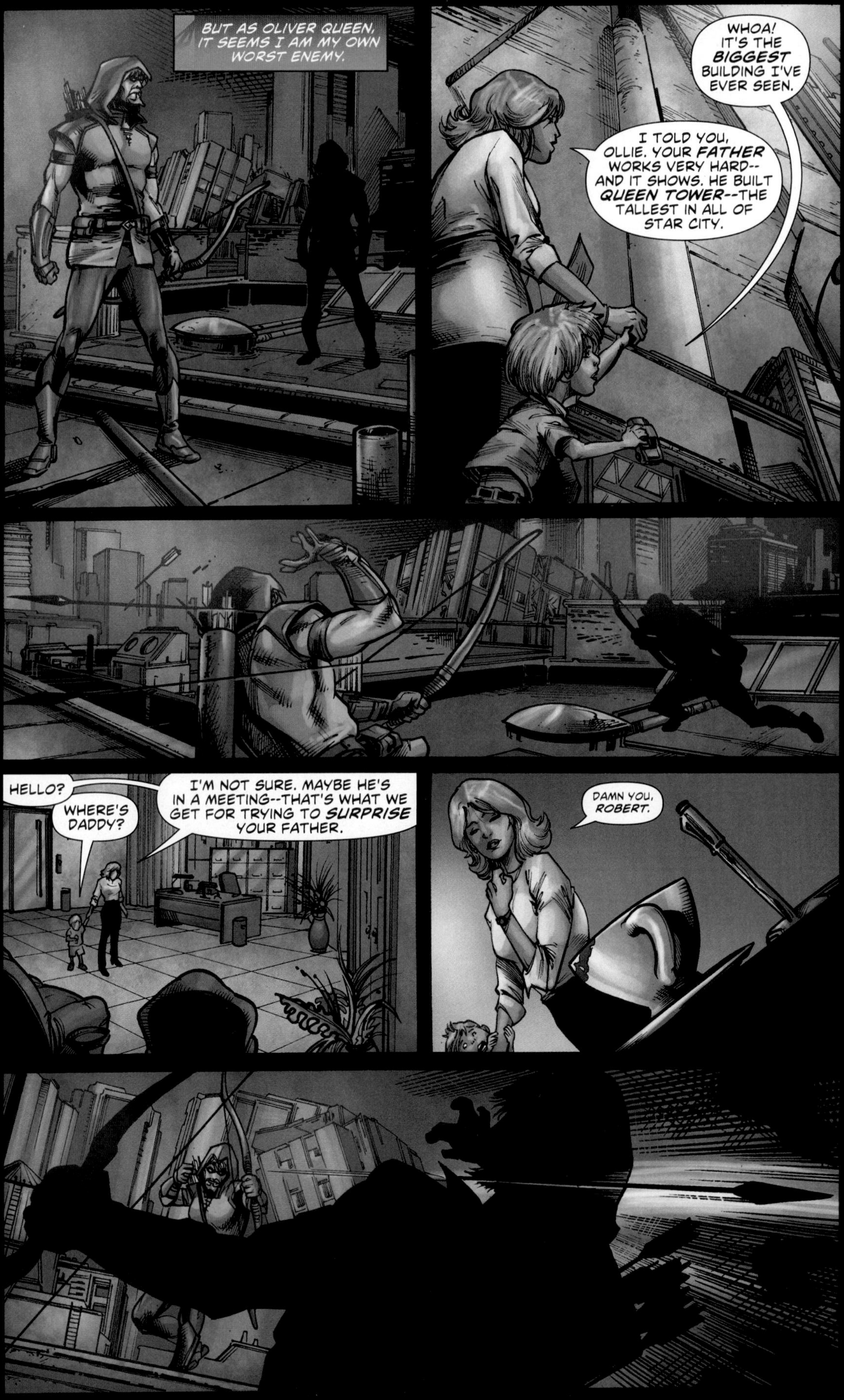
BUT AS OLIVER QUEEN, IT SEEMS I AM MY OWN WORST ENEMY.
WHOA! IT'S THE BIGGEST BUILDING I'VE EVER SEEN.
I TOLD YOU, OLLIE. YOUR FATHER WORKS VERY HARD-- AND IT SHOWS. HE BUILT QUEEN TOWER--THE TALLEST IN ALL OF STAR CITY.
HELLO?
WHERE'S DADDY?
I'M NOT SURE. MAYBE HE'S IN A MEETING--THAT'S WHAT WE GET FOR TRYING TO SURPRISE YOUR FATHER.
DAMN YOU, ROBERT.

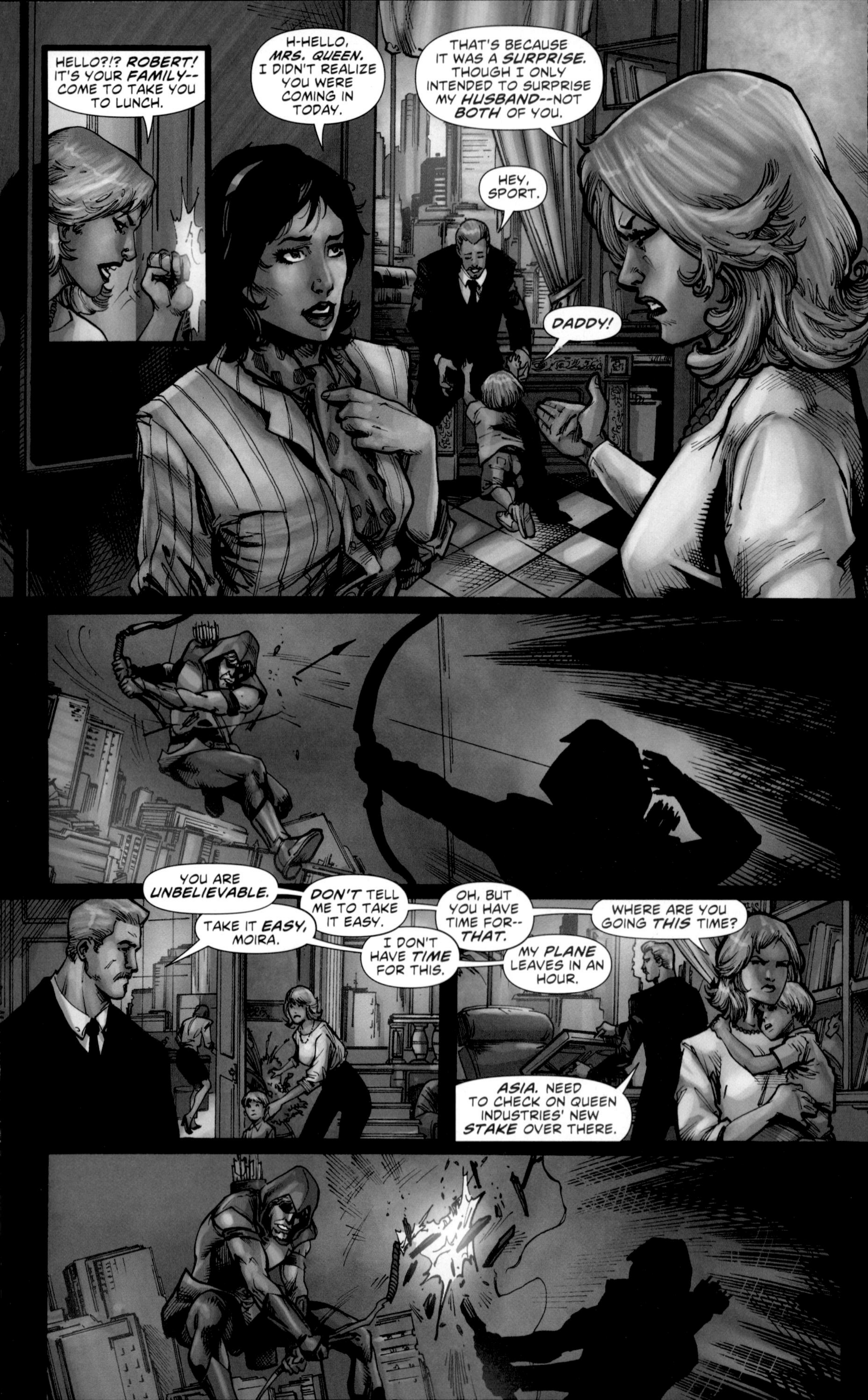

HELLO?!? ROBERT! IT'S YOUR FAMILY-- COME TO TAKE YOU TO LUNCH.
H-HELLO, MRS. QUEEN. I DIDN'T REALIZE YOU WERE COMING IN TODAY.
THAT'S BECAUSE IT WAS A SURPRISE. THOUGH I ONLY INTENDED TO SURPRISE MY HUSBAND--NOT BOTH OF YOU.
HEY, SPORT.
DADDY!
YOU ARE UNBELIEVABLE.
TAKE IT EASY, MOIRA.
DON'T TELL ME TO TAKE IT EASY.
I DON'T HAVE TIME FOR THIS.
OH, BUT YOU HAVE TIME FOR-- THAT.
MY PLANE LEAVES IN AN HOUR.
WHERE ARE YOU GOING THIS TIME?
ASIA. NEED TO CHECK ON QUEEN INDUSTRIES' NEW STAKE OVER THERE.

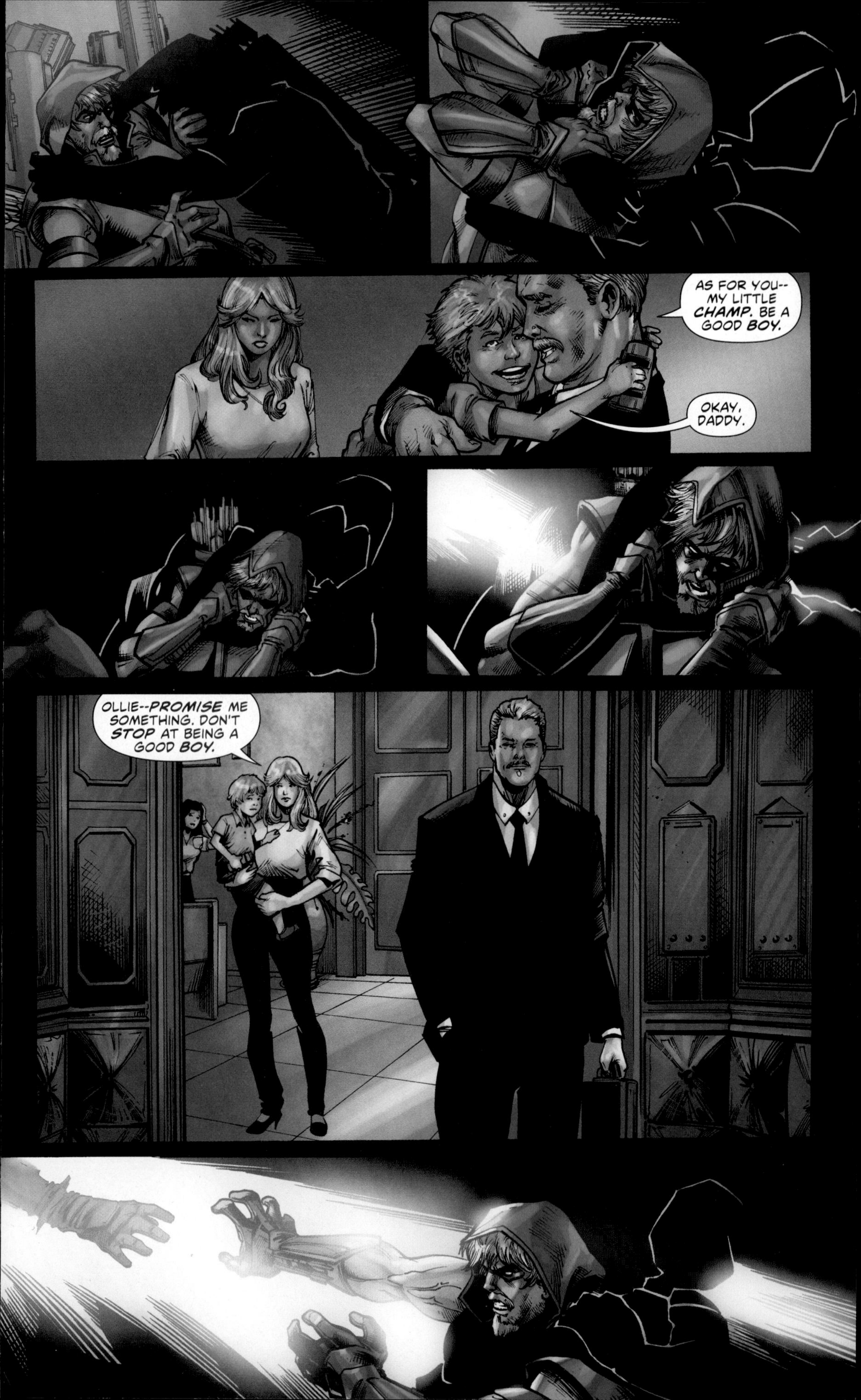
AS FOR YOU-- MY LITTLE CHAMP. BE A GOOD BOY.
OKAY, DADDY.
OLLIE--PROMISE ME SOMETHING. DON'T STOP AT BEING A GOOD BOY.

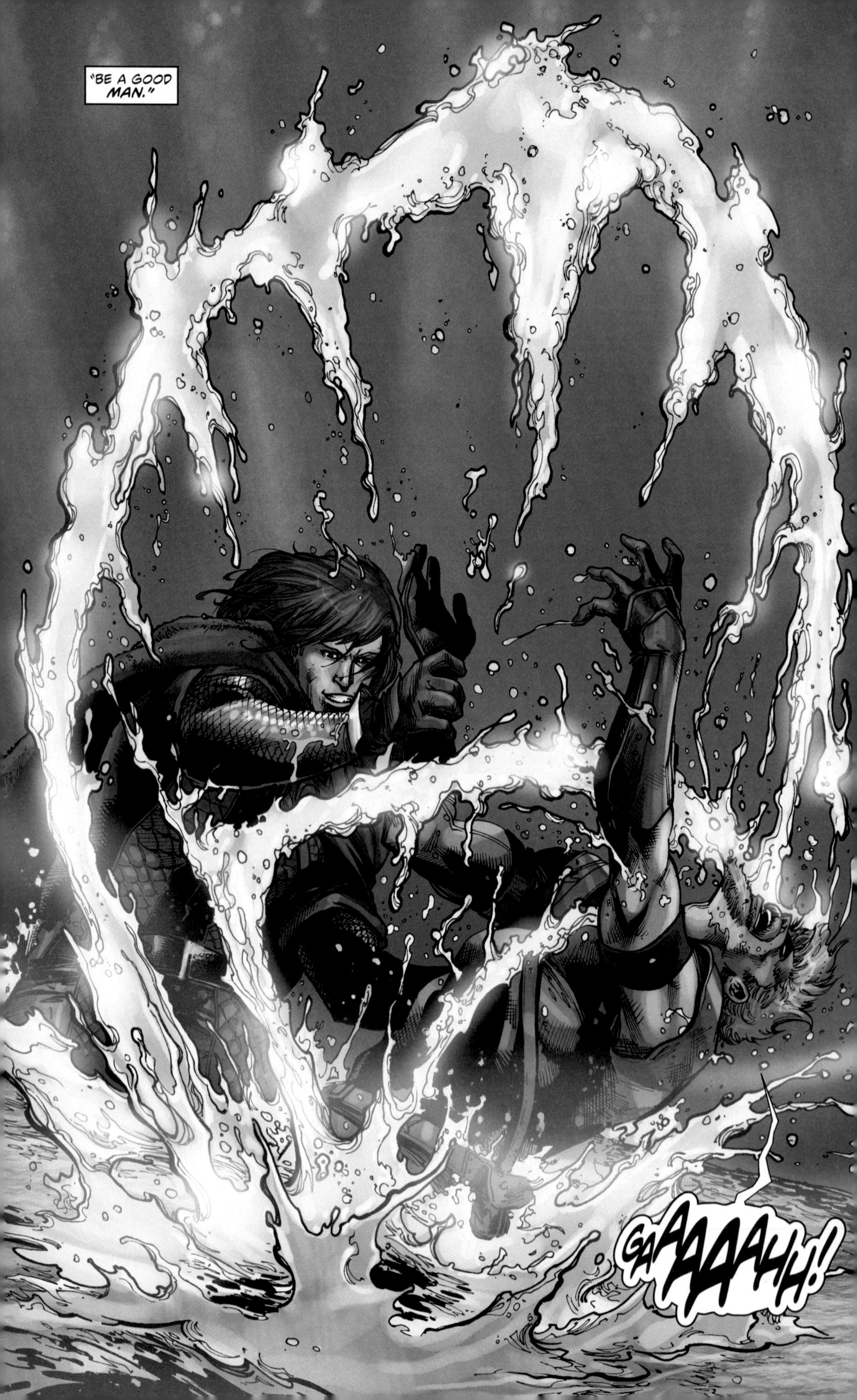
"BE A GOOD MAN."
GAAAAAAHH!

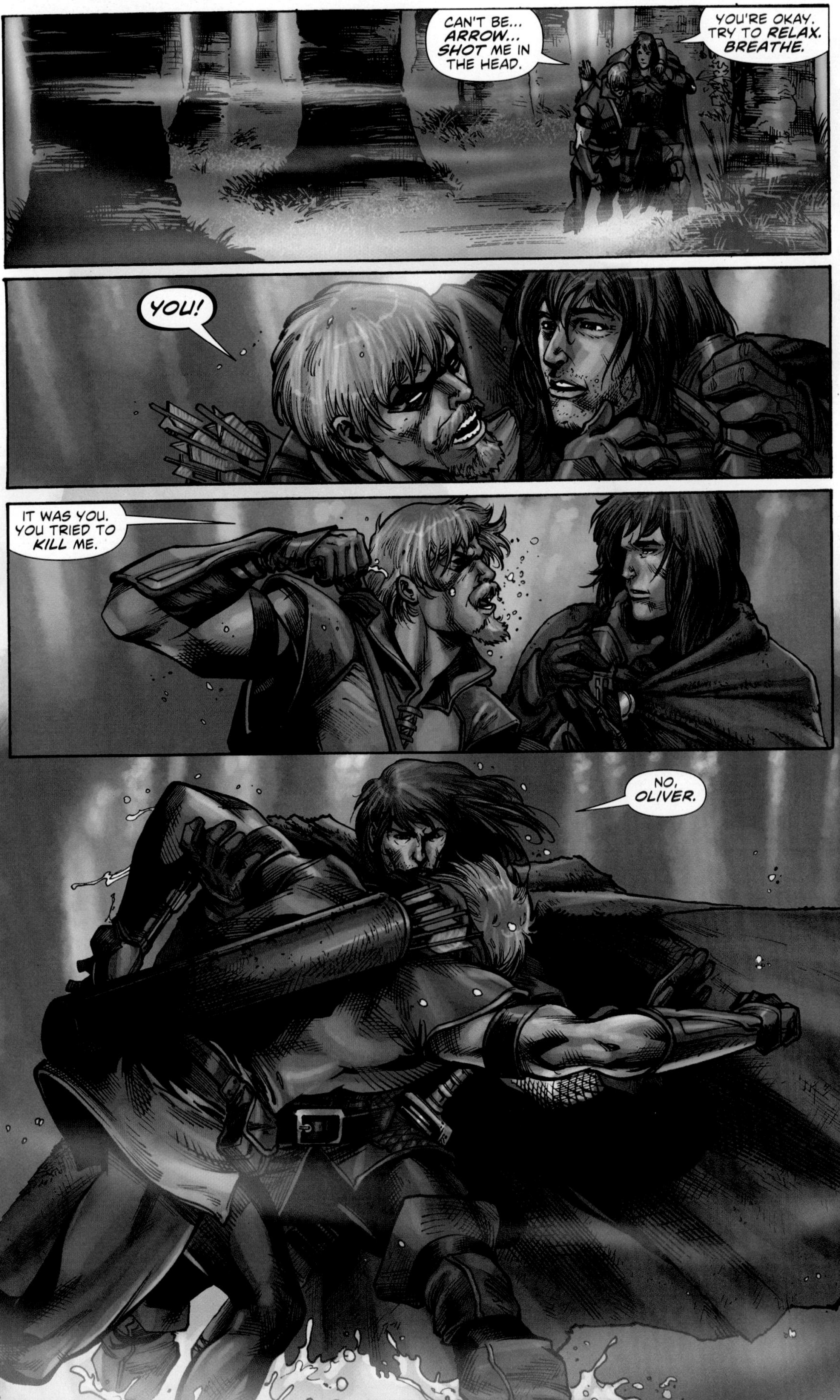
CAN'T BE... ARROW... SHOT ME IN THE HEAD.
YOU'RE OKAY. TRY TO RELAX. BREATHE.
YOU!
IT WAS YOU. YOU TRIED TO KILL ME.
NO, OLIVER.

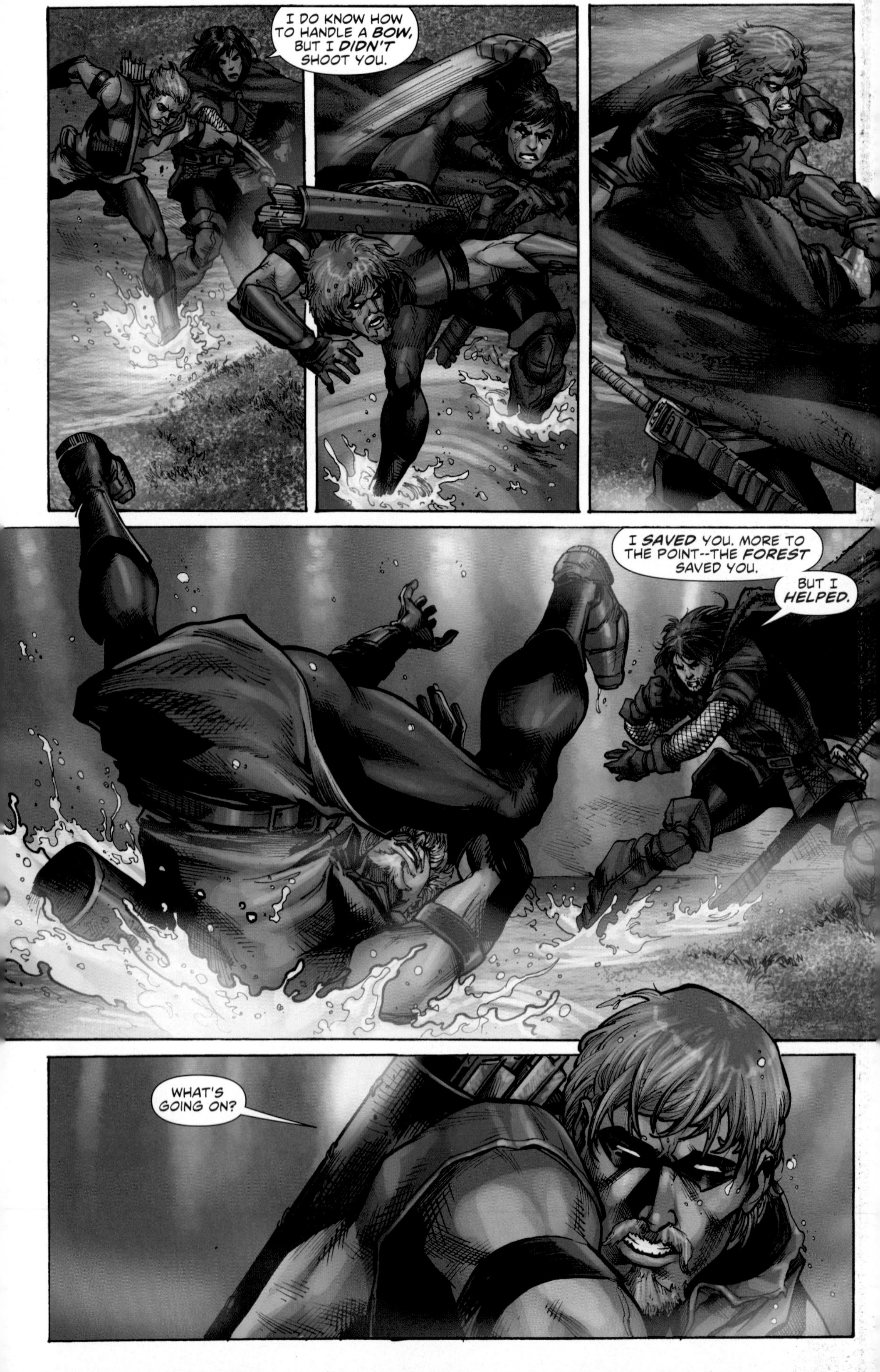
I DO KNOW HOW TO HANDLE A ***BOW,*** BUT I ***DIDN'T*** SHOOT YOU.
I ***SAVED*** YOU. MORE TO THE POINT--THE ***FOREST*** SAVED YOU.
BUT I ***HELPED.***
WHAT'S GOING ON?

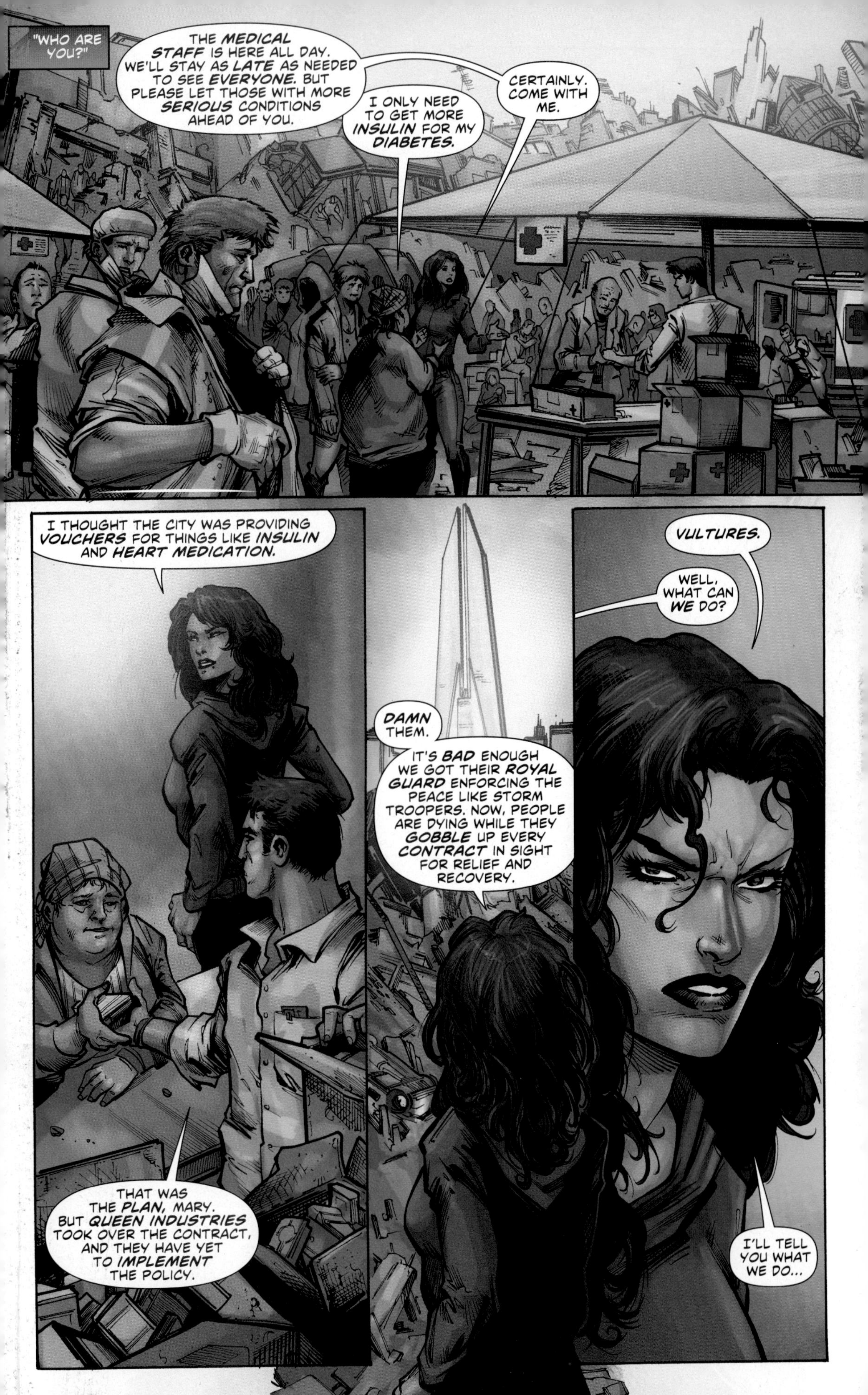
"WHO ARE YOU?"
THE MEDICAL STAFF IS HERE ALL DAY. WE'LL STAY AS LATE AS NEEDED TO SEE EVERYONE. BUT PLEASE LET THOSE WITH MORE SERIOUS CONDITIONS AHEAD OF YOU.
I ONLY NEED TO GET MORE INSULIN FOR MY DIABETES.
CERTAINLY. COME WITH ME.
I THOUGHT THE CITY WAS PROVIDING VOUCHERS FOR THINGS LIKE INSULIN AND HEART MEDICATION.
THAT WAS THE PLAN, MARY. BUT QUEEN INDUSTRIES TOOK OVER THE CONTRACT, AND THEY HAVE YET TO IMPLEMENT THE POLICY.
DAMN THEM.
IT'S BAD ENOUGH WE GOT THEIR ROYAL GUARD ENFORCING THE PEACE LIKE STORM TROOPERS. NOW, PEOPLE ARE DYING WHILE THEY GOBBLE UP EVERY CONTRACT IN SIGHT FOR RELIEF AND RECOVERY.
VULTURES.
WELL, WHAT CAN WE DO?
I'LL TELL YOU WHAT WE DO...

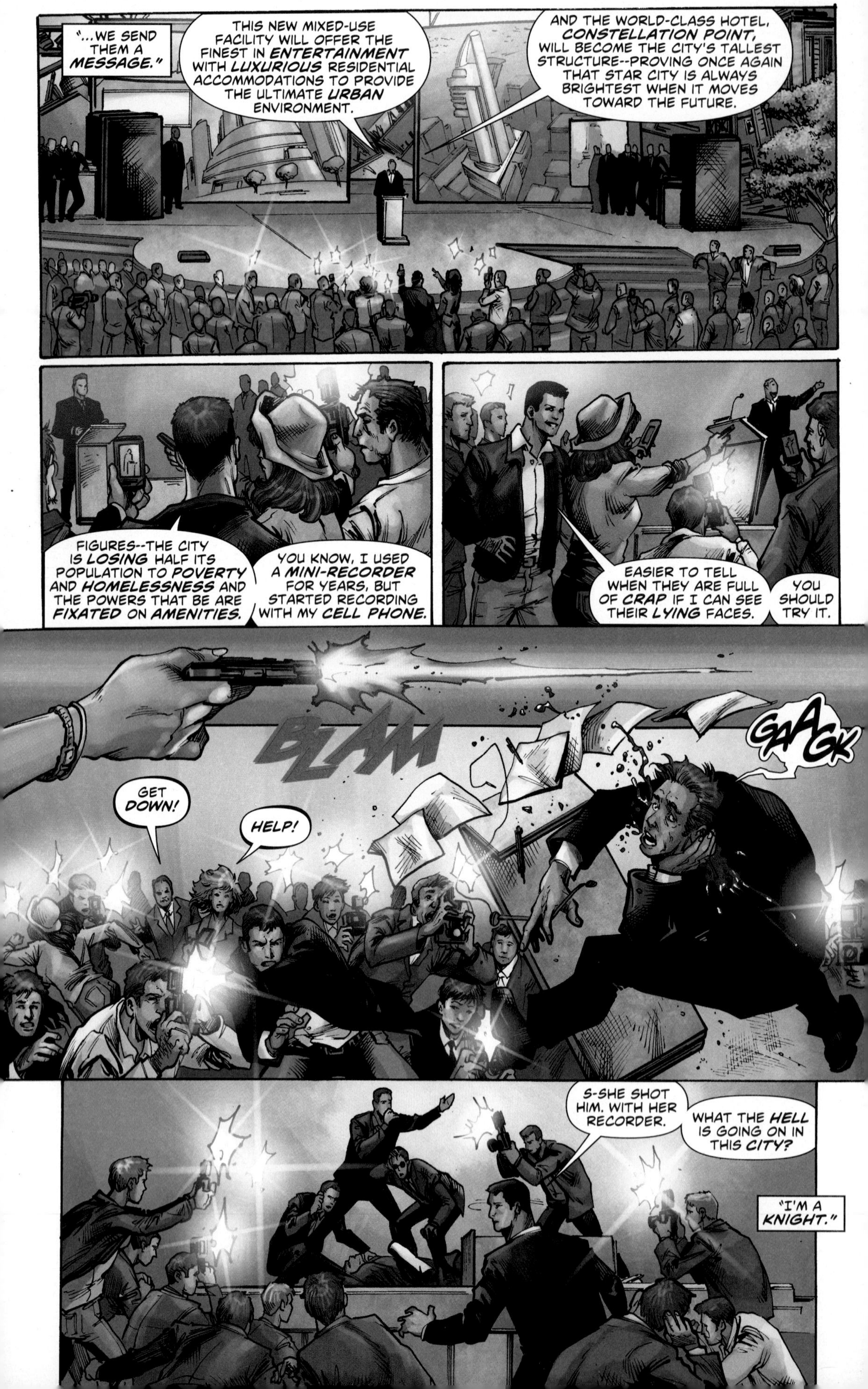
"...WE SEND THEM A MESSAGE."
THIS NEW MIXED-USE FACILITY WILL OFFER THE FINEST IN ENTERTAINMENT WITH LUXURIOUS RESIDENTIAL ACCOMMODATIONS TO PROVIDE THE ULTIMATE URBAN ENVIRONMENT.
AND THE WORLD-CLASS HOTEL, CONSTELLATION POINT, WILL BECOME THE CITY'S TALLEST STRUCTURE--PROVING ONCE AGAIN THAT STAR CITY IS ALWAYS BRIGHTEST WHEN IT MOVES TOWARD THE FUTURE.
FIGURES--THE CITY IS LOSING HALF ITS POPULATION TO POVERTY AND HOMELESSNESS AND THE POWERS THAT BE ARE FIXATED ON AMENITIES.
YOU KNOW, I USED A MINI-RECORDER FOR YEARS, BUT STARTED RECORDING WITH MY CELL PHONE.
EASIER TO TELL WHEN THEY ARE FULL OF CRAP IF I CAN SEE THEIR LYING FACES.
YOU SHOULD TRY IT.
BLAM
GAAGK
GET DOWN!
HELP!
S-SHE SHOT HIM. WITH HER RECORDER.
WHAT THE HELL IS GOING ON IN THIS CITY?
"I'M A KNIGHT."

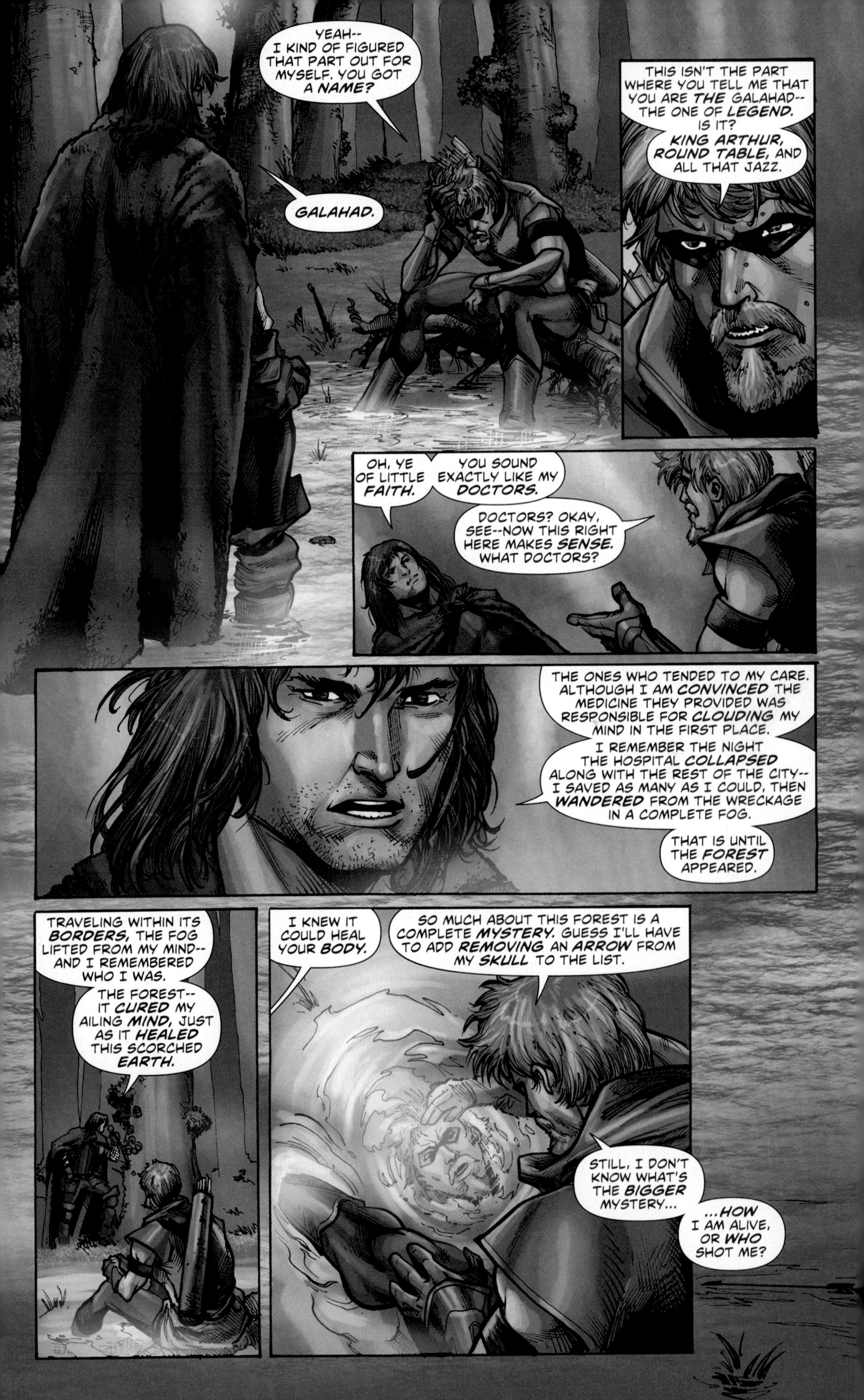
YEAH-- I KIND OF FIGURED THAT PART OUT FOR MYSELF. YOU GOT A NAME?
GALAHAD.
THIS ISN'T THE PART WHERE YOU TELL ME THAT YOU ARE THE GALAHAD-- THE ONE OF LEGEND. IS IT? KING ARTHUR, ROUND TABLE, AND ALL THAT JAZZ.
OH, YE OF LITTLE FAITH.
YOU SOUND EXACTLY LIKE MY DOCTORS.
DOCTORS? OKAY, SEE--NOW THIS RIGHT HERE MAKES SENSE. WHAT DOCTORS?
THE ONES WHO TENDED TO MY CARE. ALTHOUGH I AM CONVINCED THE MEDICINE THEY PROVIDED WAS RESPONSIBLE FOR CLOUDING MY MIND IN THE FIRST PLACE.
I REMEMBER THE NIGHT THE HOSPITAL COLLAPSED ALONG WITH THE REST OF THE CITY-- I SAVED AS MANY AS I COULD, THEN WANDERED FROM THE WRECKAGE IN A COMPLETE FOG.
THAT IS UNTIL THE FOREST APPEARED.
TRAVELING WITHIN ITS BORDERS, THE FOG LIFTED FROM MY MIND-- AND I REMEMBERED WHO I WAS.
THE FOREST-- IT CURED MY AILING MIND, JUST AS IT HEALED THIS SCORCHED EARTH.
I KNEW IT COULD HEAL YOUR BODY.
SO MUCH ABOUT THIS FOREST IS A COMPLETE MYSTERY. GUESS I'LL HAVE TO ADD REMOVING AN ARROW FROM MY SKULL TO THE LIST.
STILL, I DON'T KNOW WHAT'S THE BIGGER MYSTERY...
...HOW I AM ALIVE, OR WHO SHOT ME?

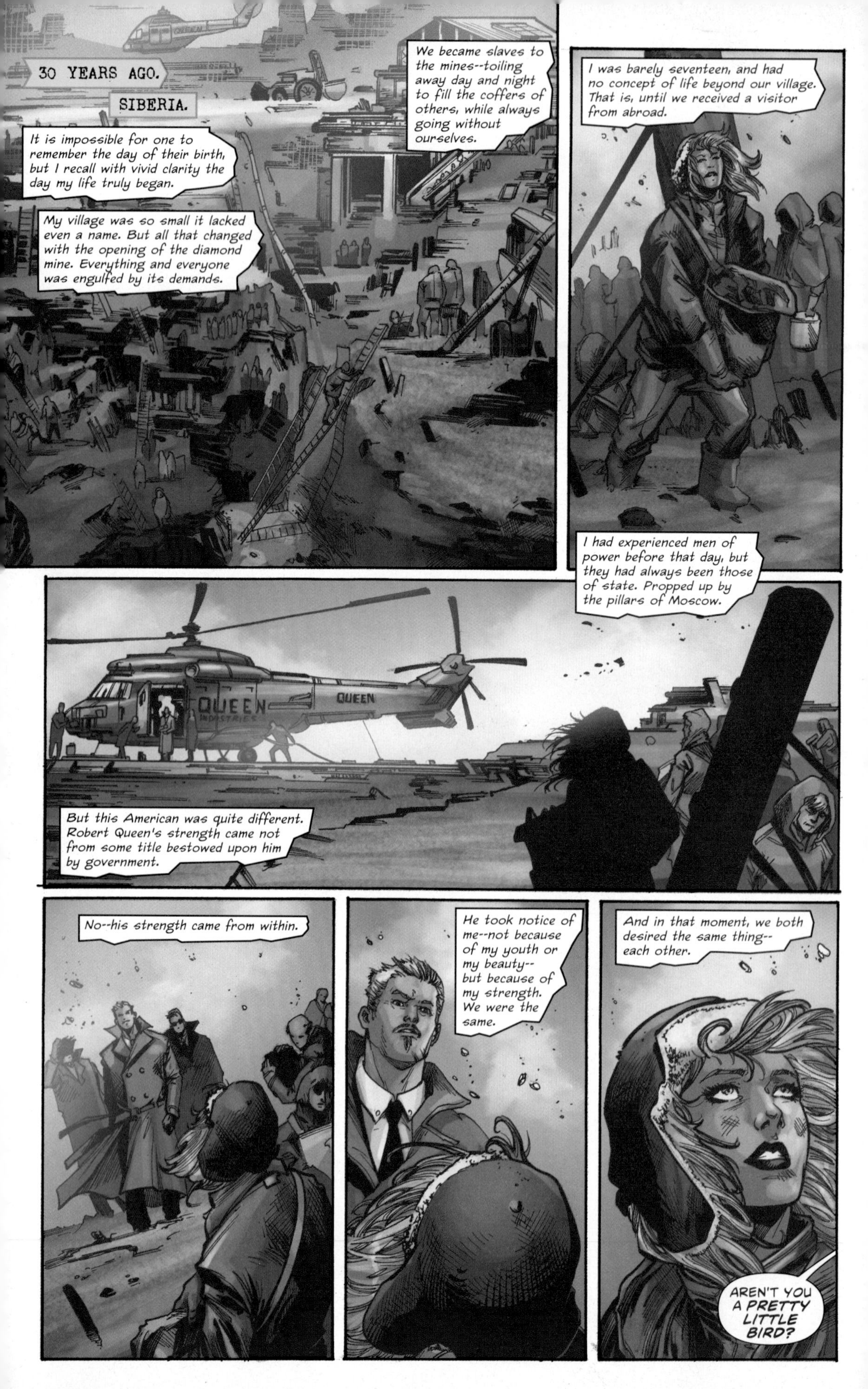

30 YEARS AGO.
SIBERIA.
It is impossible for one to remember the day of their birth, but I recall with vivid clarity the day my life truly began.
My village was so small it lacked even a name. But all that changed with the opening of the diamond mine. Everything and everyone was engulfed by its demands.
We became slaves to the mines--toiling away day and night to fill the coffers of others, while always going without ourselves.
I was barely seventeen, and had no concept of life beyond our village. That is, until we received a visitor from abroad.
I had experienced men of power before that day, but they had always been those of state. Propped up by the pillars of Moscow.
QUEEN
QUEEN
But this American was quite different. Robert Queen's strength came not from some title bestowed upon him by government.
No--his strength came from within.
He took notice of me--not because of my youth or my beauty--but because of my strength. We were the same.
And in that moment, we both desired the same thing--each other.
AREN'T YOU A PRETTY LITTLE BIRD?

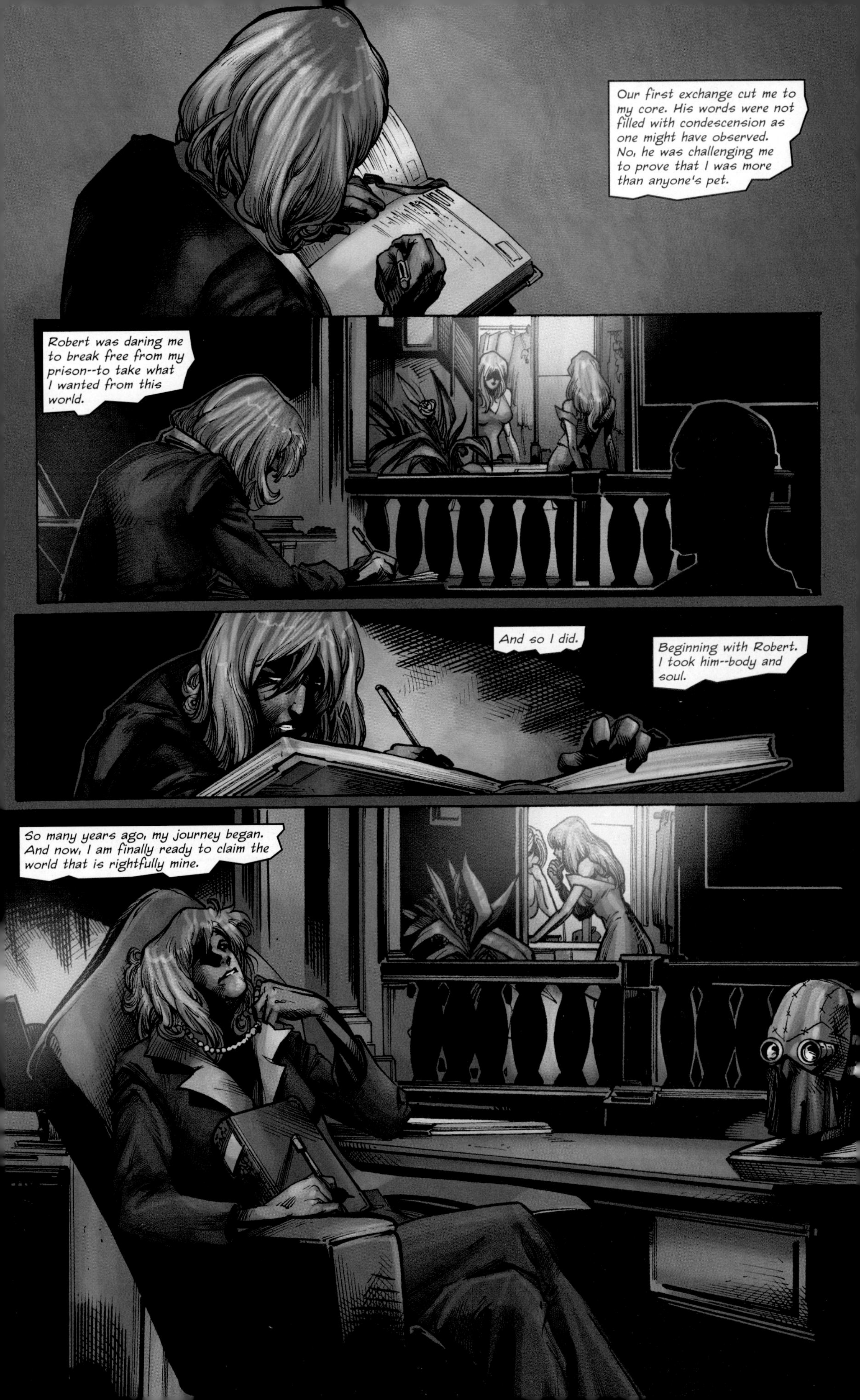
Our first exchange cut me to my core. His words were not filled with condescension as one might have observed. No, he was challenging me to prove that I was more than anyone's pet.
Robert was daring me to break free from my prison--to take what I wanted from this world.
And so I did.
Beginning with Robert. I took him--body and soul.
So many years ago, my journey began. And now, I am finally ready to claim the world that is rightfully mine.

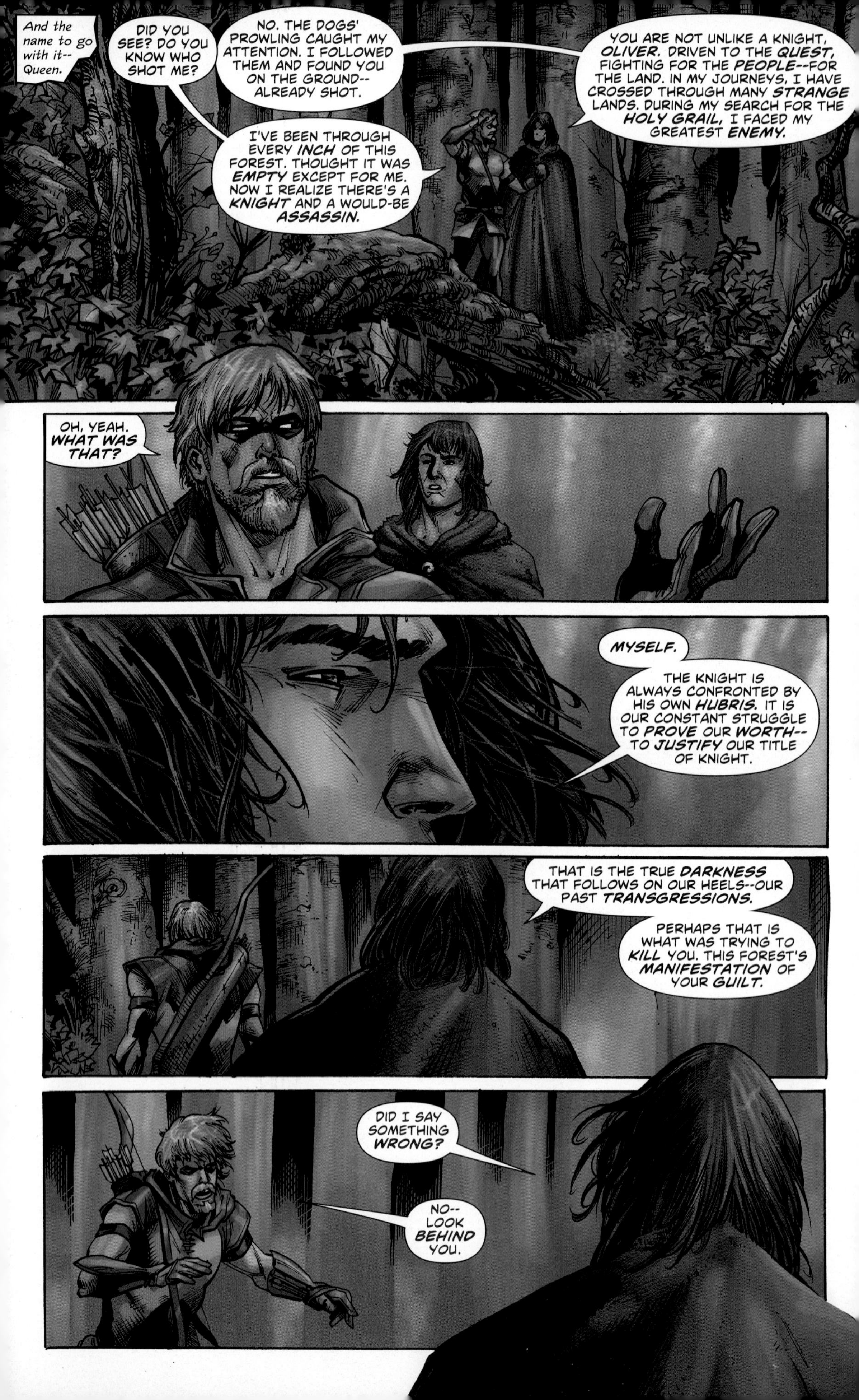
And the name to go with it-- Queen.
DID YOU SEE? DO YOU KNOW WHO SHOT ME?
NO. THE DOGS' PROWLING CAUGHT MY ATTENTION. I FOLLOWED THEM AND FOUND YOU ON THE GROUND-- ALREADY SHOT.
I'VE BEEN THROUGH EVERY INCH OF THIS FOREST. THOUGHT IT WAS EMPTY EXCEPT FOR ME. NOW I REALIZE THERE'S A KNIGHT AND A WOULD-BE ASSASSIN.
YOU ARE NOT UNLIKE A KNIGHT, OLIVER. DRIVEN TO THE QUEST, FIGHTING FOR THE PEOPLE--FOR THE LAND. IN MY JOURNEYS, I HAVE CROSSED THROUGH MANY STRANGE LANDS. DURING MY SEARCH FOR THE HOLY GRAIL, I FACED MY GREATEST ENEMY.
OH, YEAH. WHAT WAS THAT?
MYSELF.
THE KNIGHT IS ALWAYS CONFRONTED BY HIS OWN HUBRIS. IT IS OUR CONSTANT STRUGGLE TO PROVE OUR WORTH-- TO JUSTIFY OUR TITLE OF KNIGHT.
THAT IS THE TRUE DARKNESS THAT FOLLOWS ON OUR HEELS--OUR PAST TRANSGRESSIONS.
PERHAPS THAT IS WHAT WAS TRYING TO KILL YOU. THIS FOREST'S MANIFESTATION OF YOUR GUILT.
DID I SAY SOMETHING WRONG?
NO-- LOOK BEHIND YOU.

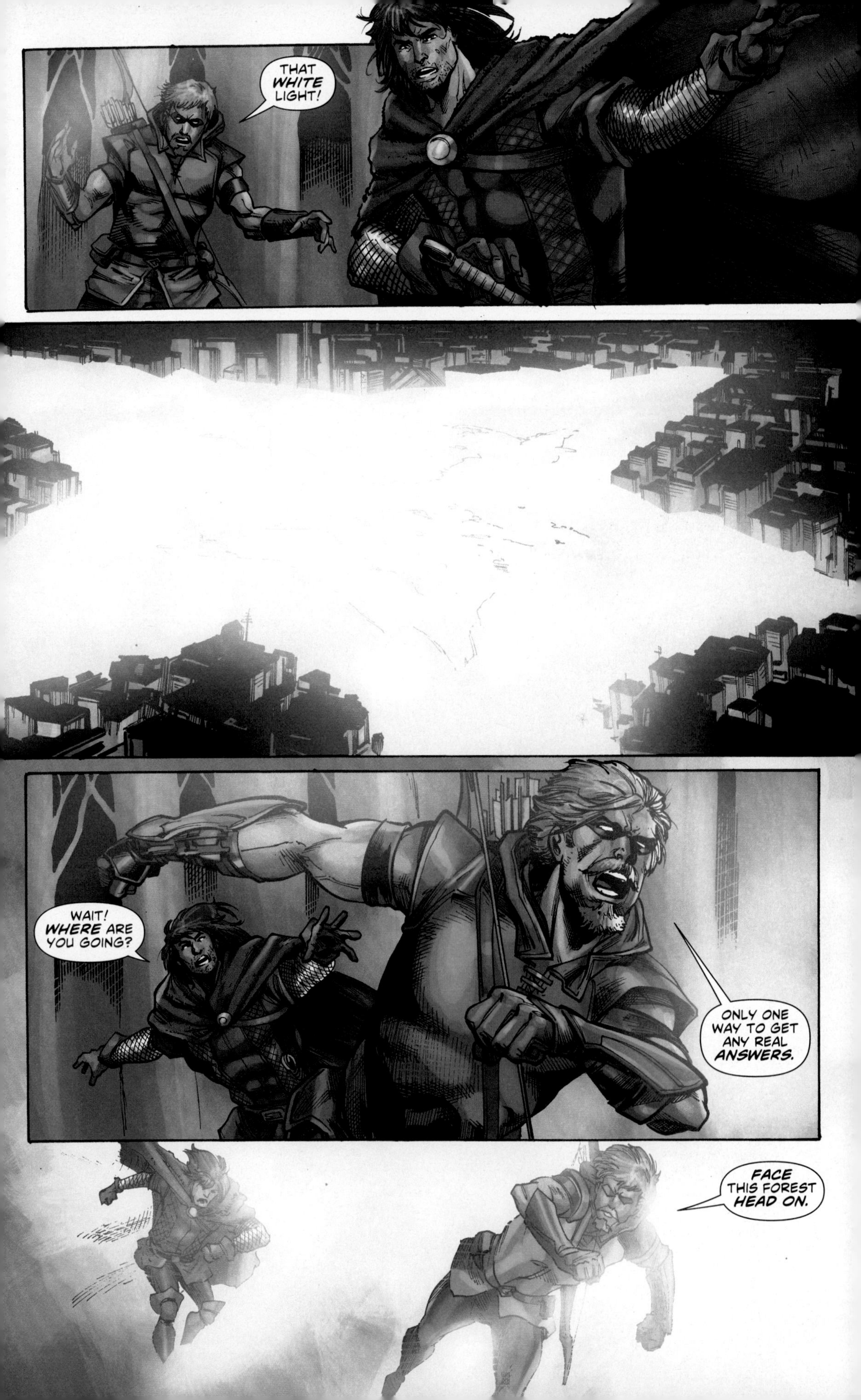
THAT WHITE LIGHT!
WAIT! WHERE ARE YOU GOING?
ONLY ONE WAY TO GET ANY REAL ANSWERS.
FACE THIS FOREST HEAD ON.

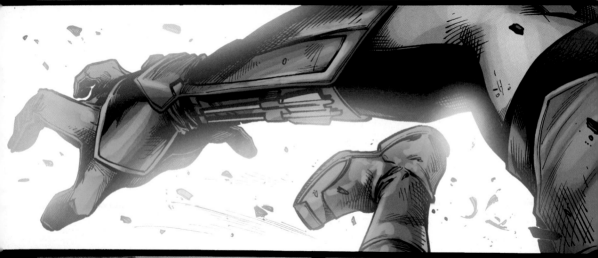

I SEE THE CHANGE AS THE LEAVES TURN BROWN, THEN BRITTLE, THEN FALL ALTOGETHER.

I FEEL THE CHANGE AS THE COLD WINTER WIND BRUSHES ACROSS MY FACE-- BRINGING WITH IT BLANKETS OF SNOW.

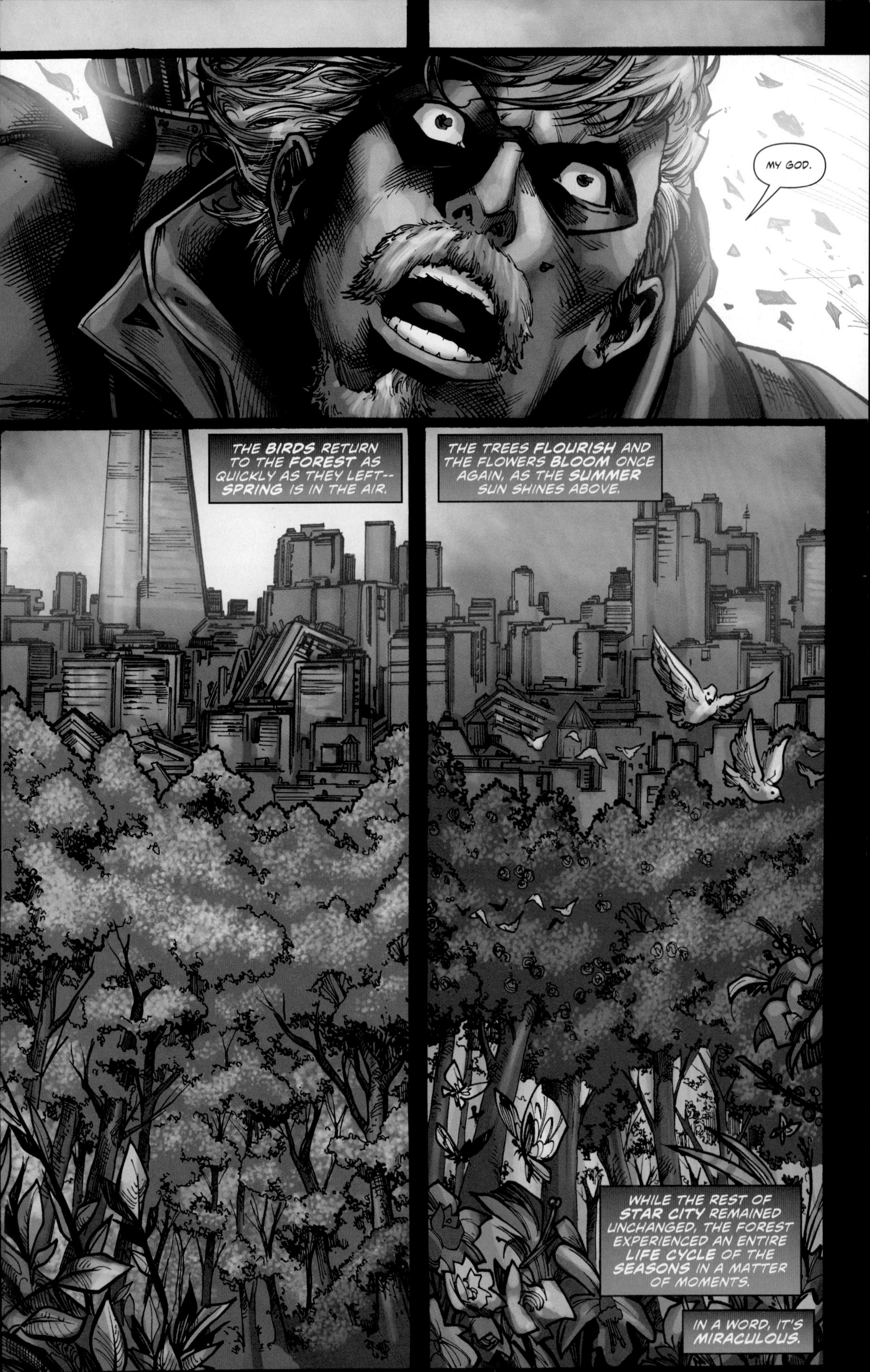
MY GOD.
THE BIRDS RETURN TO THE FOREST AS QUICKLY AS THEY LEFT--SPRING IS IN THE AIR.
THE TREES FLOURISH AND THE FLOWERS BLOOM ONCE AGAIN, AS THE SUMMER SUN SHINES ABOVE.
WHILE THE REST OF STAR CITY REMAINED UNCHANGED, THE FOREST EXPERIENCED AN ENTIRE LIFE CYCLE OF THE SEASONS IN A MATTER OF MOMENTS.
IN A WORD, IT'S MIRACULOUS.

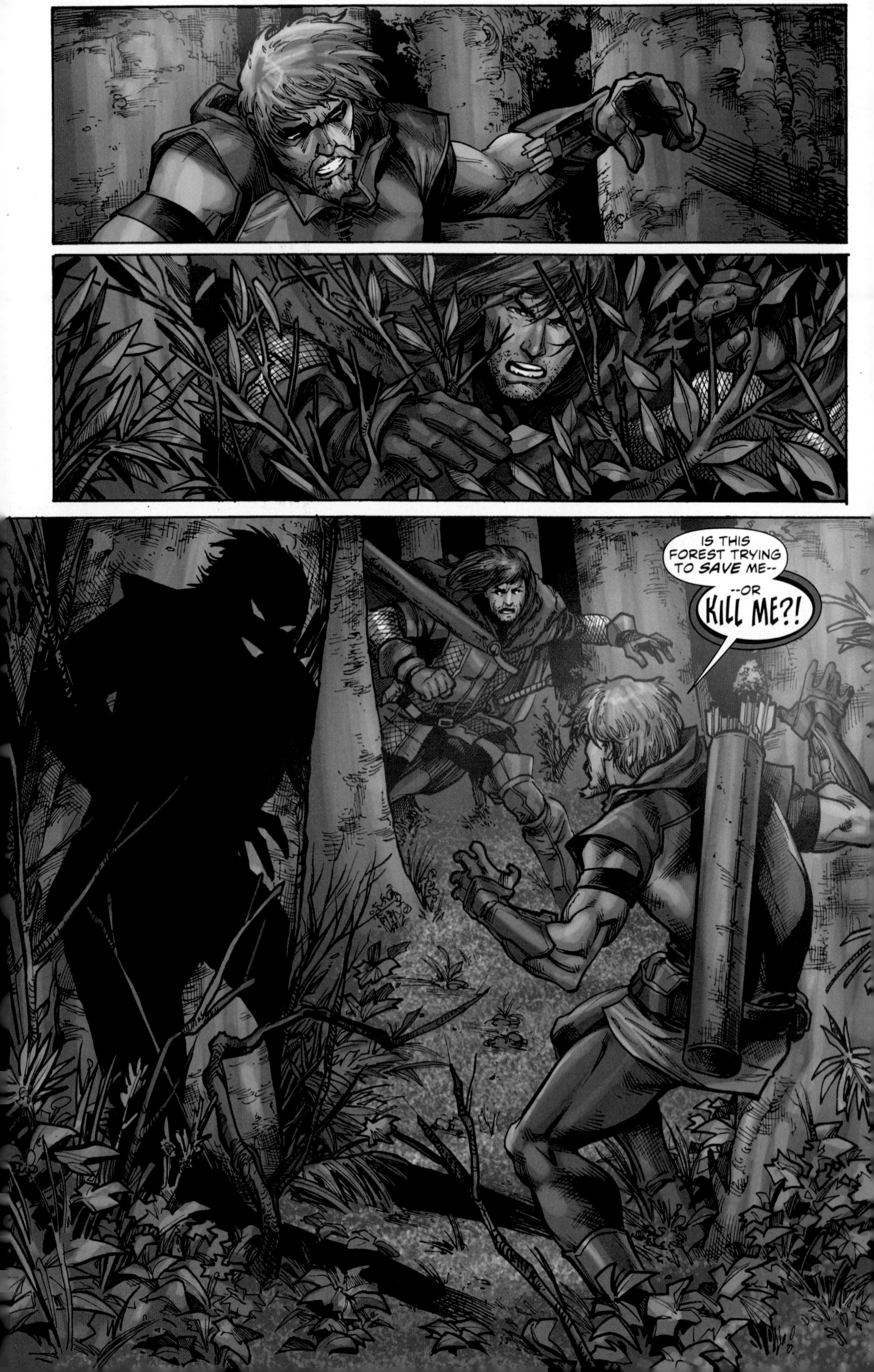
IS THIS FOREST TRYING TO SAVE ME--
--OR KILL ME?!

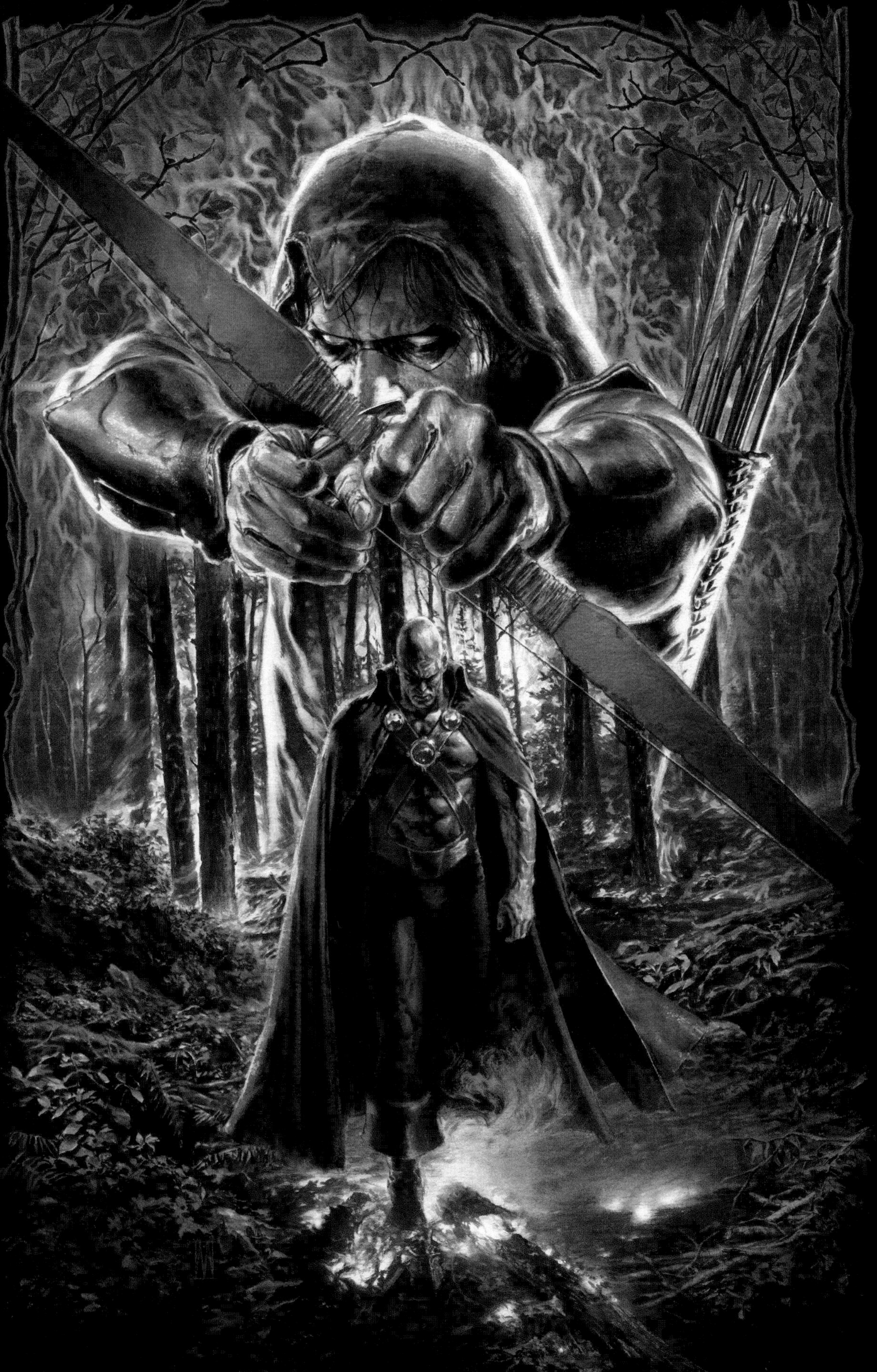

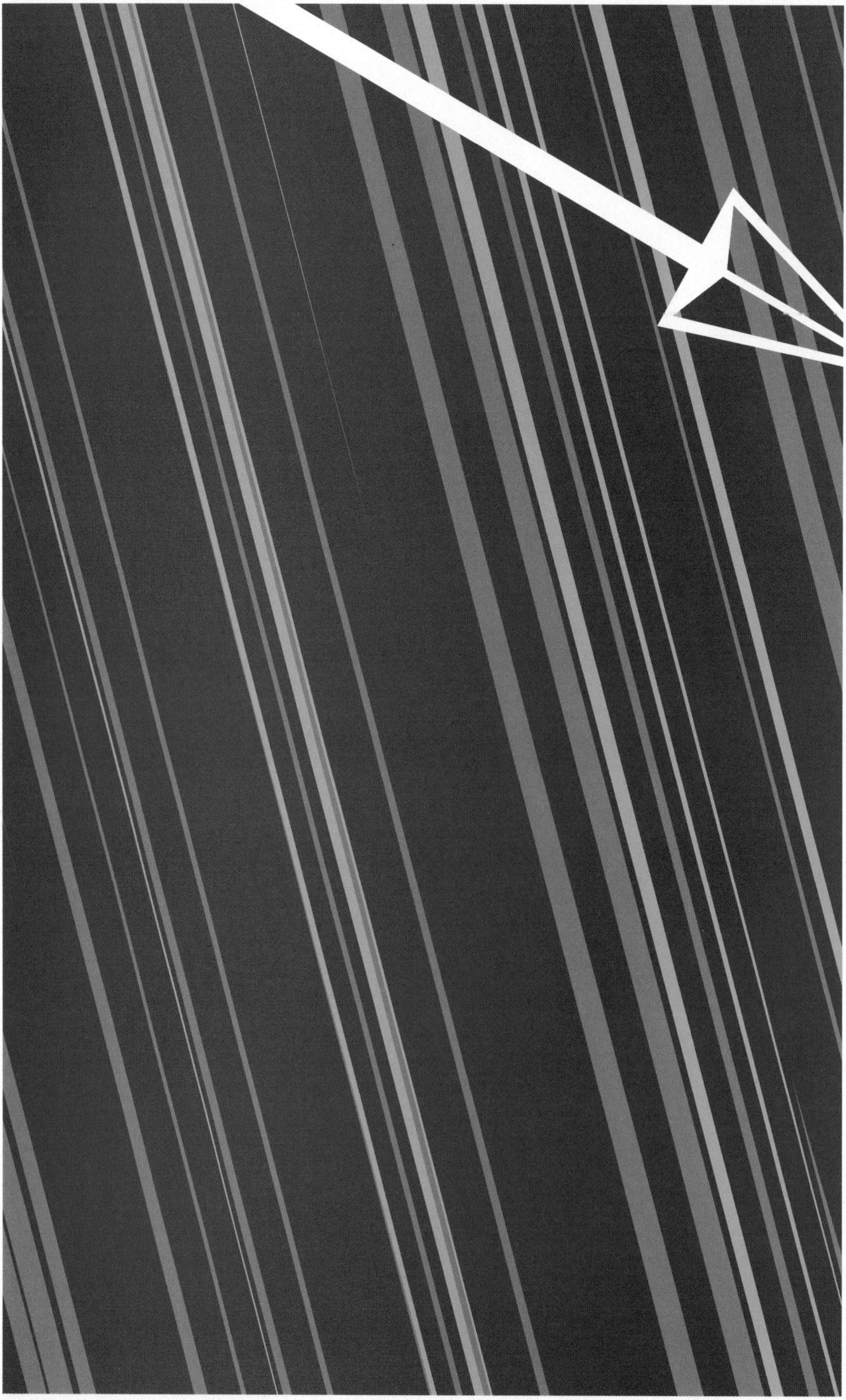

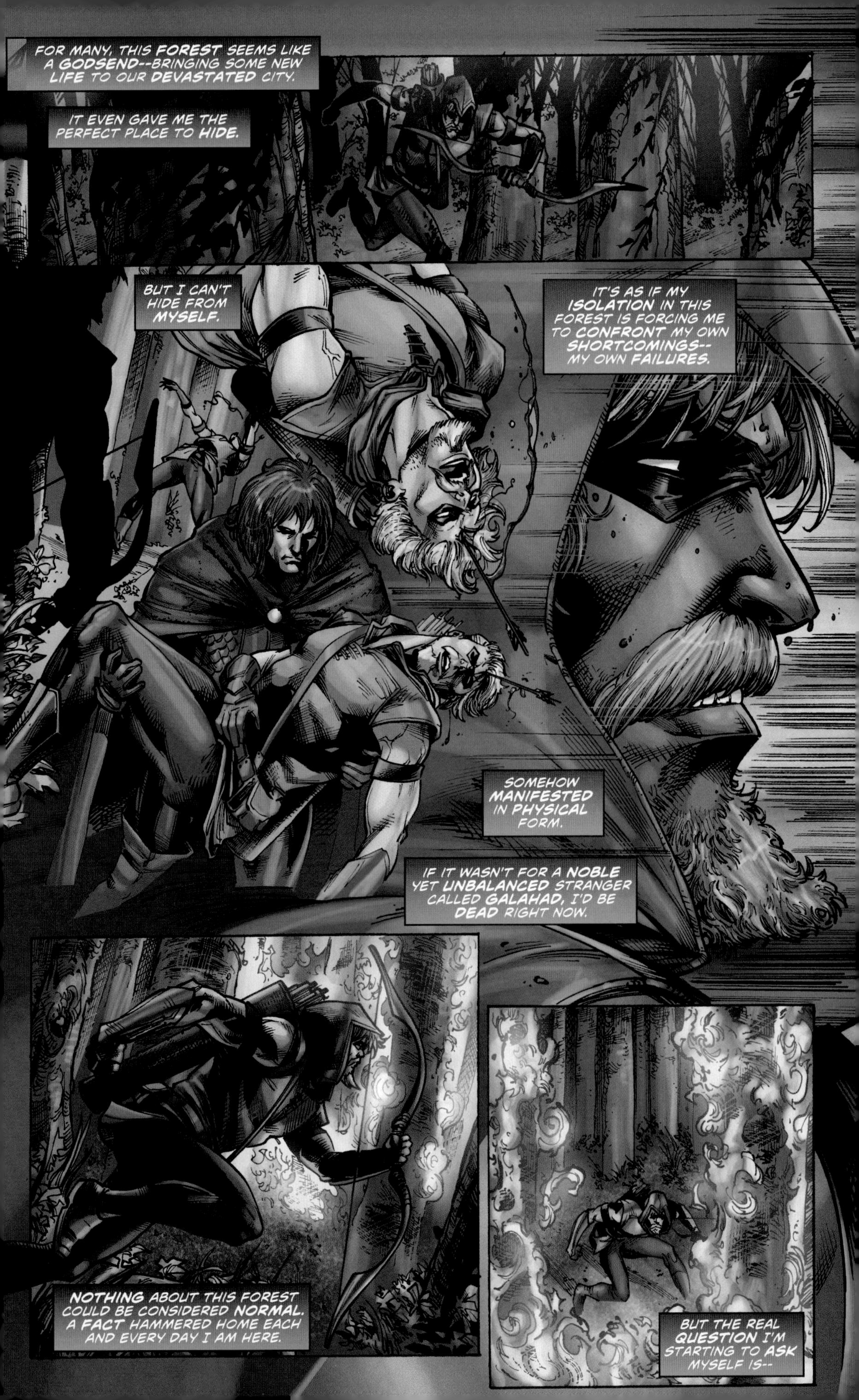
FOR MANY, THIS FOREST SEEMS LIKE A GODSEND--BRINGING SOME NEW LIFE TO OUR DEVASTATED CITY.
IT EVEN GAVE ME THE PERFECT PLACE TO HIDE.
BUT I CAN'T HIDE FROM MYSELF.
IT'S AS IF MY ISOLATION IN THIS FOREST IS FORCING ME TO CONFRONT MY OWN SHORTCOMINGS-- MY OWN FAILURES.
SOMEHOW MANIFESTED IN PHYSICAL FORM.
IF IT WASN'T FOR A NOBLE YET UNBALANCED STRANGER CALLED GALAHAD, I'D BE DEAD RIGHT NOW.
NOTHING ABOUT THIS FOREST COULD BE CONSIDERED NORMAL. A FACT HAMMERED HOME EACH AND EVERY DAY I AM HERE.
BUT THE REAL QUESTION I'M STARTING TO ASK MYSELF IS--

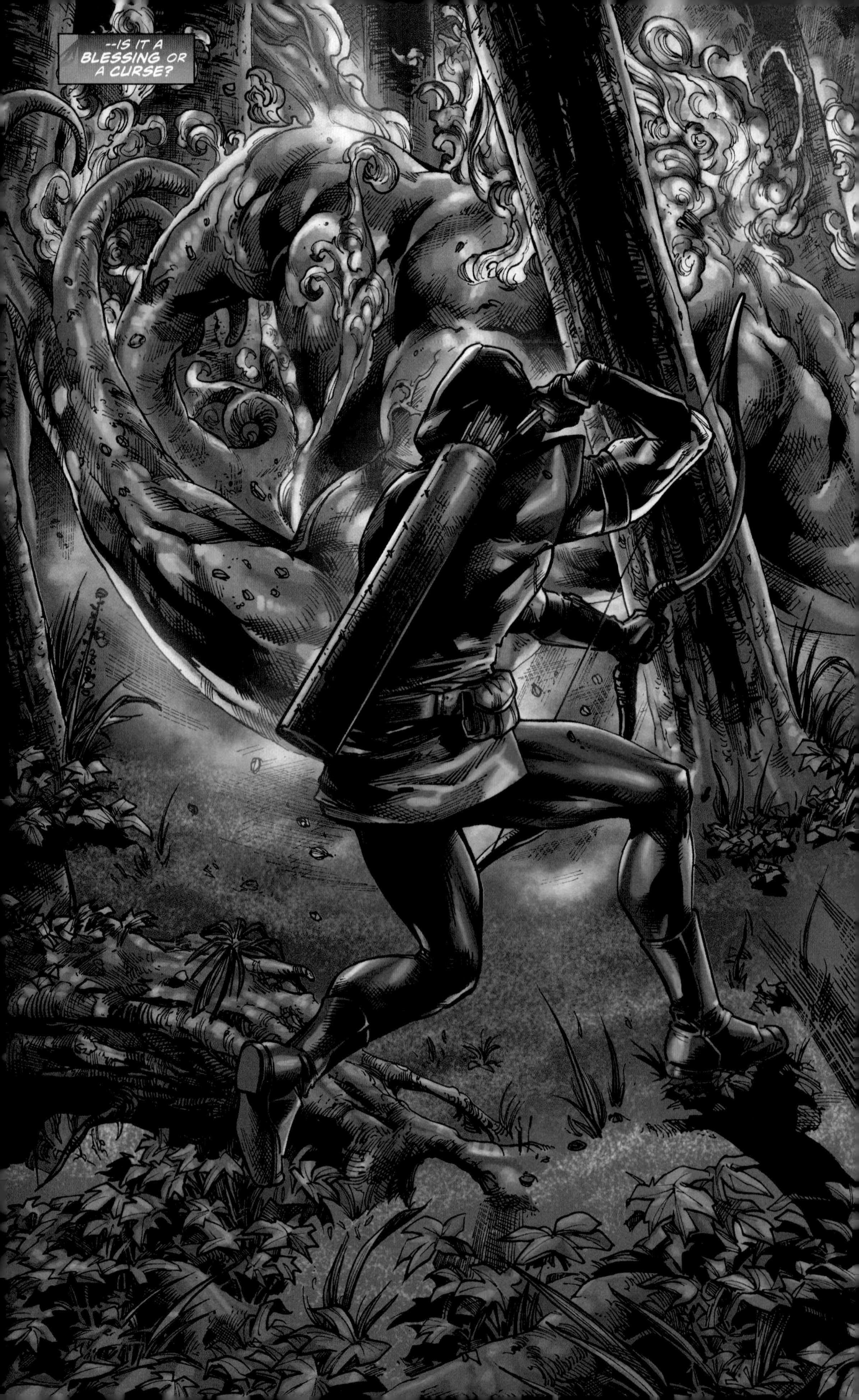
--IS IT A BLESSING OR A CURSE?

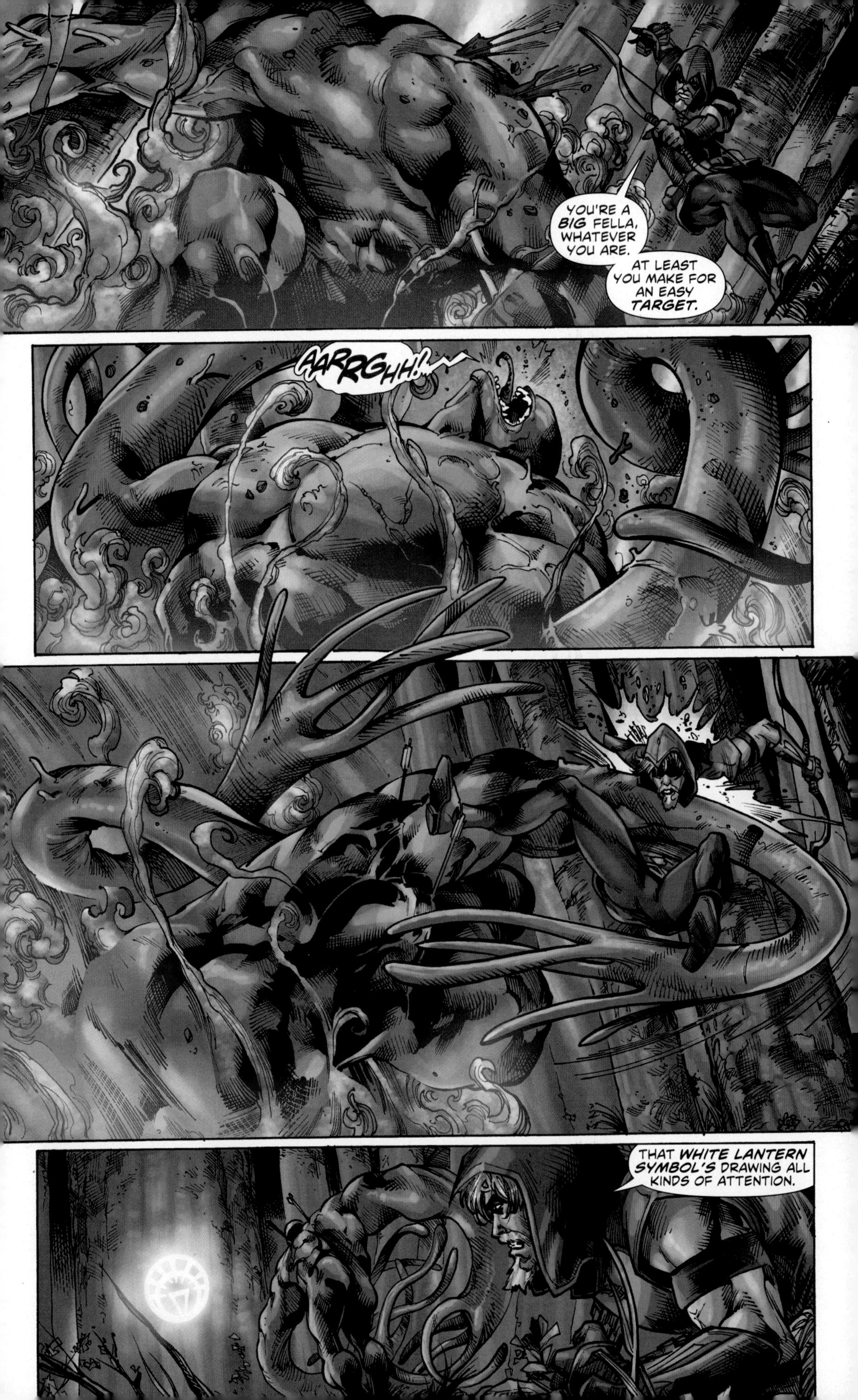
YOU'RE A BIG FELLA, WHATEVER YOU ARE.
AT LEAST YOU MAKE FOR AN EASY TARGET.
AARRGHH!
THAT WHITE LANTERN SYMBOL'S DRAWING ALL KINDS OF ATTENTION.

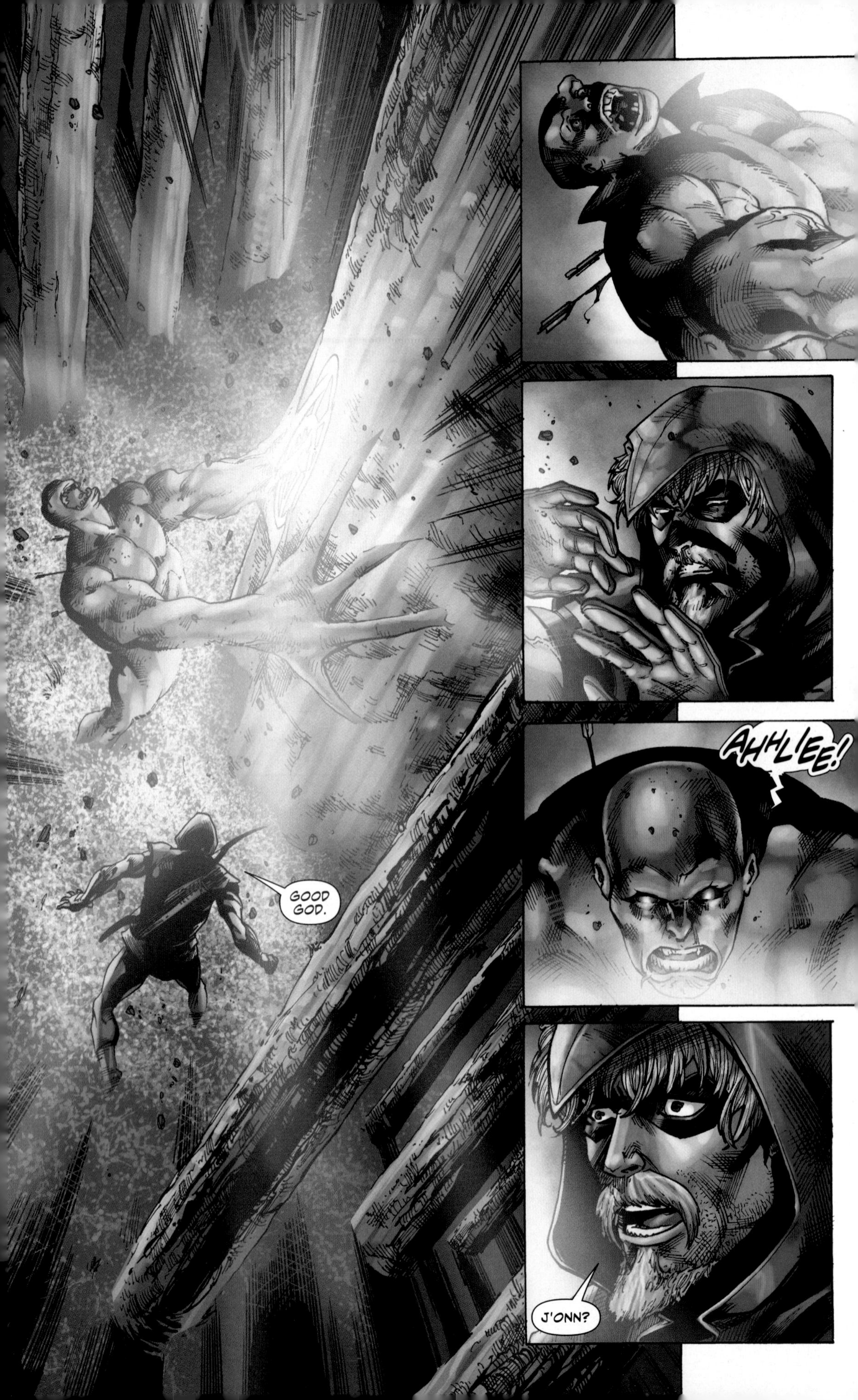
GOOD GOD.
AHHLIEE!
J'ONN?

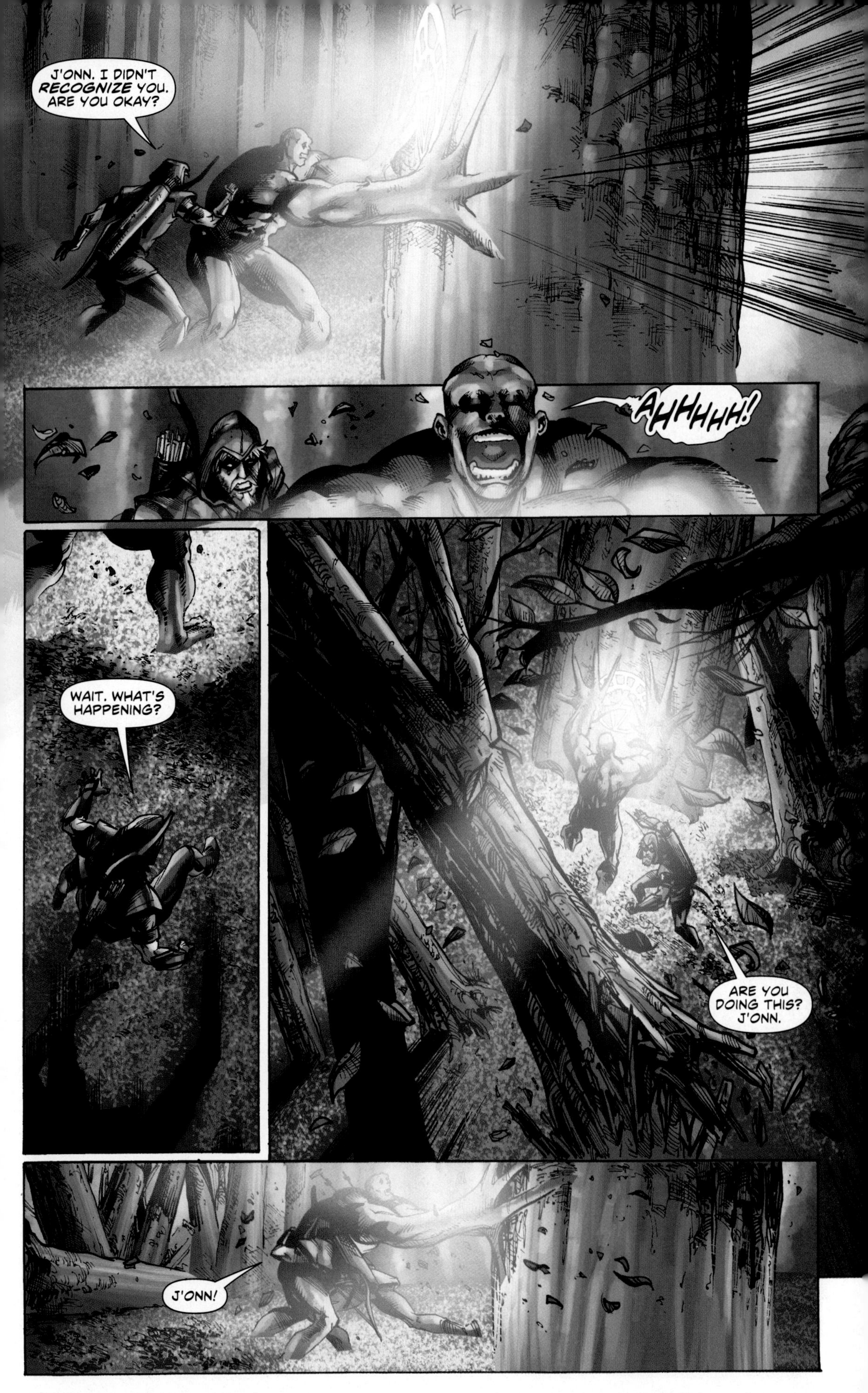
J'ONN. I DIDN'T *RECOGNIZE* YOU. ARE YOU OKAY?
AHHHHH!
WAIT. WHAT'S HAPPENING?
ARE YOU DOING THIS? J'ONN.
J'ONN!

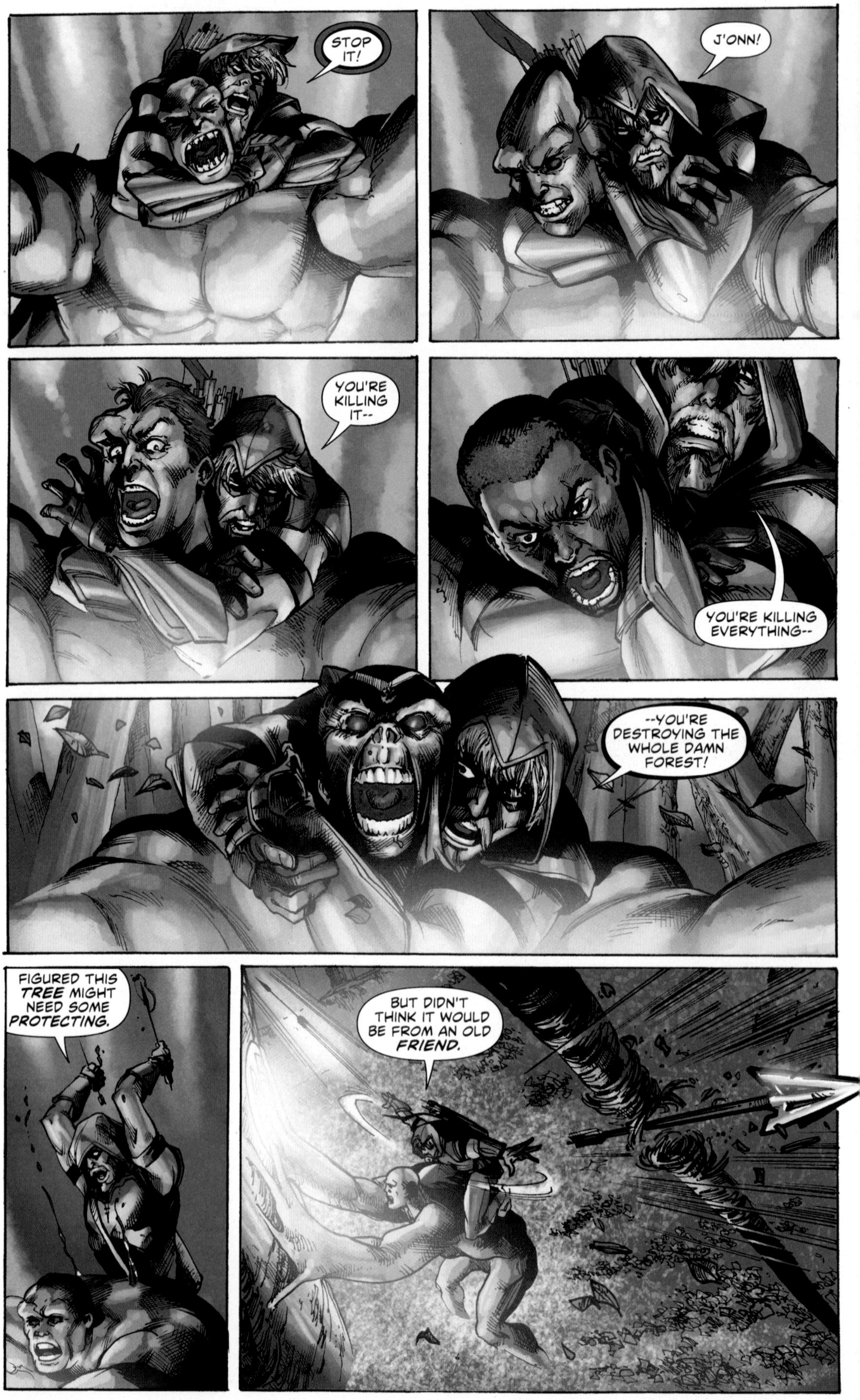
STOP IT!
J'ONN!
YOU'RE KILLING IT--
YOU'RE KILLING EVERYTHING--
--YOU'RE DESTROYING THE WHOLE DAMN FOREST!
FIGURED THIS TREE MIGHT NEED SOME PROTECTING.
BUT DIDN'T THINK IT WOULD BE FROM AN OLD FRIEND.

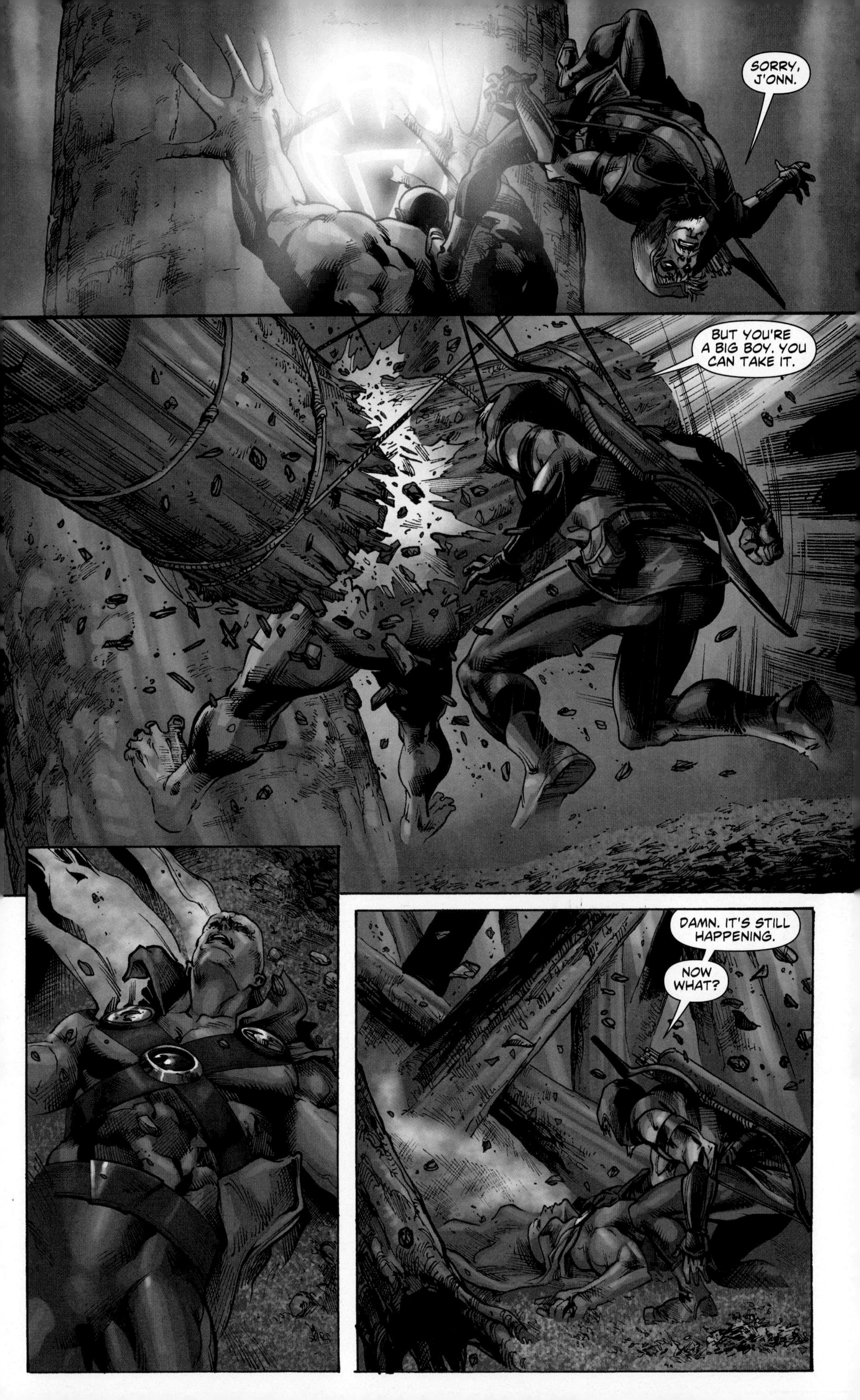
SORRY, J'ONN.
BUT YOU'RE A BIG BOY. YOU CAN TAKE IT.
DAMN. IT'S STILL HAPPENING.
NOW WHAT?

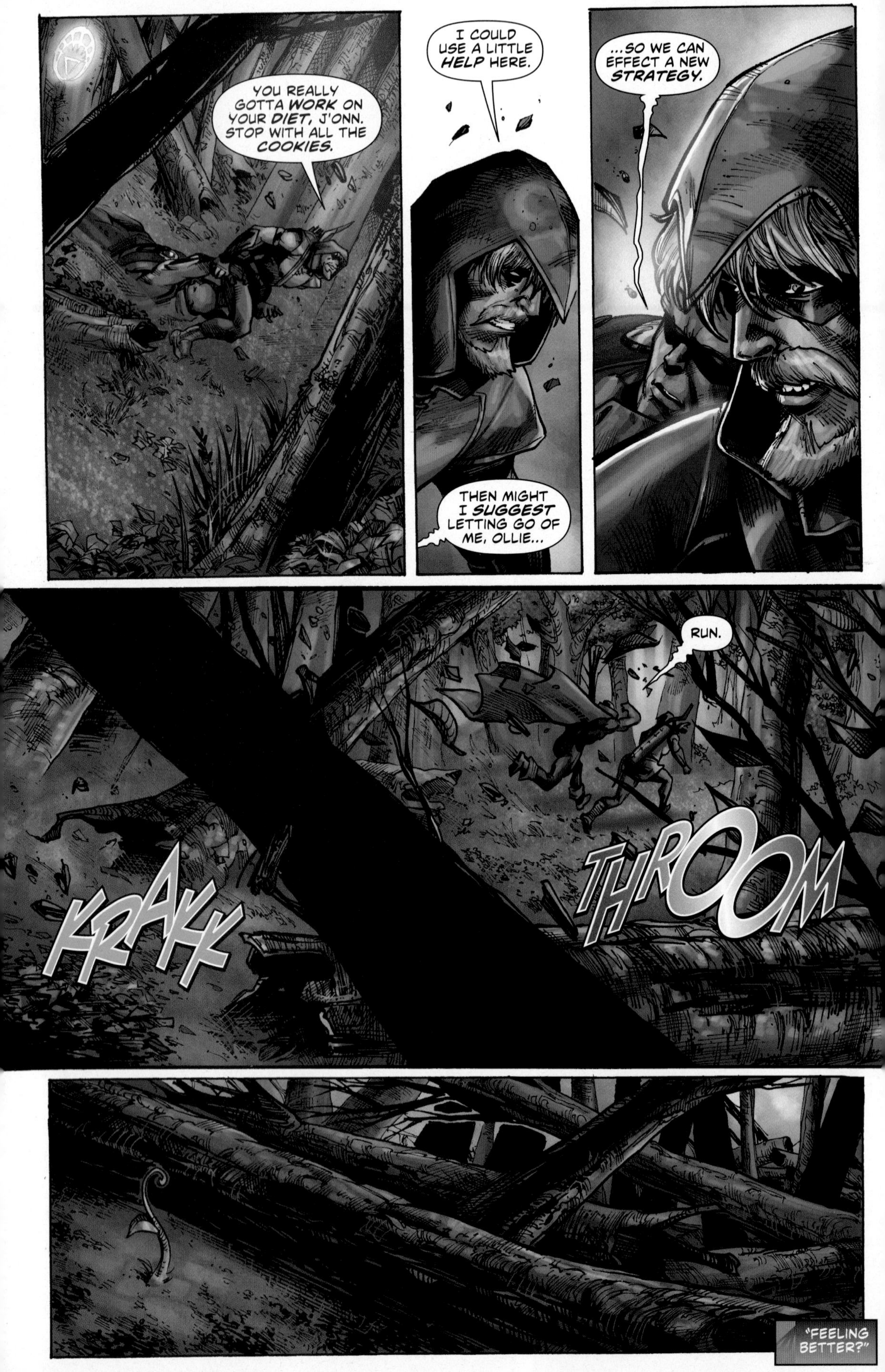

YOU REALLY GOTTA WORK ON YOUR DIET, J'ONN. STOP WITH ALL THE COOKIES.
I COULD USE A LITTLE HELP HERE.
THEN MIGHT I SUGGEST LETTING GO OF ME, OLLIE...
...SO WE CAN EFFECT A NEW STRATEGY.
RUN.
KRAKK
THROOM
"FEELING BETTER?"

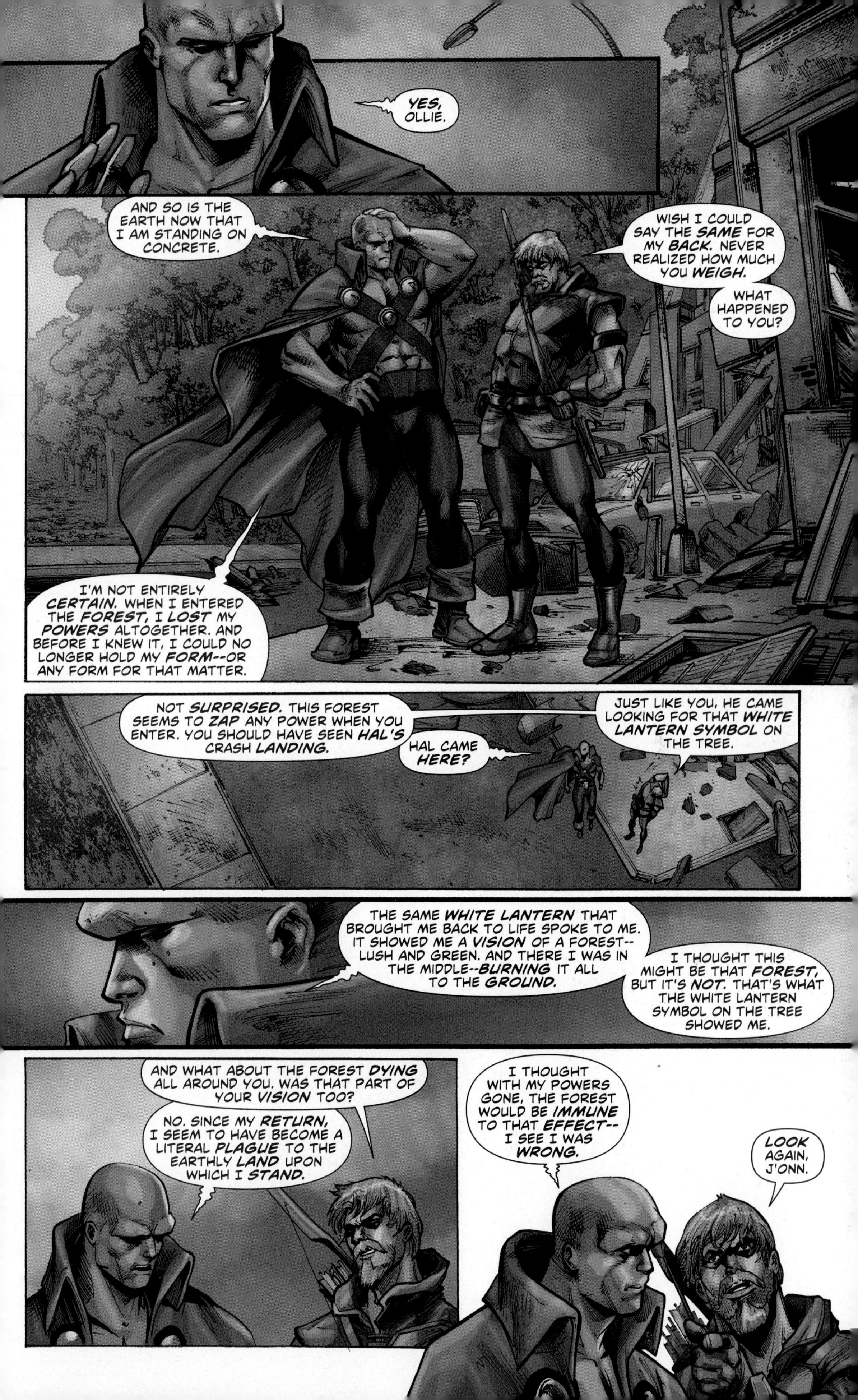
YES, OLLIE.
AND SO IS THE EARTH NOW THAT I AM STANDING ON CONCRETE.
WISH I COULD SAY THE SAME FOR MY BACK. NEVER REALIZED HOW MUCH YOU WEIGH.
WHAT HAPPENED TO YOU?
I'M NOT ENTIRELY CERTAIN. WHEN I ENTERED THE FOREST, I LOST MY POWERS ALTOGETHER. AND BEFORE I KNEW IT, I COULD NO LONGER HOLD MY FORM--OR ANY FORM FOR THAT MATTER.
NOT SURPRISED. THIS FOREST SEEMS TO ZAP ANY POWER WHEN YOU ENTER. YOU SHOULD HAVE SEEN HAL'S CRASH LANDING.
HAL CAME HERE?
JUST LIKE YOU, HE CAME LOOKING FOR THAT WHITE LANTERN SYMBOL ON THE TREE.
THE SAME WHITE LANTERN THAT BROUGHT ME BACK TO LIFE SPOKE TO ME. IT SHOWED ME A VISION OF A FOREST--LUSH AND GREEN. AND THERE I WAS IN THE MIDDLE--BURNING IT ALL TO THE GROUND.
I THOUGHT THIS MIGHT BE THAT FOREST, BUT IT'S NOT. THAT'S WHAT THE WHITE LANTERN SYMBOL ON THE TREE SHOWED ME.
AND WHAT ABOUT THE FOREST DYING ALL AROUND YOU. WAS THAT PART OF YOUR VISION TOO?
NO. SINCE MY RETURN, I SEEM TO HAVE BECOME A LITERAL PLAGUE TO THE EARTHLY LAND UPON WHICH I STAND.
I THOUGHT WITH MY POWERS GONE, THE FOREST WOULD BE IMMUNE TO THAT EFFECT--I SEE I WAS WRONG.
LOOK AGAIN, J'ONN.

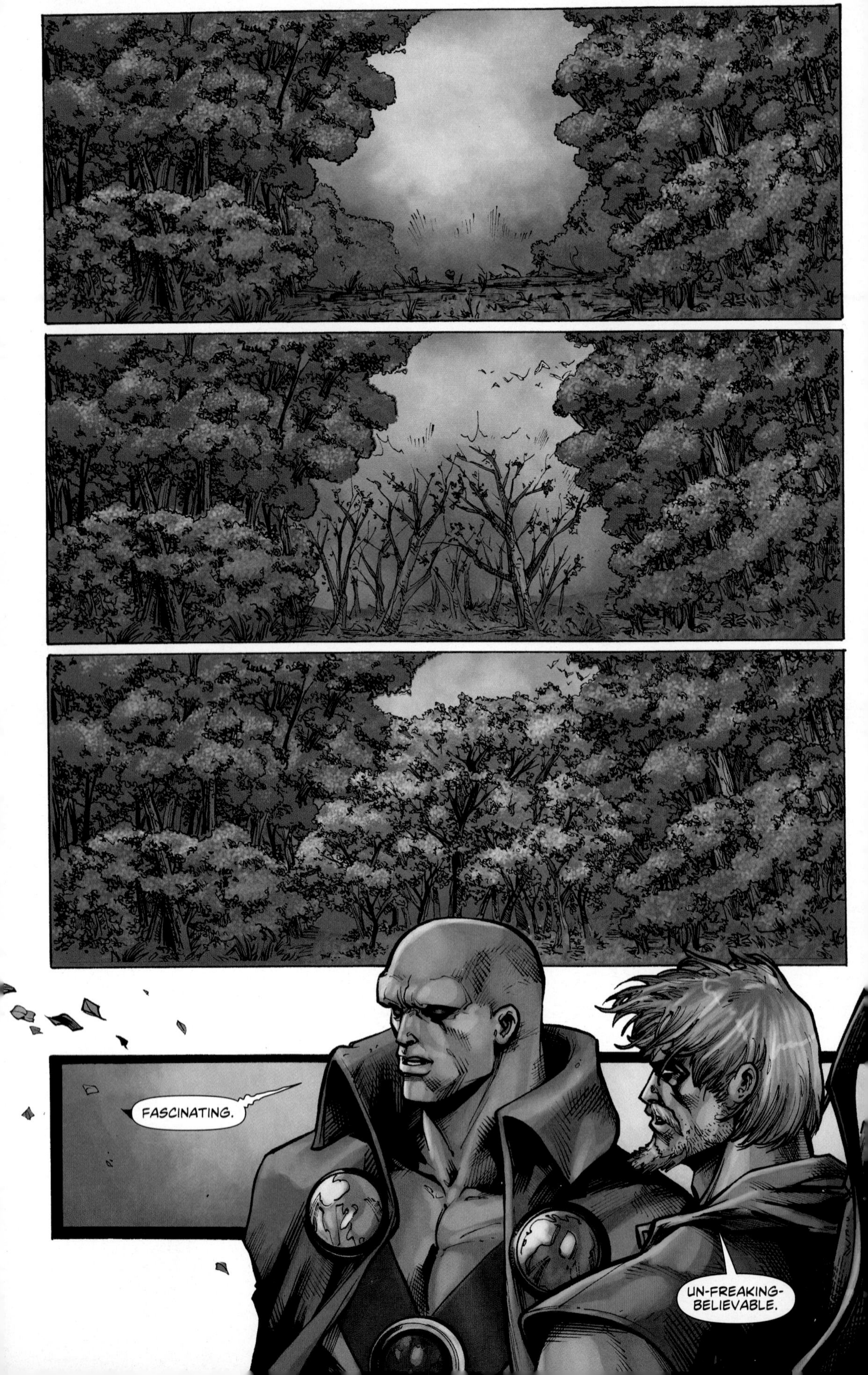
FASCINATING.
UN-FREAKING-BELIEVABLE.

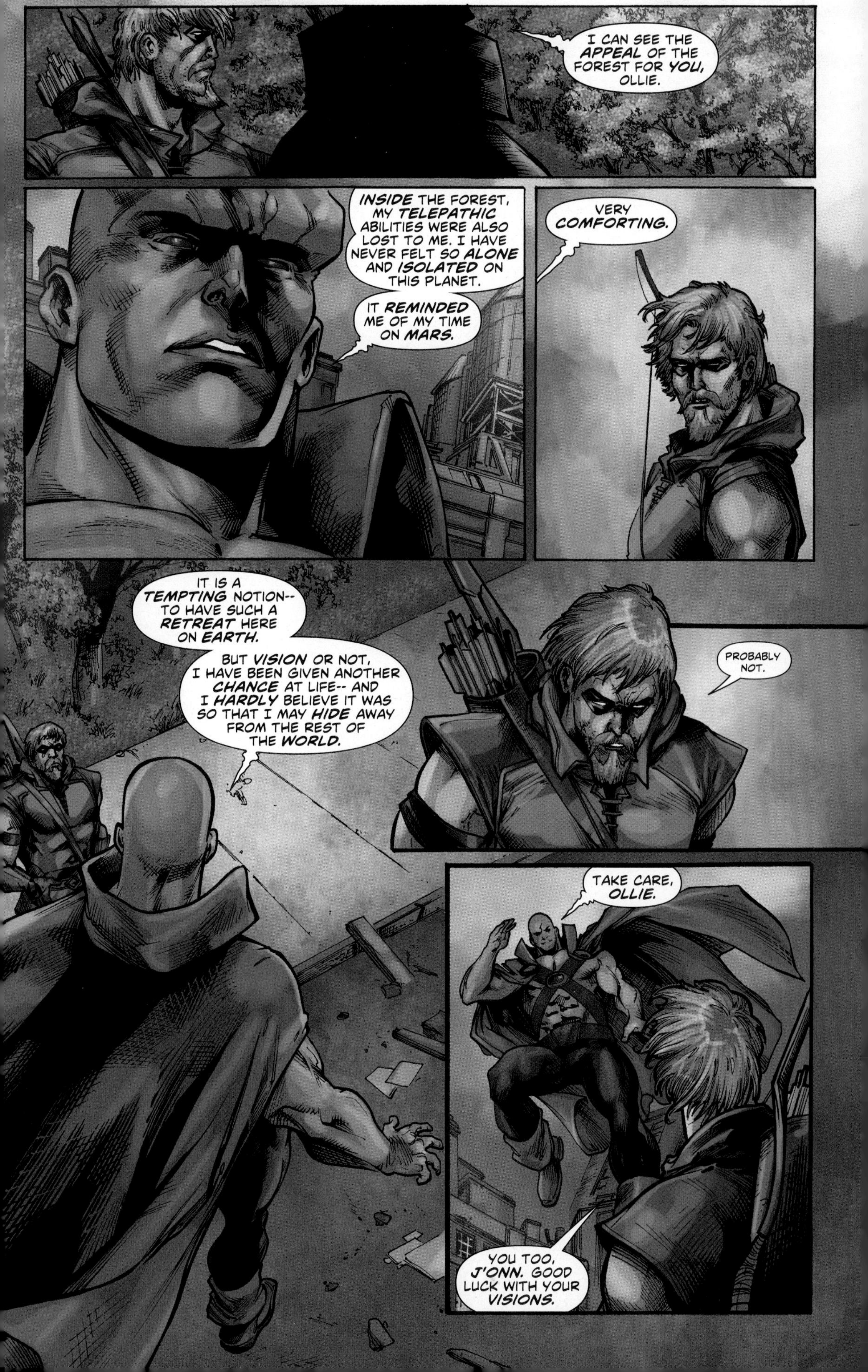
I CAN SEE THE APPEAL OF THE FOREST FOR YOU, OLLIE.
INSIDE THE FOREST, MY TELEPATHIC ABILITIES WERE ALSO LOST TO ME. I HAVE NEVER FELT SO ALONE AND ISOLATED ON THIS PLANET.
IT REMINDED ME OF MY TIME ON MARS.
VERY COMFORTING.
IT IS A TEMPTING NOTION-- TO HAVE SUCH A RETREAT HERE ON EARTH.
BUT VISION OR NOT, I HAVE BEEN GIVEN ANOTHER CHANCE AT LIFE-- AND I HARDLY BELIEVE IT WAS SO THAT I MAY HIDE AWAY FROM THE REST OF THE WORLD.
PROBABLY NOT.
TAKE CARE, OLLIE.
YOU TOO, J'ONN. GOOD LUCK WITH YOUR VISIONS.

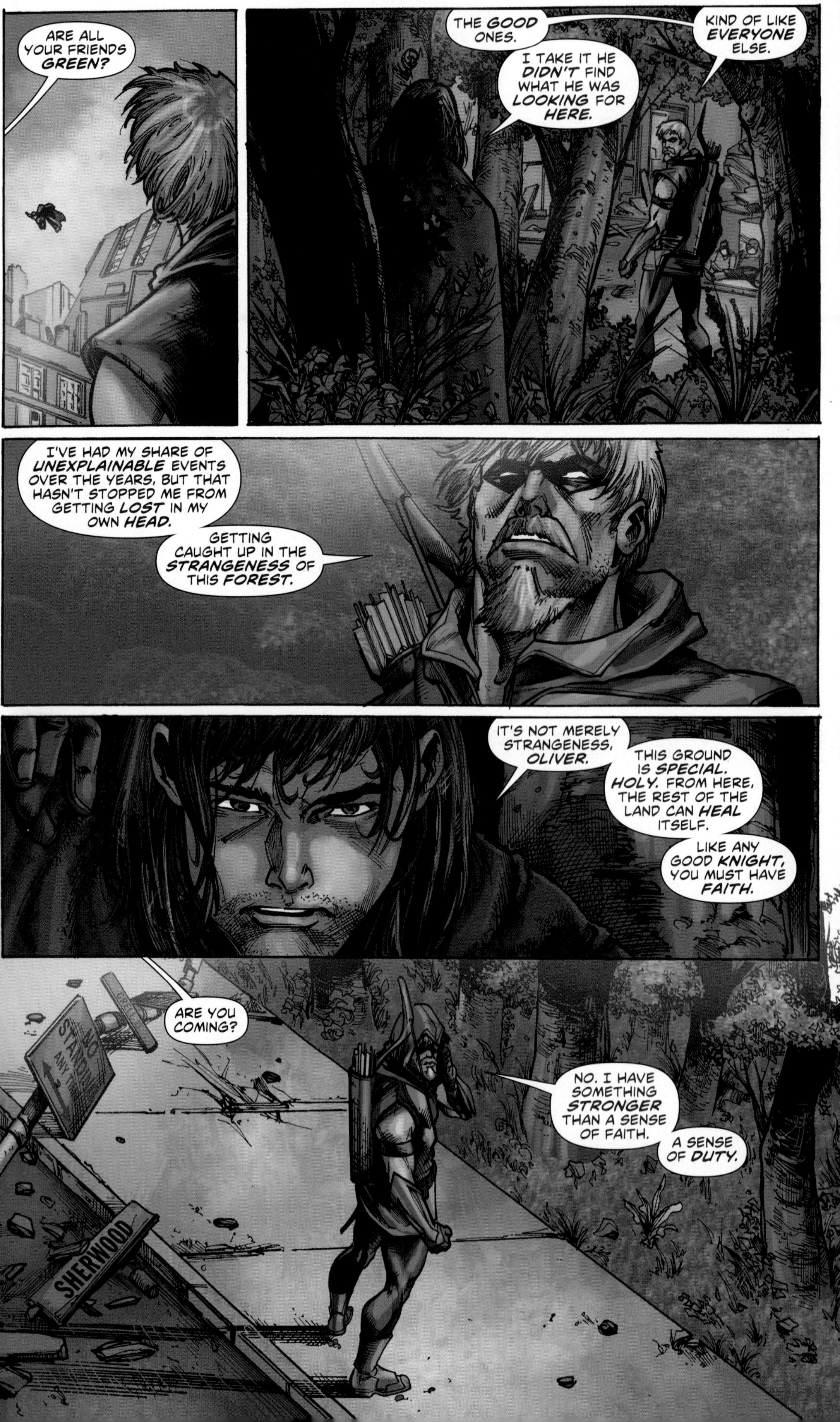

ARE ALL YOUR FRIENDS GREEN?
THE GOOD ONES.
KIND OF LIKE EVERYONE ELSE.
I TAKE IT HE DIDN'T FIND WHAT HE WAS LOOKING FOR HERE.
I'VE HAD MY SHARE OF UNEXPLAINABLE EVENTS OVER THE YEARS, BUT THAT HASN'T STOPPED ME FROM GETTING LOST IN MY OWN HEAD.
GETTING CAUGHT UP IN THE STRANGENESS OF THIS FOREST.
IT'S NOT MERELY STRANGENESS, OLIVER.
THIS GROUND IS SPECIAL. HOLY. FROM HERE, THE REST OF THE LAND CAN HEAL ITSELF.
LIKE ANY GOOD KNIGHT, YOU MUST HAVE FAITH.
ARE YOU COMING?
NO. I HAVE SOMETHING STRONGER THAN A SENSE OF FAITH.
A SENSE OF DUTY.
GRELL
SHERWOOD

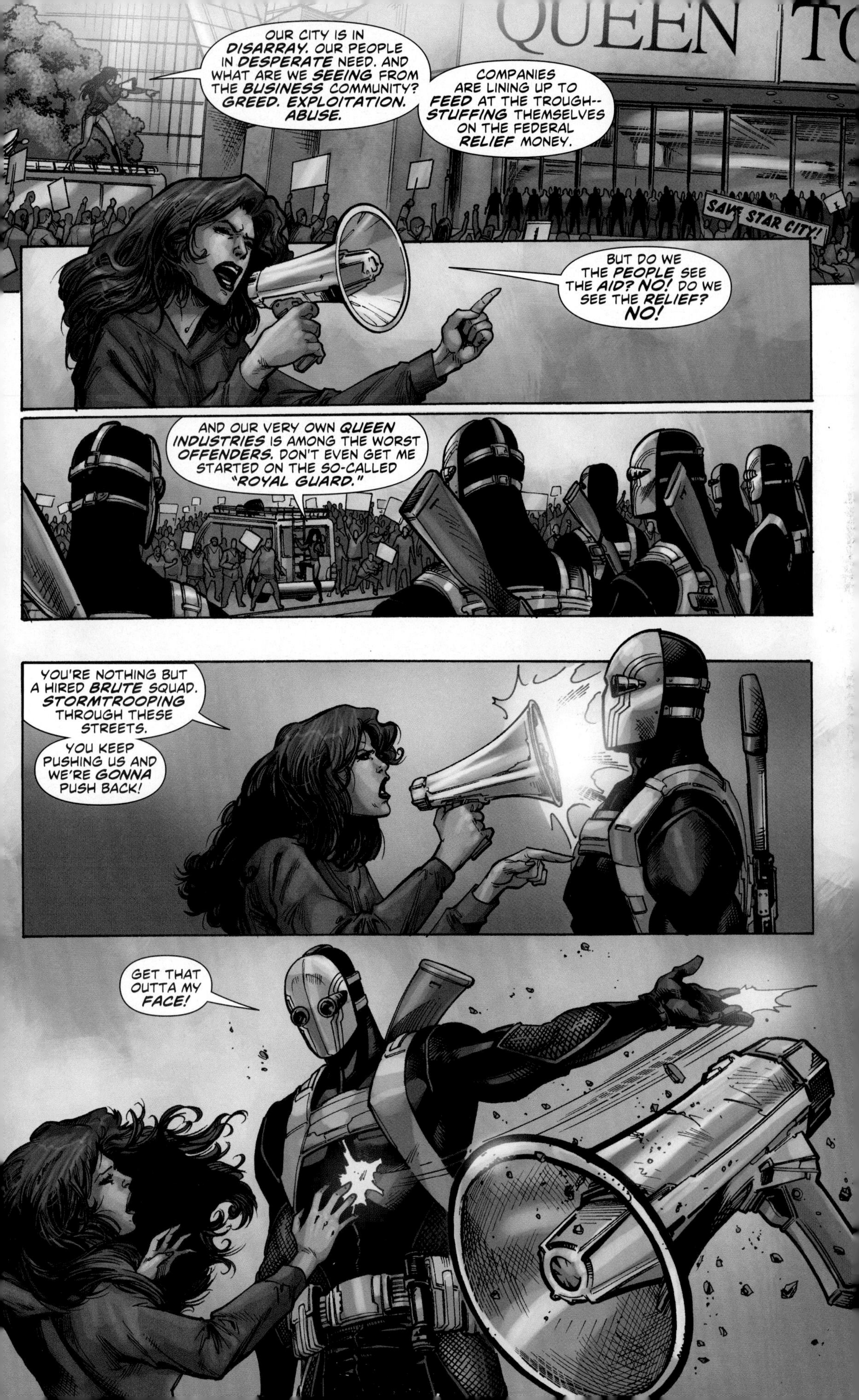
QUEEN TO
OUR CITY IS IN DISARRAY. OUR PEOPLE IN DESPERATE NEED. AND WHAT ARE WE SEEING FROM THE BUSINESS COMMUNITY? GREED. EXPLOITATION. ABUSE.
COMPANIES ARE LINING UP TO FEED AT THE TROUGH-- STUFFING THEMSELVES ON THE FEDERAL RELIEF MONEY.
SAVE STAR CITY!
BUT DO WE THE PEOPLE SEE THE AID? NO! DO WE SEE THE RELIEF? NO!
AND OUR VERY OWN QUEEN INDUSTRIES IS AMONG THE WORST OFFENDERS. DON'T EVEN GET ME STARTED ON THE SO-CALLED "ROYAL GUARD."
YOU'RE NOTHING BUT A HIRED BRUTE SQUAD. STORMTROOPING THROUGH THESE STREETS.
YOU KEEP PUSHING US AND WE'RE GONNA PUSH BACK!
GET THAT OUTTA MY FACE!

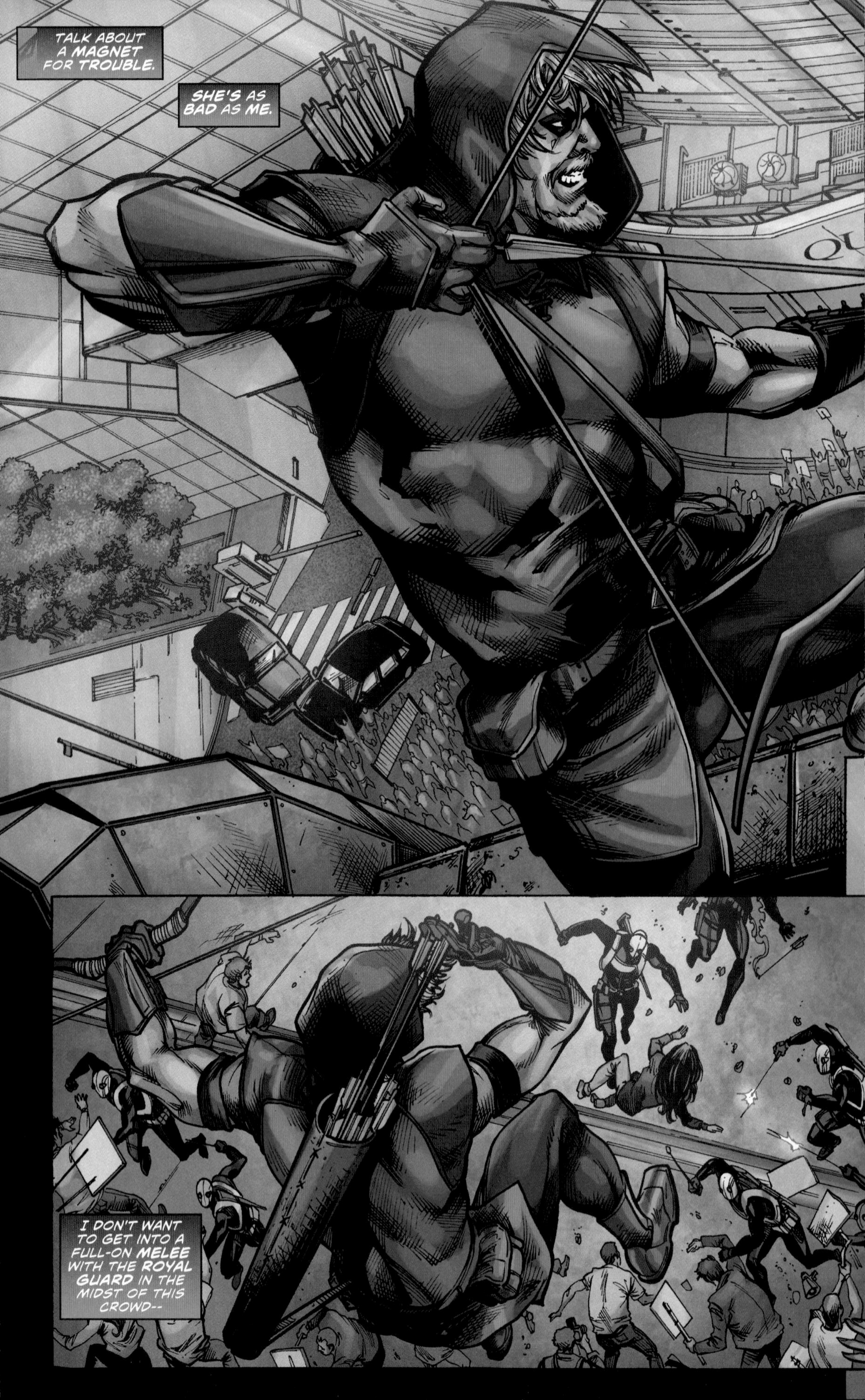
TALK ABOUT A MAGNET FOR TROUBLE.
SHE'S AS BAD AS ME.
I DON'T WANT TO GET INTO A FULL-ON MELEE WITH THE ROYAL GUARD IN THE MIDST OF THIS CROWD--

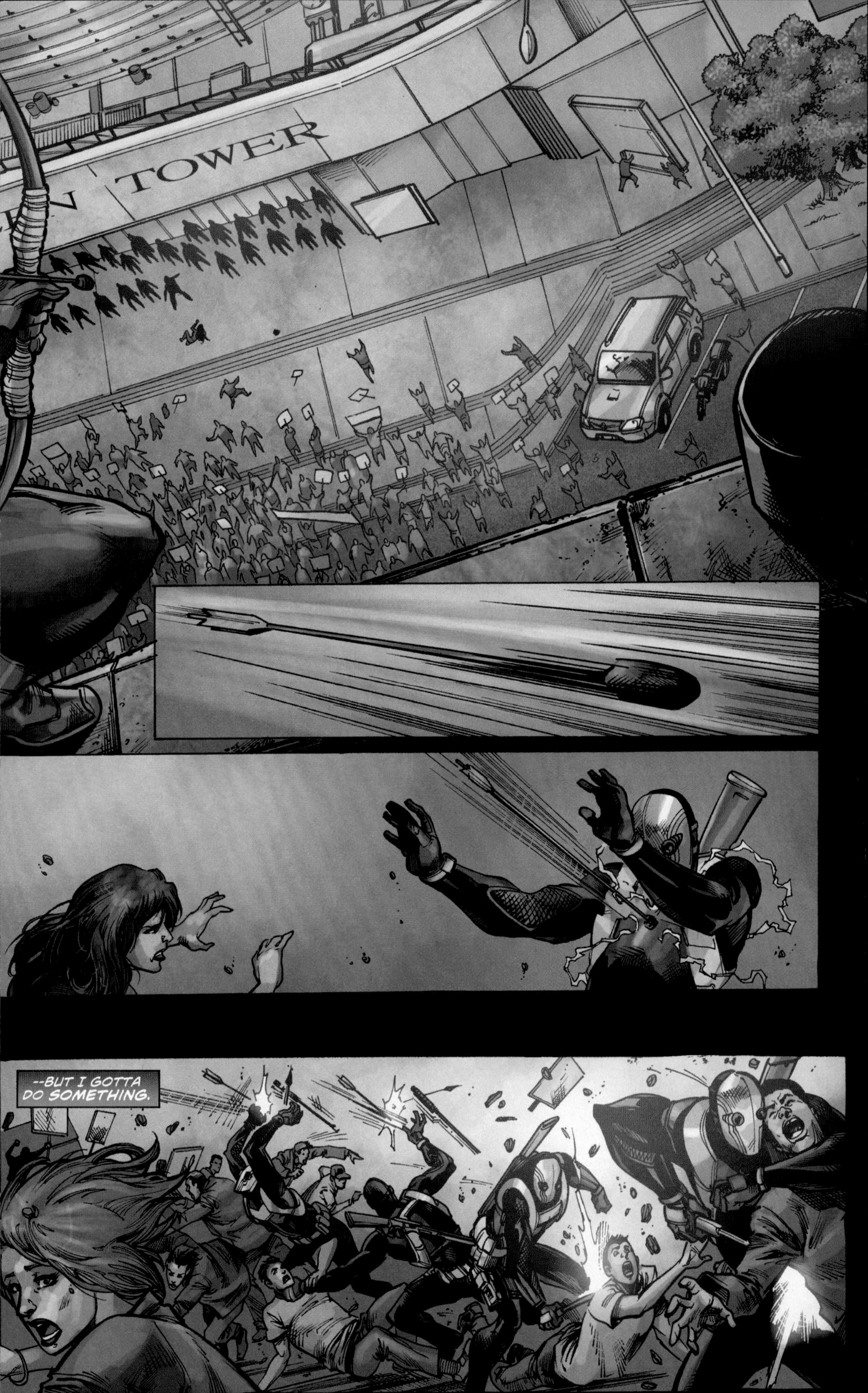

TOWER
--BUT I GOTTA DO SOMETHING.

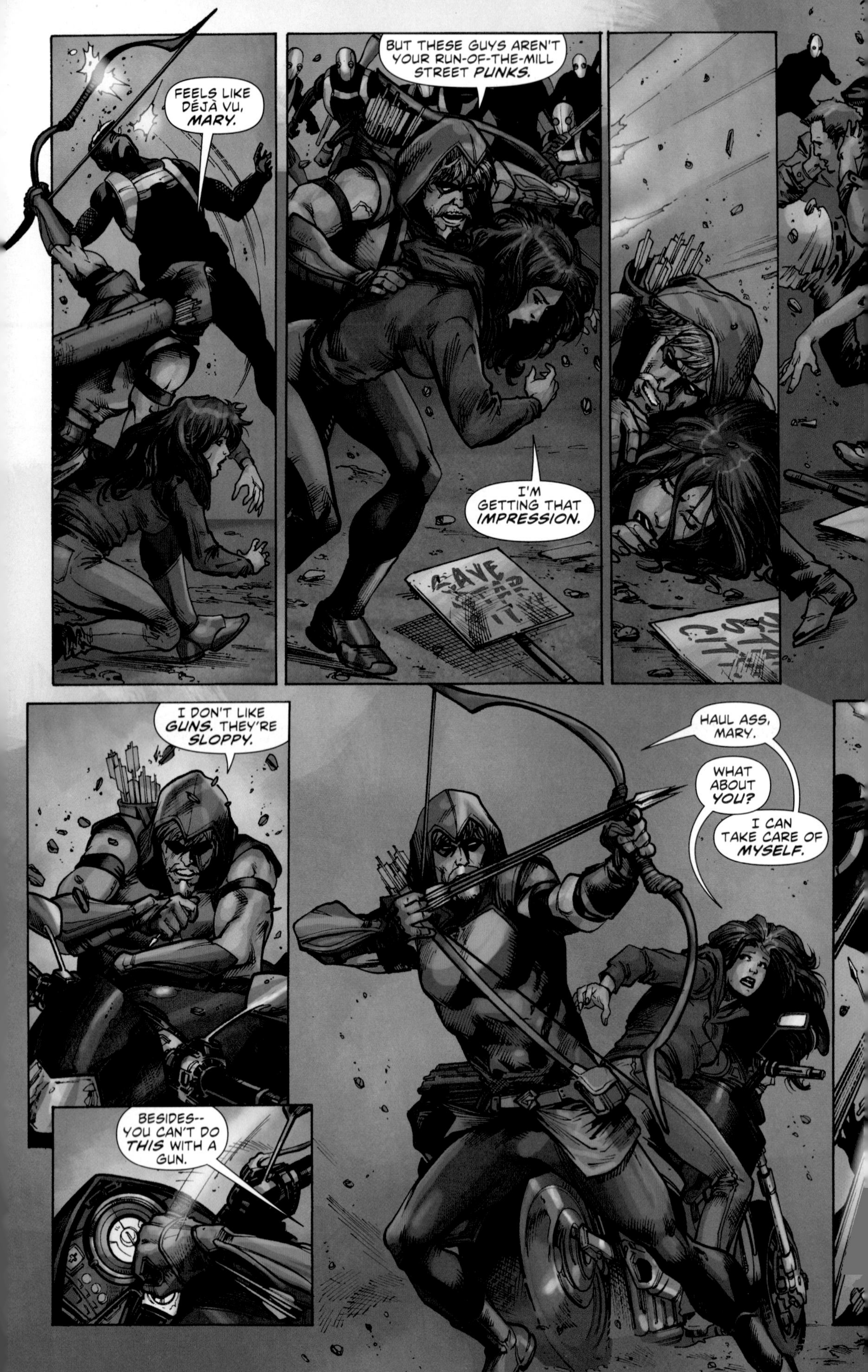
FEELS LIKE DÉJÀ VU, MARY.
BUT THESE GUYS AREN'T YOUR RUN-OF-THE-MILL STREET PUNKS.
I'M GETTING THAT IMPRESSION.
I DON'T LIKE GUNS. THEY'RE SLOPPY.
BESIDES-- YOU CAN'T DO THIS WITH A GUN.
HAUL ASS, MARY.
WHAT ABOUT YOU?
I CAN TAKE CARE OF MYSELF.

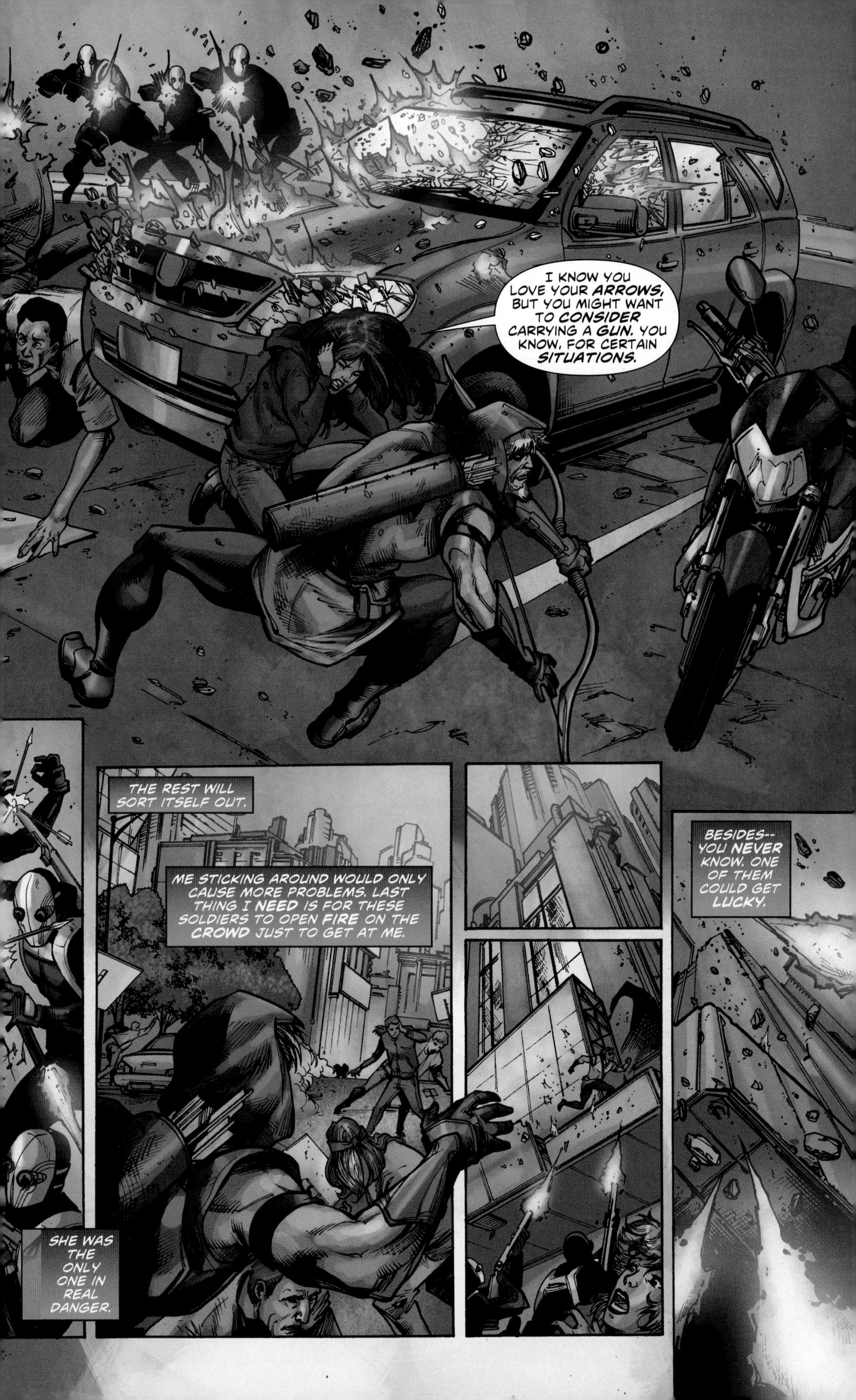
I KNOW YOU LOVE YOUR ARROWS, BUT YOU MIGHT WANT TO CONSIDER CARRYING A GUN. YOU KNOW, FOR CERTAIN SITUATIONS.
SHE WAS THE ONLY ONE IN REAL DANGER.
THE REST WILL SORT ITSELF OUT.
ME STICKING AROUND WOULD ONLY CAUSE MORE PROBLEMS. LAST THING I NEED IS FOR THESE SOLDIERS TO OPEN FIRE ON THE CROWD JUST TO GET AT ME.
BESIDES-- YOU NEVER KNOW. ONE OF THEM COULD GET LUCKY.

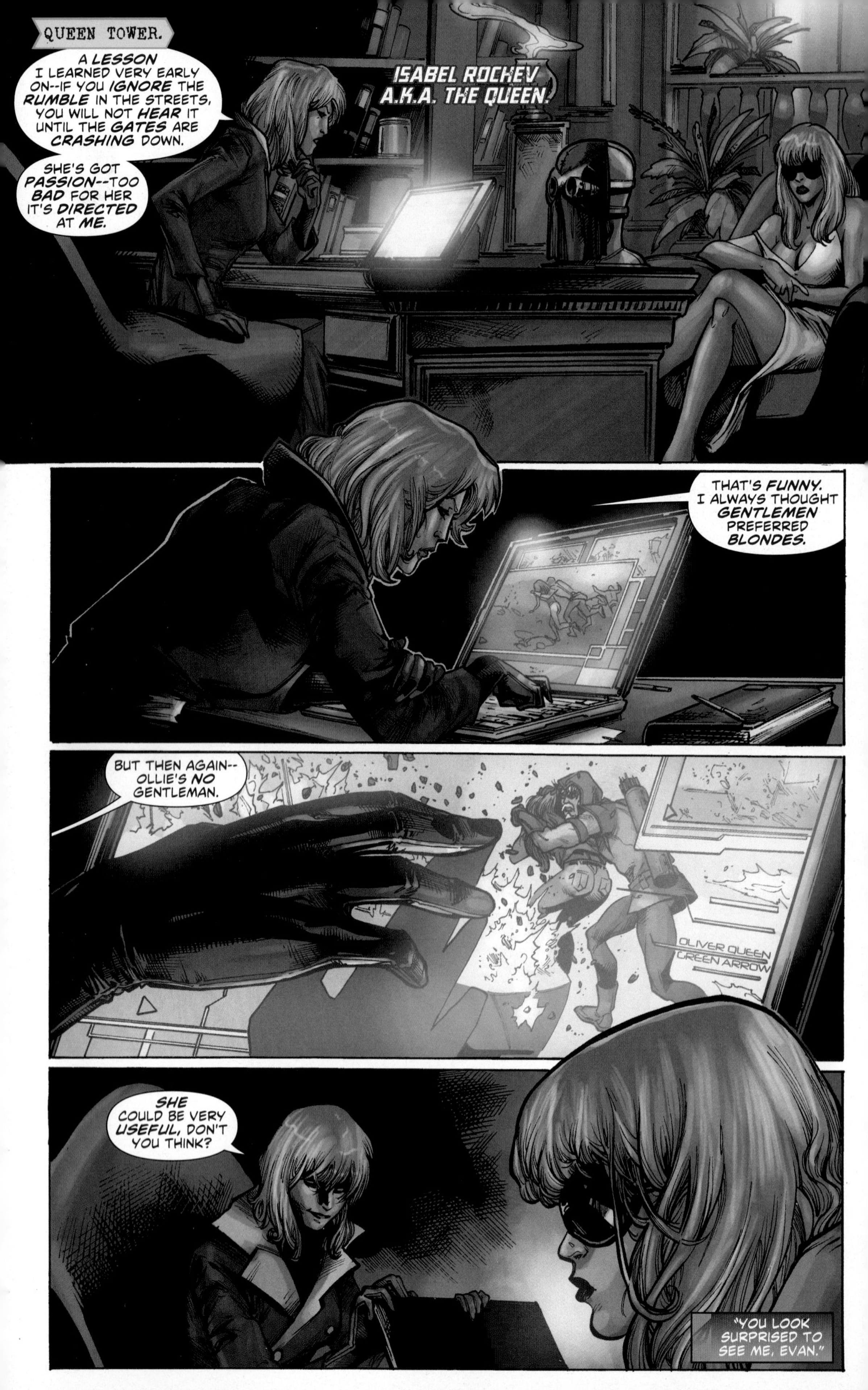
QUEEN TOWER.
A LESSON I LEARNED VERY EARLY ON--IF YOU IGNORE THE RUMBLE IN THE STREETS, YOU WILL NOT HEAR IT UNTIL THE GATES ARE CRASHING DOWN.
ISABEL ROCHEV A.K.A. THE QUEEN.
SHE'S GOT PASSION--TOO BAD FOR HER IT'S DIRECTED AT ME.
THAT'S FUNNY. I ALWAYS THOUGHT GENTLEMEN PREFERRED BLONDES.
BUT THEN AGAIN--OLLIE'S NO GENTLEMAN.
OLIVER QUEEN
GREEN ARROW
SHE COULD BE VERY USEFUL, DON'T YOU THINK?
"YOU LOOK SURPRISED TO SEE ME, EVAN."

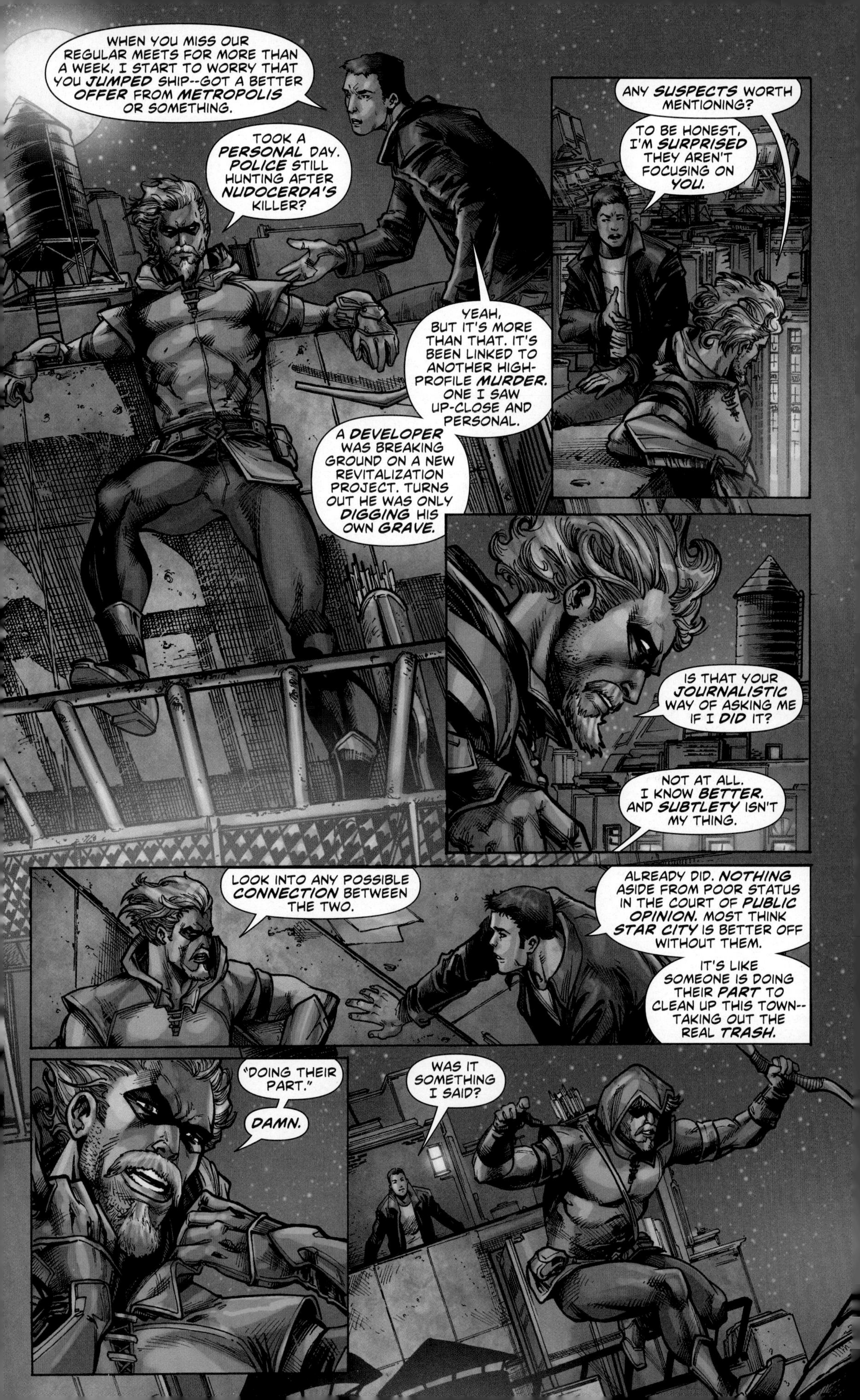
WHEN YOU MISS OUR REGULAR MEETS FOR MORE THAN A WEEK, I START TO WORRY THAT YOU JUMPED SHIP--GOT A BETTER OFFER FROM METROPOLIS OR SOMETHING.
TOOK A PERSONAL DAY. POLICE STILL HUNTING AFTER NUDOCERDA'S KILLER?
YEAH, BUT IT'S MORE THAN THAT. IT'S BEEN LINKED TO ANOTHER HIGH-PROFILE MURDER. ONE I SAW UP-CLOSE AND PERSONAL.
A DEVELOPER WAS BREAKING GROUND ON A NEW REVITALIZATION PROJECT. TURNS OUT HE WAS ONLY DIGGING HIS OWN GRAVE.
ANY SUSPECTS WORTH MENTIONING?
TO BE HONEST, I'M SURPRISED THEY AREN'T FOCUSING ON YOU.
IS THAT YOUR JOURNALISTIC WAY OF ASKING ME IF I DID IT?
NOT AT ALL. I KNOW BETTER. AND SUBTLETY ISN'T MY THING.
LOOK INTO ANY POSSIBLE CONNECTION BETWEEN THE TWO.
ALREADY DID. NOTHING ASIDE FROM POOR STATUS IN THE COURT OF PUBLIC OPINION. MOST THINK STAR CITY IS BETTER OFF WITHOUT THEM.
IT'S LIKE SOMEONE IS DOING THEIR PART TO CLEAN UP THIS TOWN--TAKING OUT THE REAL TRASH.
"DOING THEIR PART."
DAMN.
WAS IT SOMETHING I SAID?

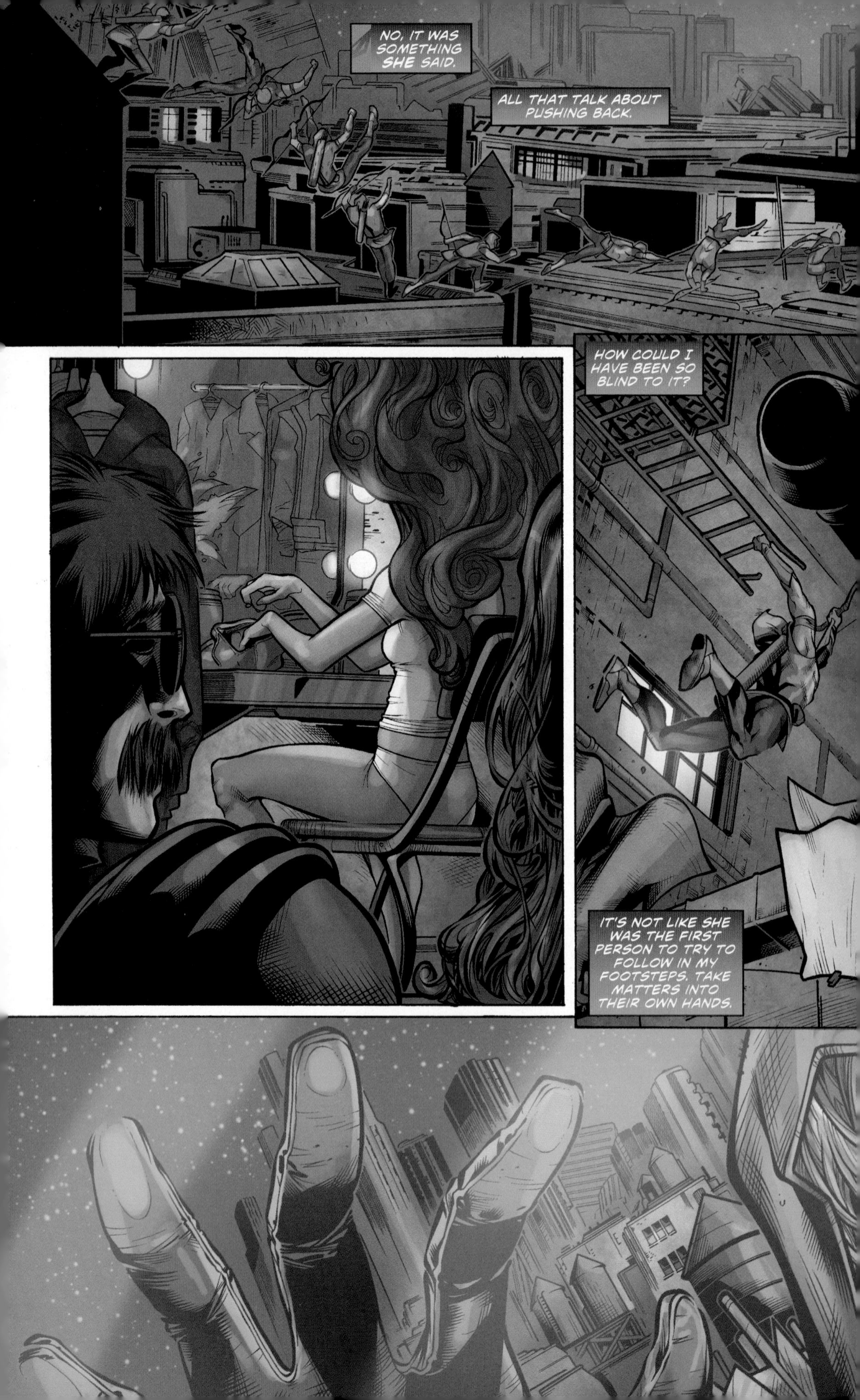
NO, IT WAS SOMETHING SHE SAID.
ALL THAT TALK ABOUT PUSHING BACK.
HOW COULD I HAVE BEEN SO BLIND TO IT?
IT'S NOT LIKE SHE WAS THE FIRST PERSON TO TRY TO FOLLOW IN MY FOOTSTEPS. TAKE MATTERS INTO THEIR OWN HANDS.

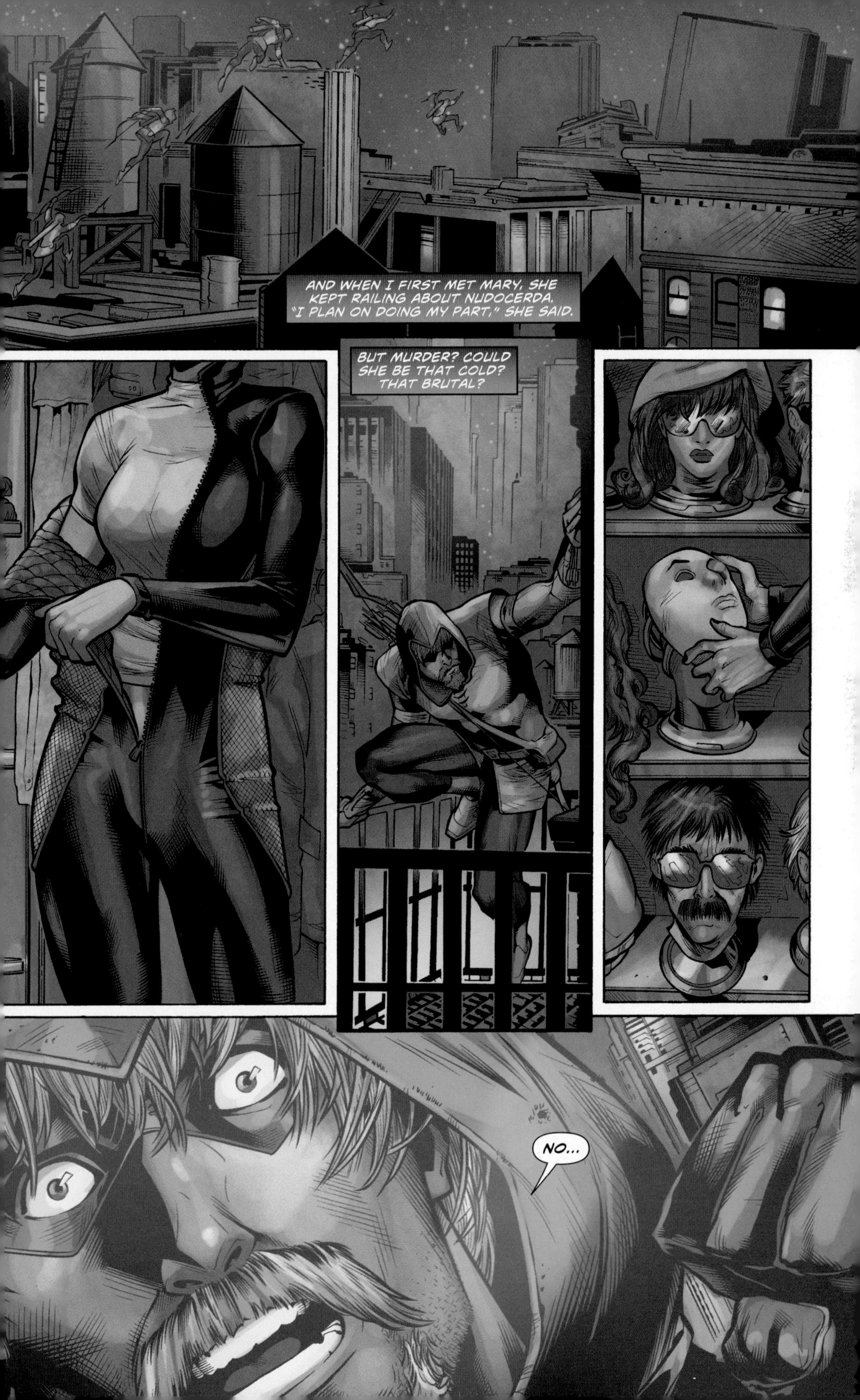
AND WHEN I FIRST MET MARY, SHE KEPT RAILING ABOUT NUDOCERDA. "I PLAN ON DOING MY PART," SHE SAID.
BUT MURDER? COULD SHE BE THAT COLD? THAT BRUTAL?
NO...

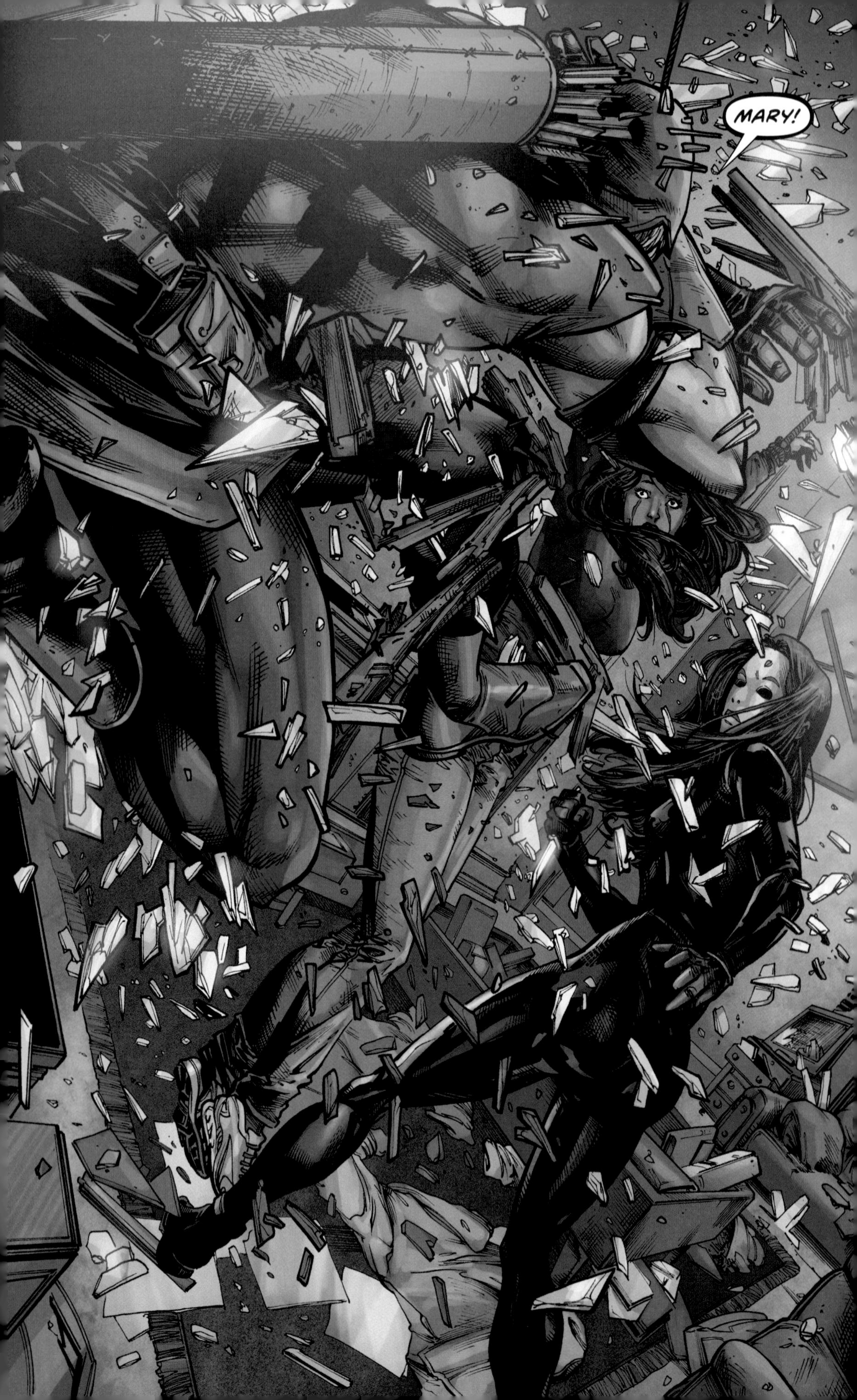
MARY!

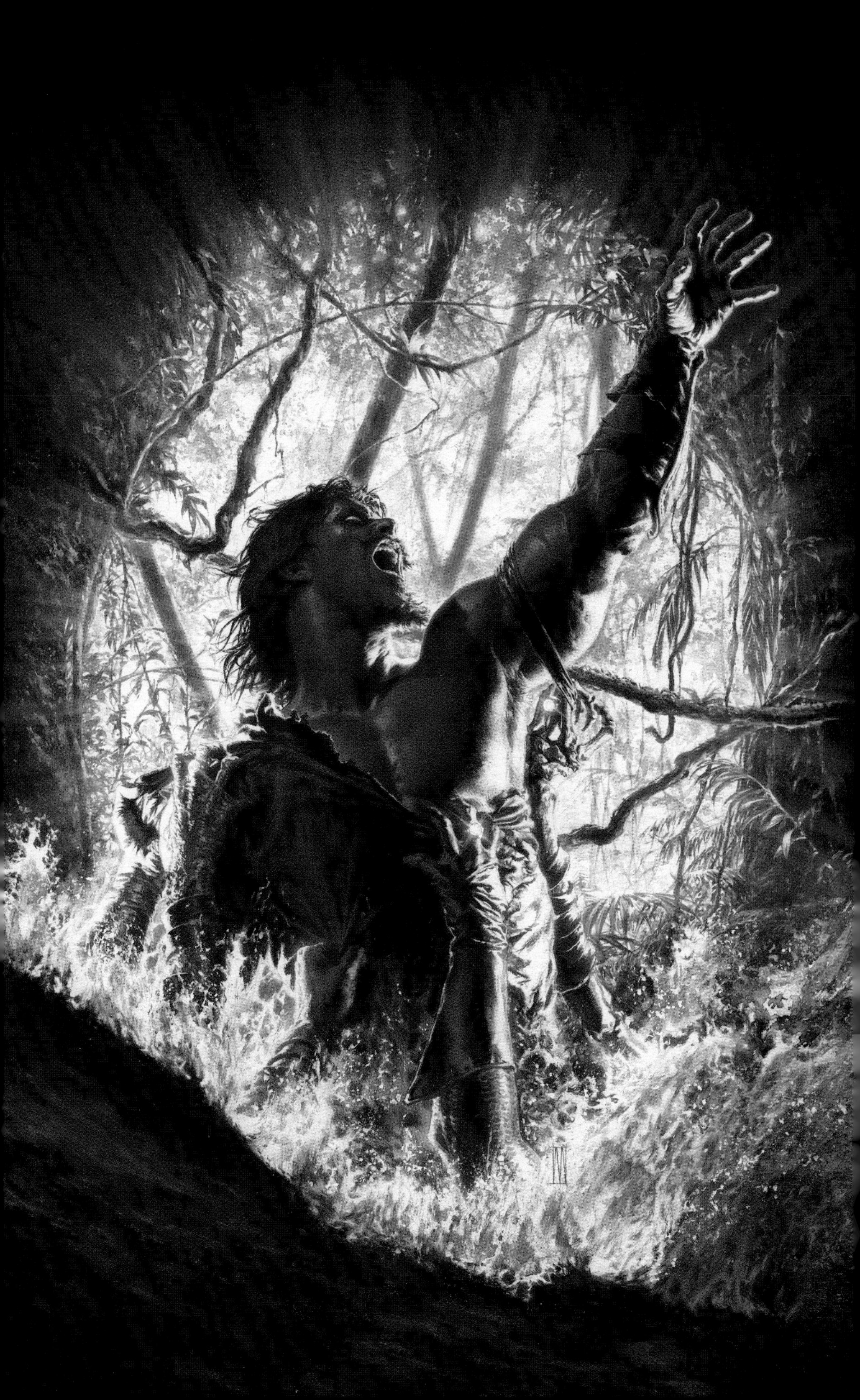

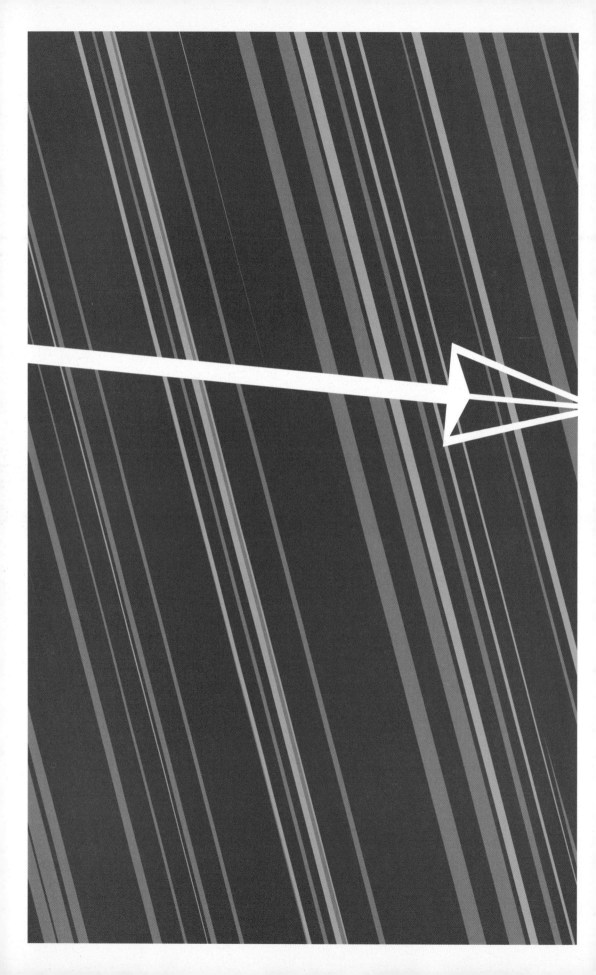

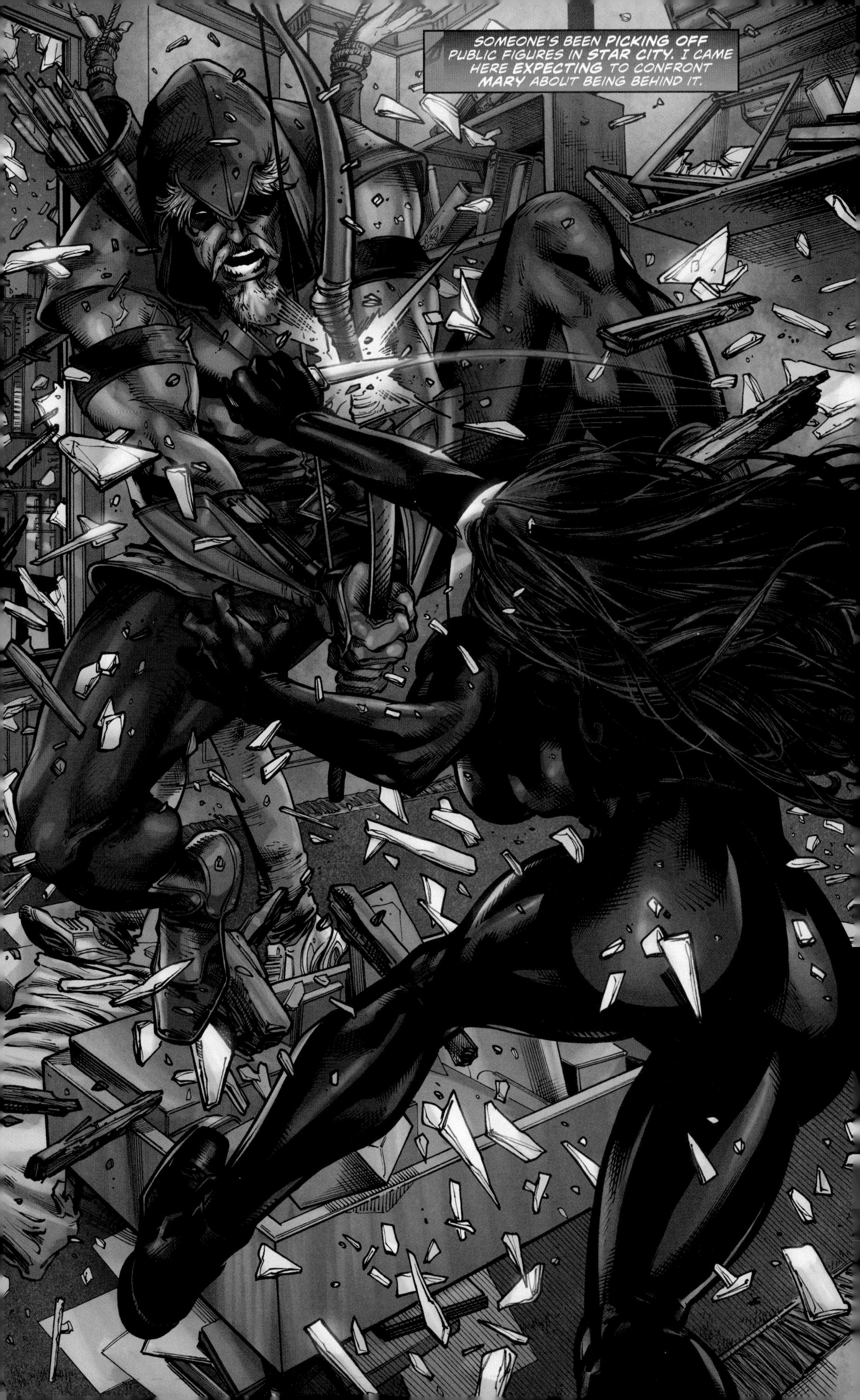
SOMEONE'S BEEN PICKING OFF PUBLIC FIGURES IN STAR CITY. I CAME HERE EXPECTING TO CONFRONT MARY ABOUT BEING BEHIND IT.

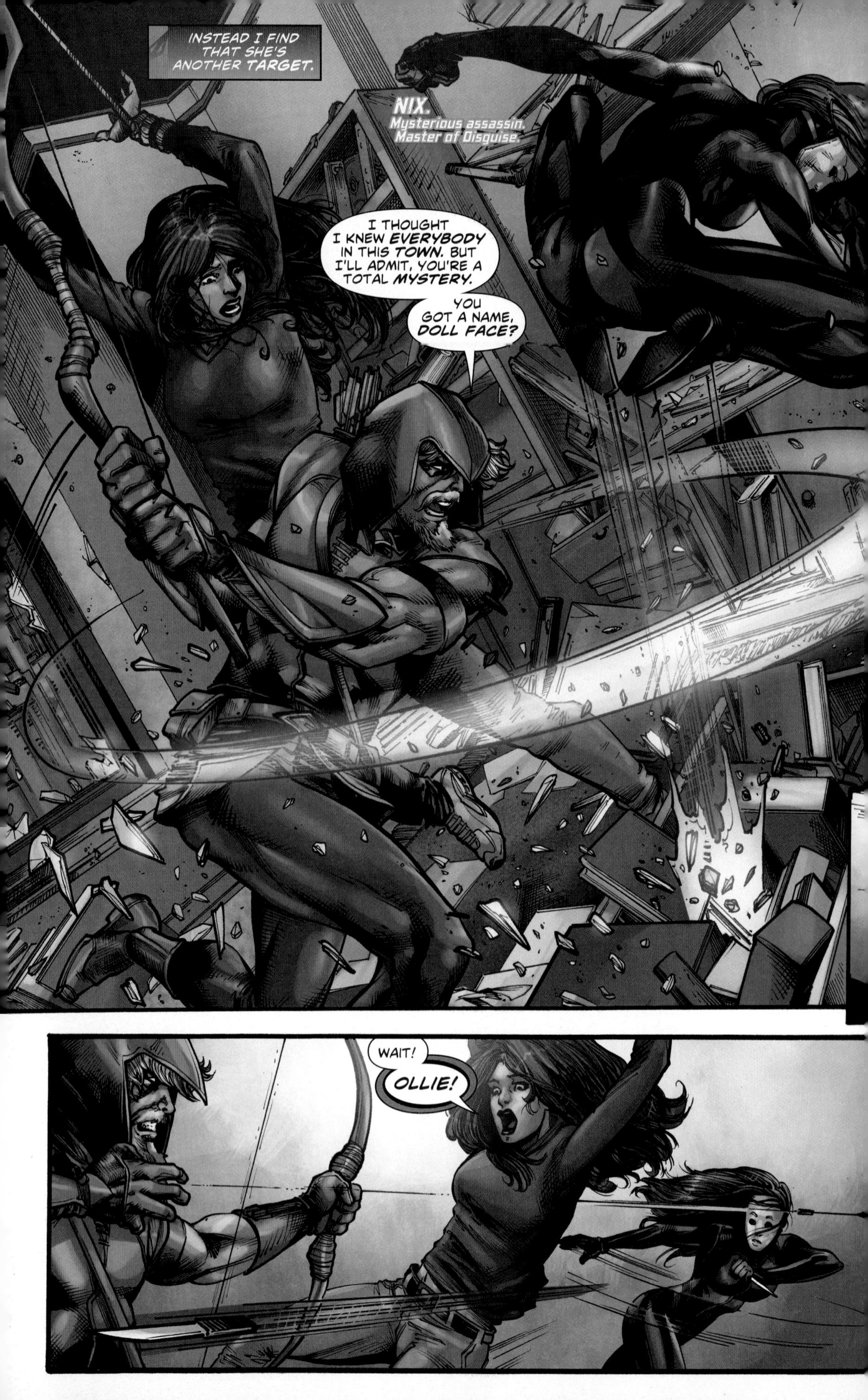
INSTEAD I FIND THAT SHE'S ANOTHER TARGET.
NIX.
Mysterious assassin. Master of Disguise.
I THOUGHT I KNEW EVERYBODY IN THIS TOWN. BUT I'LL ADMIT, YOU'RE A TOTAL MYSTERY.
YOU GOT A NAME, DOLL FACE?
WAIT!
OLLIE!

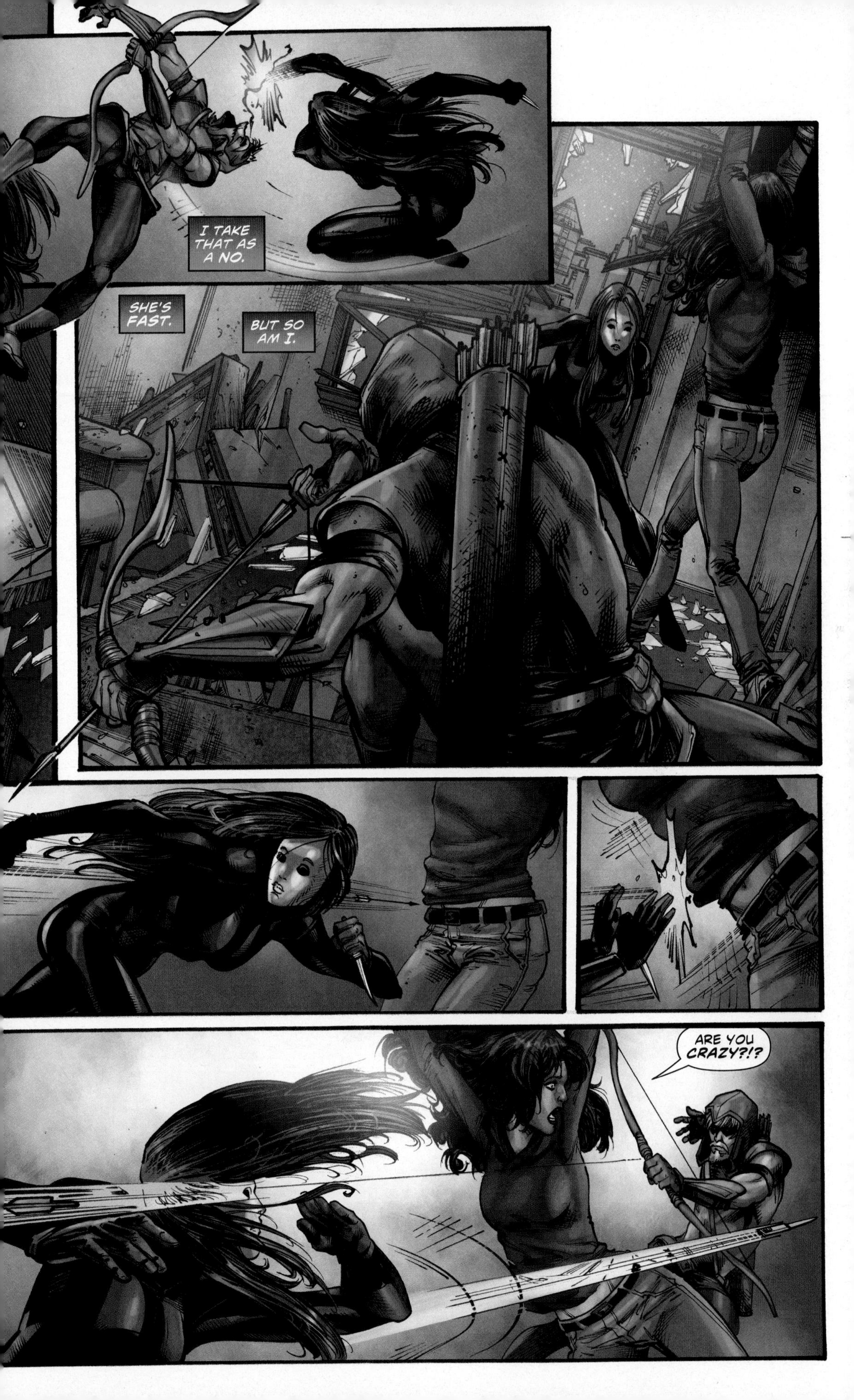
I TAKE THAT AS A NO.
SHE'S FAST.
BUT SO AM I.
ARE YOU CRAZY?!?

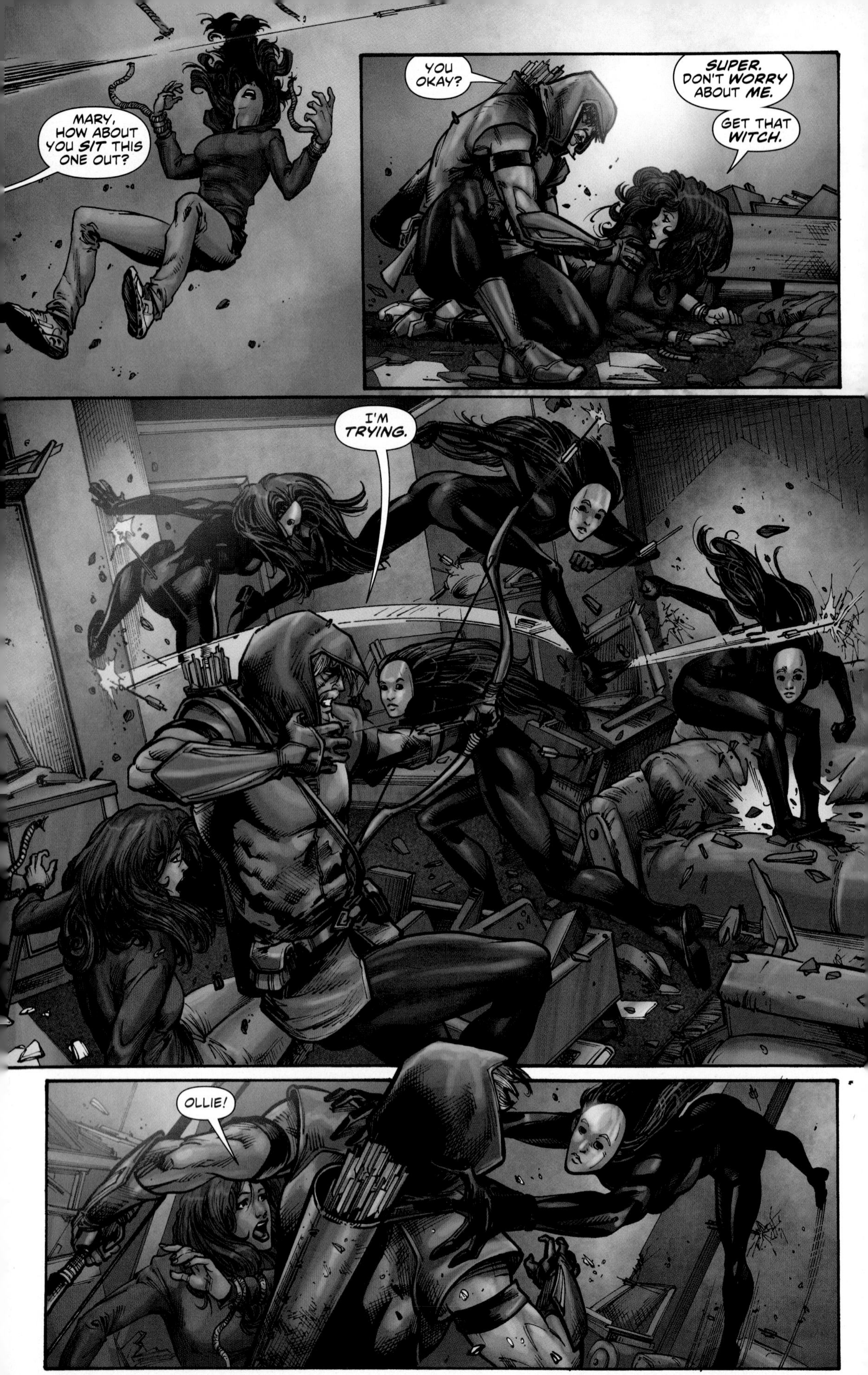
MARY, HOW ABOUT YOU SIT THIS ONE OUT?
YOU OKAY?
SUPER. DON'T WORRY ABOUT ME.
GET THAT WITCH.
I'M TRYING.
OLLIE!

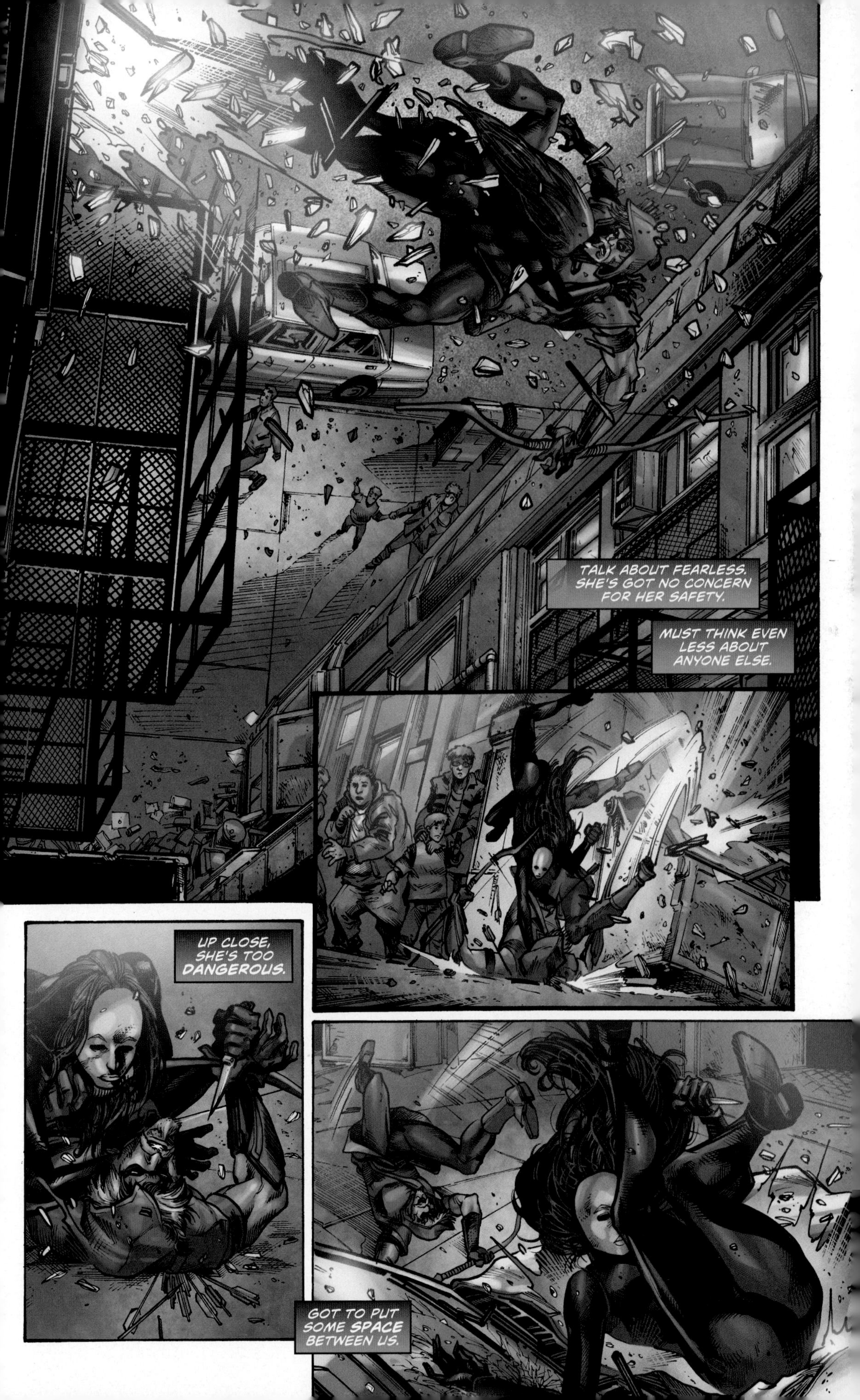
TALK ABOUT FEARLESS. SHE'S GOT NO CONCERN FOR HER SAFETY.
MUST THINK EVEN LESS ABOUT ANYONE ELSE.
UP CLOSE, SHE'S TOO DANGEROUS.
GOT TO PUT SOME SPACE BETWEEN US.

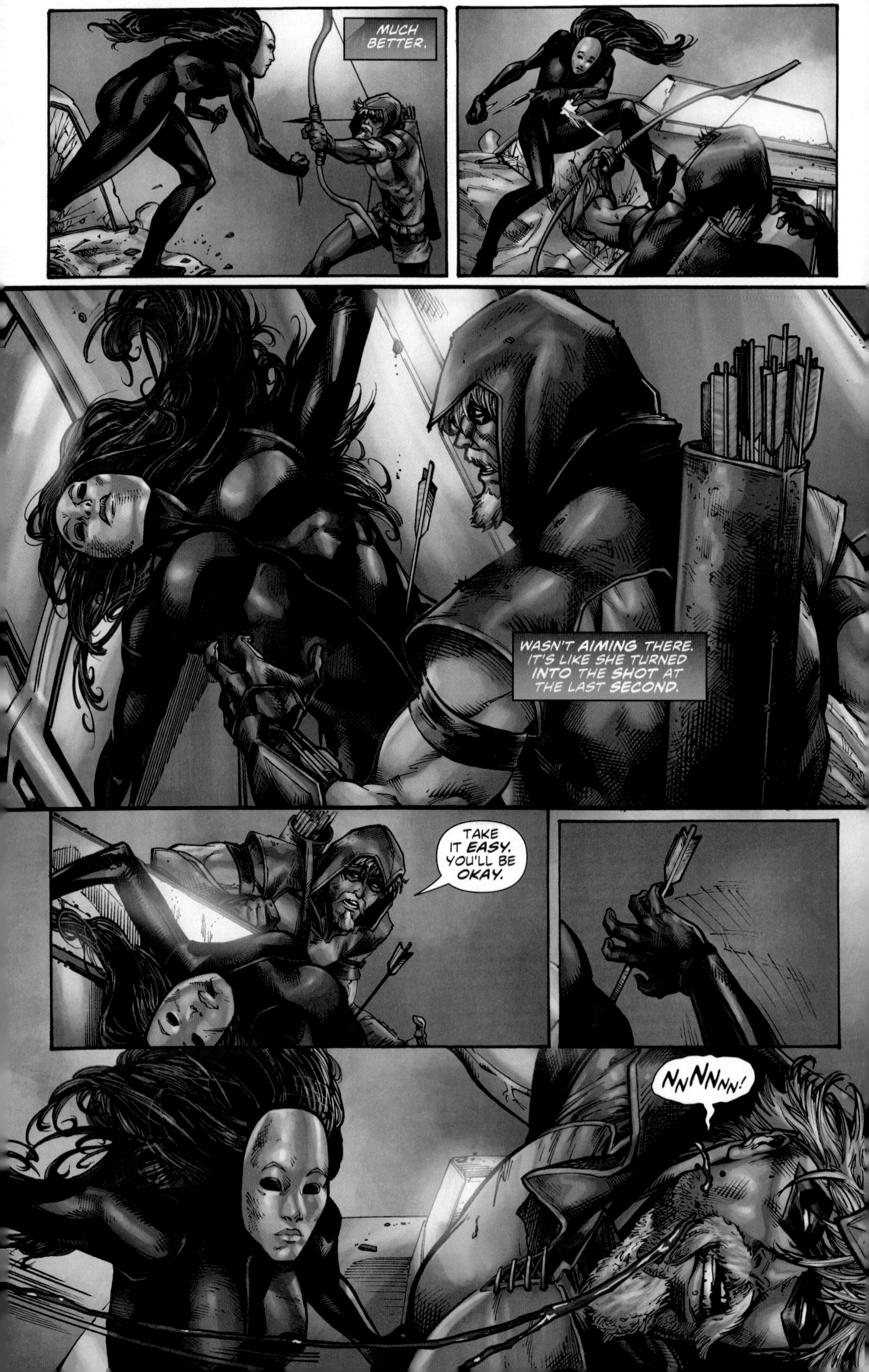
MUCH BETTER.
WASN'T AIMING THERE. IT'S LIKE SHE TURNED INTO THE SHOT AT THE LAST SECOND.
TAKE IT EASY. YOU'LL BE OKAY.
NNNNNN!

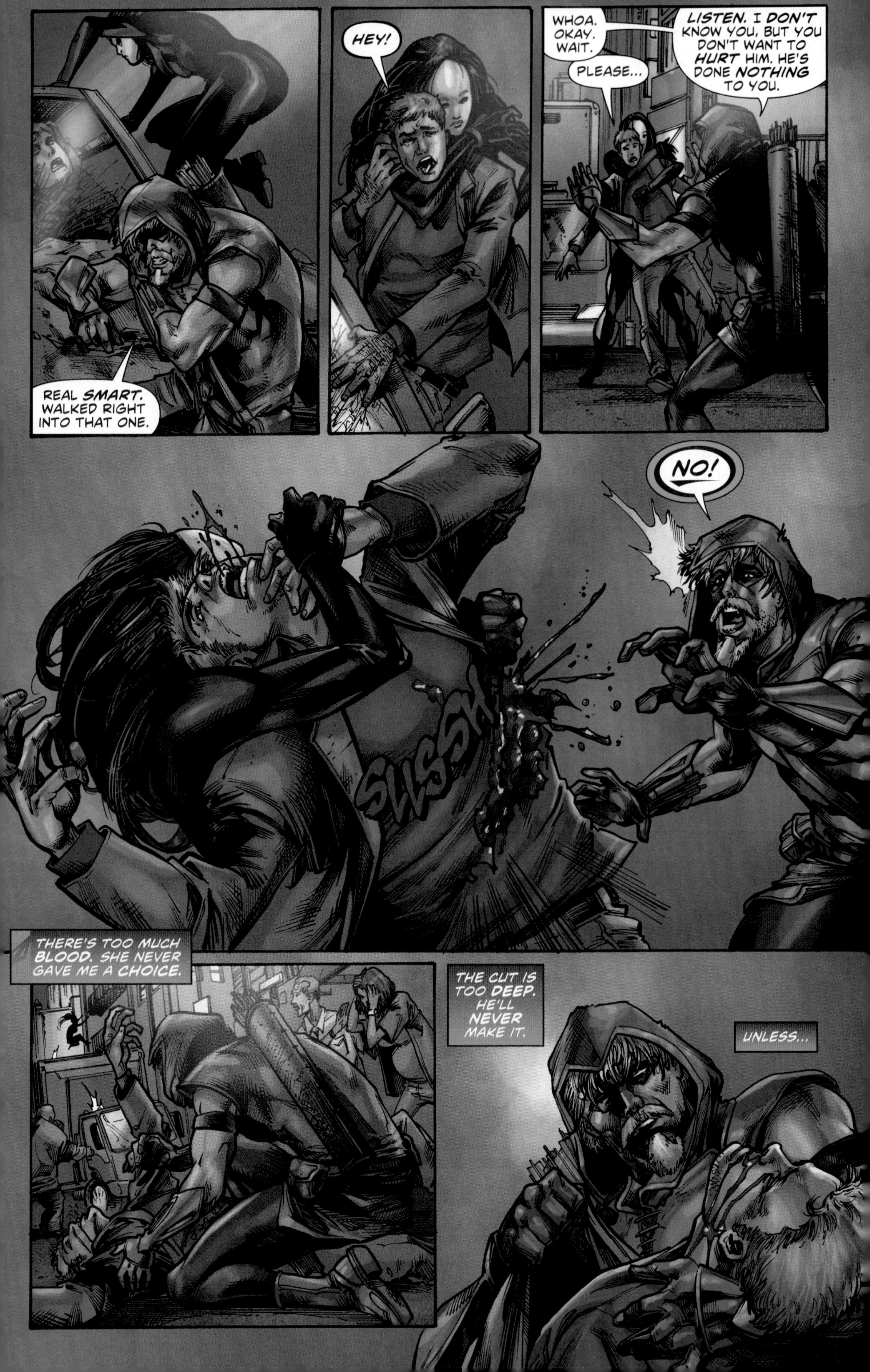
REAL SMART. WALKED RIGHT INTO THAT ONE.
HEY!
WHOA. OKAY. WAIT.
PLEASE...
LISTEN. I DON'T KNOW YOU, BUT YOU DON'T WANT TO HURT HIM. HE'S DONE NOTHING TO YOU.
NO!
SLISSH
THERE'S TOO MUCH BLOOD. SHE NEVER GAVE ME A CHOICE.
THE CUT IS TOO DEEP. HE'LL NEVER MAKE IT.
UNLESS...

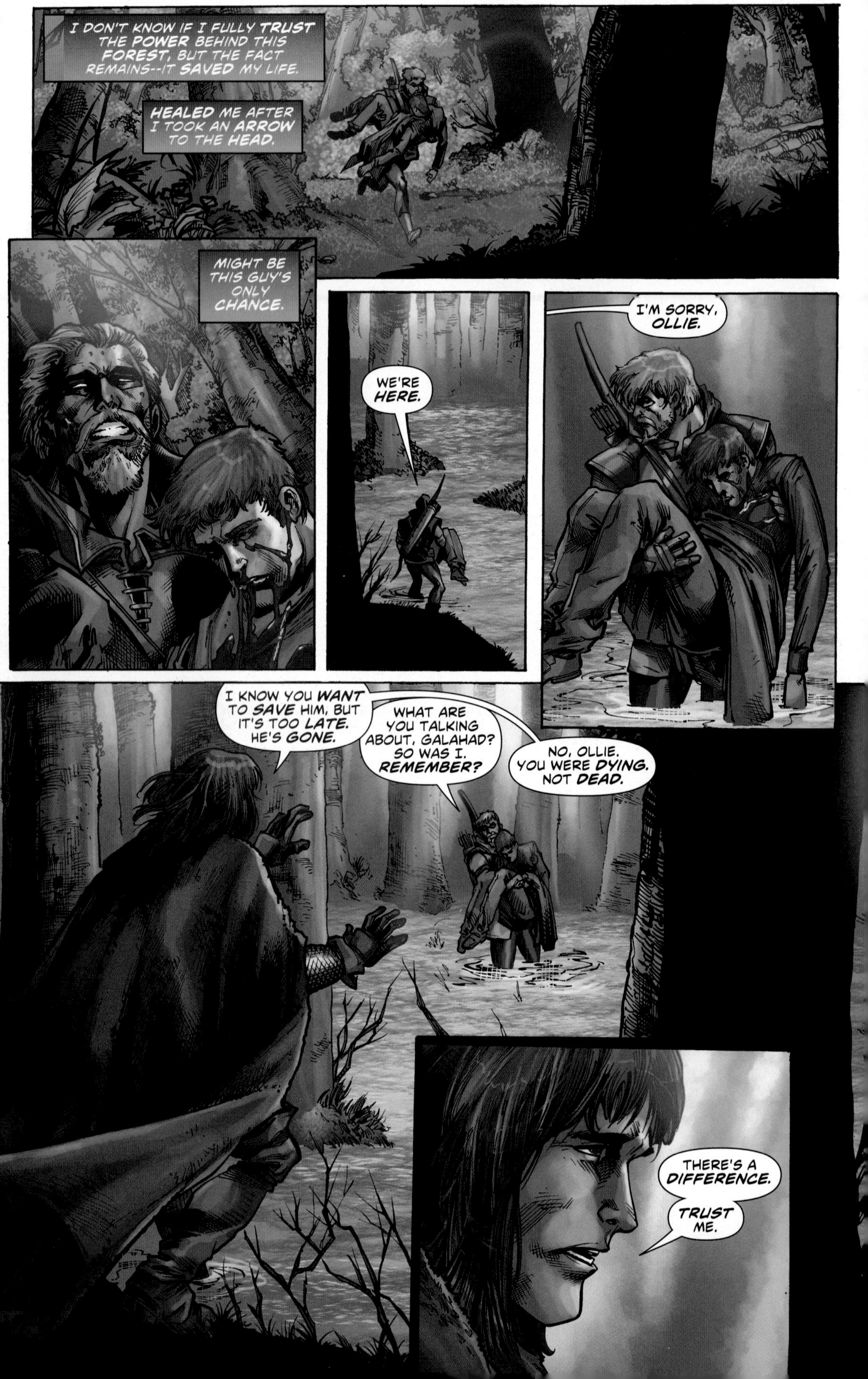
I DON'T KNOW IF I FULLY TRUST THE POWER BEHIND THIS FOREST, BUT THE FACT REMAINS--IT SAVED MY LIFE.
HEALED ME AFTER I TOOK AN ARROW TO THE HEAD.
MIGHT BE THIS GUY'S ONLY CHANCE.
WE'RE HERE.
I'M SORRY, OLLIE.
I KNOW YOU WANT TO SAVE HIM, BUT IT'S TOO LATE. HE'S GONE.
WHAT ARE YOU TALKING ABOUT, GALAHAD? SO WAS I. REMEMBER?
NO, OLLIE. YOU WERE DYING. NOT DEAD.
THERE'S A DIFFERENCE.
TRUST ME.

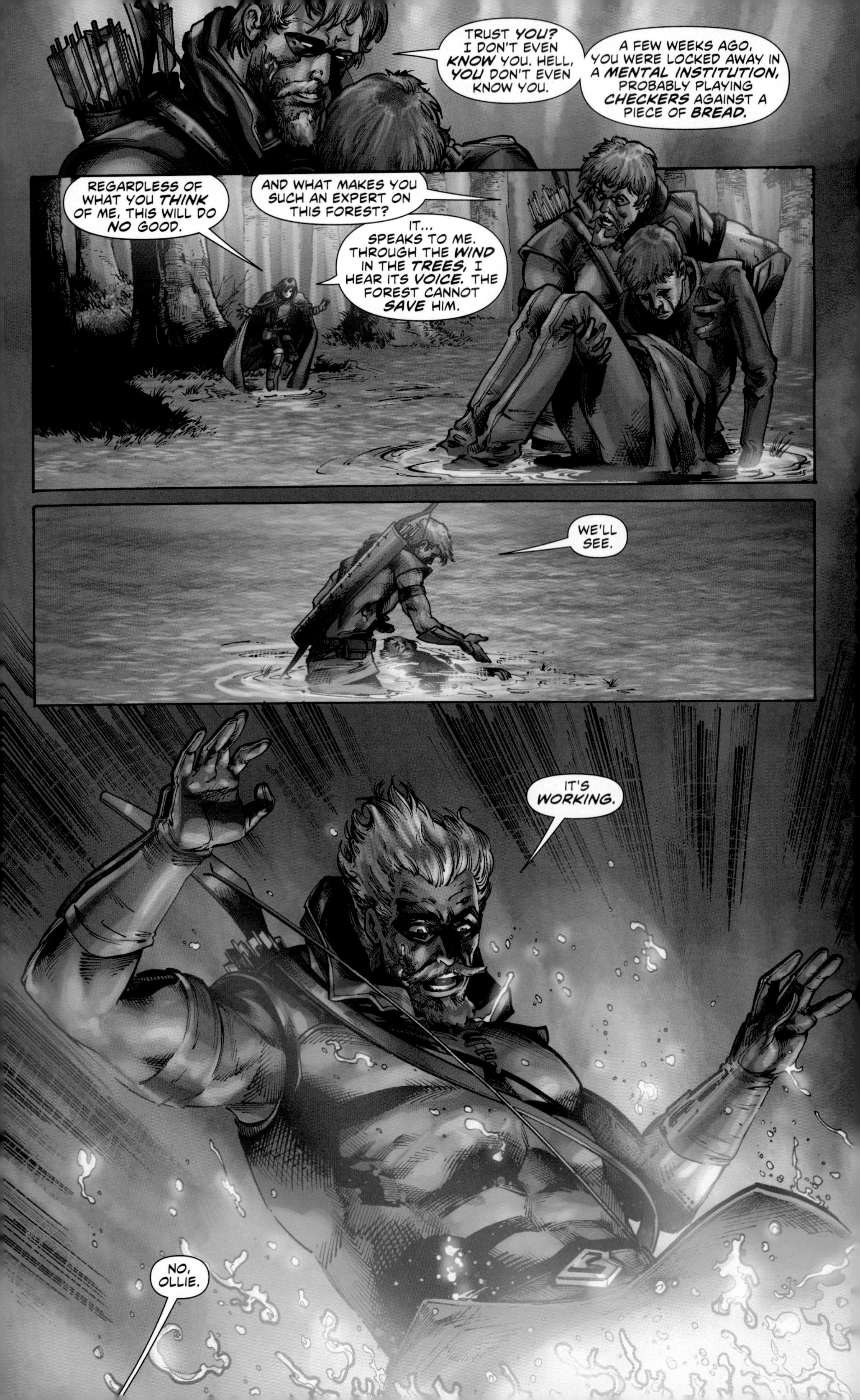

TRUST YOU? I DON'T EVEN KNOW YOU. HELL, YOU DON'T EVEN KNOW YOU.
A FEW WEEKS AGO, YOU WERE LOCKED AWAY IN A MENTAL INSTITUTION, PROBABLY PLAYING CHECKERS AGAINST A PIECE OF BREAD.
REGARDLESS OF WHAT YOU THINK OF ME, THIS WILL DO NO GOOD.
AND WHAT MAKES YOU SUCH AN EXPERT ON THIS FOREST?
IT... SPEAKS TO ME. THROUGH THE WIND IN THE TREES, I HEAR ITS VOICE. THE FOREST CANNOT SAVE HIM.
WE'LL SEE.
IT'S WORKING.
NO, OLLIE.

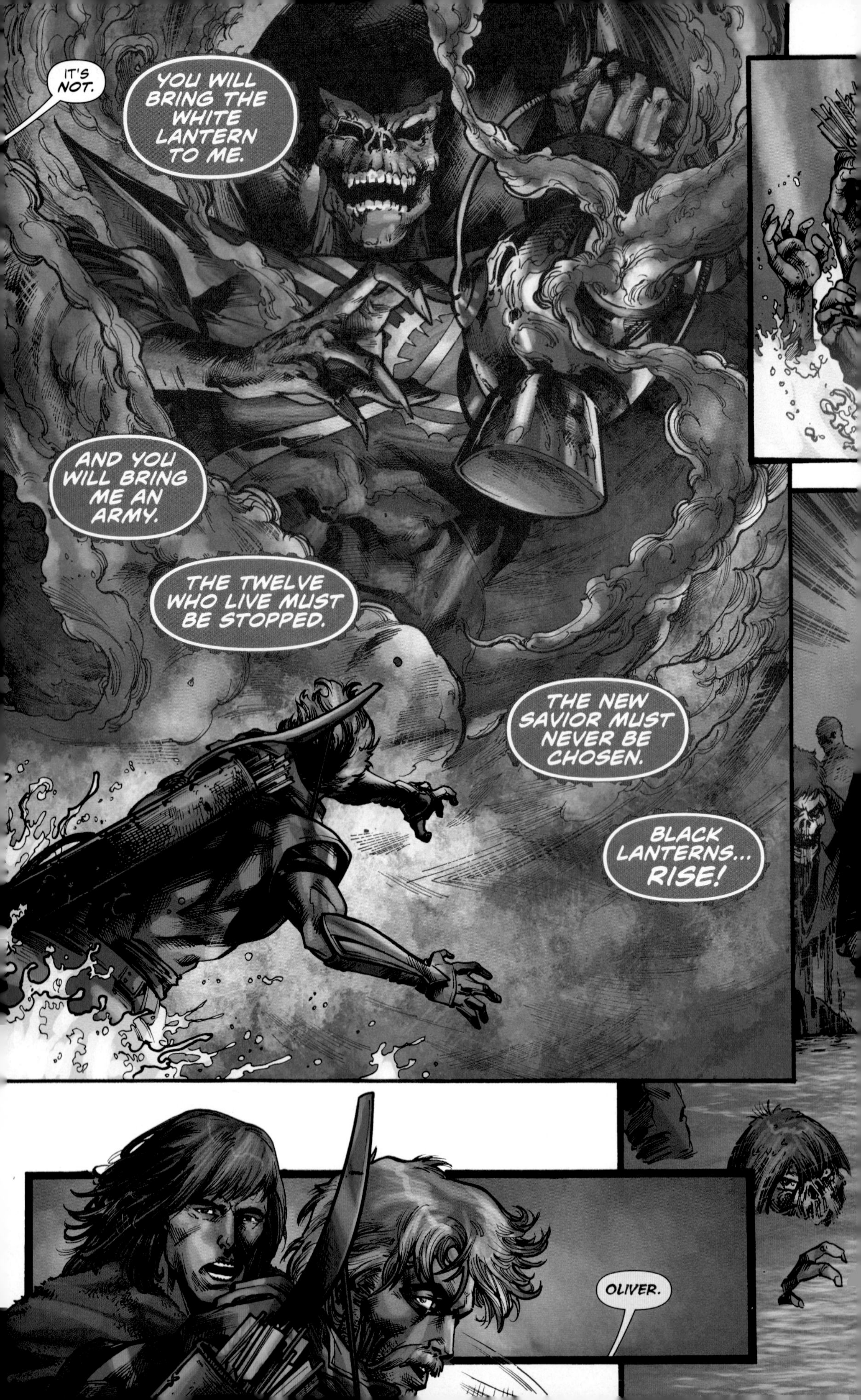
IT'S NOT.
YOU WILL BRING THE WHITE LANTERN TO ME.
AND YOU WILL BRING ME AN ARMY.
THE TWELVE WHO LIVE MUST BE STOPPED.
THE NEW SAVIOR MUST NEVER BE CHOSEN.
BLACK LANTERNS... RISE!
OLIVER.

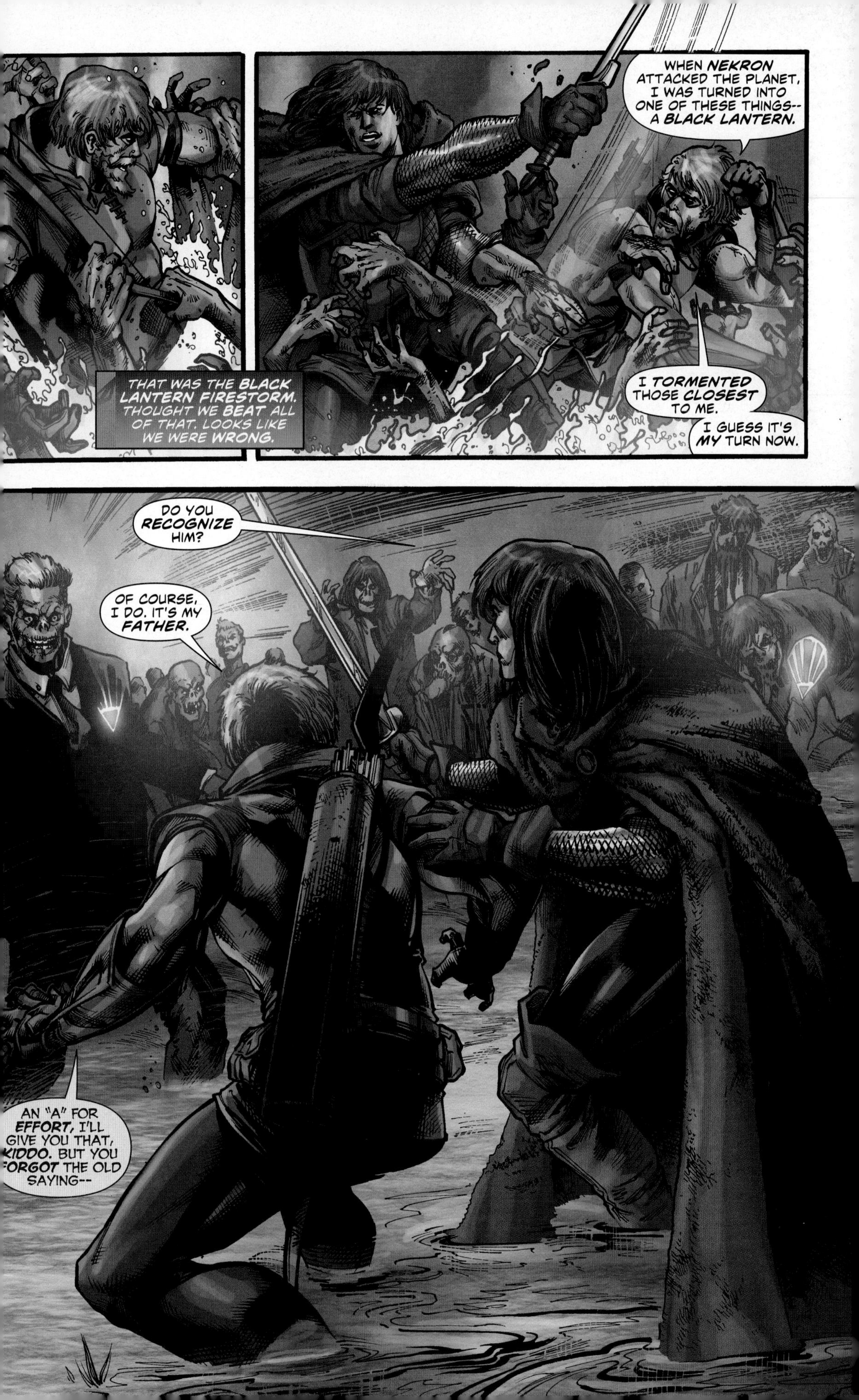
THAT WAS THE BLACK LANTERN FIRESTORM. THOUGHT WE BEAT ALL OF THAT. LOOKS LIKE WE WERE WRONG.
WHEN NEKRON ATTACKED THE PLANET, I WAS TURNED INTO ONE OF THESE THINGS-- A BLACK LANTERN.
I TORMENTED THOSE CLOSEST TO ME.
I GUESS IT'S MY TURN NOW.
DO YOU RECOGNIZE HIM?
OF COURSE, I DO. IT'S MY FATHER.
AN "A" FOR EFFORT, I'LL GIVE YOU THAT, KIDDO. BUT YOU FORGOT THE OLD SAYING--

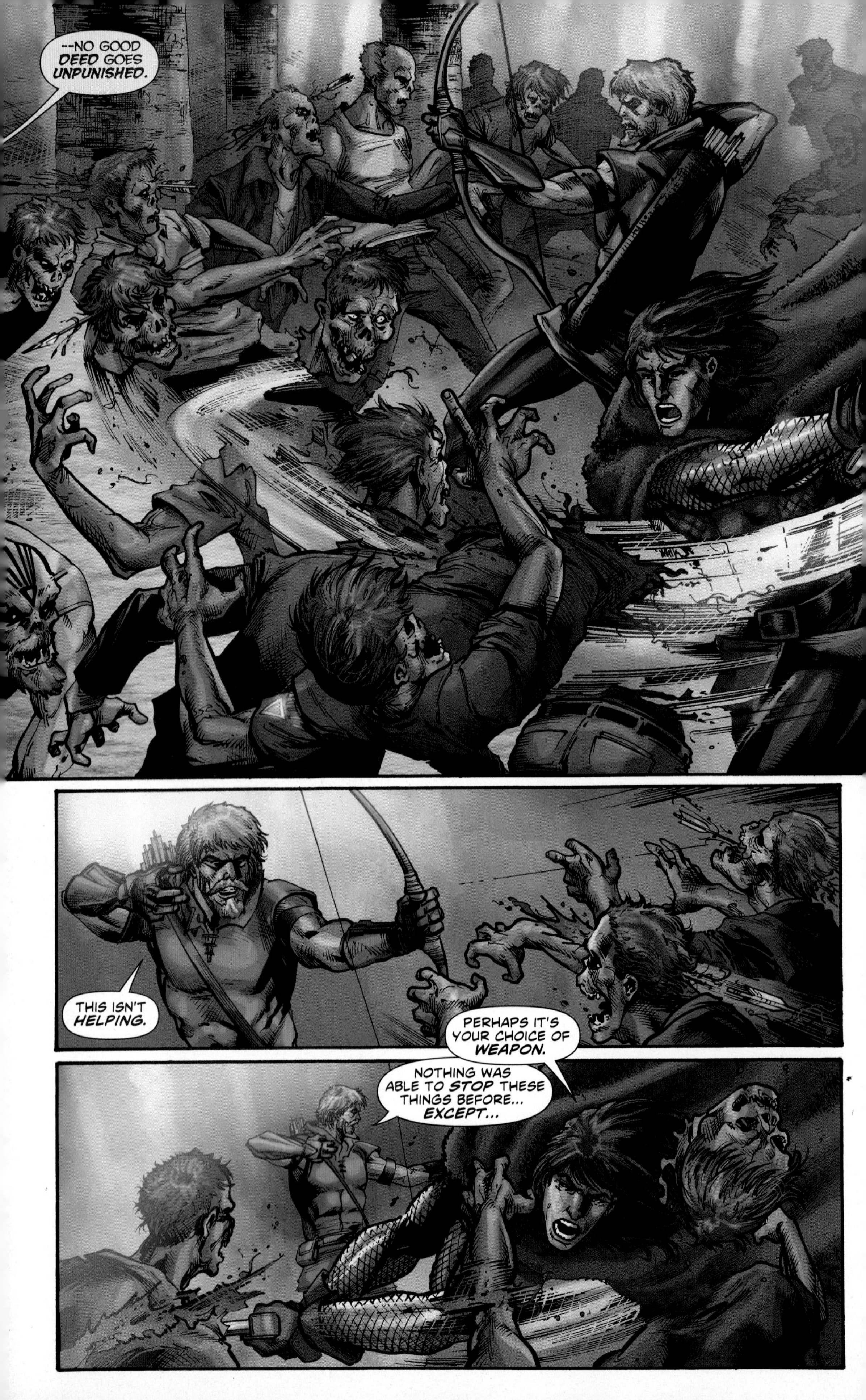
--NO GOOD DEED GOES UNPUNISHED.
THIS ISN'T HELPING.
PERHAPS IT'S YOUR CHOICE OF WEAPON.
NOTHING WAS ABLE TO STOP THESE THINGS BEFORE... EXCEPT...

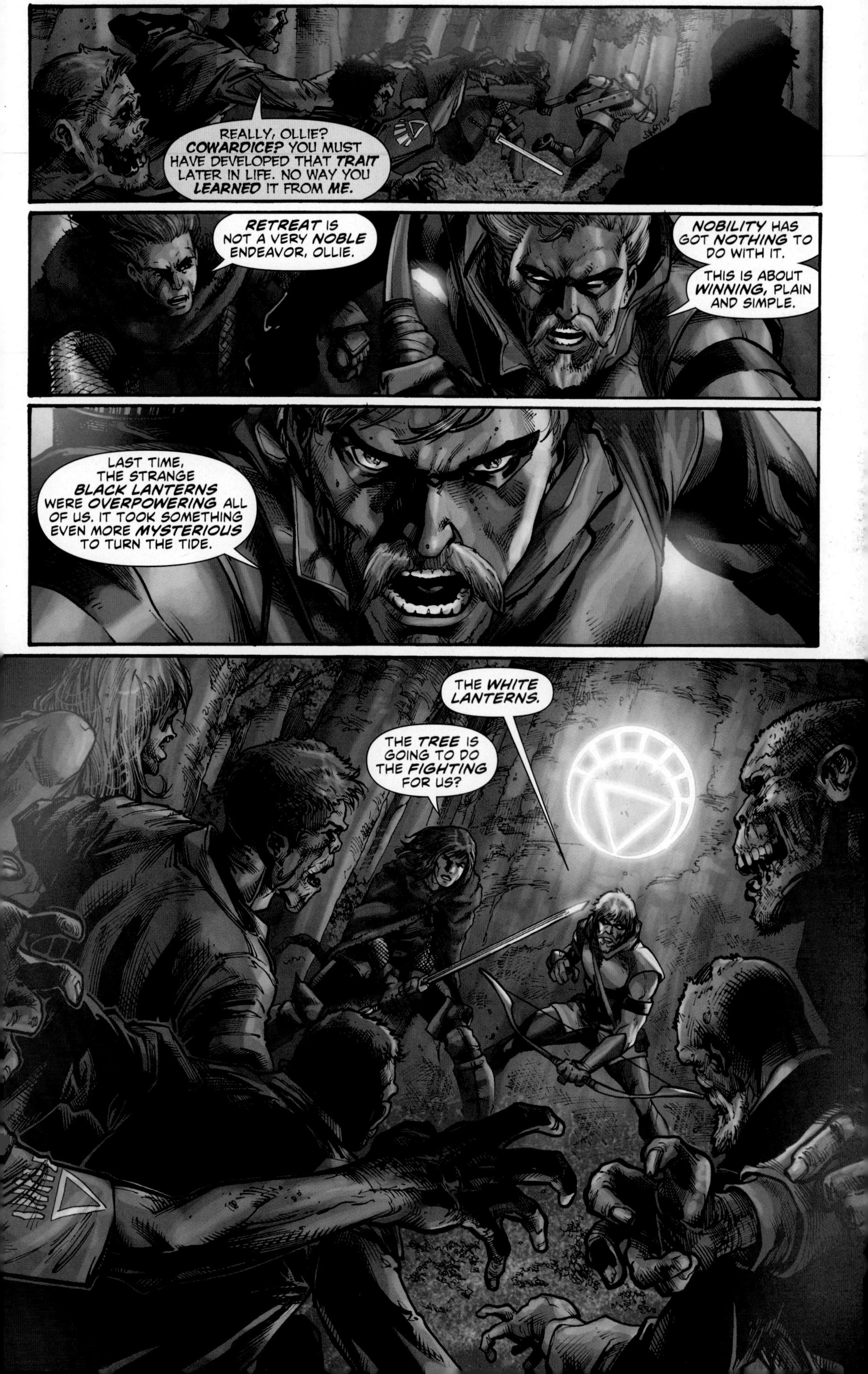
REALLY, OLLIE? COWARDICE? YOU MUST HAVE DEVELOPED THAT TRAIT LATER IN LIFE. NO WAY YOU LEARNED IT FROM ME.
RETREAT IS NOT A VERY NOBLE ENDEAVOR, OLLIE.
NOBILITY HAS GOT NOTHING TO DO WITH IT.
THIS IS ABOUT WINNING, PLAIN AND SIMPLE.
LAST TIME, THE STRANGE BLACK LANTERNS WERE OVERPOWERING ALL OF US. IT TOOK SOMETHING EVEN MORE MYSTERIOUS TO TURN THE TIDE.
THE WHITE LANTERNS.
THE TREE IS GOING TO DO THE FIGHTING FOR US?

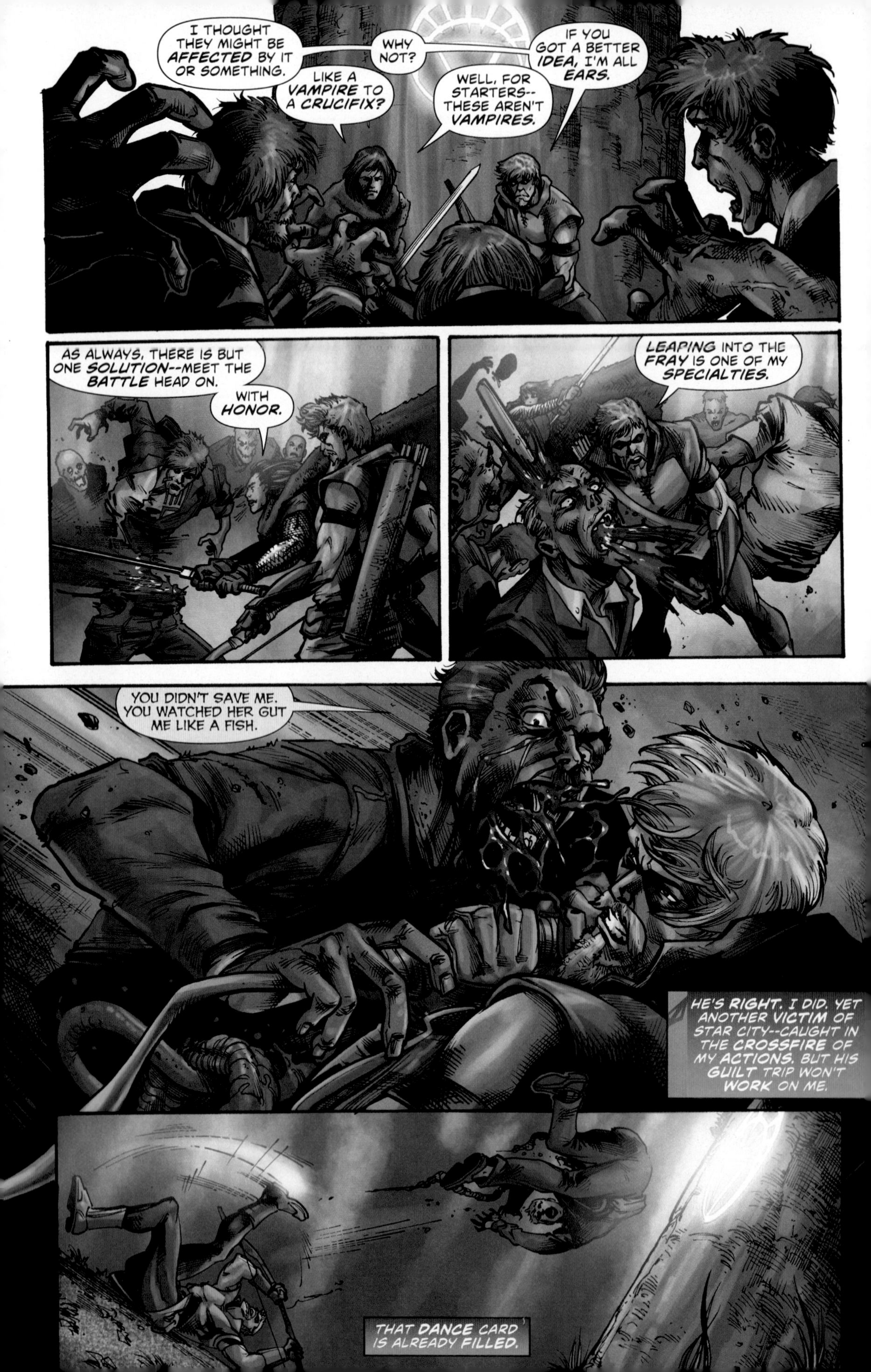

I THOUGHT THEY MIGHT BE AFFECTED BY IT OR SOMETHING.
WHY NOT?
IF YOU GOT A BETTER IDEA, I'M ALL EARS.
LIKE A VAMPIRE TO A CRUCIFIX?
WELL, FOR STARTERS-- THESE AREN'T VAMPIRES.
AS ALWAYS, THERE IS BUT ONE SOLUTION--MEET THE BATTLE HEAD ON.
WITH HONOR.
LEAPING INTO THE FRAY IS ONE OF MY SPECIALTIES.
YOU DIDN'T SAVE ME. YOU WATCHED HER GUT ME LIKE A FISH.
HE'S RIGHT. I DID. YET ANOTHER VICTIM OF STAR CITY--CAUGHT IN THE CROSSFIRE OF MY ACTIONS. BUT HIS GUILT TRIP WON'T WORK ON ME.
THAT DANCE CARD IS ALREADY FILLED.

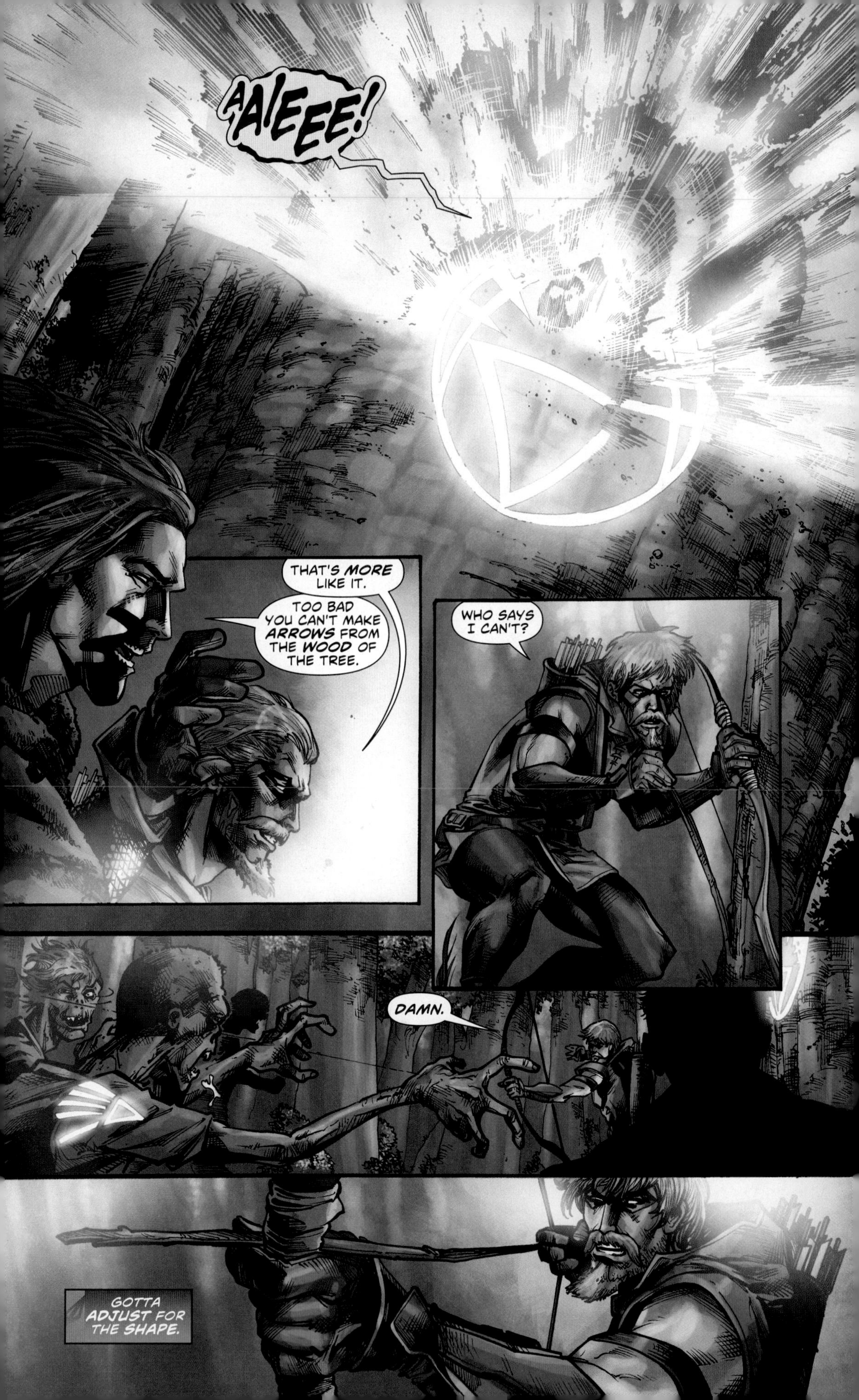
AAIEEE!
THAT'S MORE LIKE IT.
TOO BAD YOU CAN'T MAKE ARROWS FROM THE WOOD OF THE TREE.
WHO SAYS I CAN'T?
DAMN.
GOTTA ADJUST FOR THE SHAPE.

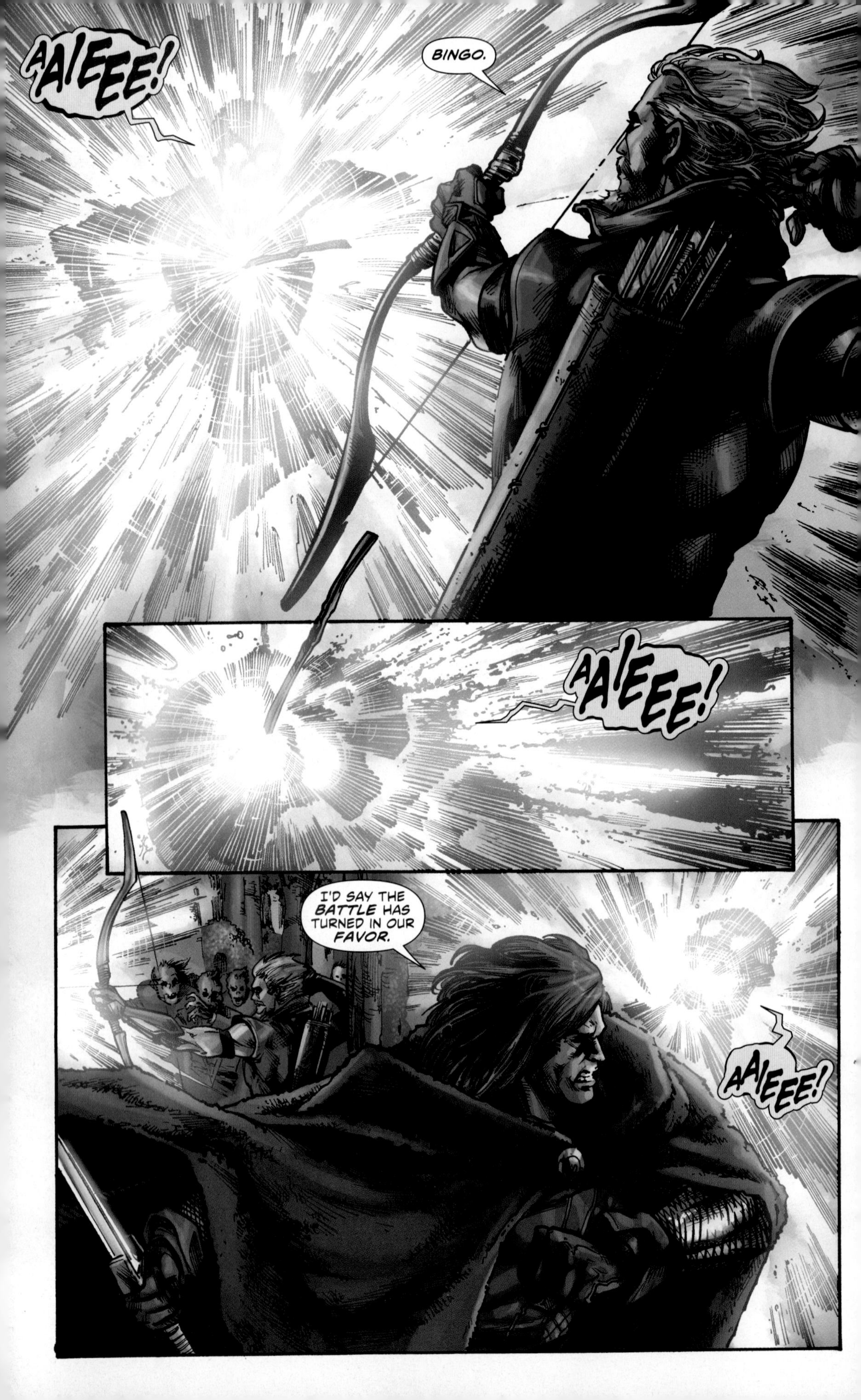
AAIEEE!
BINGO.
AAIEEE!
I'D SAY THE BATTLE HAS TURNED IN OUR FAVOR.
AAIEEE!

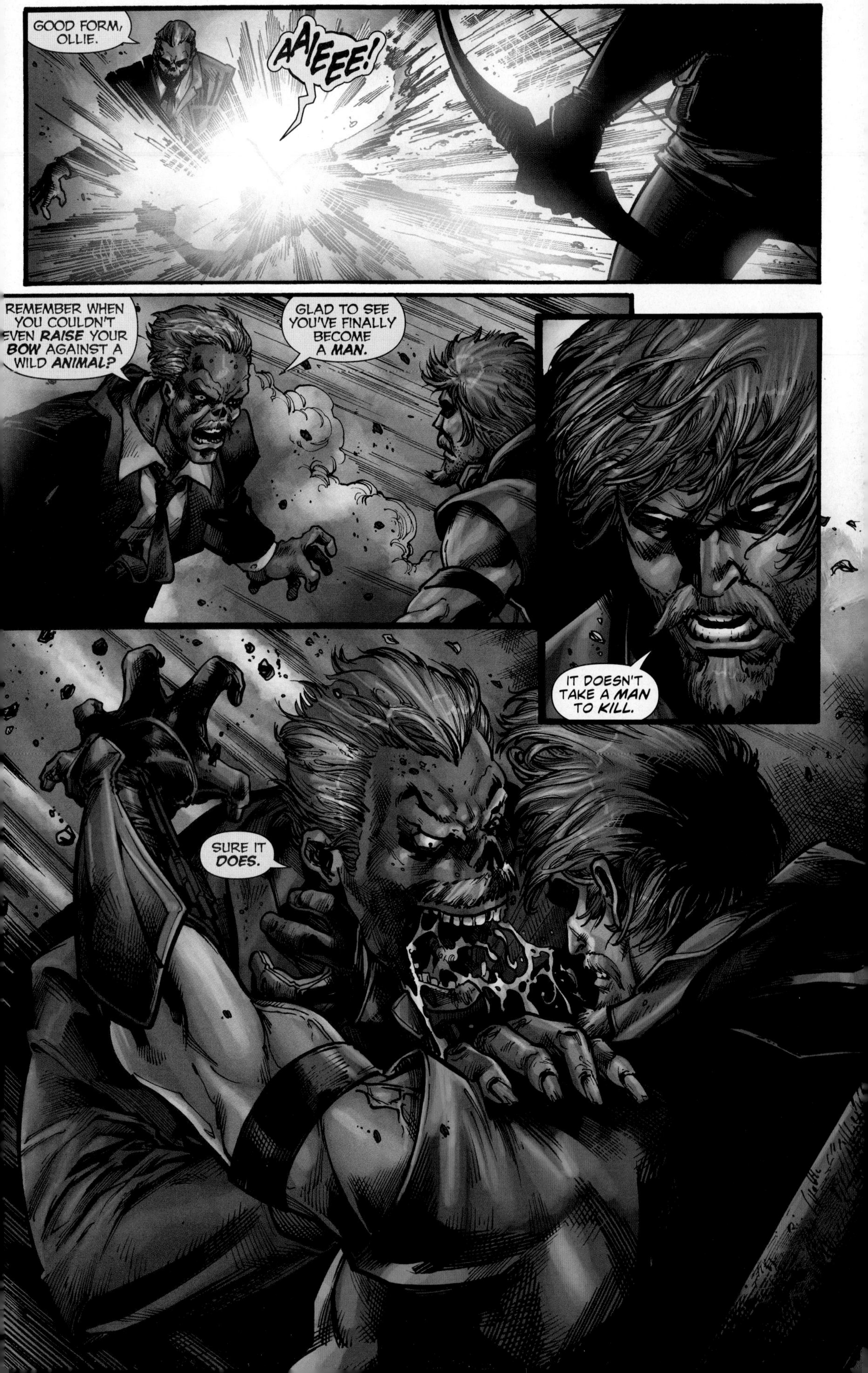

GOOD FORM, OLLIE.
AAIEEE!
REMEMBER WHEN YOU COULDN'T EVEN RAISE YOUR BOW AGAINST A WILD ANIMAL?
GLAD TO SEE YOU'VE FINALLY BECOME A MAN.
IT DOESN'T TAKE A MAN TO KILL.
SURE IT DOES.

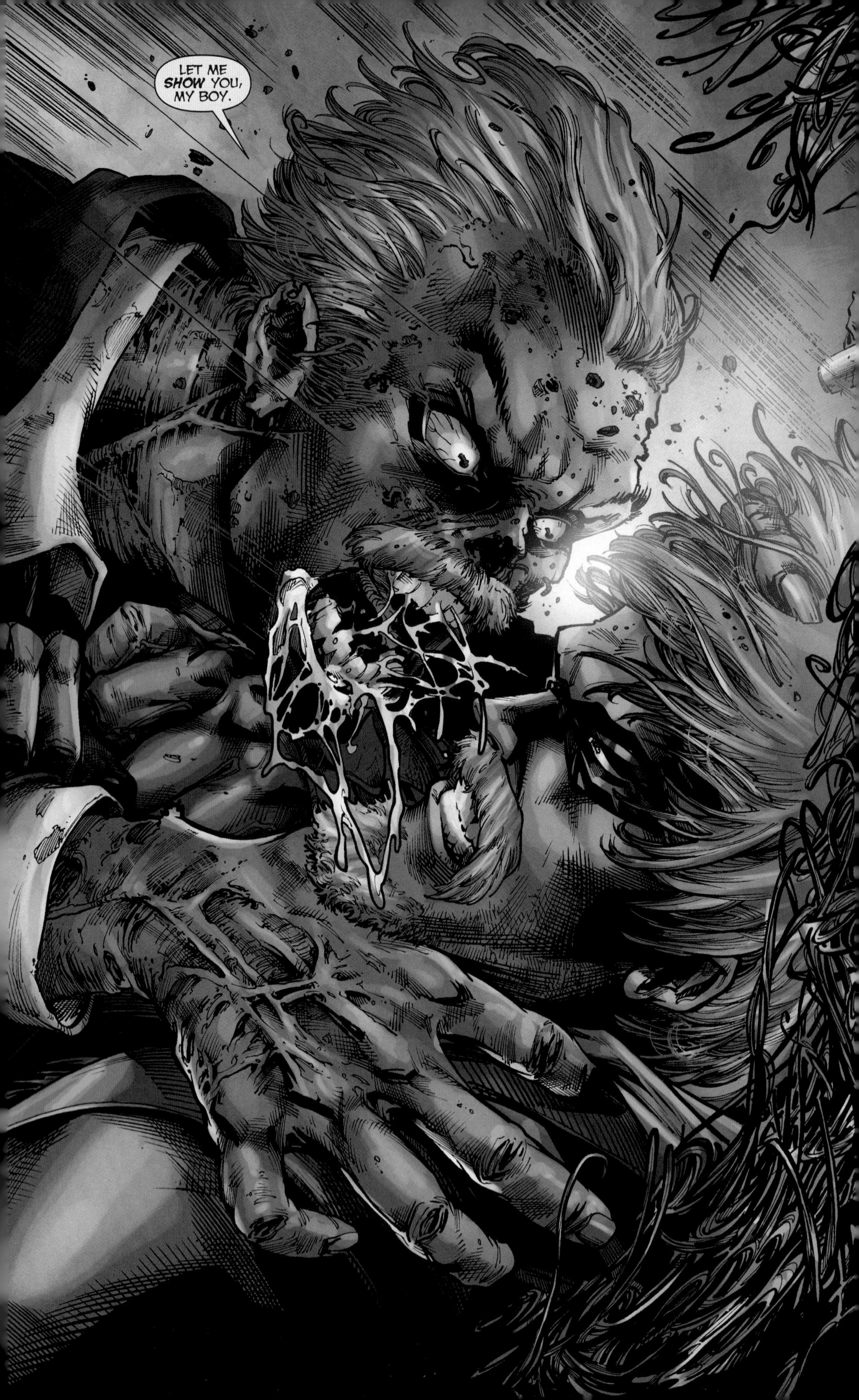
LET ME SHOW YOU, MY BOY.

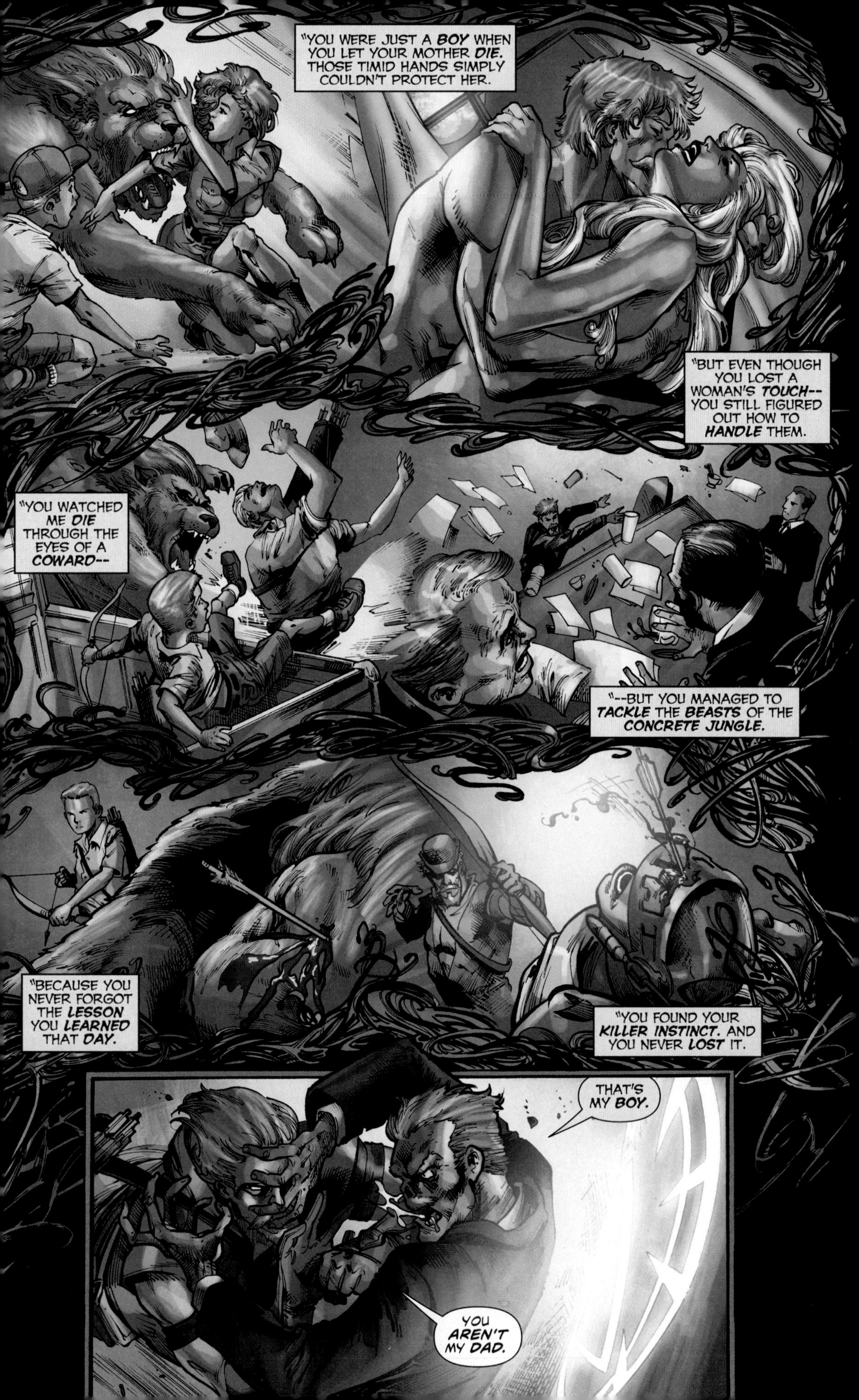
"YOU WERE JUST A BOY WHEN YOU LET YOUR MOTHER DIE. THOSE TIMID HANDS SIMPLY COULDN'T PROTECT HER.
"BUT EVEN THOUGH YOU LOST A WOMAN'S TOUCH-- YOU STILL FIGURED OUT HOW TO HANDLE THEM.
"YOU WATCHED ME DIE THROUGH THE EYES OF A COWARD--
"--BUT YOU MANAGED TO TACKLE THE BEASTS OF THE CONCRETE JUNGLE.
"BECAUSE YOU NEVER FORGOT THE LESSON YOU LEARNED THAT DAY.
"YOU FOUND YOUR KILLER INSTINCT. AND YOU NEVER LOST IT.
THAT'S MY BOY.
YOU AREN'T MY DAD.

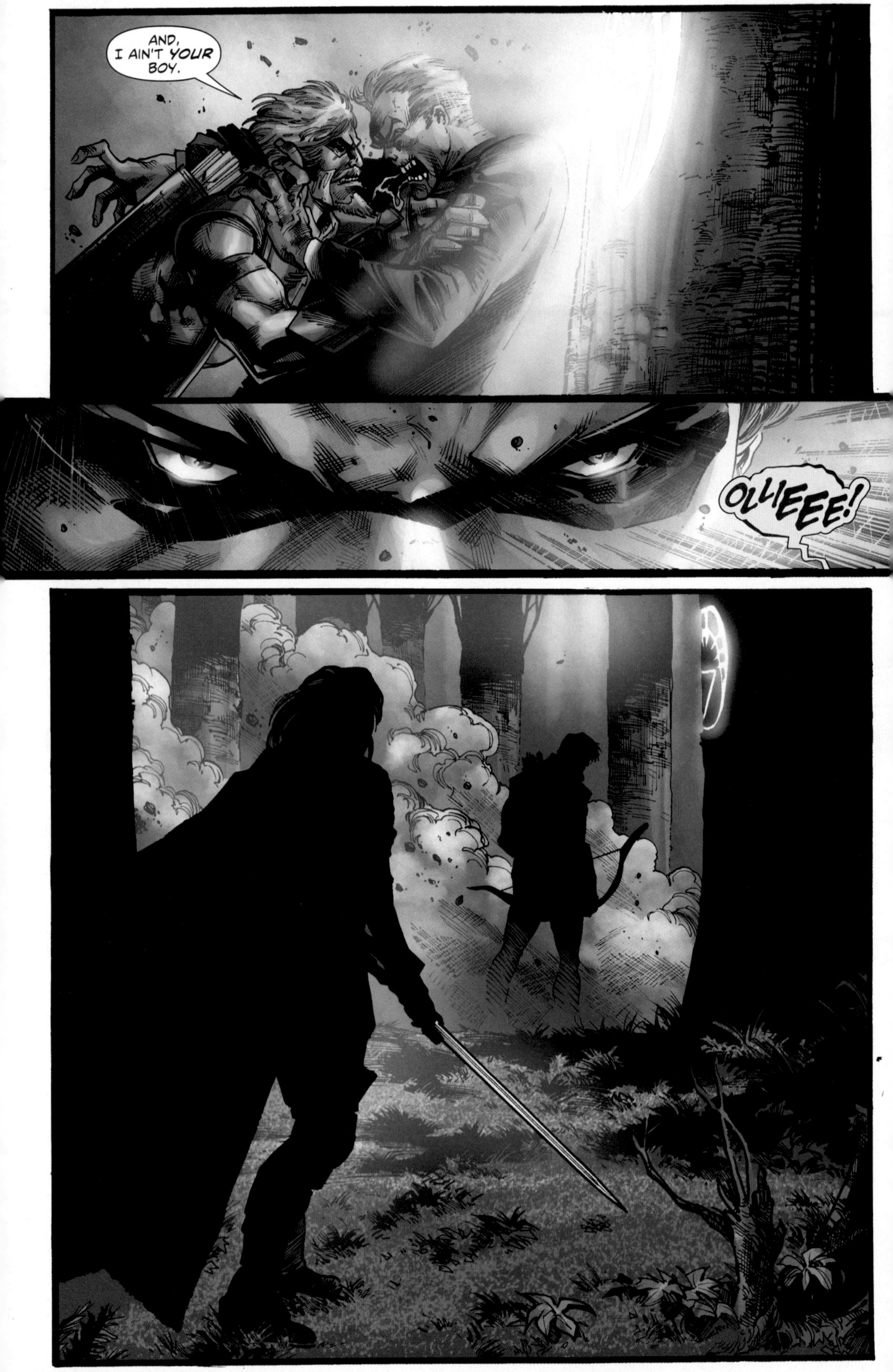
AND, I AIN'T YOUR BOY.
OLLIEEE!

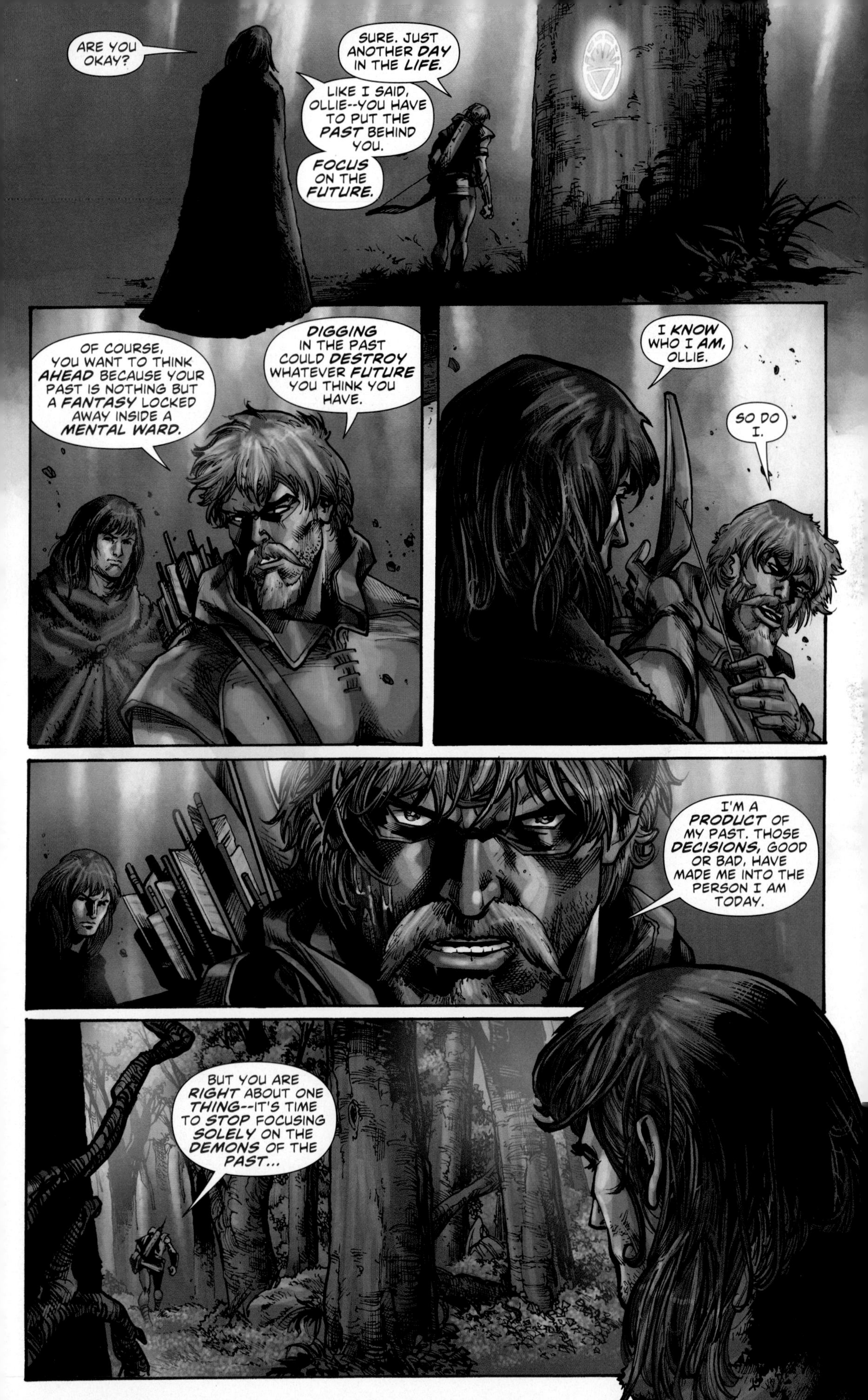
ARE YOU OKAY?
SURE. JUST ANOTHER DAY IN THE LIFE.
LIKE I SAID, OLLIE--YOU HAVE TO PUT THE PAST BEHIND YOU.
FOCUS ON THE FUTURE.
OF COURSE, YOU WANT TO THINK AHEAD BECAUSE YOUR PAST IS NOTHING BUT A FANTASY LOCKED AWAY INSIDE A MENTAL WARD.
DIGGING IN THE PAST COULD DESTROY WHATEVER FUTURE YOU THINK YOU HAVE.
I KNOW WHO I AM, OLLIE.
SO DO I.
I'M A PRODUCT OF MY PAST. THOSE DECISIONS, GOOD OR BAD, HAVE MADE ME INTO THE PERSON I AM TODAY.
BUT YOU ARE RIGHT ABOUT ONE THING--IT'S TIME TO STOP FOCUSING SOLELY ON THE DEMONS OF THE PAST...

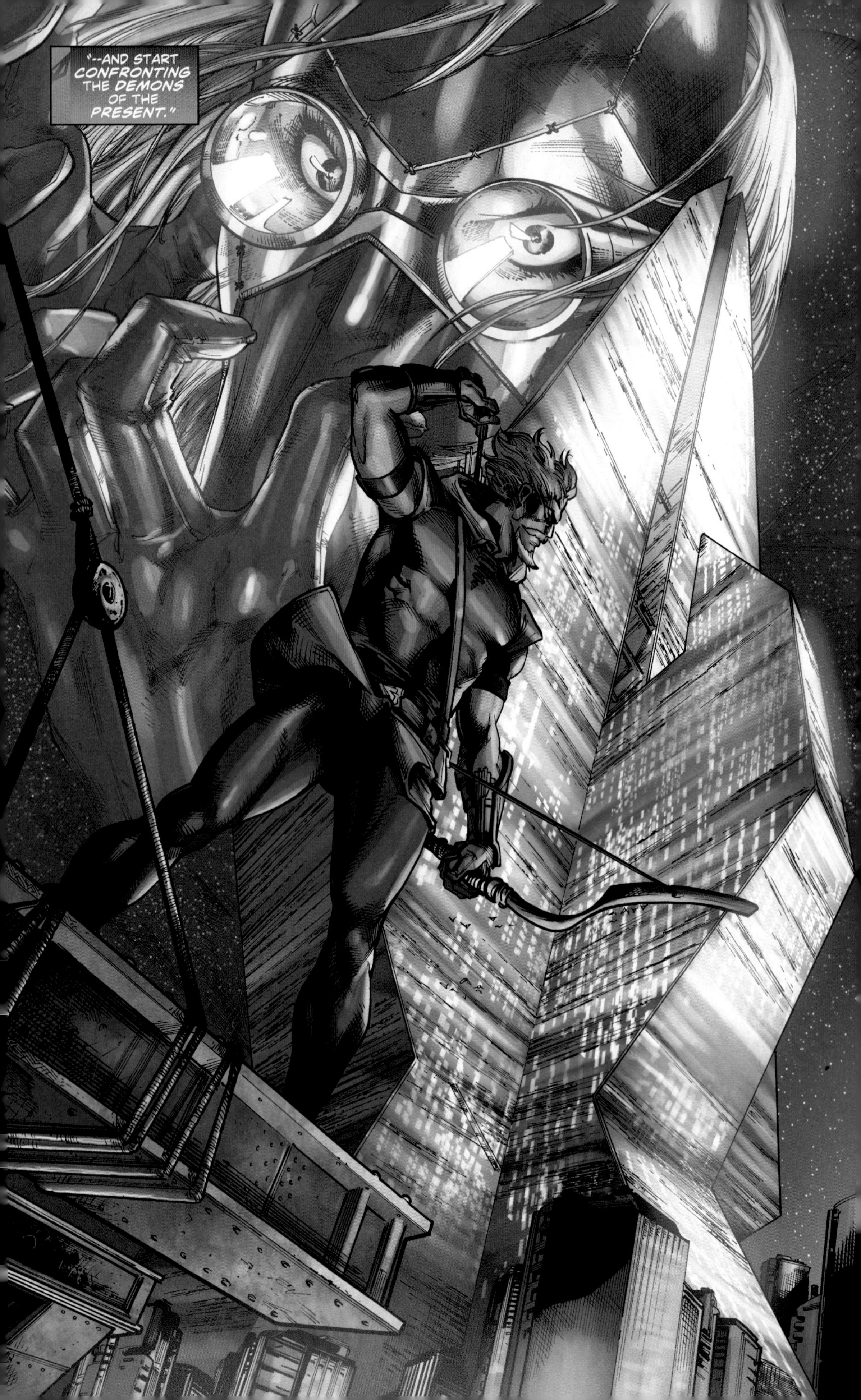
"--AND START CONFRONTING THE DEMONS OF THE PRESENT."

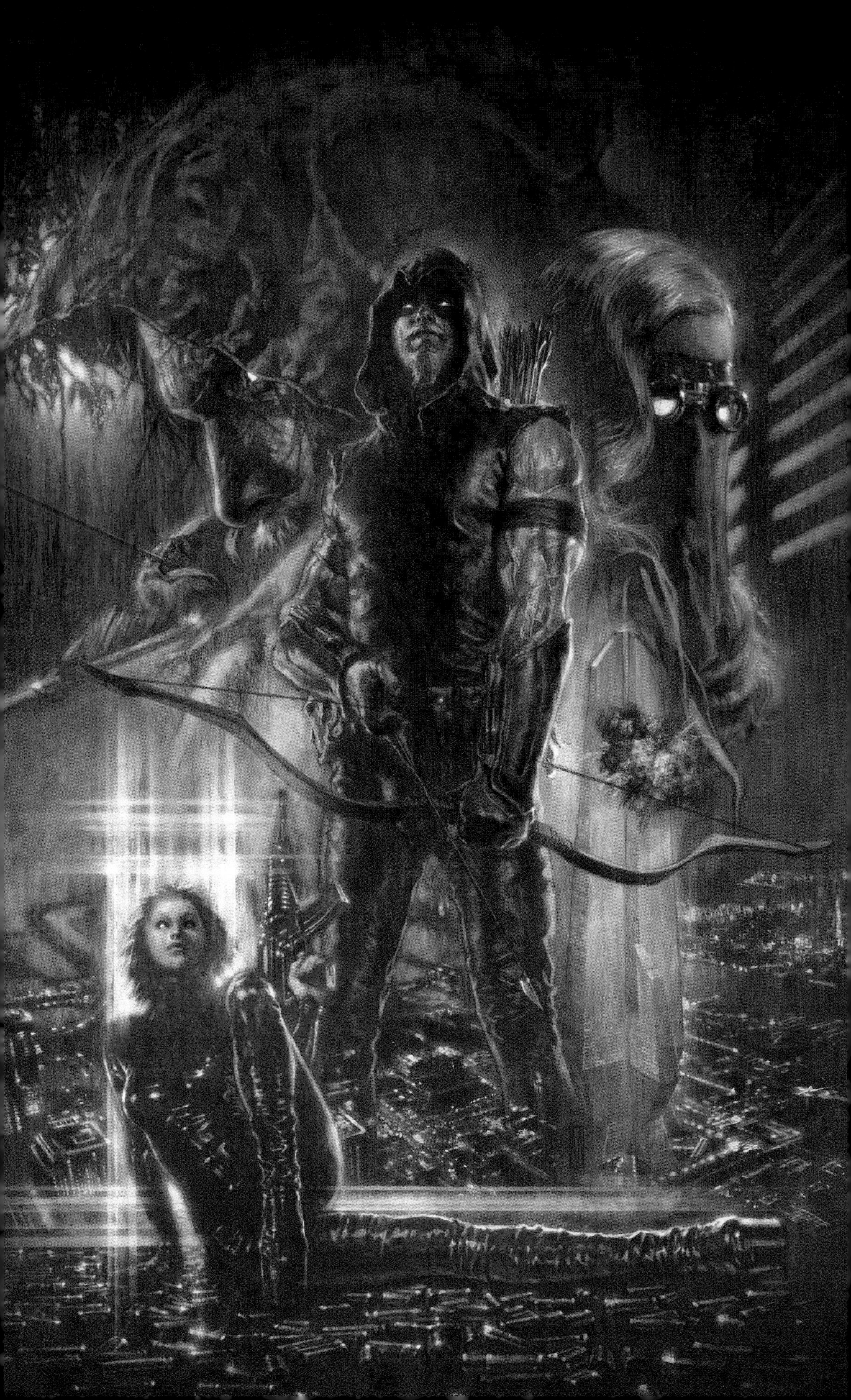

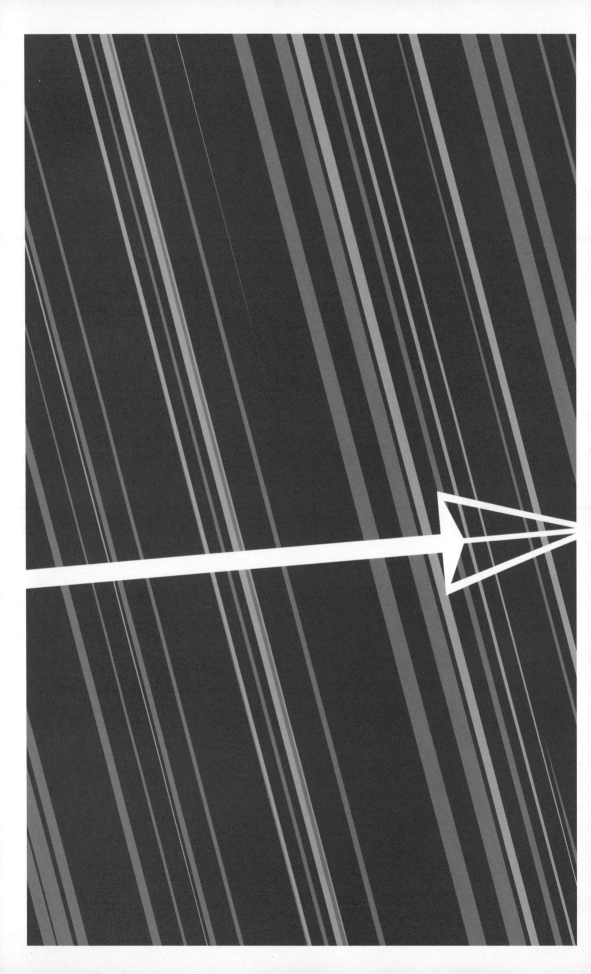

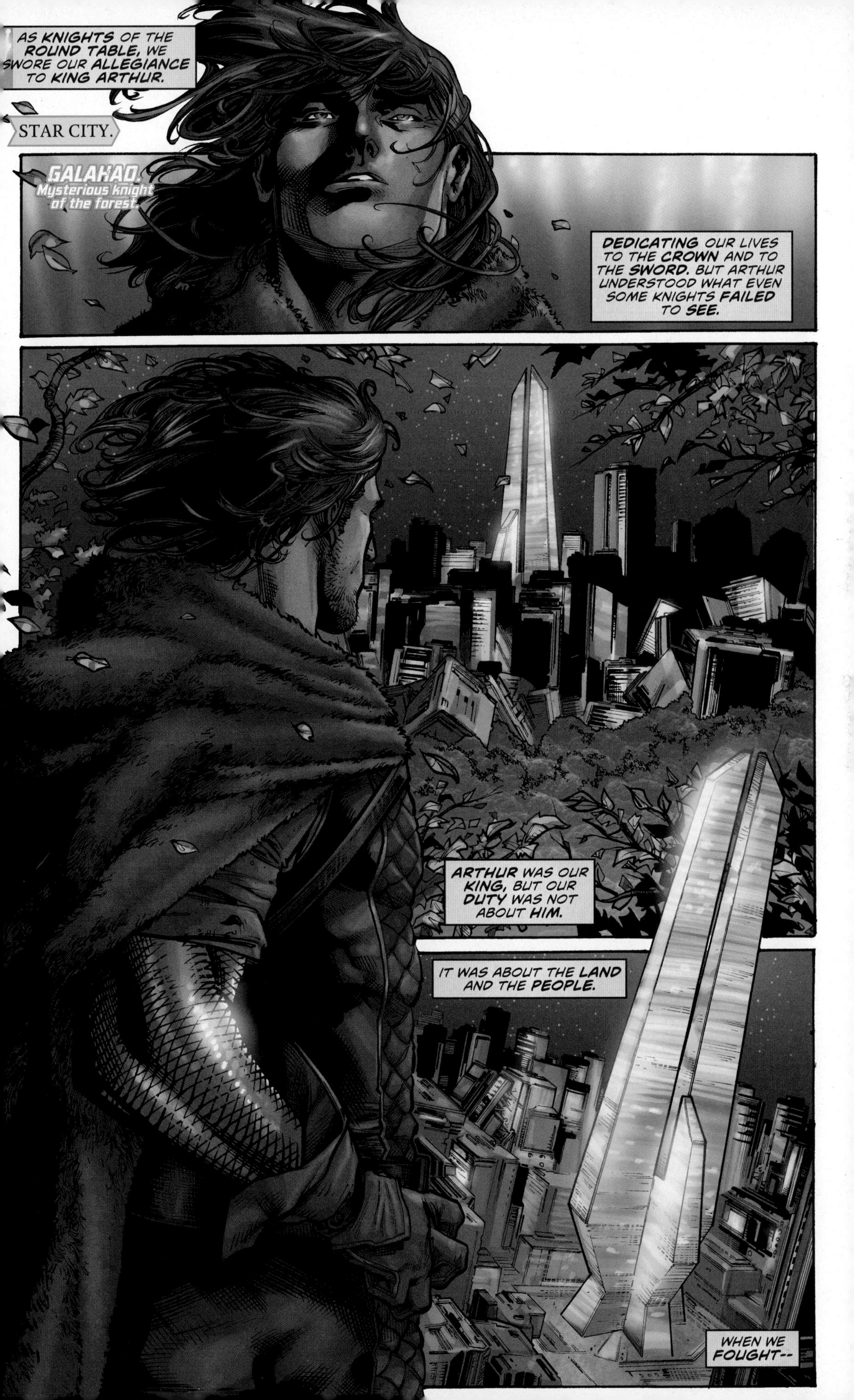
AS KNIGHTS OF THE ROUND TABLE, WE SWORE OUR ALLEGIANCE TO KING ARTHUR.
STAR CITY.
GALAHAD. Mysterious knight of the forest.
DEDICATING OUR LIVES TO THE CROWN AND TO THE SWORD. BUT ARTHUR UNDERSTOOD WHAT EVEN SOME KNIGHTS FAILED TO SEE.
ARTHUR WAS OUR KING, BUT OUR DUTY WAS NOT ABOUT HIM.
IT WAS ABOUT THE LAND AND THE PEOPLE.
WHEN WE FOUGHT--

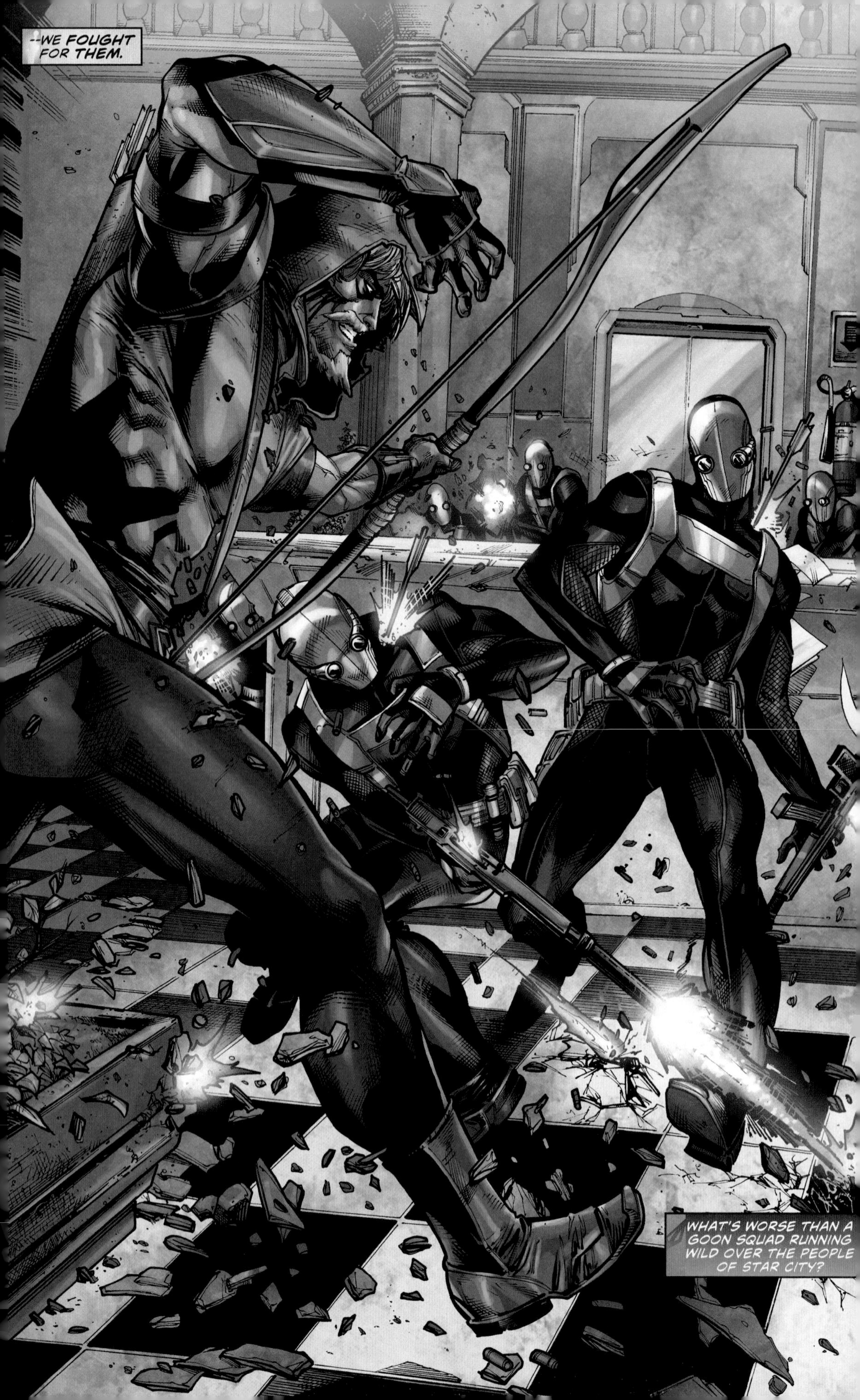
--WE FOUGHT FOR THEM.
WHAT'S WORSE THAN A GOON SQUAD RUNNING WILD OVER THE PEOPLE OF STAR CITY?

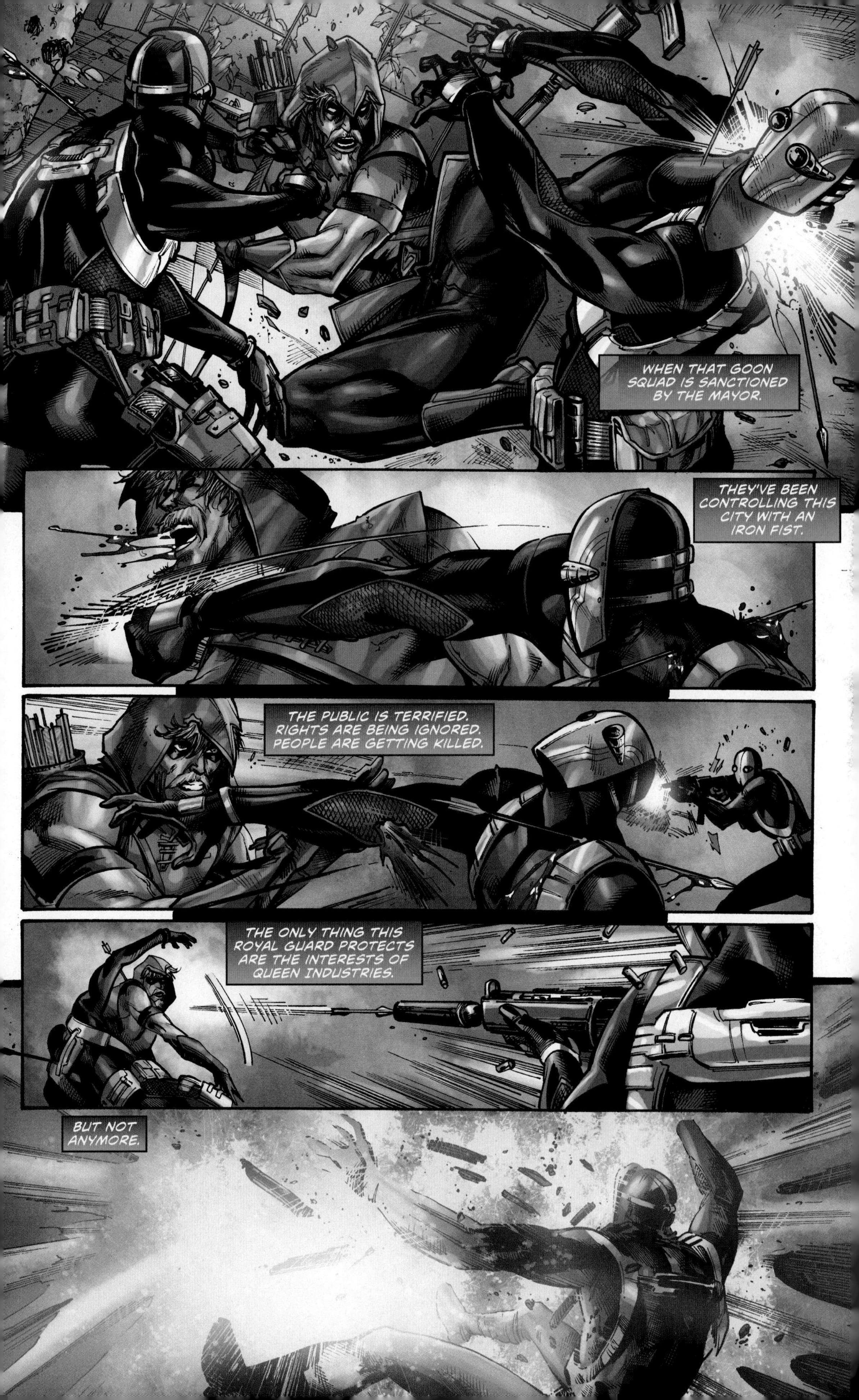
WHEN THAT GOON SQUAD IS SANCTIONED BY THE MAYOR.
THEY'VE BEEN CONTROLLING THIS CITY WITH AN IRON FIST.
THE PUBLIC IS TERRIFIED. RIGHTS ARE BEING IGNORED. PEOPLE ARE GETTING KILLED.
THE ONLY THING THIS ROYAL GUARD PROTECTS ARE THE INTERESTS OF QUEEN INDUSTRIES.
BUT NOT ANYMORE.

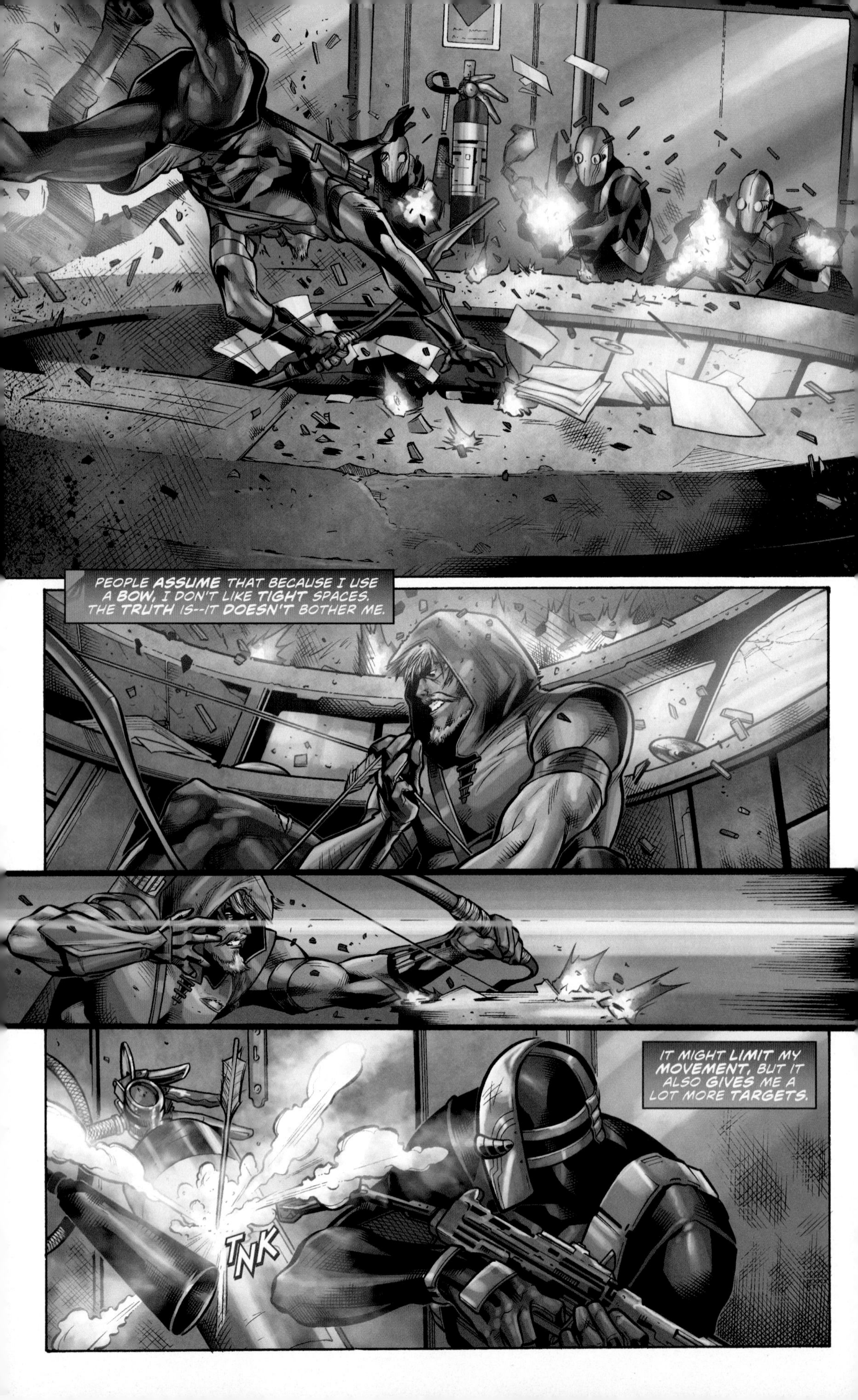
PEOPLE ASSUME THAT BECAUSE I USE A BOW, I DON'T LIKE TIGHT SPACES. THE TRUTH IS--IT DOESN'T BOTHER ME.
IT MIGHT LIMIT MY MOVEMENT, BUT IT ALSO GIVES ME A LOT MORE TARGETS.
TNK

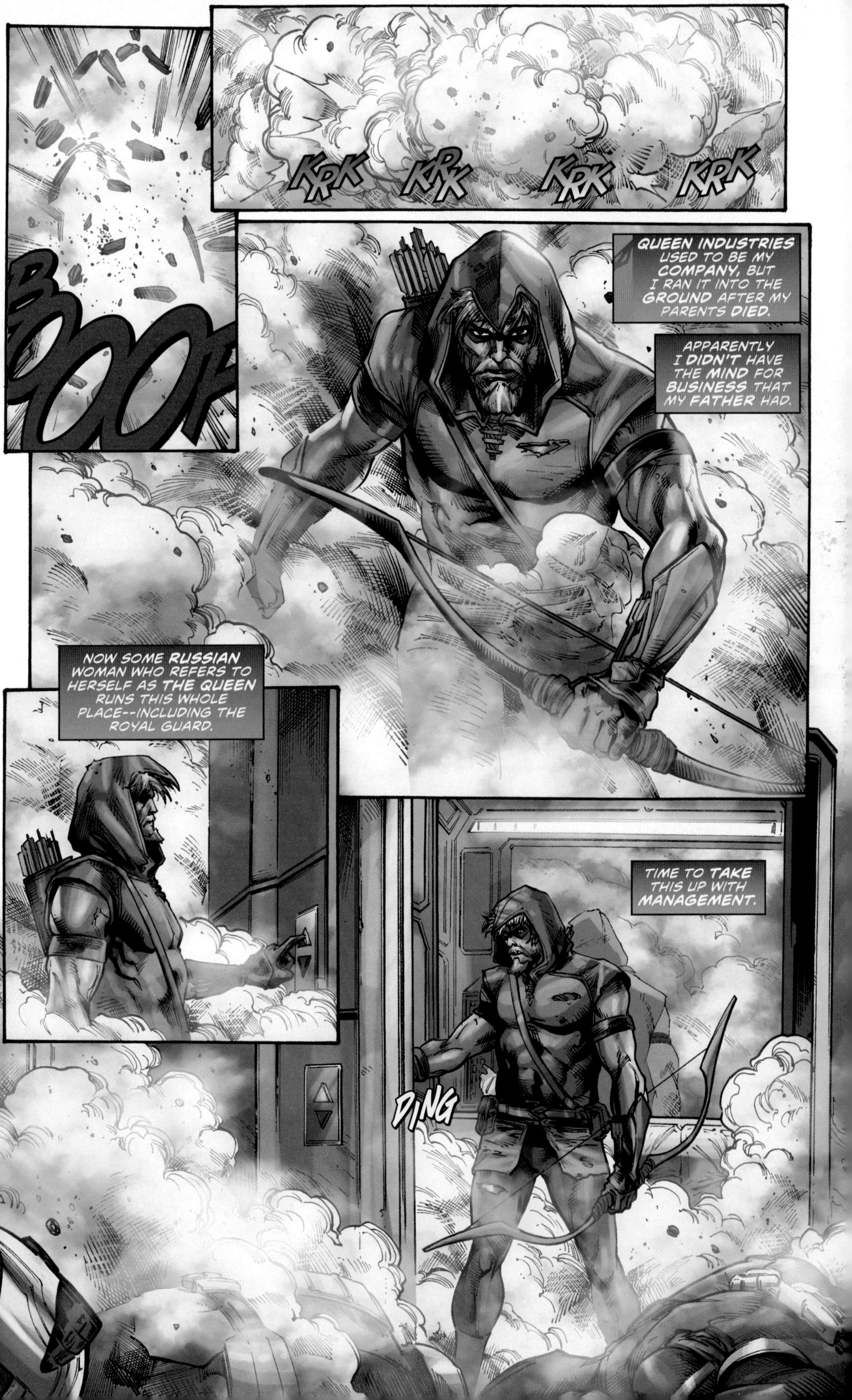
BOOOF
KRK KRK KRK KRK
QUEEN INDUSTRIES USED TO BE MY COMPANY, BUT I RAN IT INTO THE GROUND AFTER MY PARENTS DIED.
APPARENTLY I DIDN'T HAVE THE MIND FOR BUSINESS THAT MY FATHER HAD.
NOW SOME RUSSIAN WOMAN WHO REFERS TO HERSELF AS THE QUEEN RUNS THIS WHOLE PLACE--INCLUDING THE ROYAL GUARD.
TIME TO TAKE THIS UP WITH MANAGEMENT.
DING

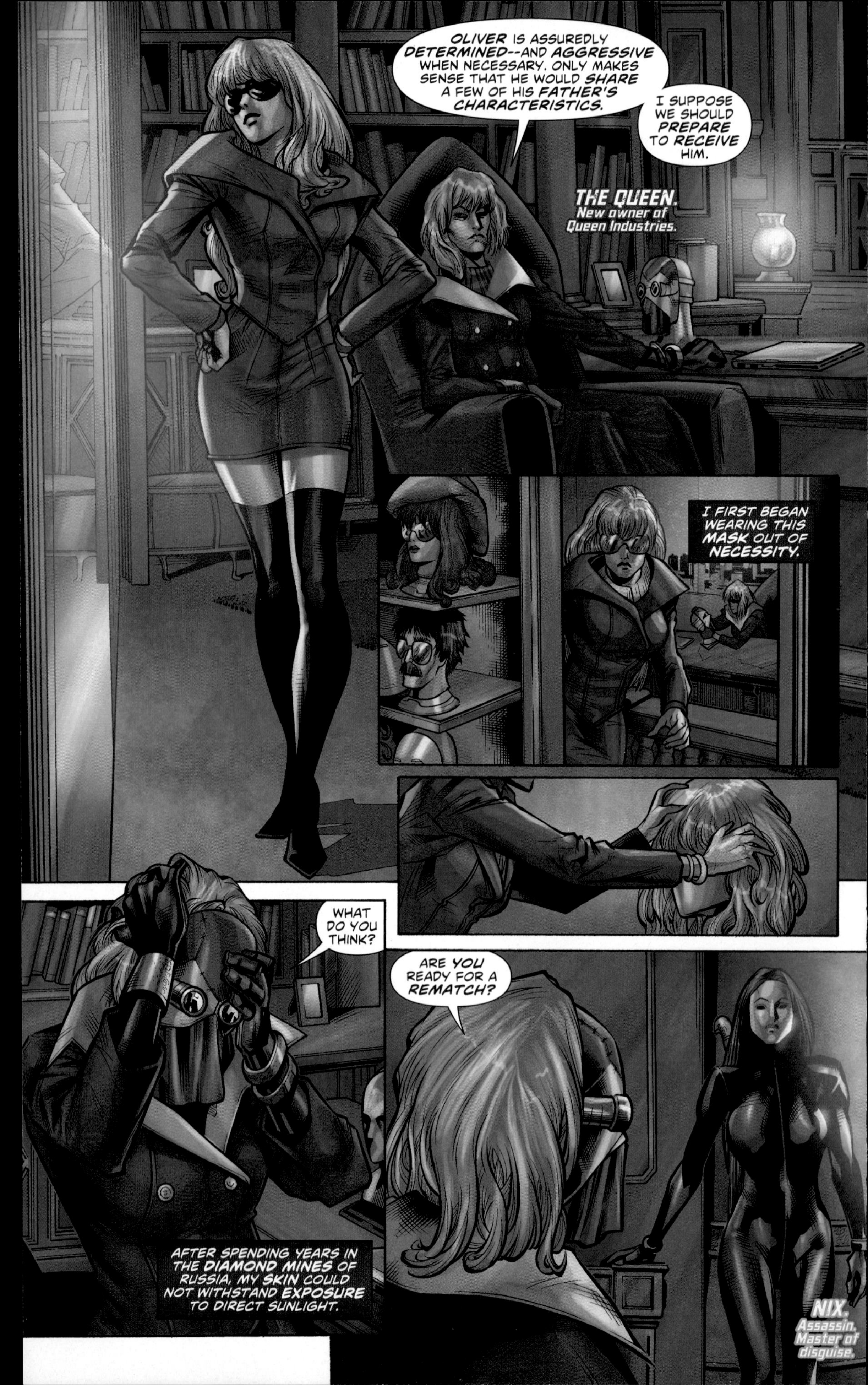
OLIVER IS ASSUREDLY DETERMINED--AND AGGRESSIVE WHEN NECESSARY. ONLY MAKES SENSE THAT HE WOULD SHARE A FEW OF HIS FATHER'S CHARACTERISTICS.
I SUPPOSE WE SHOULD PREPARE TO RECEIVE HIM.
THE QUEEN. New owner of Queen Industries.
I FIRST BEGAN WEARING THIS MASK OUT OF NECESSITY.
AFTER SPENDING YEARS IN THE DIAMOND MINES OF RUSSIA, MY SKIN COULD NOT WITHSTAND EXPOSURE TO DIRECT SUNLIGHT.
WHAT DO YOU THINK?
ARE YOU READY FOR A REMATCH?
NIX. Assassin. Master of disguise.

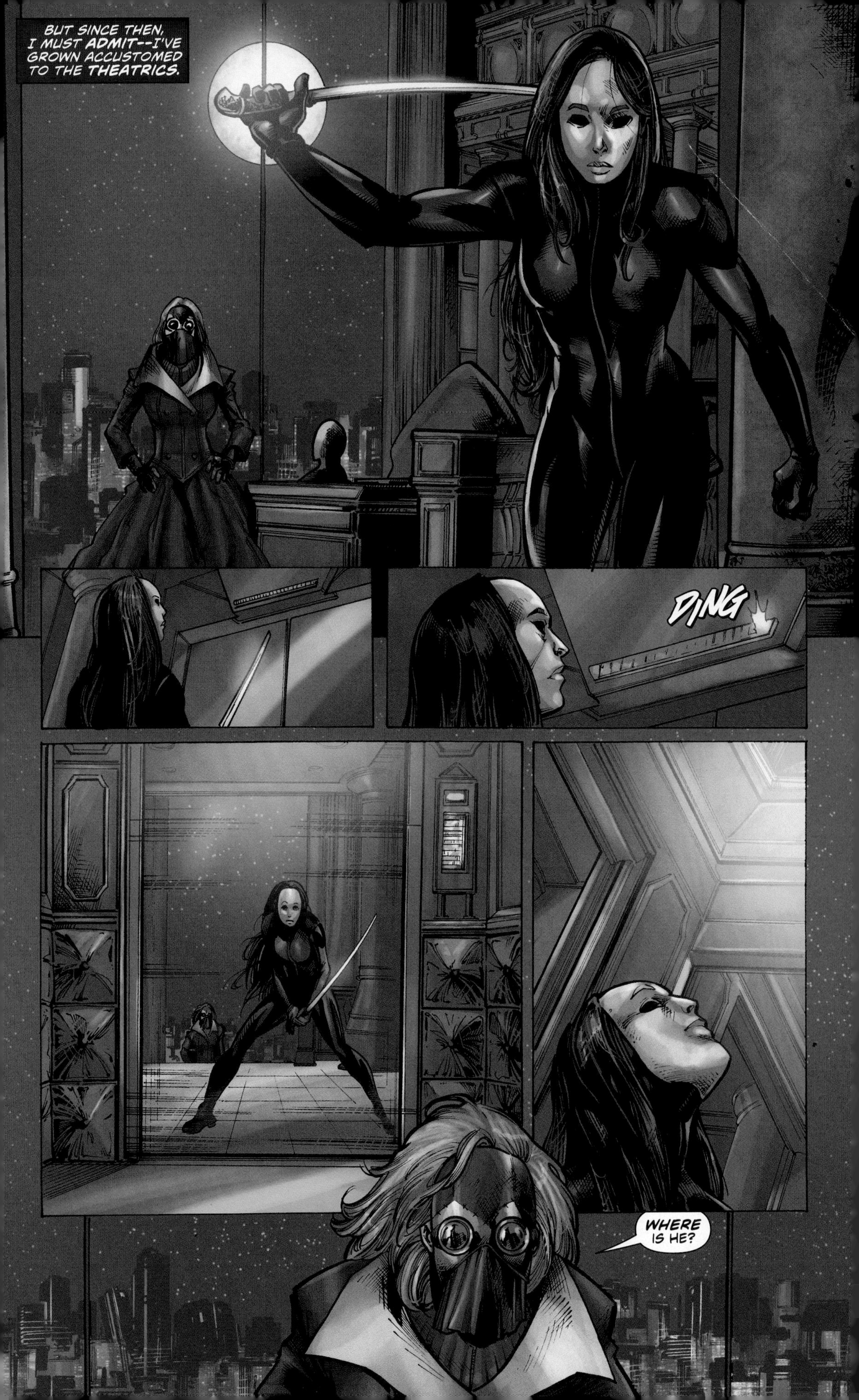
BUT SINCE THEN, I MUST ADMIT--I'VE GROWN ACCUSTOMED TO THE THEATRICS.
DING
WHERE IS HE?

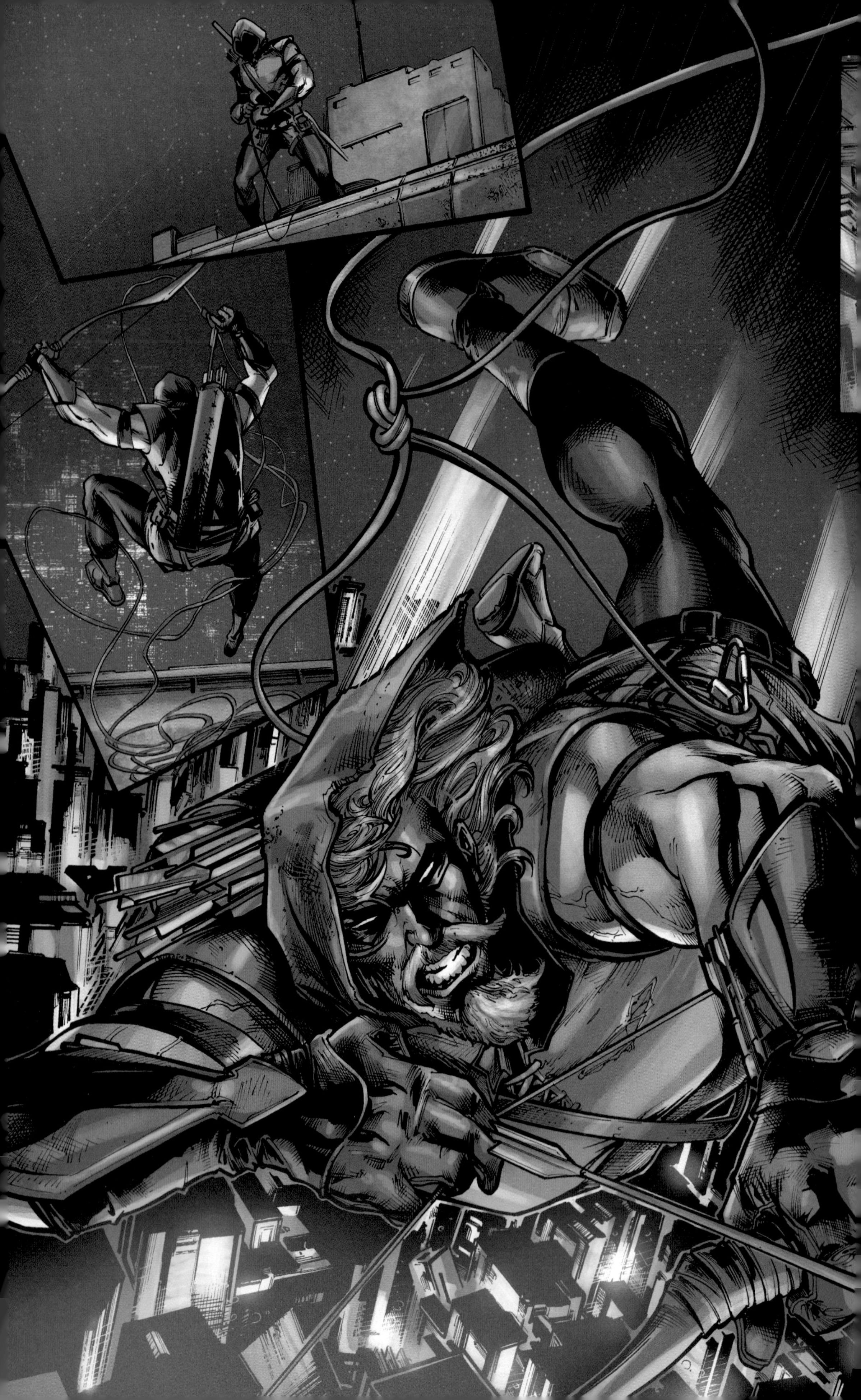

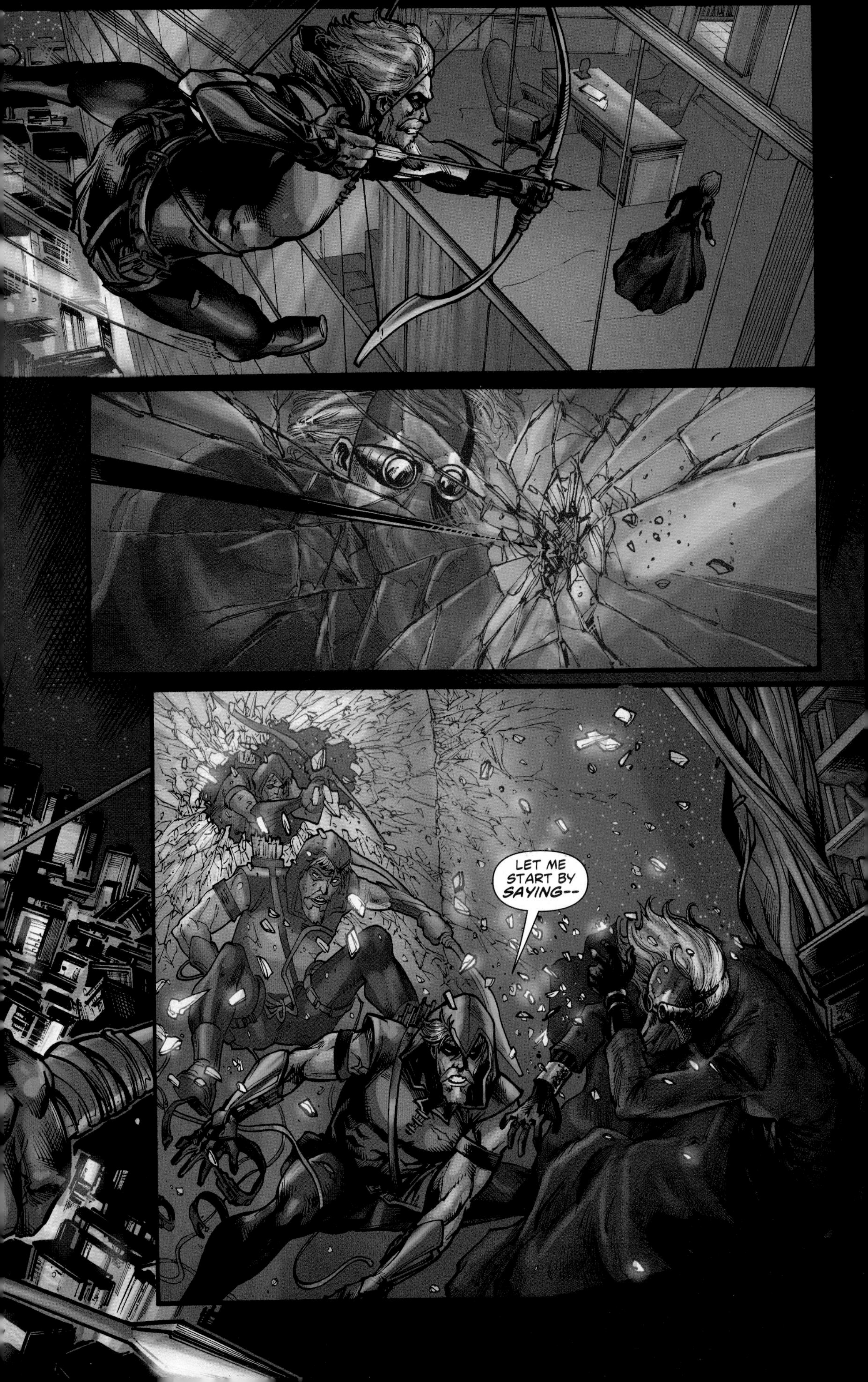
LET ME START BY SAYING--

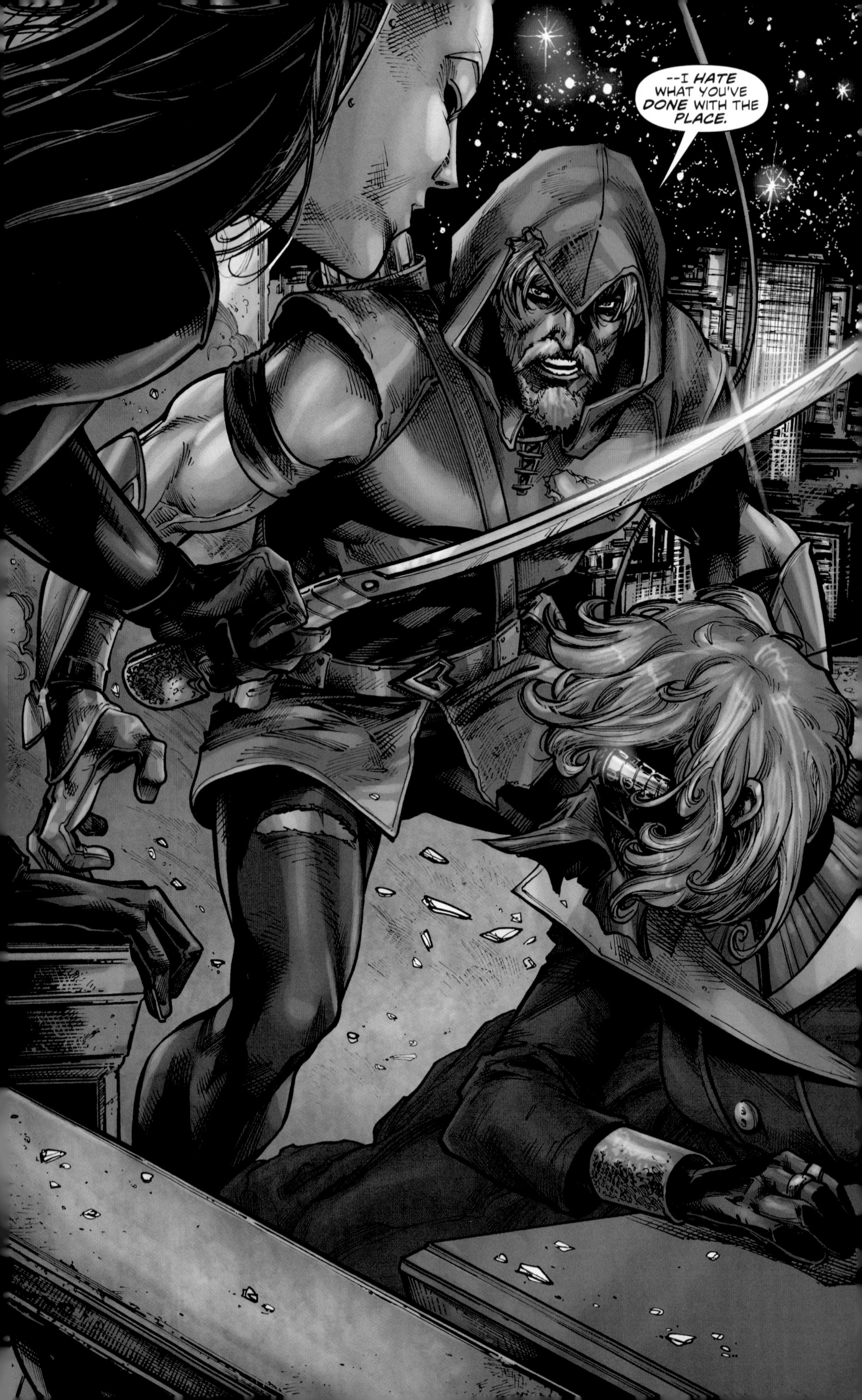
--I HATE WHAT YOU'VE DONE WITH THE PLACE.

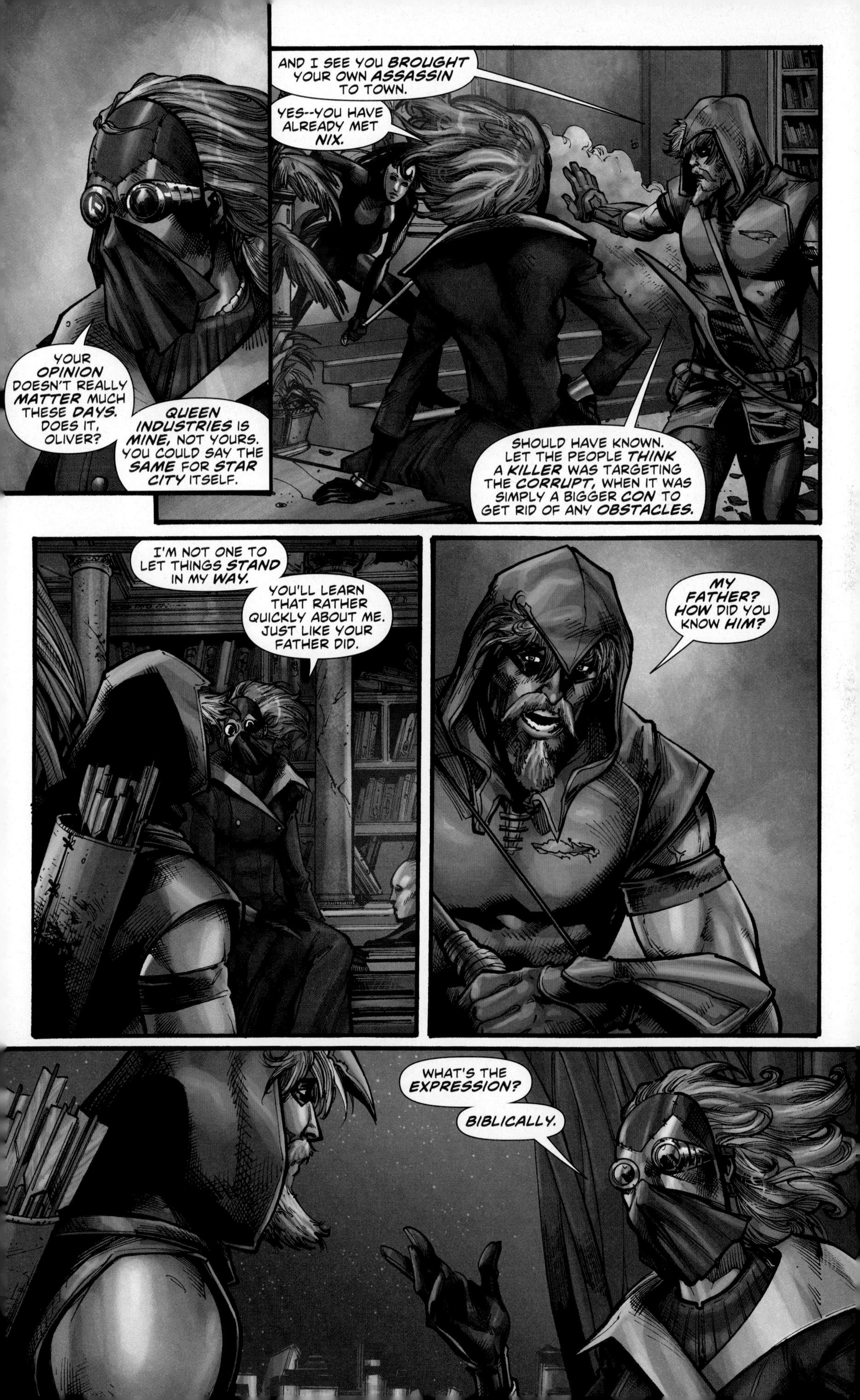
YOUR OPINION DOESN'T REALLY MATTER MUCH THESE DAYS. DOES IT, OLIVER?
QUEEN INDUSTRIES IS MINE, NOT YOURS. YOU COULD SAY THE SAME FOR STAR CITY ITSELF.
AND I SEE YOU BROUGHT YOUR OWN ASSASSIN TO TOWN.
YES--YOU HAVE ALREADY MET NIX.
SHOULD HAVE KNOWN. LET THE PEOPLE THINK A KILLER WAS TARGETING THE CORRUPT, WHEN IT WAS SIMPLY A BIGGER CON TO GET RID OF ANY OBSTACLES.
I'M NOT ONE TO LET THINGS STAND IN MY WAY.
YOU'LL LEARN THAT RATHER QUICKLY ABOUT ME. JUST LIKE YOUR FATHER DID.
MY FATHER? HOW DID YOU KNOW HIM?
WHAT'S THE EXPRESSION?
BIBLICALLY.

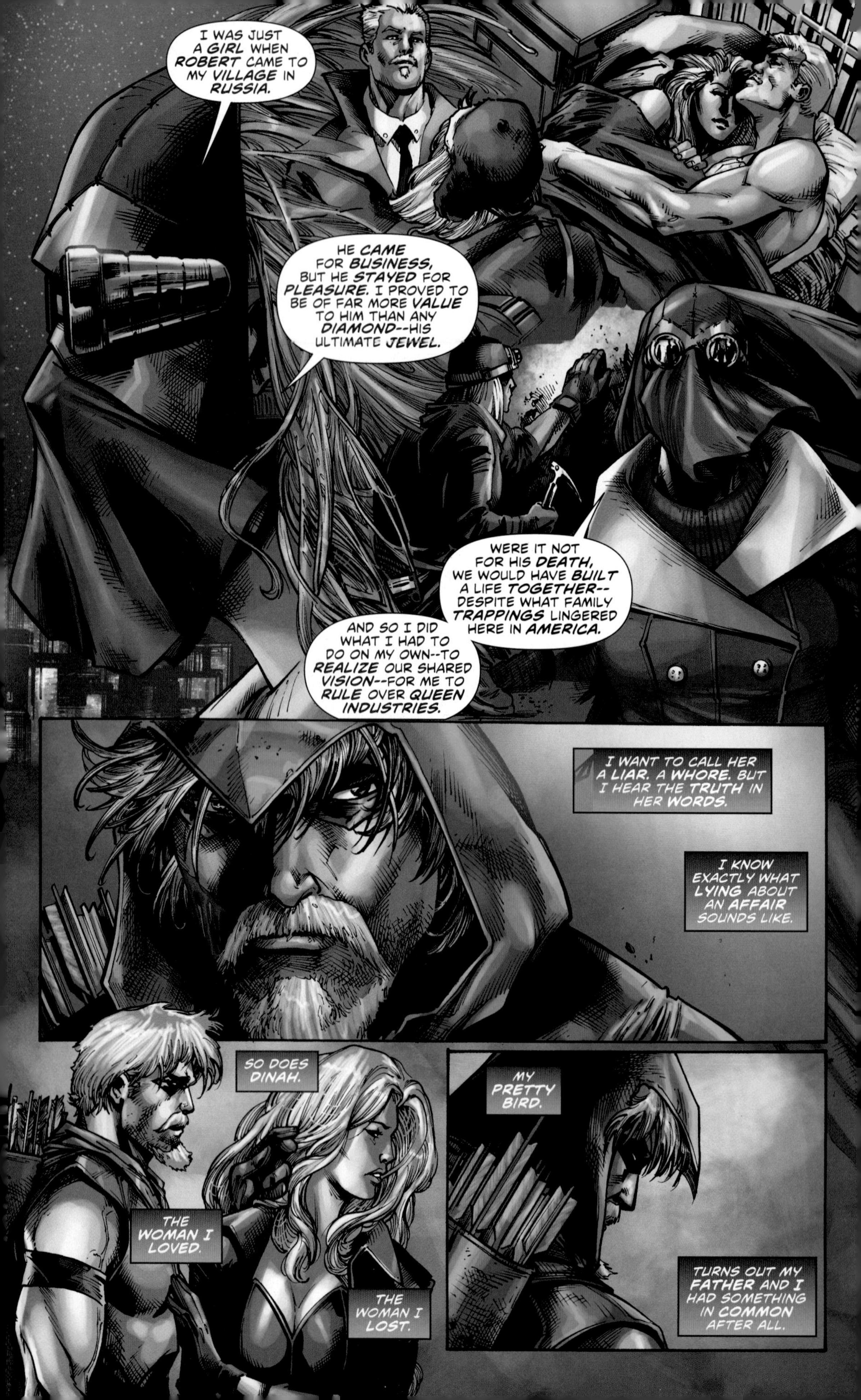

I WAS JUST A GIRL WHEN ROBERT CAME TO MY VILLAGE IN RUSSIA.
HE CAME FOR BUSINESS, BUT HE STAYED FOR PLEASURE. I PROVED TO BE OF FAR MORE VALUE TO HIM THAN ANY DIAMOND--HIS ULTIMATE JEWEL.
WERE IT NOT FOR HIS DEATH, WE WOULD HAVE BUILT A LIFE TOGETHER--DESPITE WHAT FAMILY TRAPPINGS LINGERED HERE IN AMERICA.
AND SO I DID WHAT I HAD TO DO ON MY OWN--TO REALIZE OUR SHARED VISION--FOR ME TO RULE OVER QUEEN INDUSTRIES.
I WANT TO CALL HER A LIAR. A WHORE. BUT I HEAR THE TRUTH IN HER WORDS.
I KNOW EXACTLY WHAT LYING ABOUT AN AFFAIR SOUNDS LIKE.
SO DOES DINAH.
THE WOMAN I LOVED.
THE WOMAN I LOST.
MY PRETTY BIRD.
TURNS OUT MY FATHER AND I HAD SOMETHING IN COMMON AFTER ALL.

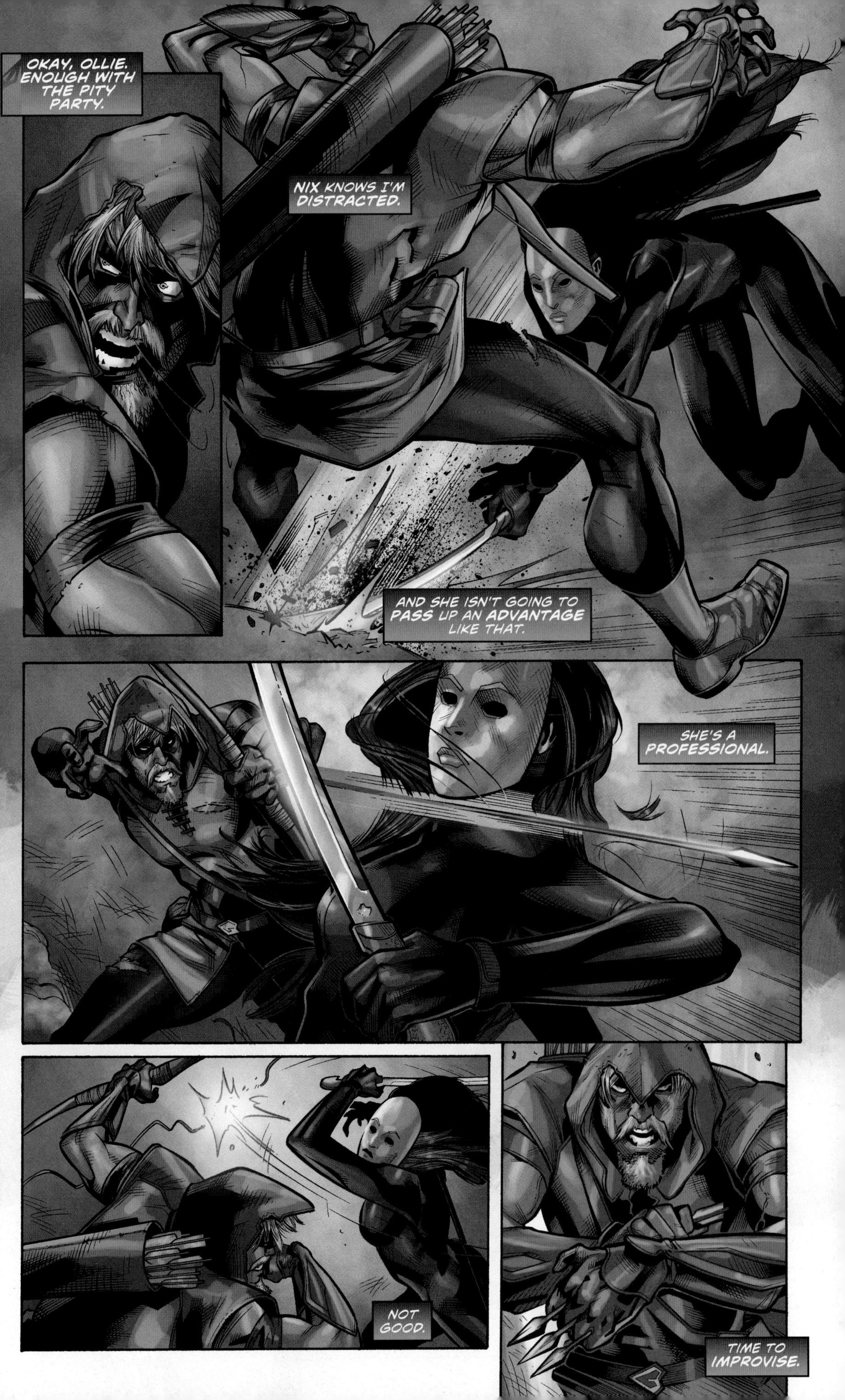
OKAY, OLLIE. ENOUGH WITH THE PITY PARTY.
NIX KNOWS I'M DISTRACTED.
AND SHE ISN'T GOING TO PASS UP AN ADVANTAGE LIKE THAT.
SHE'S A PROFESSIONAL.
NOT GOOD.
TIME TO IMPROVISE.

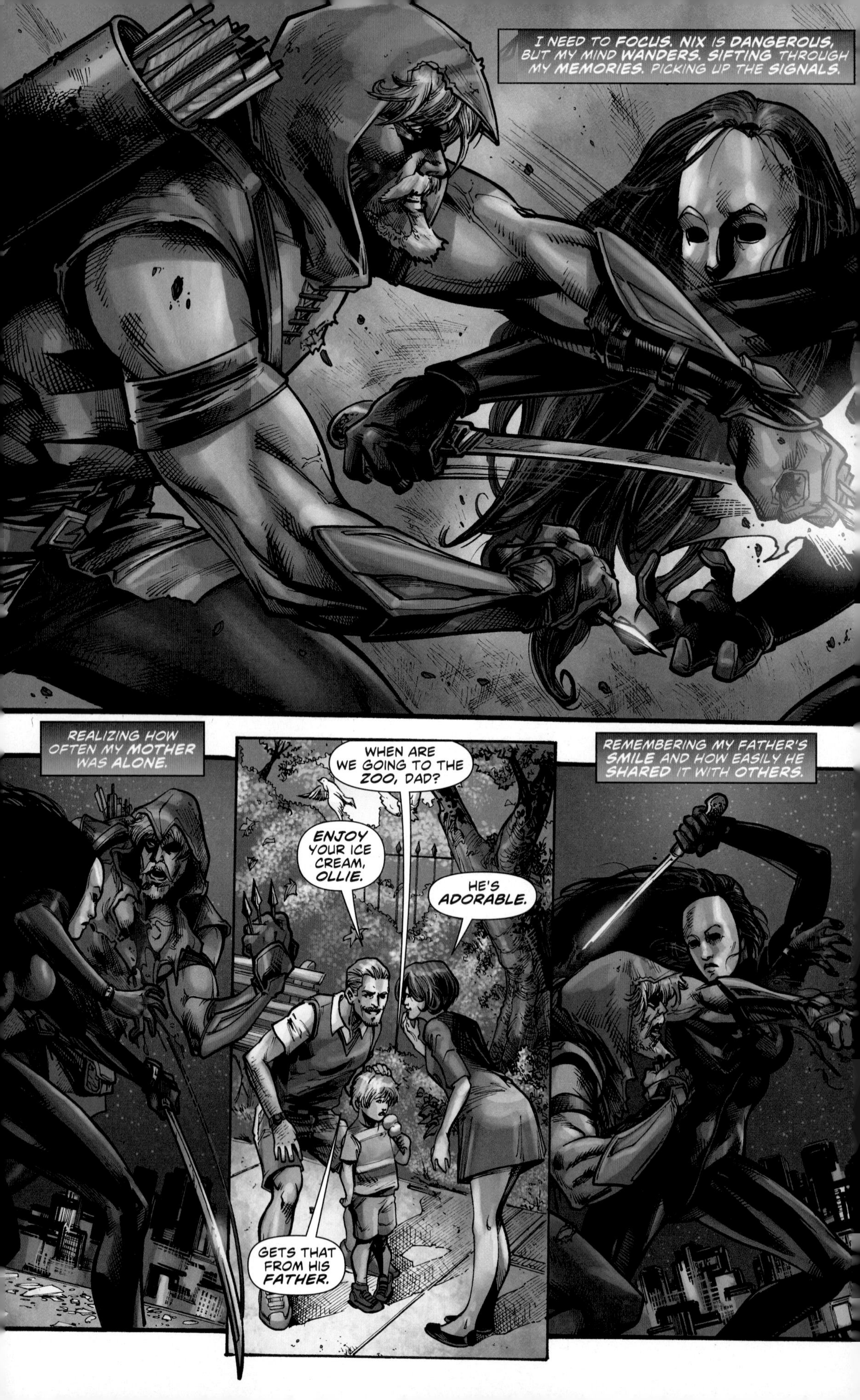
I NEED TO FOCUS. NIX IS DANGEROUS, BUT MY MIND WANDERS. SIFTING THROUGH MY MEMORIES. PICKING UP THE SIGNALS.
REALIZING HOW OFTEN MY MOTHER WAS ALONE.
WHEN ARE WE GOING TO THE ZOO, DAD?
ENJOY YOUR ICE CREAM, OLLIE.
HE'S ADORABLE.
GETS THAT FROM HIS FATHER.
REMEMBERING MY FATHER'S SMILE AND HOW EASILY HE SHARED IT WITH OTHERS.

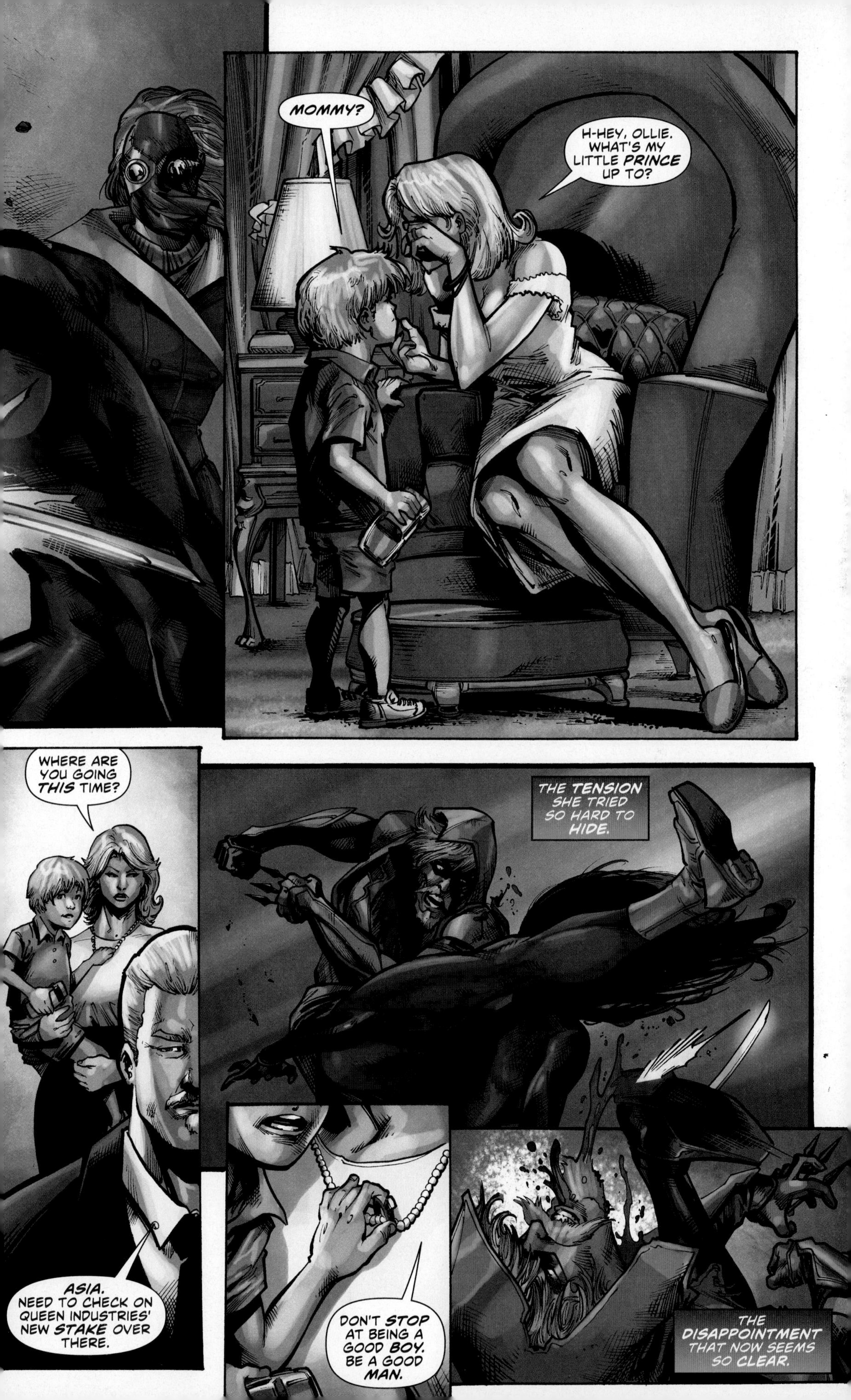
MOMMY?
H-HEY, OLLIE. WHAT'S MY LITTLE PRINCE UP TO?
WHERE ARE YOU GOING THIS TIME?
THE TENSION SHE TRIED SO HARD TO HIDE.
ASIA. NEED TO CHECK ON QUEEN INDUSTRIES' NEW STAKE OVER THERE.
DON'T STOP AT BEING A GOOD BOY. BE A GOOD MAN.
THE DISAPPOINTMENT THAT NOW SEEMS SO CLEAR.

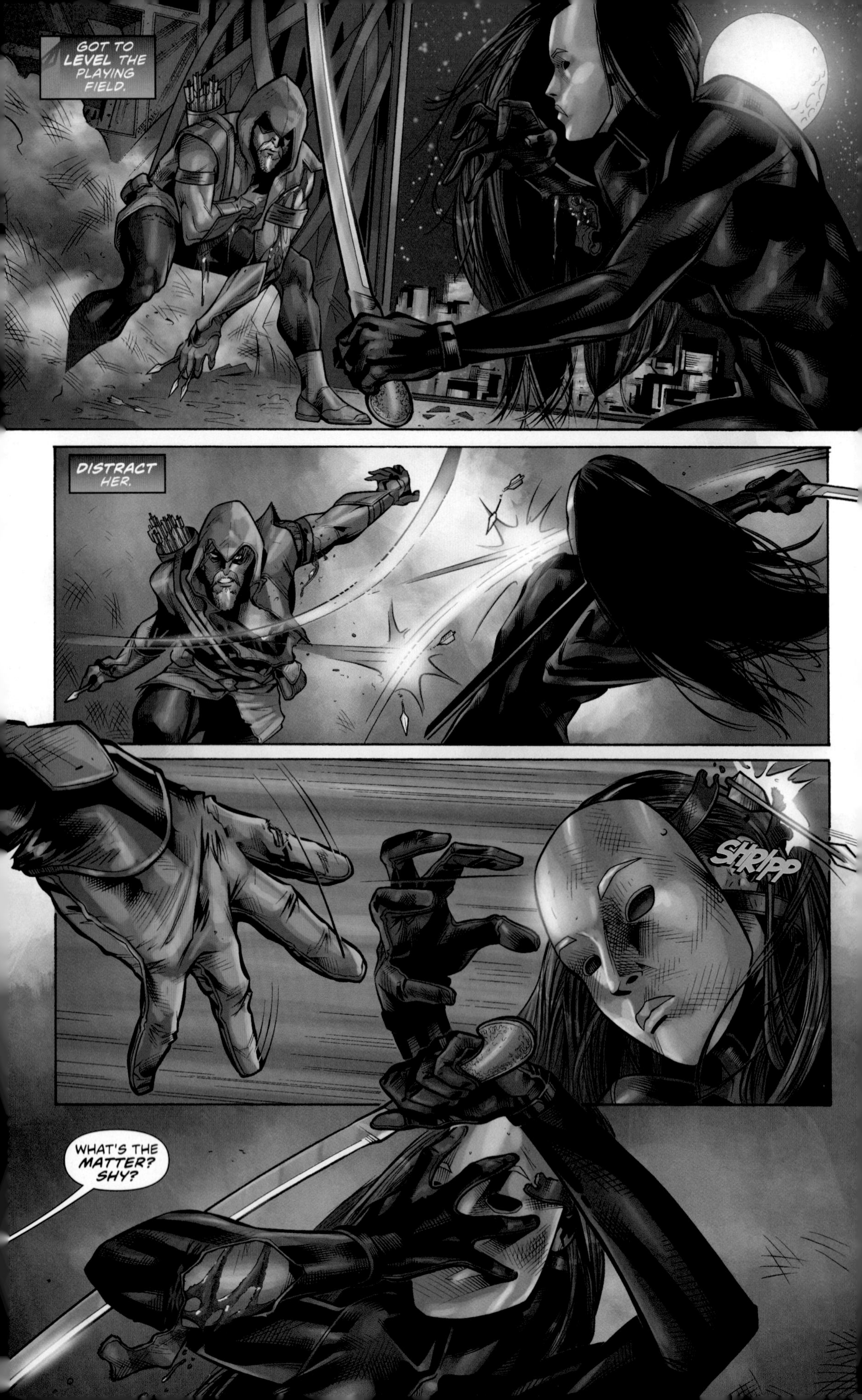
GOT TO LEVEL THE PLAYING FIELD.
DISTRACT HER.
SHRIPP
WHAT'S THE MATTER? SHY?

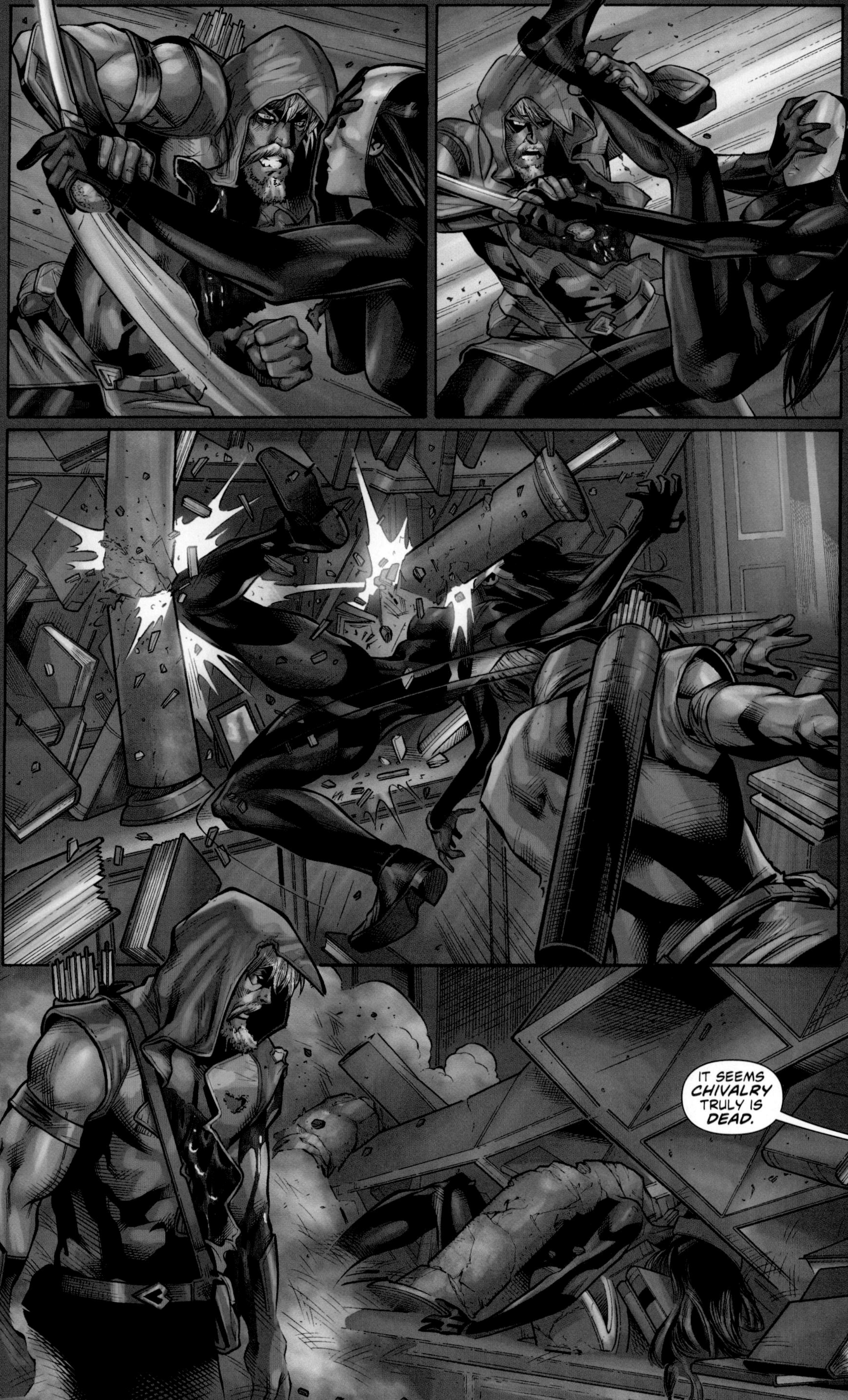
IT SEEMS CHIVALRY TRULY IS DEAD.

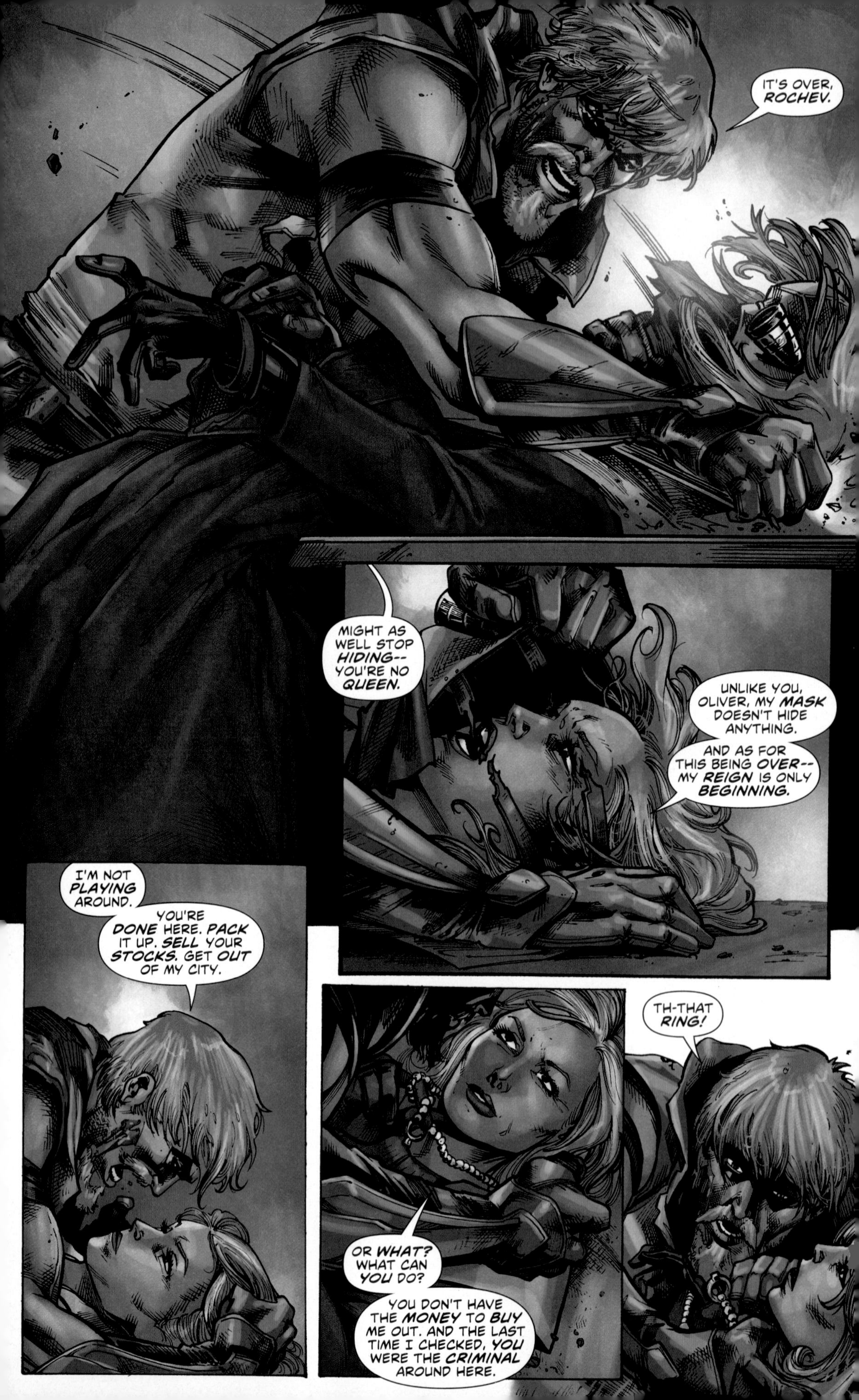

IT'S OVER, ROCHEV.
MIGHT AS WELL STOP HIDING-- YOU'RE NO QUEEN.
UNLIKE YOU, OLIVER, MY MASK DOESN'T HIDE ANYTHING.
AND AS FOR THIS BEING OVER-- MY REIGN IS ONLY BEGINNING.
I'M NOT PLAYING AROUND.
YOU'RE DONE HERE. PACK IT UP. SELL YOUR STOCKS. GET OUT OF MY CITY.
OR WHAT? WHAT CAN YOU DO?
YOU DON'T HAVE THE MONEY TO BUY ME OUT. AND THE LAST TIME I CHECKED, YOU WERE THE CRIMINAL AROUND HERE.
TH-THAT RING!

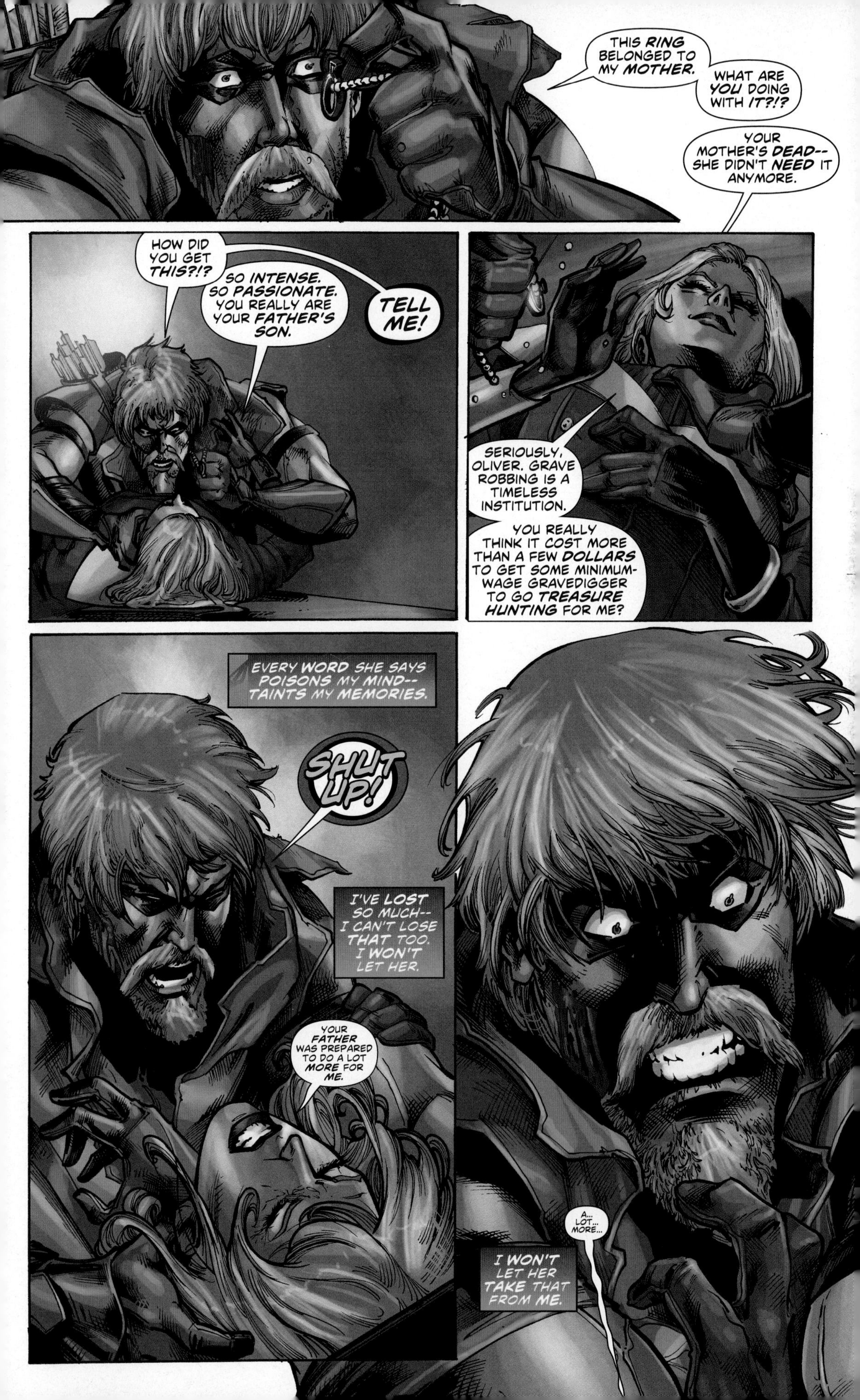
THIS RING BELONGED TO MY MOTHER.
WHAT ARE YOU DOING WITH IT?!?
YOUR MOTHER'S DEAD-- SHE DIDN'T NEED IT ANYMORE.
HOW DID YOU GET THIS?!?
SO INTENSE. SO PASSIONATE. YOU REALLY ARE YOUR FATHER'S SON.
TELL ME!
SERIOUSLY, OLIVER. GRAVE ROBBING IS A TIMELESS INSTITUTION.
YOU REALLY THINK IT COST MORE THAN A FEW DOLLARS TO GET SOME MINIMUM-WAGE GRAVEDIGGER TO GO TREASURE HUNTING FOR ME?
EVERY WORD SHE SAYS POISONS MY MIND-- TAINTS MY MEMORIES.
SHUT UP!
I'VE LOST SO MUCH-- I CAN'T LOSE THAT TOO. I WON'T LET HER.
YOUR FATHER WAS PREPARED TO DO A LOT MORE FOR ME.
A... LOT... MORE...
I WON'T LET HER TAKE THAT FROM ME.

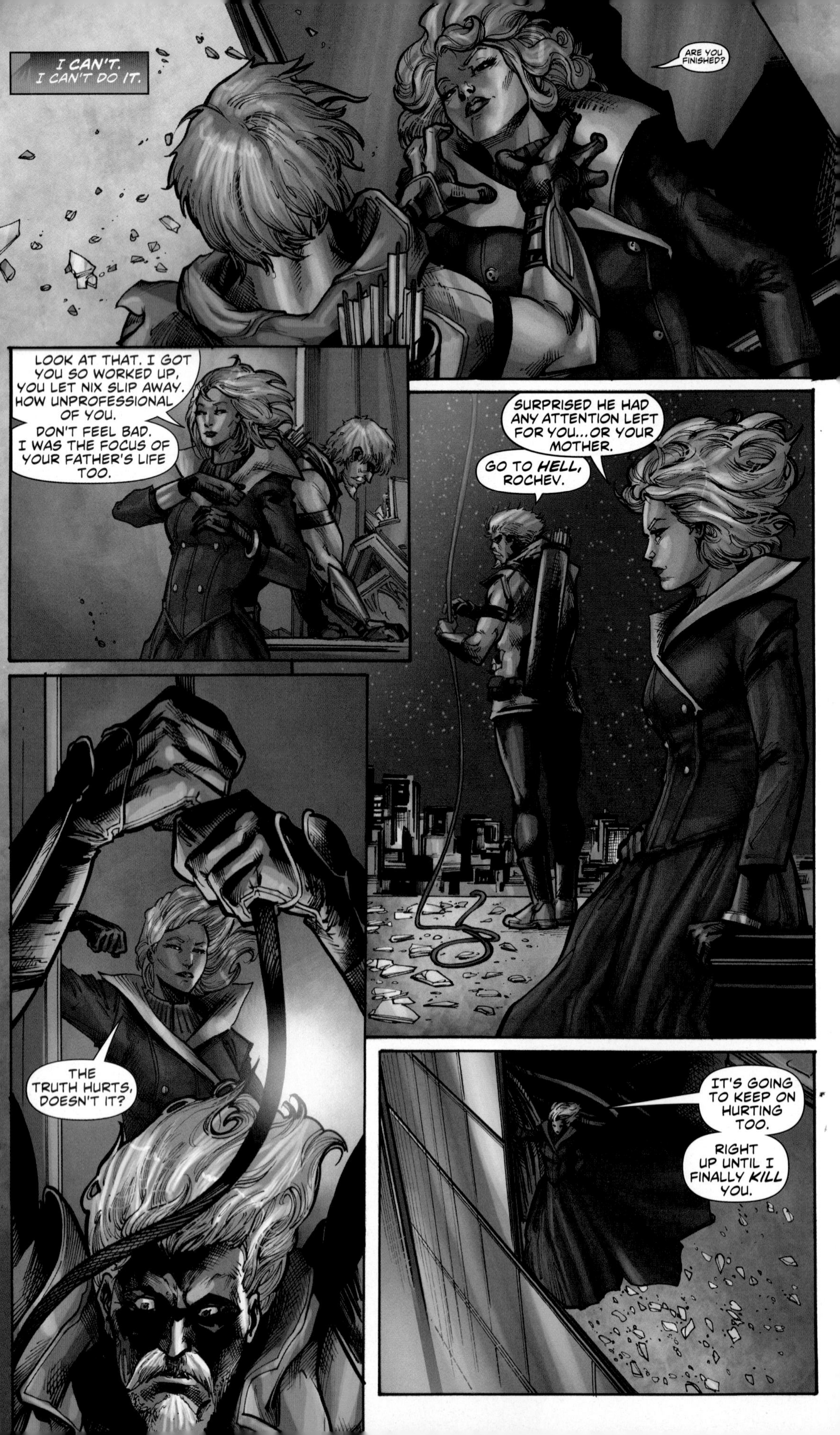
I CAN'T. I CAN'T DO IT.
ARE YOU FINISHED?
LOOK AT THAT. I GOT YOU SO WORKED UP, YOU LET NIX SLIP AWAY. HOW UNPROFESSIONAL OF YOU.
DON'T FEEL BAD. I WAS THE FOCUS OF YOUR FATHER'S LIFE TOO.
SURPRISED HE HAD ANY ATTENTION LEFT FOR YOU...OR YOUR MOTHER.
GO TO HELL, ROCHEV.
THE TRUTH HURTS, DOESN'T IT?
IT'S GOING TO KEEP ON HURTING TOO.
RIGHT UP UNTIL I FINALLY KILL YOU.

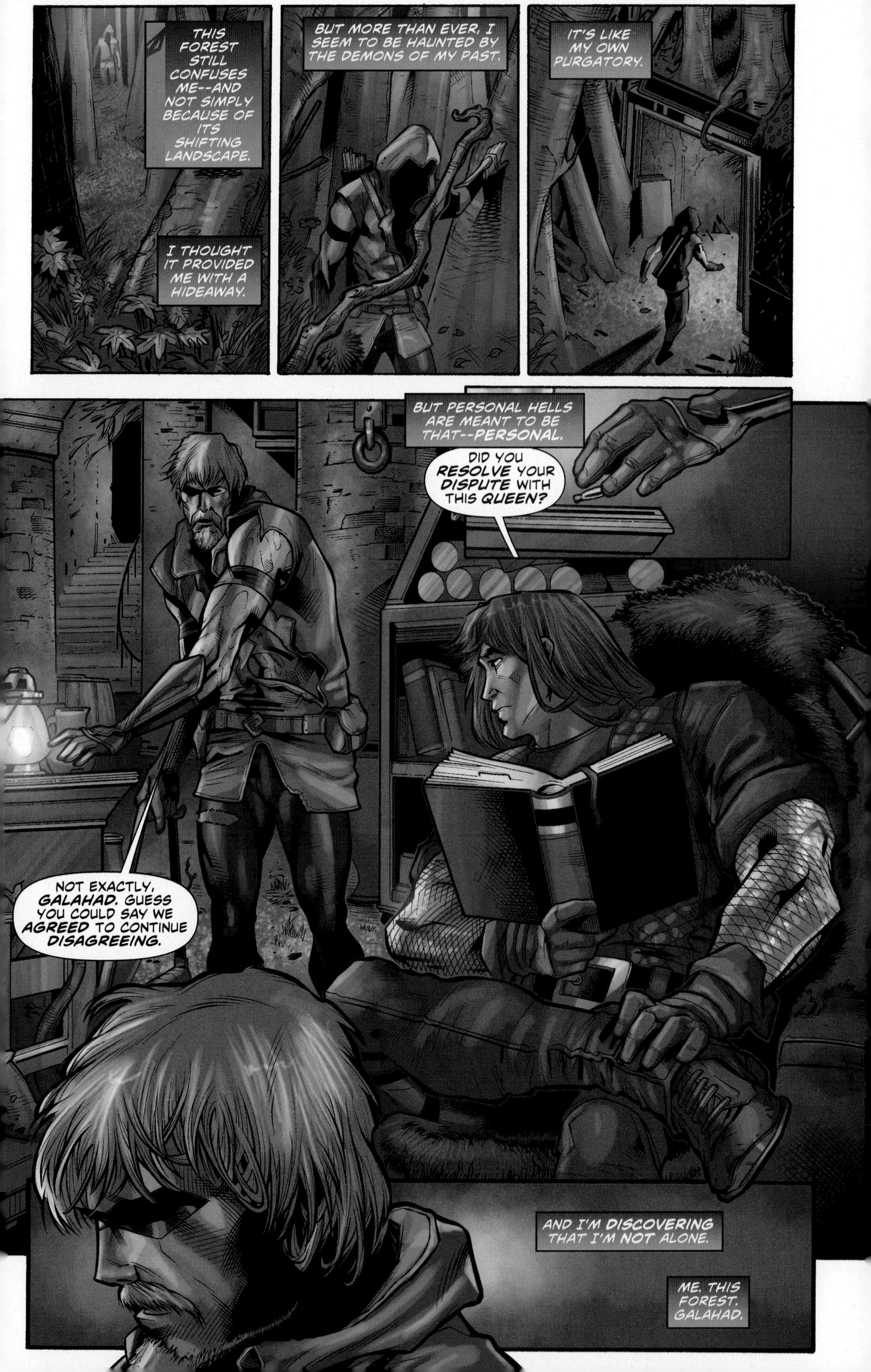
THIS FOREST STILL CONFUSES ME--AND NOT SIMPLY BECAUSE OF ITS SHIFTING LANDSCAPE.
I THOUGHT IT PROVIDED ME WITH A HIDEAWAY.
BUT MORE THAN EVER, I SEEM TO BE HAUNTED BY THE DEMONS OF MY PAST.
IT'S LIKE MY OWN PURGATORY.
BUT PERSONAL HELLS ARE MEANT TO BE THAT--PERSONAL.
DID YOU RESOLVE YOUR DISPUTE WITH THIS QUEEN?
NOT EXACTLY, GALAHAD. GUESS YOU COULD SAY WE AGREED TO CONTINUE DISAGREEING.
AND I'M DISCOVERING THAT I'M NOT ALONE.
ME. THIS FOREST. GALAHAD.

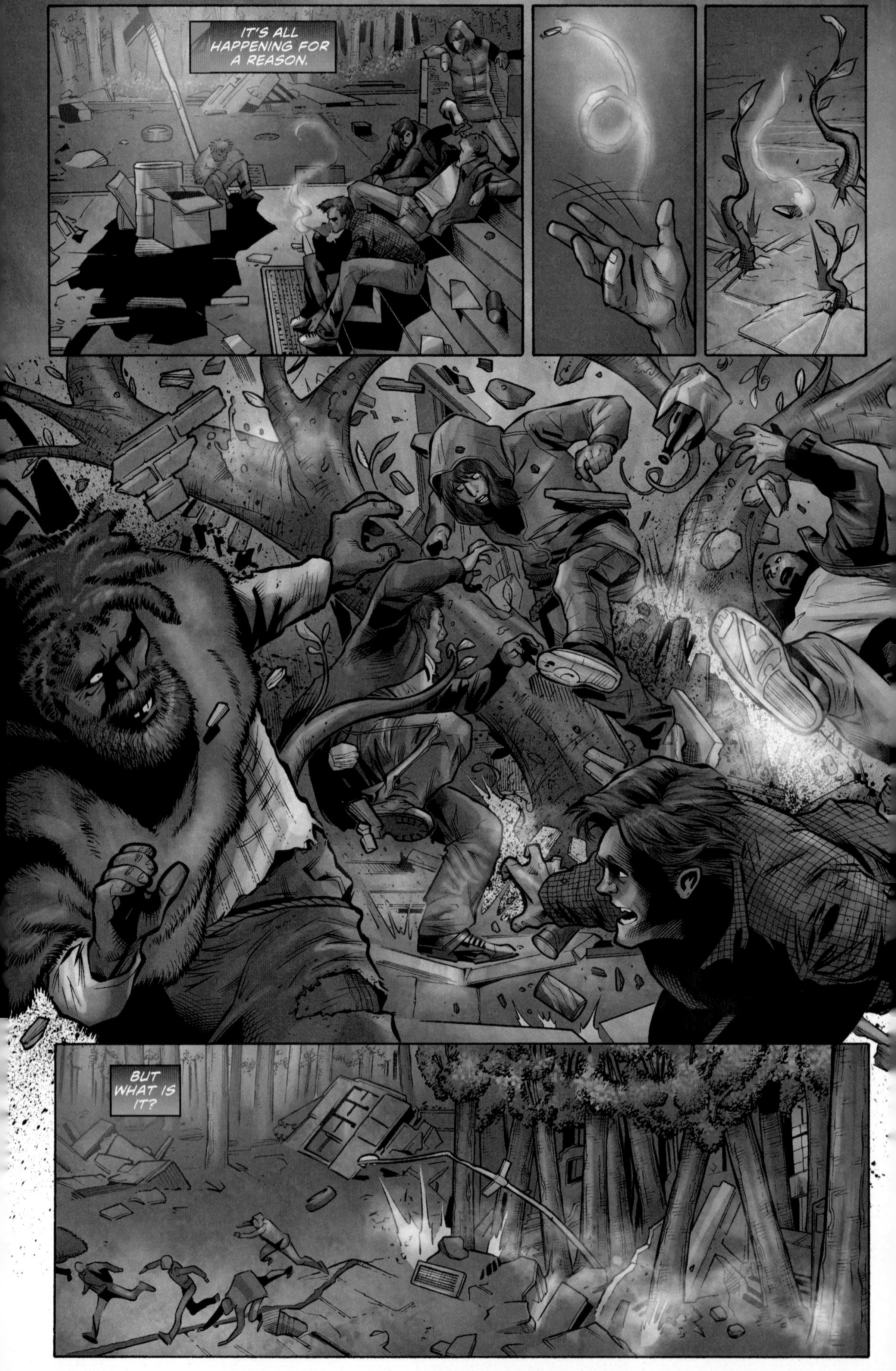
IT'S ALL HAPPENING FOR A REASON.
BUT WHAT IS IT?

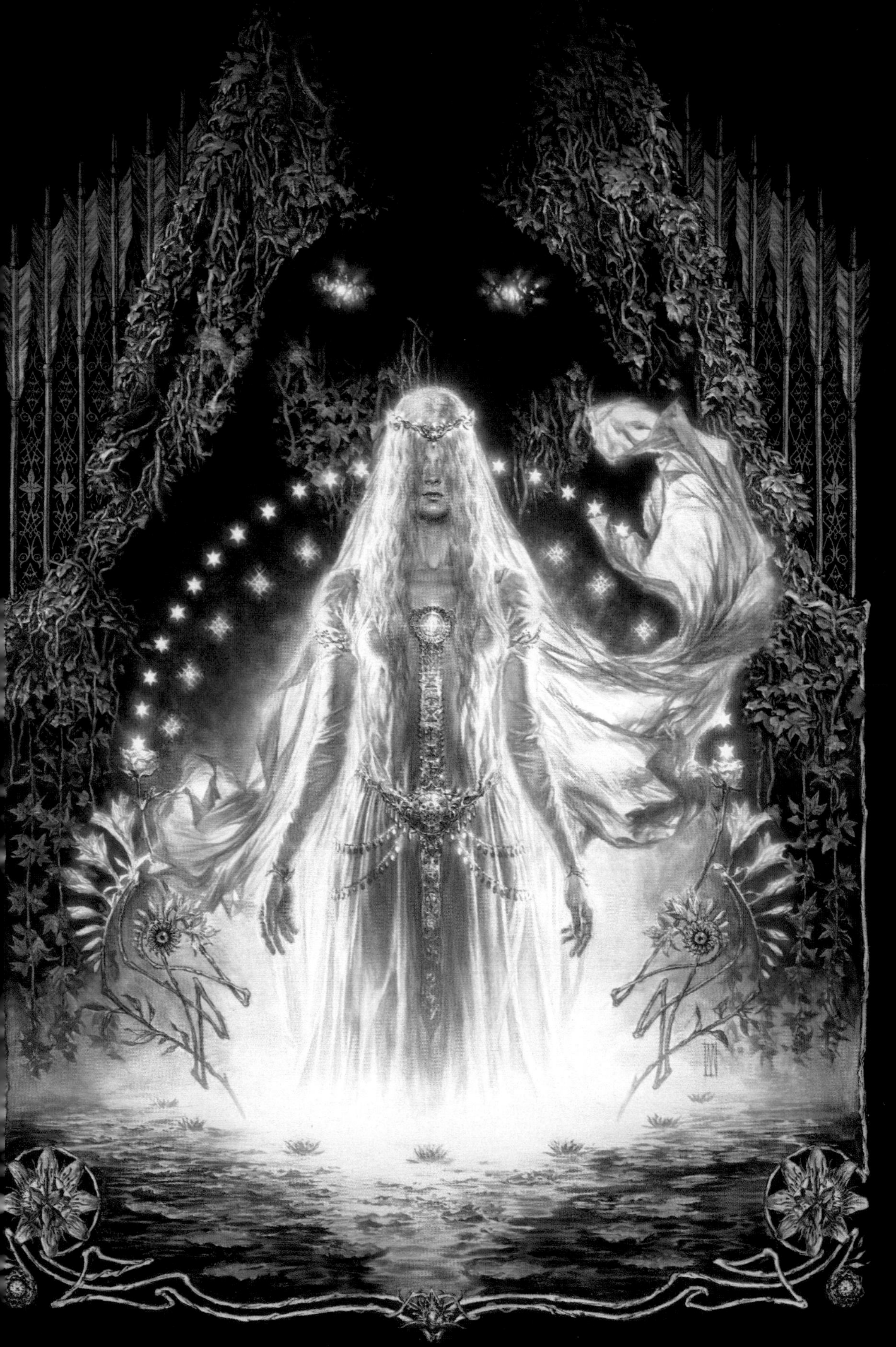

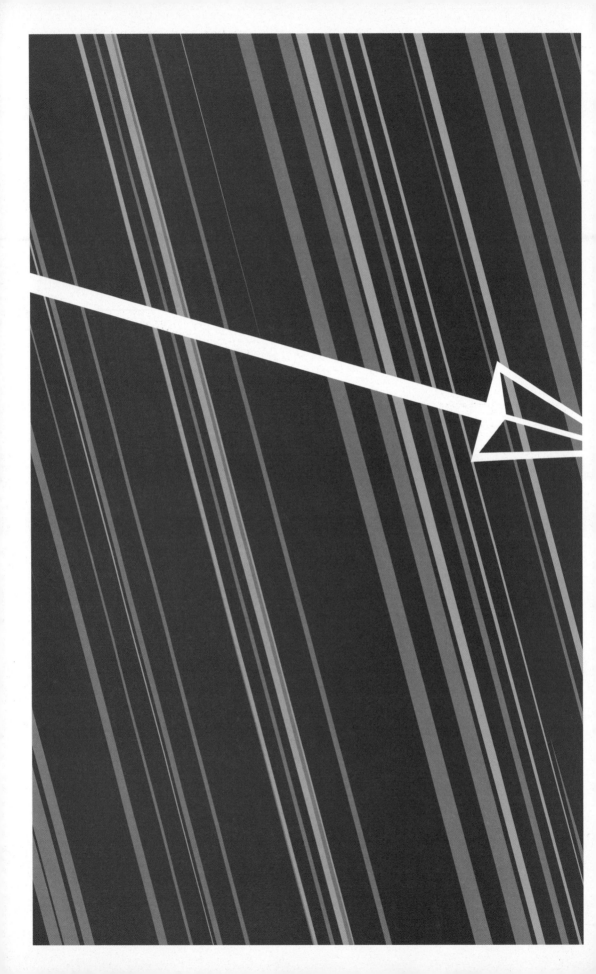

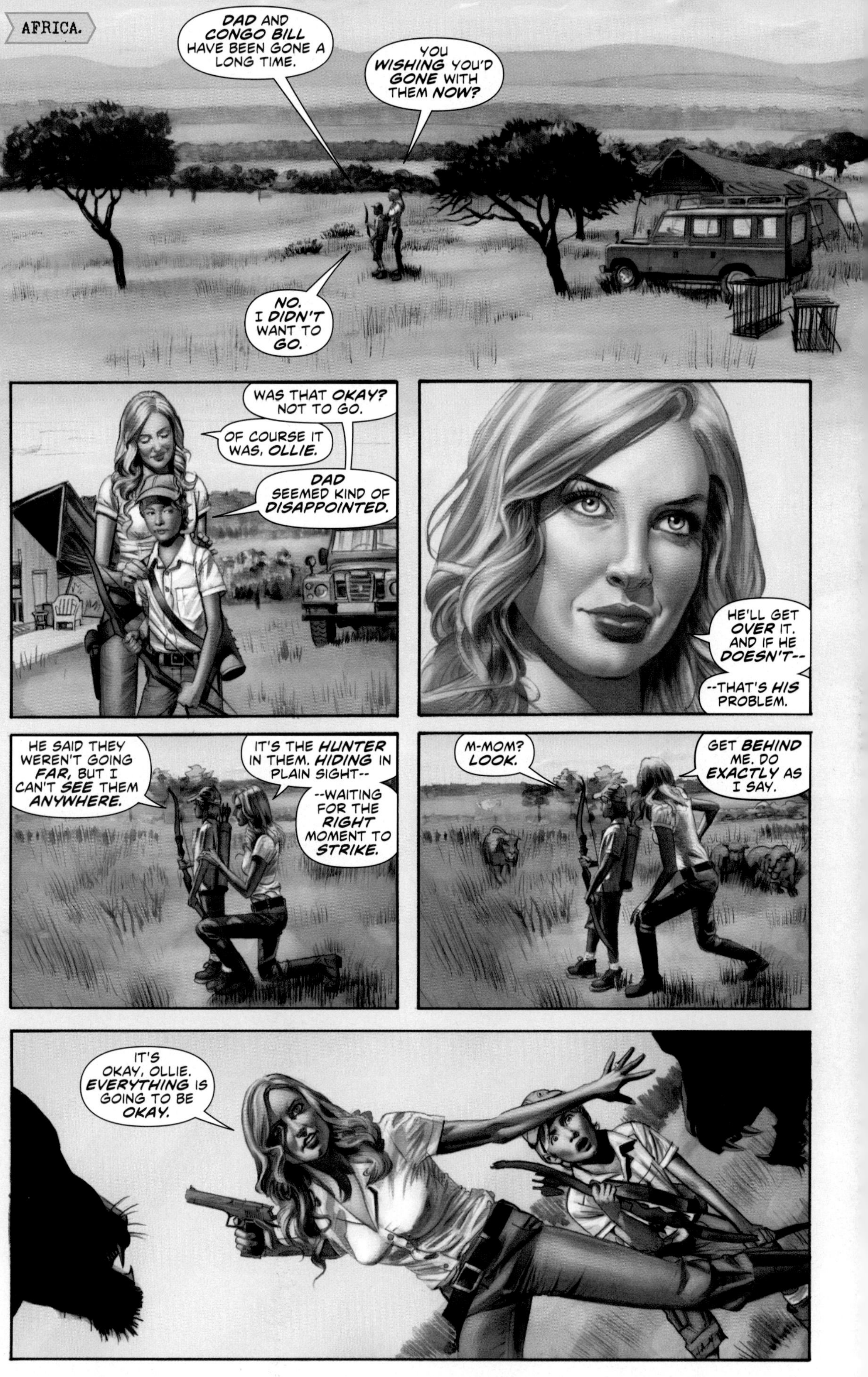
AFRICA.
DAD AND CONGO BILL HAVE BEEN GONE A LONG TIME.
YOU WISHING YOU'D GONE WITH THEM NOW?
NO. I DIDN'T WANT TO GO.
WAS THAT OKAY? NOT TO GO.
OF COURSE IT WAS, OLLIE.
DAD SEEMED KIND OF DISAPPOINTED.
HE'LL GET OVER IT. AND IF HE DOESN'T--
--THAT'S HIS PROBLEM.
HE SAID THEY WEREN'T GOING FAR, BUT I CAN'T SEE THEM ANYWHERE.
IT'S THE HUNTER IN THEM. HIDING IN PLAIN SIGHT--
--WAITING FOR THE RIGHT MOMENT TO STRIKE.
M-MOM? LOOK.
GET BEHIND ME. DO EXACTLY AS I SAY.
IT'S OKAY, OLLIE. EVERYTHING IS GOING TO BE OKAY.

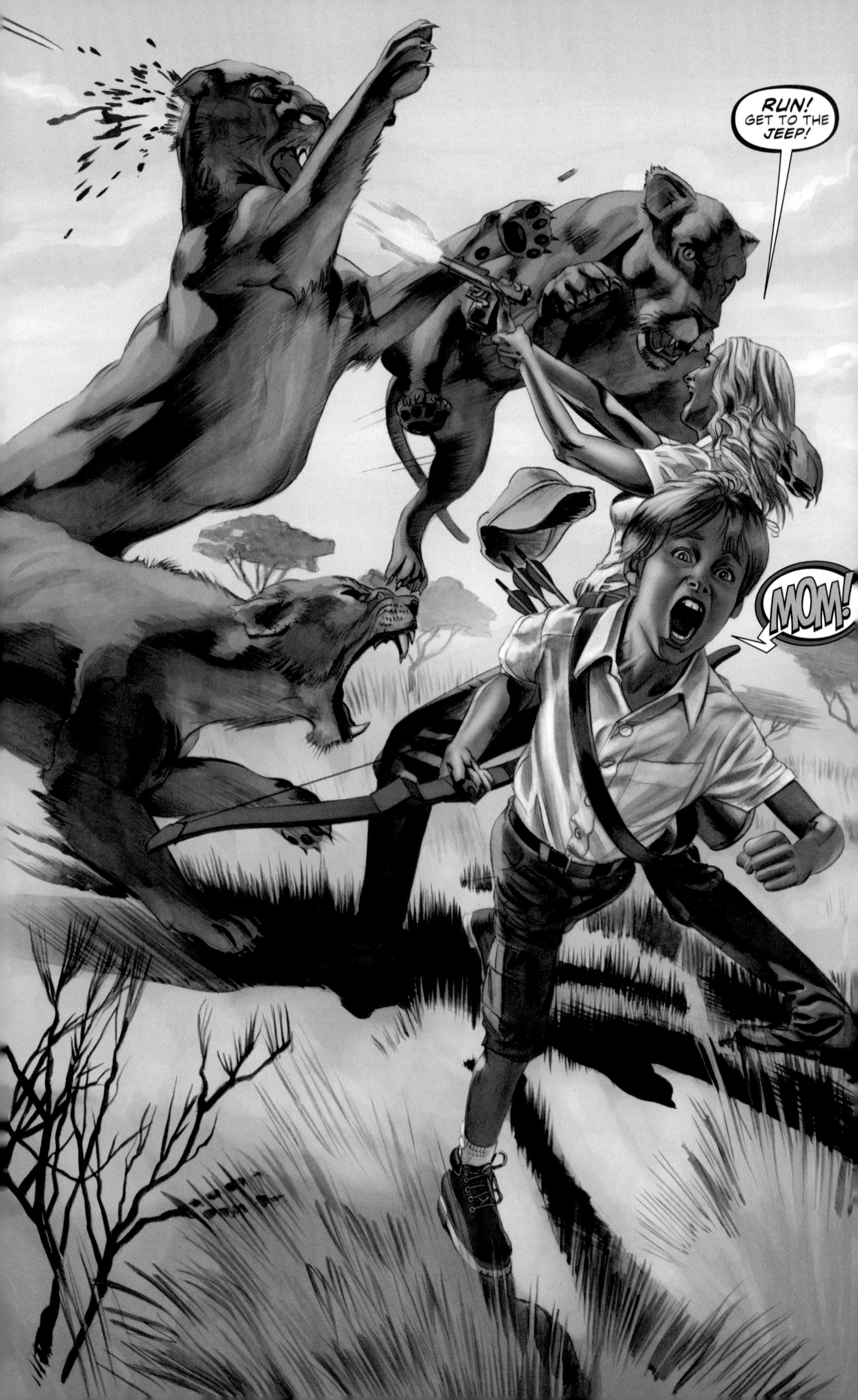
RUN! GET TO THE JEEP!
MOM!

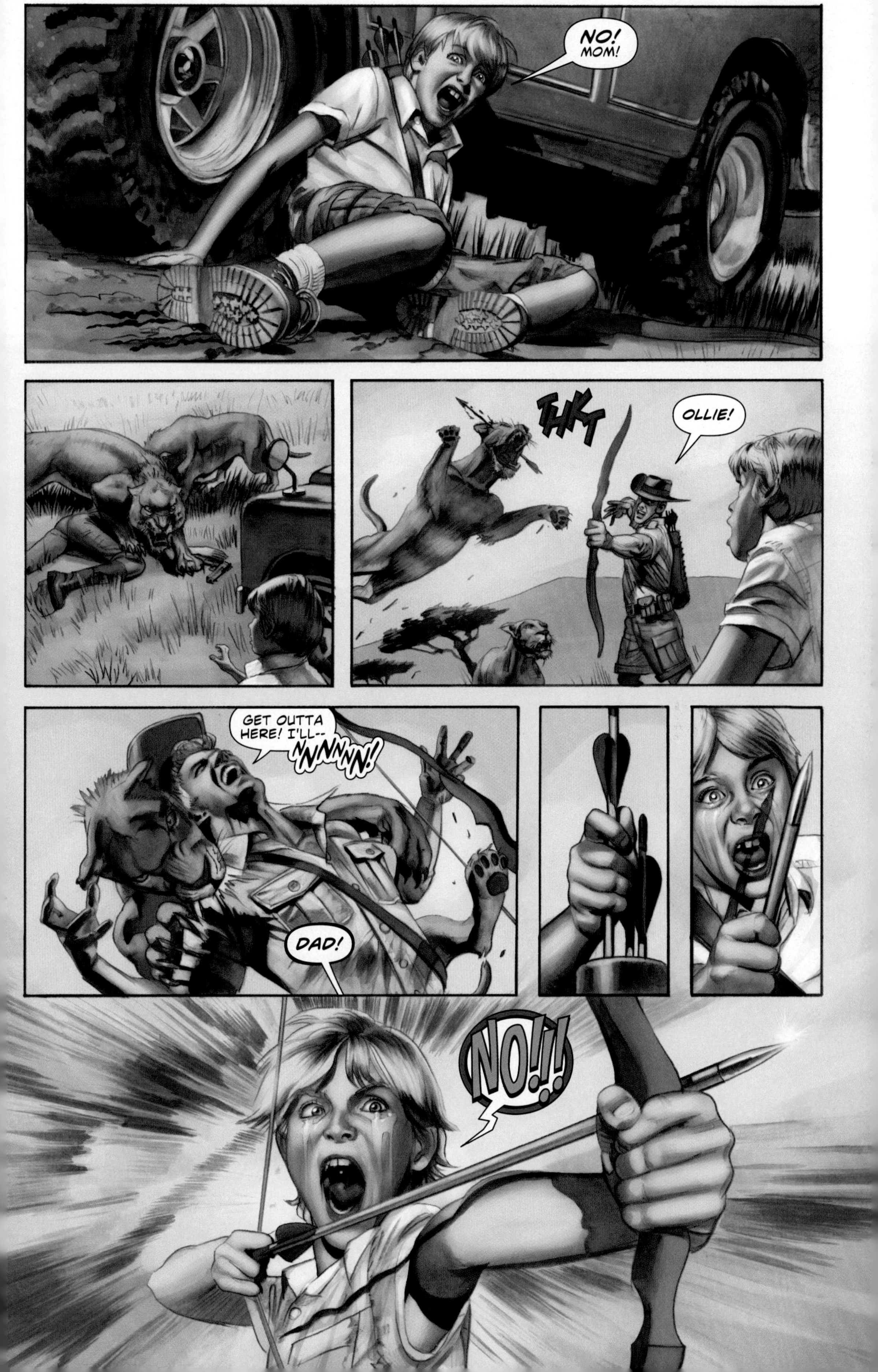
NO! MOM!
THKT
OLLIE!
GET OUTTA HERE! I'LL-- NNNNNN!
DAD!
NO!!!

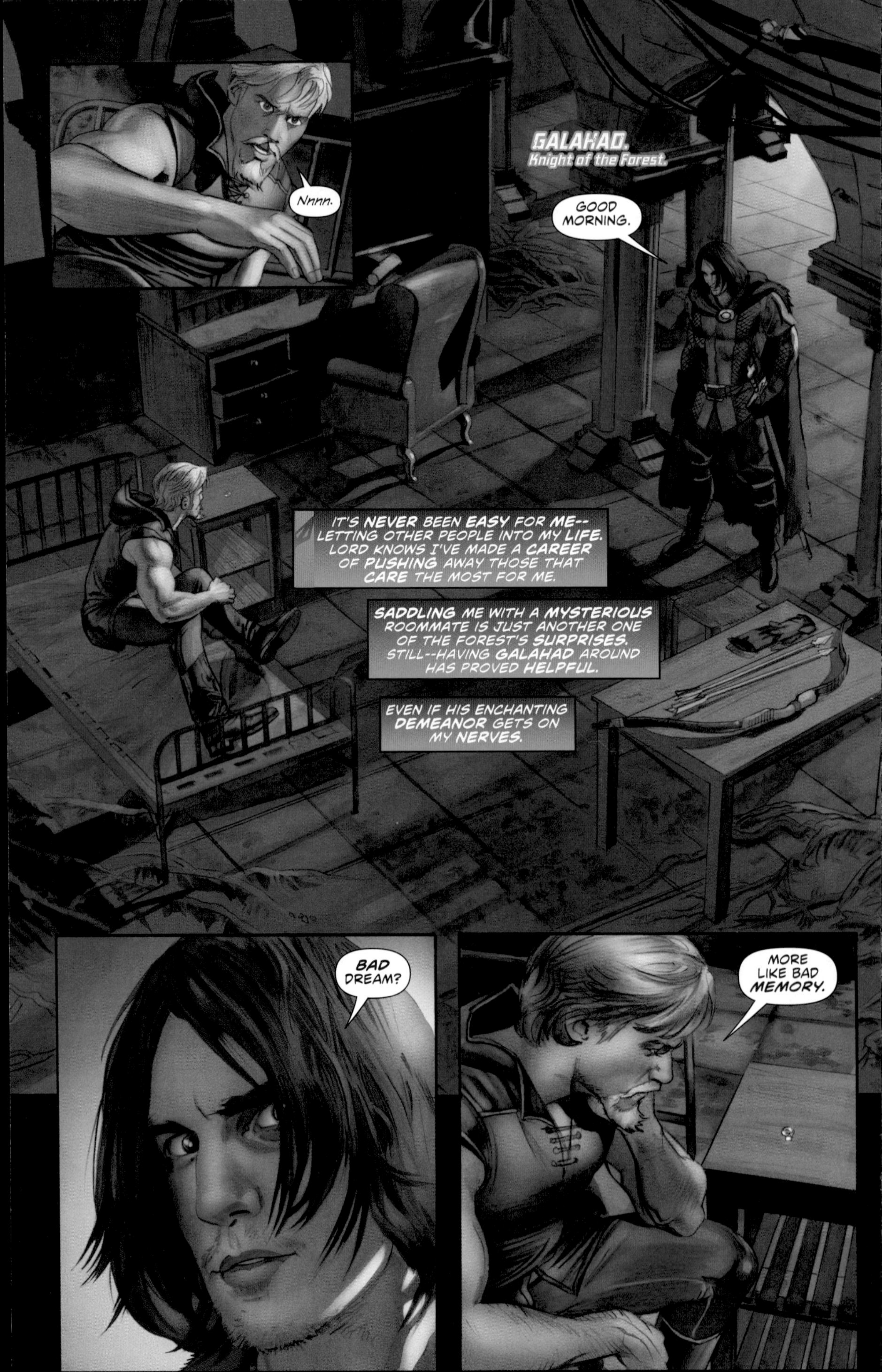
Nnnn.
GALAHAD.
Knight of the Forest.
GOOD MORNING.
IT'S NEVER BEEN EASY FOR ME--LETTING OTHER PEOPLE INTO MY LIFE. LORD KNOWS I'VE MADE A CAREER OF PUSHING AWAY THOSE THAT CARE THE MOST FOR ME.
SADDLING ME WITH A MYSTERIOUS ROOMMATE IS JUST ANOTHER ONE OF THE FOREST'S SURPRISES. STILL--HAVING GALAHAD AROUND HAS PROVED HELPFUL.
EVEN IF HIS ENCHANTING DEMEANOR GETS ON MY NERVES.
BAD DREAM?
MORE LIKE BAD MEMORY.

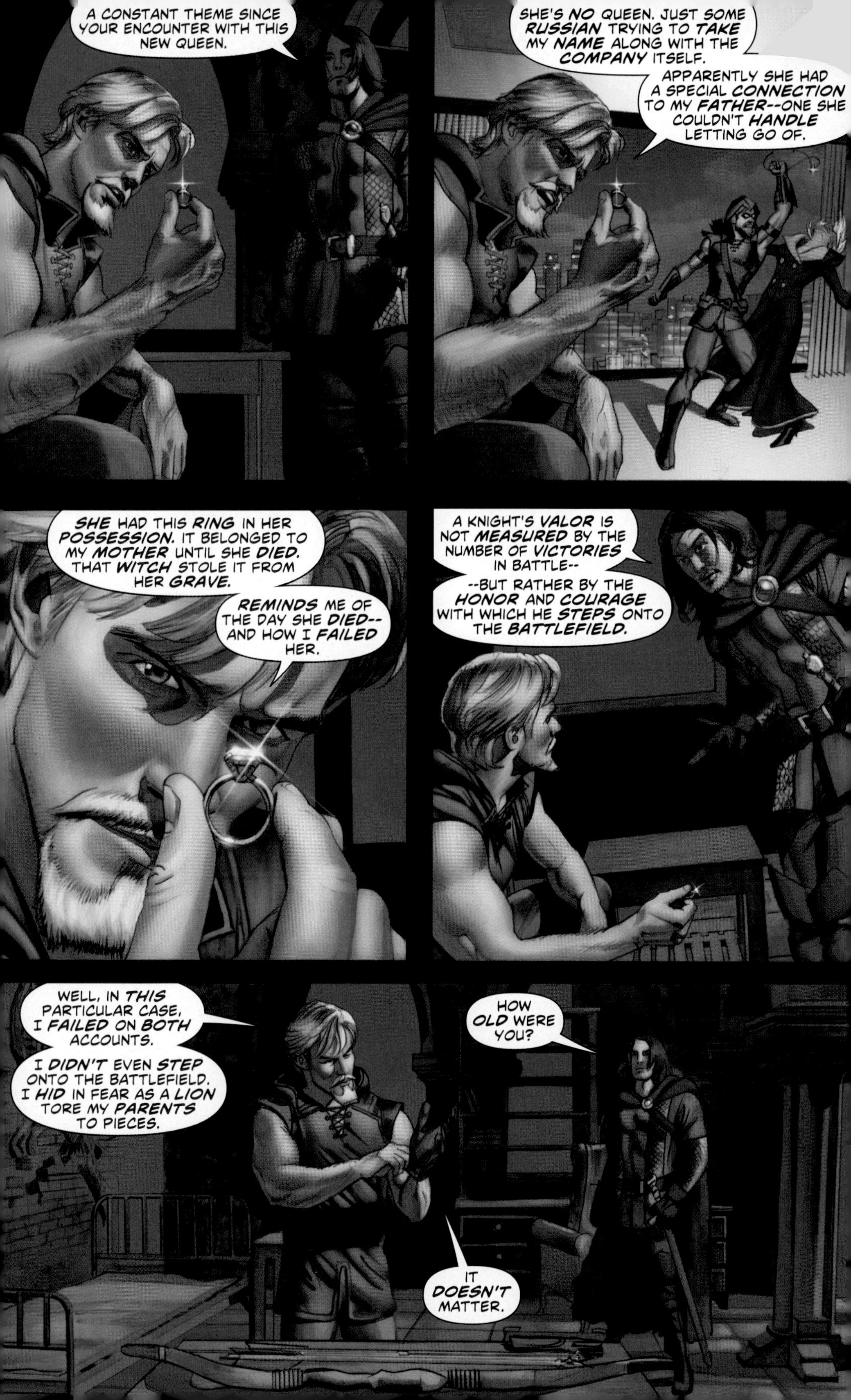
A CONSTANT THEME SINCE YOUR ENCOUNTER WITH THIS NEW QUEEN.
SHE'S NO QUEEN. JUST SOME RUSSIAN TRYING TO TAKE MY NAME ALONG WITH THE COMPANY ITSELF.
APPARENTLY SHE HAD A SPECIAL CONNECTION TO MY FATHER--ONE SHE COULDN'T HANDLE LETTING GO OF.
SHE HAD THIS RING IN HER POSSESSION. IT BELONGED TO MY MOTHER UNTIL SHE DIED. THAT WITCH STOLE IT FROM HER GRAVE.
REMINDS ME OF THE DAY SHE DIED-- AND HOW I FAILED HER.
A KNIGHT'S VALOR IS NOT MEASURED BY THE NUMBER OF VICTORIES IN BATTLE--
--BUT RATHER BY THE HONOR AND COURAGE WITH WHICH HE STEPS ONTO THE BATTLEFIELD.
WELL, IN THIS PARTICULAR CASE, I FAILED ON BOTH ACCOUNTS.
I DIDN'T EVEN STEP ONTO THE BATTLEFIELD. I HID IN FEAR AS A LION TORE MY PARENTS TO PIECES.
HOW OLD WERE YOU?
IT DOESN'T MATTER.

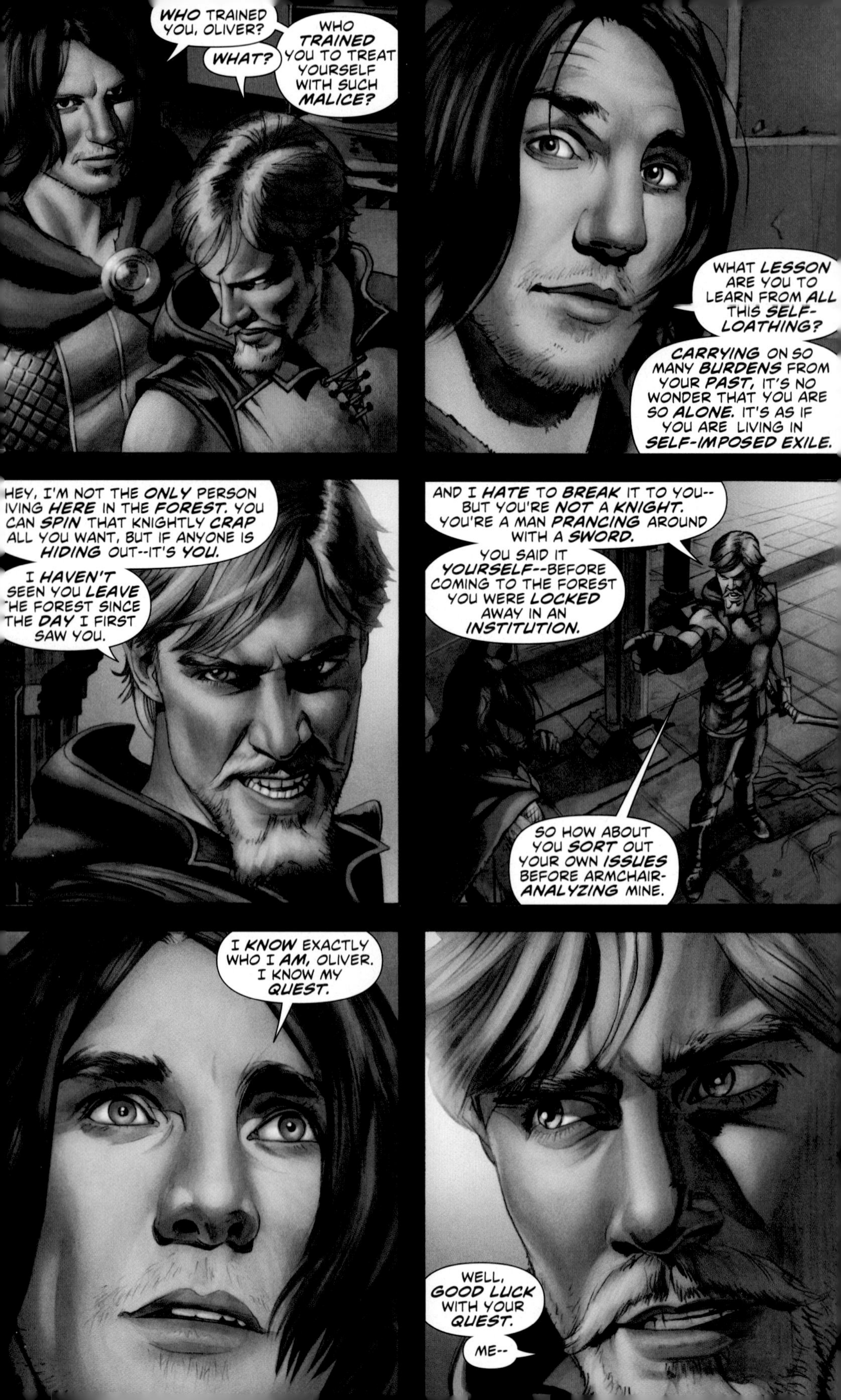
WHO TRAINED YOU, OLIVER?
WHAT?
WHO TRAINED YOU TO TREAT YOURSELF WITH SUCH MALICE?
WHAT LESSON ARE YOU TO LEARN FROM ALL THIS SELF-LOATHING?
CARRYING ON SO MANY BURDENS FROM YOUR PAST, IT'S NO WONDER THAT YOU ARE SO ALONE. IT'S AS IF YOU ARE LIVING IN SELF-IMPOSED EXILE.
HEY, I'M NOT THE ONLY PERSON LIVING HERE IN THE FOREST. YOU CAN SPIN THAT KNIGHTLY CRAP ALL YOU WANT, BUT IF ANYONE IS HIDING OUT--IT'S YOU.
I HAVEN'T SEEN YOU LEAVE THE FOREST SINCE THE DAY I FIRST SAW YOU.
AND I HATE TO BREAK IT TO YOU-- BUT YOU'RE NOT A KNIGHT. YOU'RE A MAN PRANCING AROUND WITH A SWORD.
YOU SAID IT YOURSELF--BEFORE COMING TO THE FOREST YOU WERE LOCKED AWAY IN AN INSTITUTION.
SO HOW ABOUT YOU SORT OUT YOUR OWN ISSUES BEFORE ARMCHAIR-ANALYZING MINE.
I KNOW EXACTLY WHO I AM, OLIVER. I KNOW MY QUEST.
WELL, GOOD LUCK WITH YOUR QUEST.
ME--

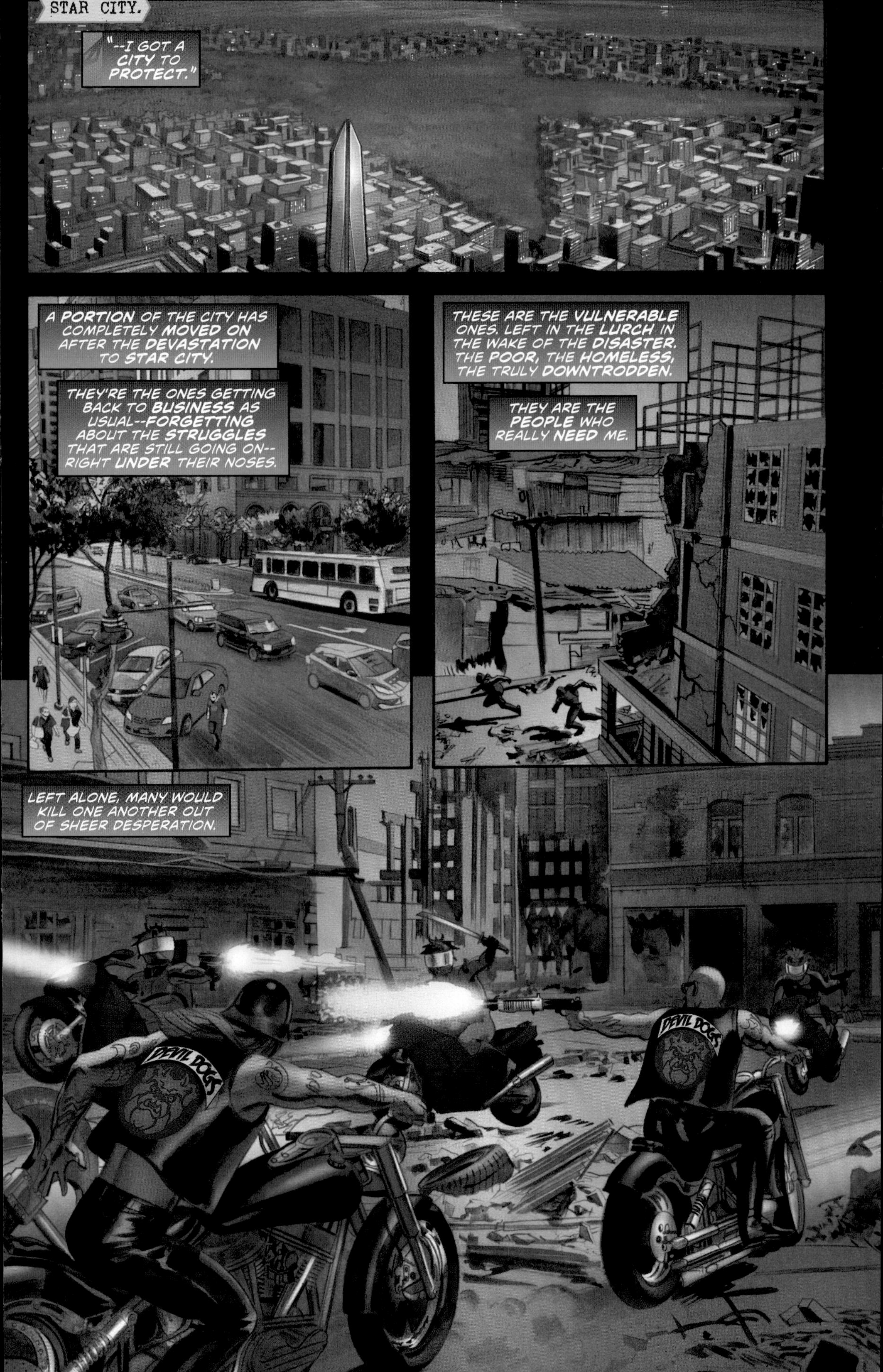
STAR CITY.
"--I GOT A CITY TO PROTECT."
A PORTION OF THE CITY HAS COMPLETELY MOVED ON AFTER THE DEVASTATION TO STAR CITY.
THEY'RE THE ONES GETTING BACK TO BUSINESS AS USUAL--FORGETTING ABOUT THE STRUGGLES THAT ARE STILL GOING ON--RIGHT UNDER THEIR NOSES.
THESE ARE THE VULNERABLE ONES. LEFT IN THE LURCH IN THE WAKE OF THE DISASTER. THE POOR, THE HOMELESS, THE TRULY DOWNTRODDEN.
THEY ARE THE PEOPLE WHO REALLY NEED ME.
LEFT ALONE, MANY WOULD KILL ONE ANOTHER OUT OF SHEER DESPERATION.
DEVIL DOGS
DEVIL DOGS

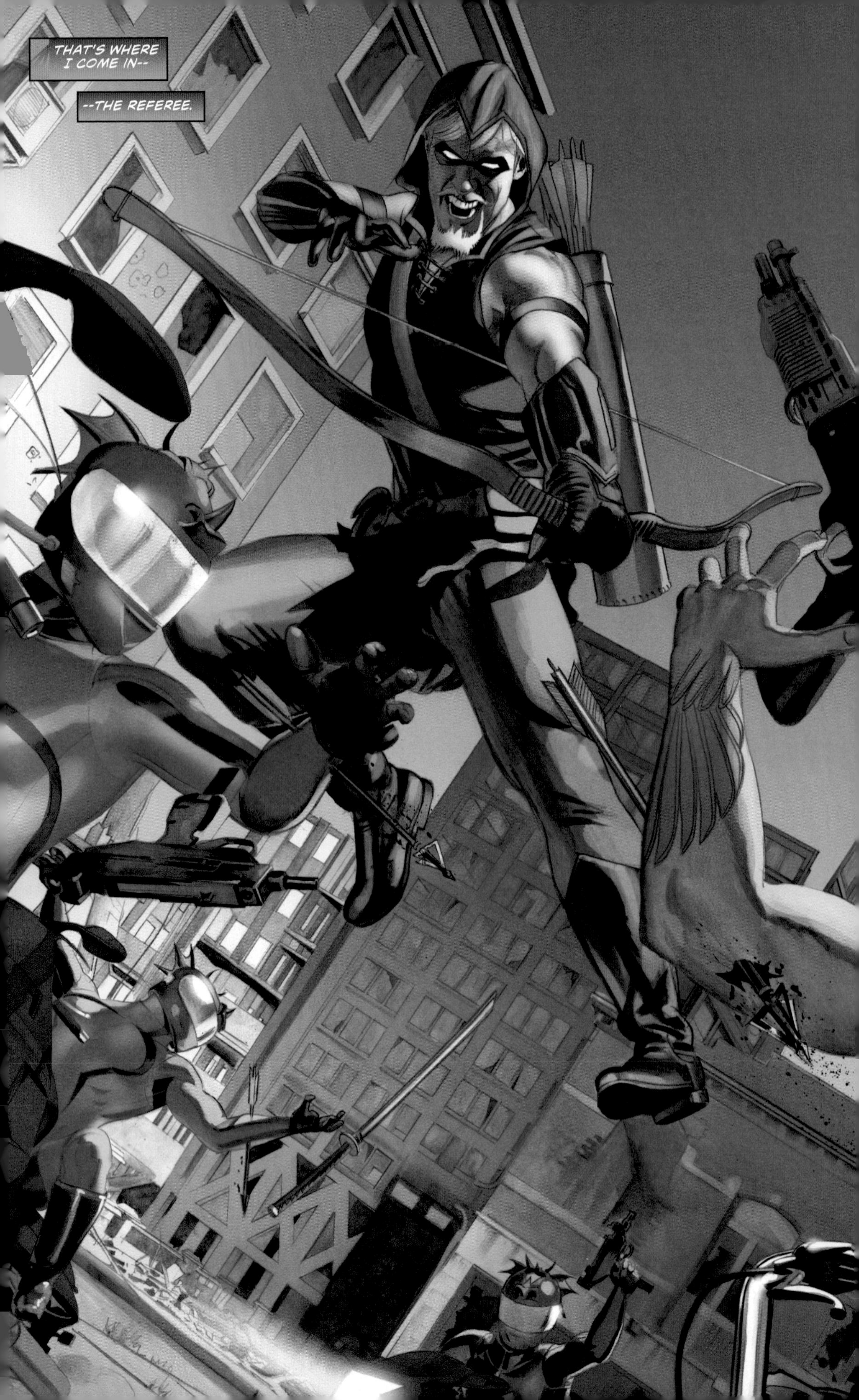
THAT'S WHERE I COME IN--
--THE REFEREE.

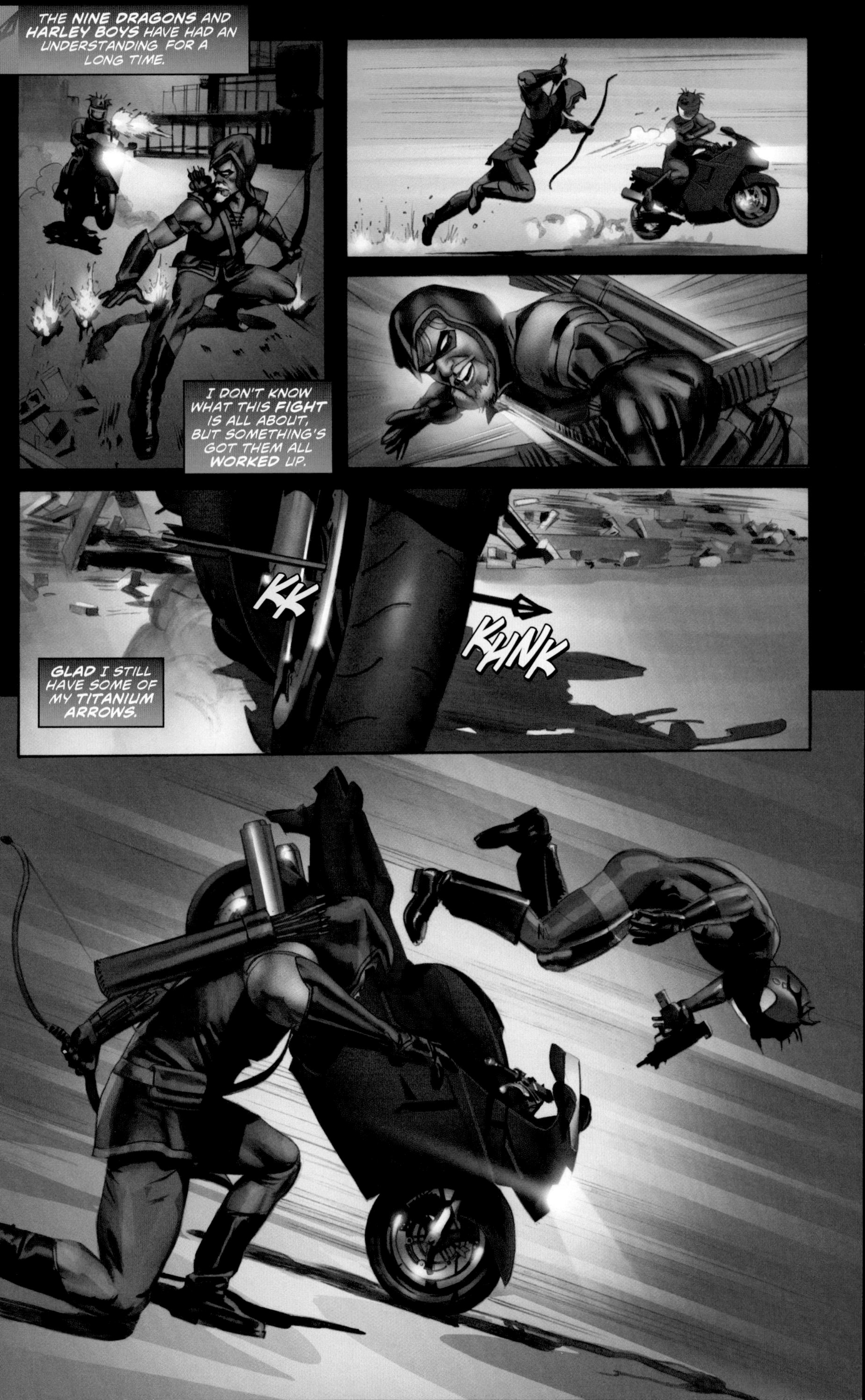
THE NINE DRAGONS AND HARLEY BOYS HAVE HAD AN UNDERSTANDING FOR A LONG TIME.
I DON'T KNOW WHAT THIS FIGHT IS ALL ABOUT, BUT SOMETHING'S GOT THEM ALL WORKED UP.
KK
KHNK
GLAD I STILL HAVE SOME OF MY TITANIUM ARROWS.

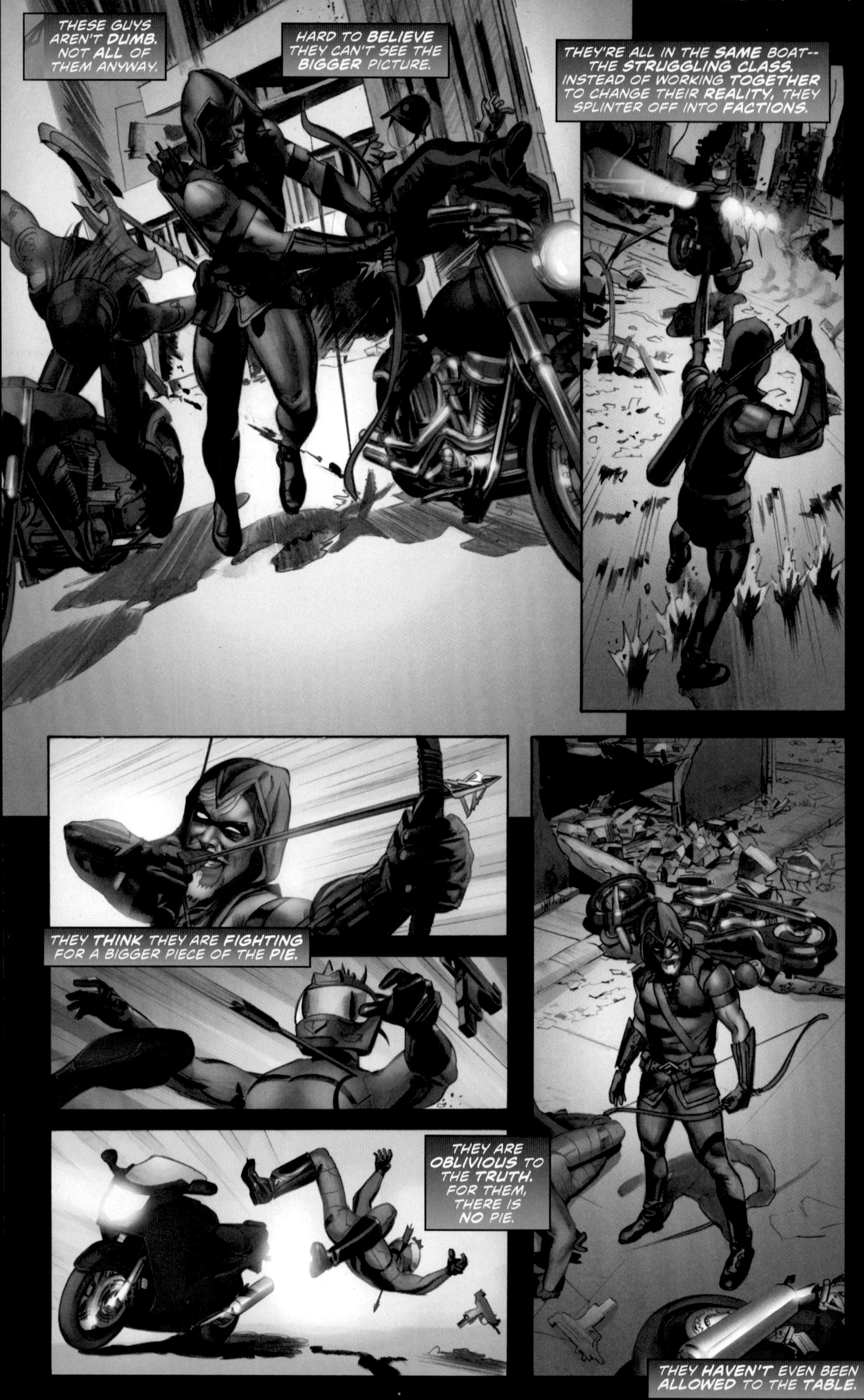
THESE GUYS AREN'T DUMB. NOT ALL OF THEM ANYWAY.
HARD TO BELIEVE THEY CAN'T SEE THE BIGGER PICTURE.
THEY'RE ALL IN THE SAME BOAT-- THE STRUGGLING CLASS. INSTEAD OF WORKING TOGETHER TO CHANGE THEIR REALITY, THEY SPLINTER OFF INTO FACTIONS.
THEY THINK THEY ARE FIGHTING FOR A BIGGER PIECE OF THE PIE.
THEY ARE OBLIVIOUS TO THE TRUTH. FOR THEM, THERE IS NO PIE.
THEY HAVEN'T EVEN BEEN ALLOWED TO THE TABLE.

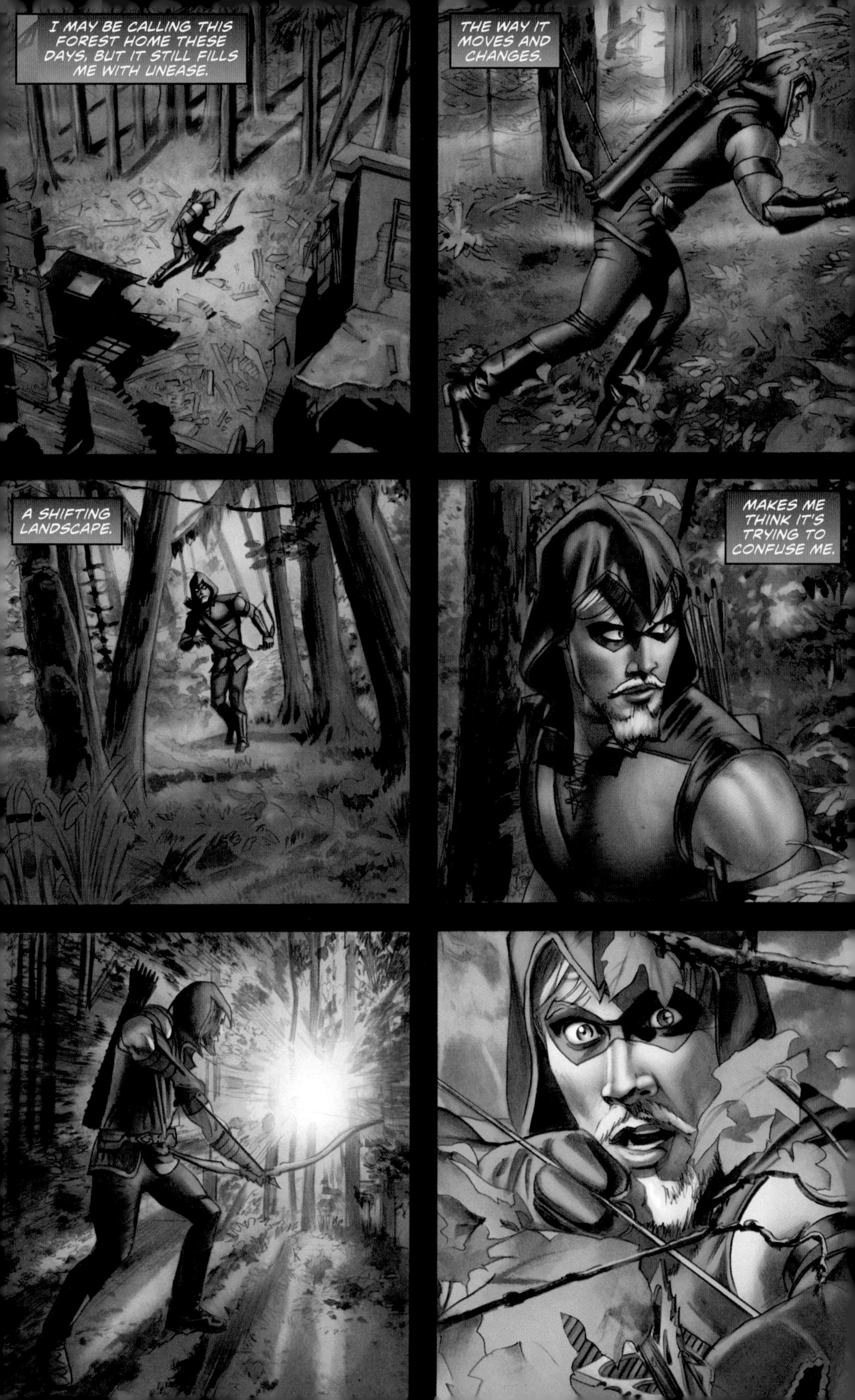
I MAY BE CALLING THIS FOREST HOME THESE DAYS, BUT IT STILL FILLS ME WITH UNEASE.
THE WAY IT MOVES AND CHANGES.
A SHIFTING LANDSCAPE.
MAKES ME THINK IT'S TRYING TO CONFUSE ME.

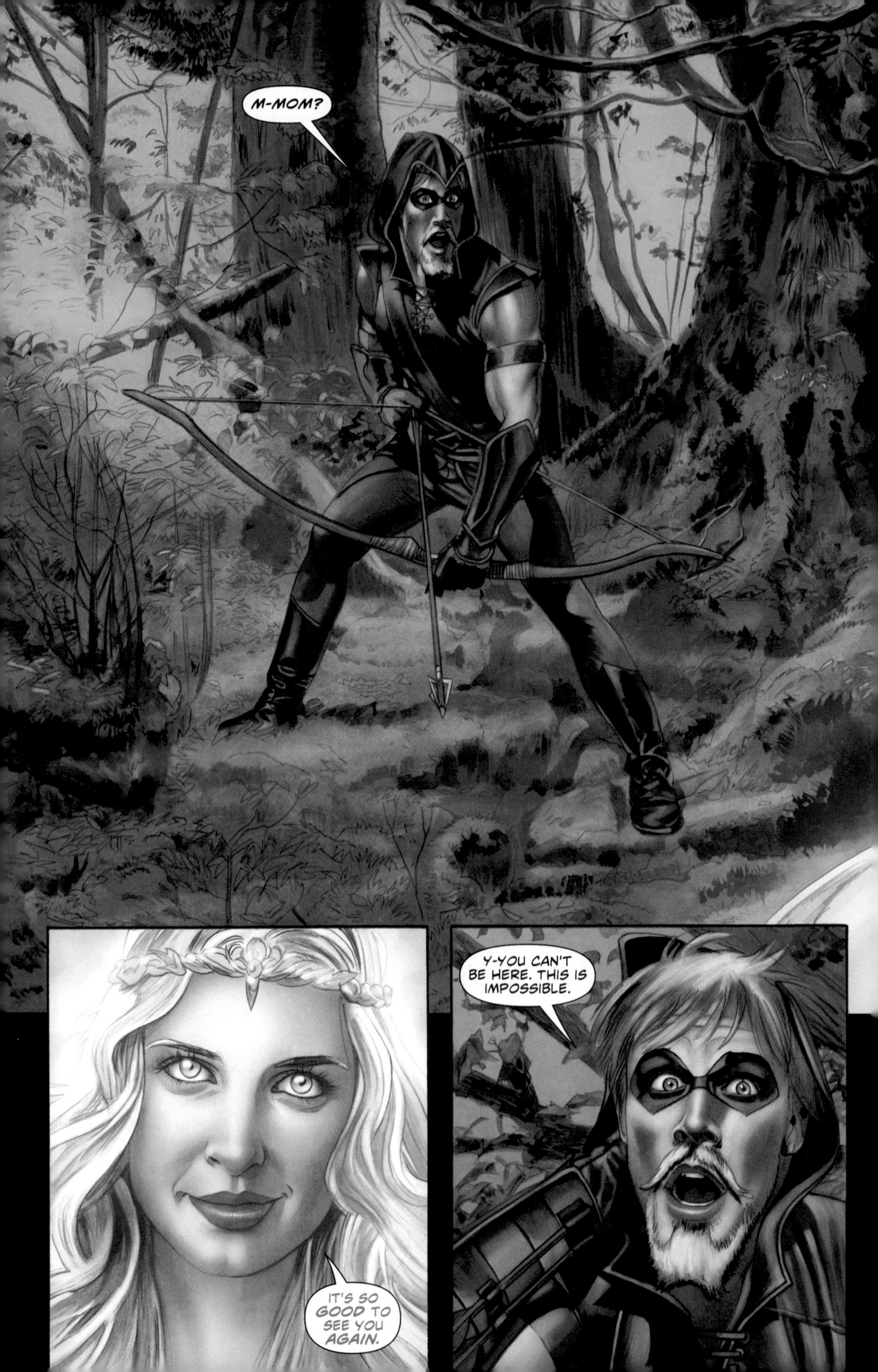
M-MOM?
IT'S SO GOOD TO SEE YOU AGAIN.
Y-YOU CAN'T BE HERE. THIS IS IMPOSSIBLE.

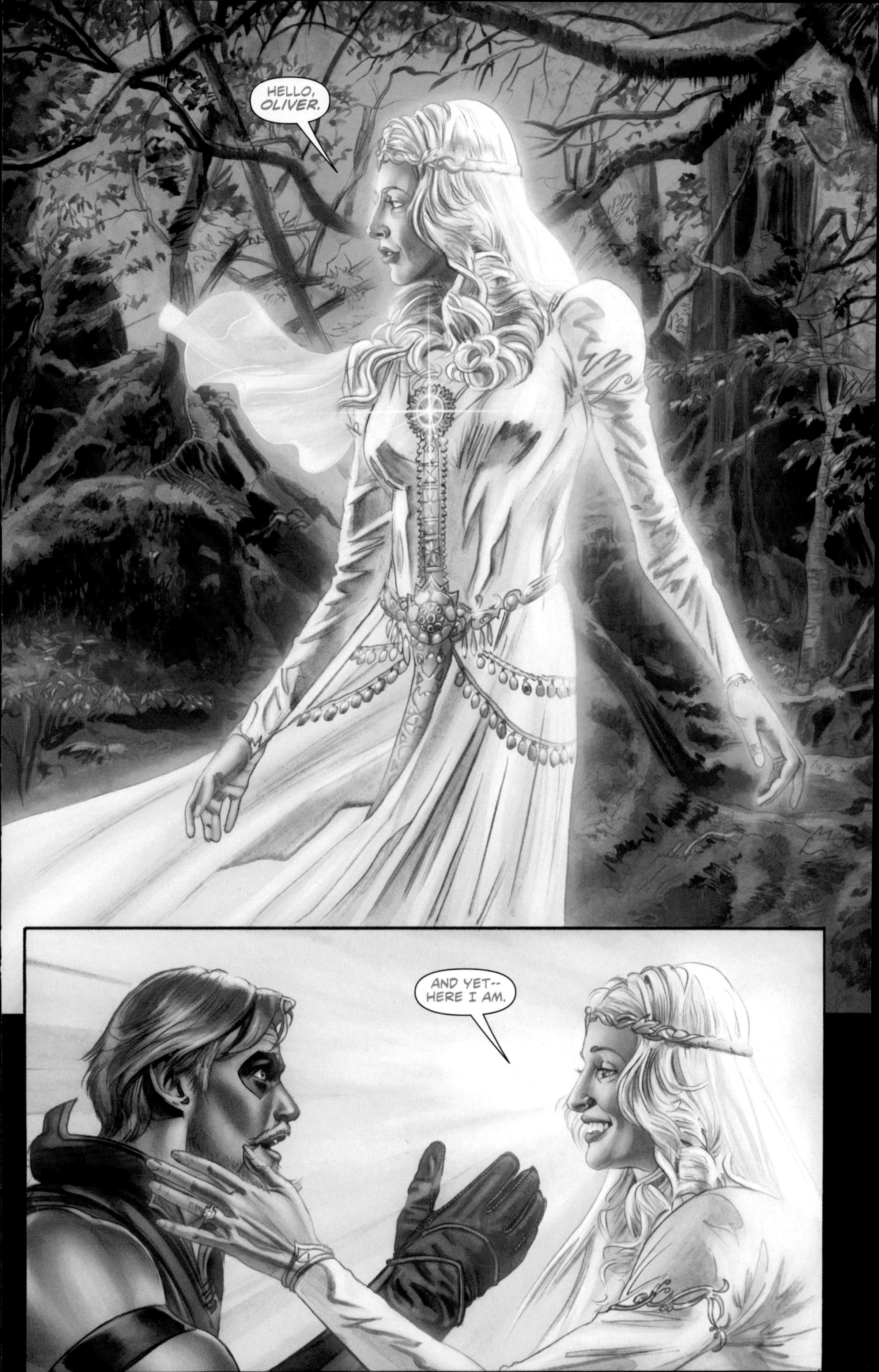
HELLO, OLIVER.
AND YET-- HERE I AM.

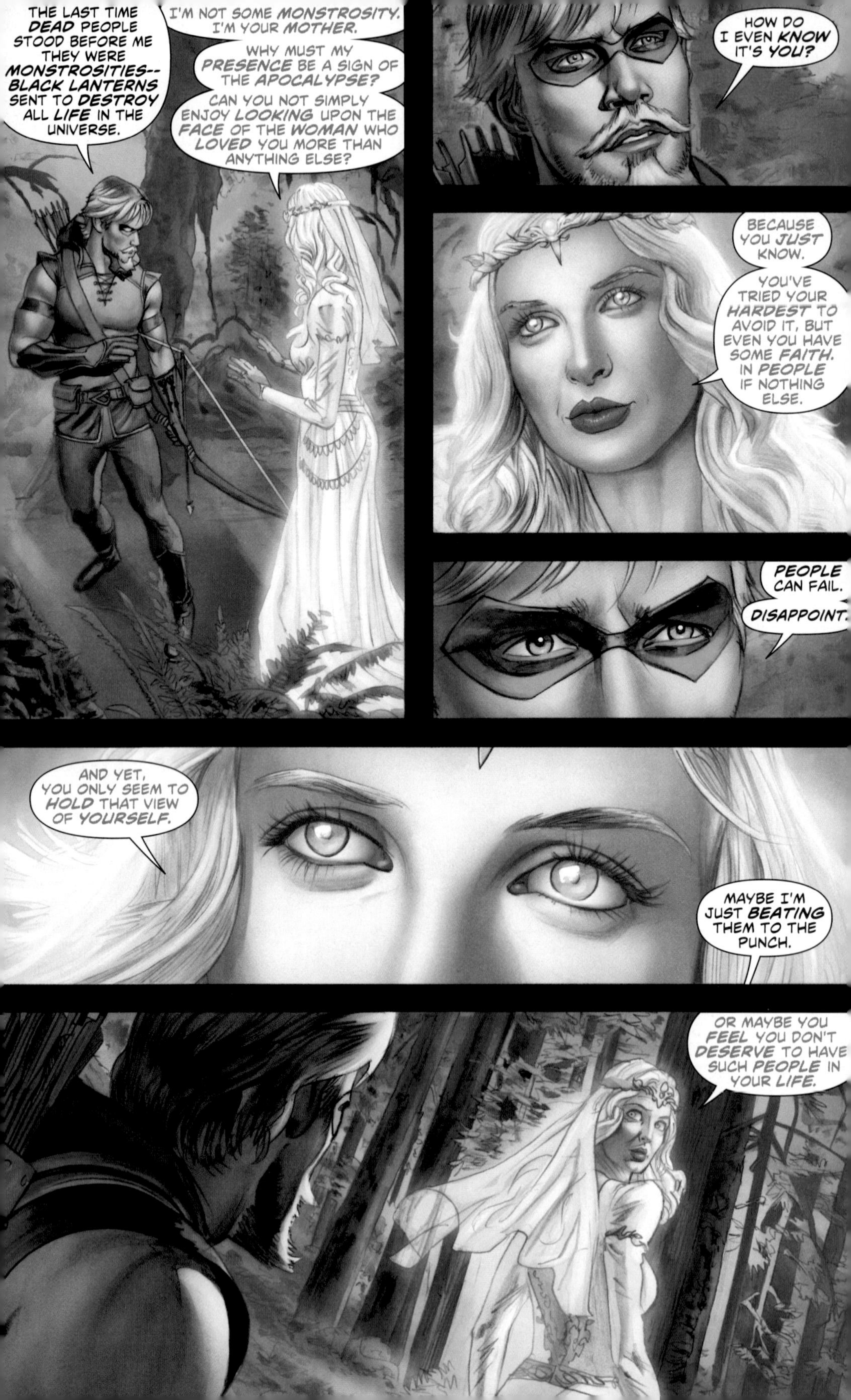
THE LAST TIME DEAD PEOPLE STOOD BEFORE ME THEY WERE MONSTROSITIES-- BLACK LANTERNS SENT TO DESTROY ALL LIFE IN THE UNIVERSE.
I'M NOT SOME MONSTROSITY. I'M YOUR MOTHER.
WHY MUST MY PRESENCE BE A SIGN OF THE APOCALYPSE?
CAN YOU NOT SIMPLY ENJOY LOOKING UPON THE FACE OF THE WOMAN WHO LOVED YOU MORE THAN ANYTHING ELSE?
HOW DO I EVEN KNOW IT'S YOU?
BECAUSE YOU JUST KNOW.
YOU'VE TRIED YOUR HARDEST TO AVOID IT, BUT EVEN YOU HAVE SOME FAITH. IN PEOPLE IF NOTHING ELSE.
PEOPLE CAN FAIL.
DISAPPOINT.
AND YET, YOU ONLY SEEM TO HOLD THAT VIEW OF YOURSELF.
MAYBE I'M JUST BEATING THEM TO THE PUNCH.
OR MAYBE YOU FEEL YOU DON'T DESERVE TO HAVE SUCH PEOPLE IN YOUR LIFE.

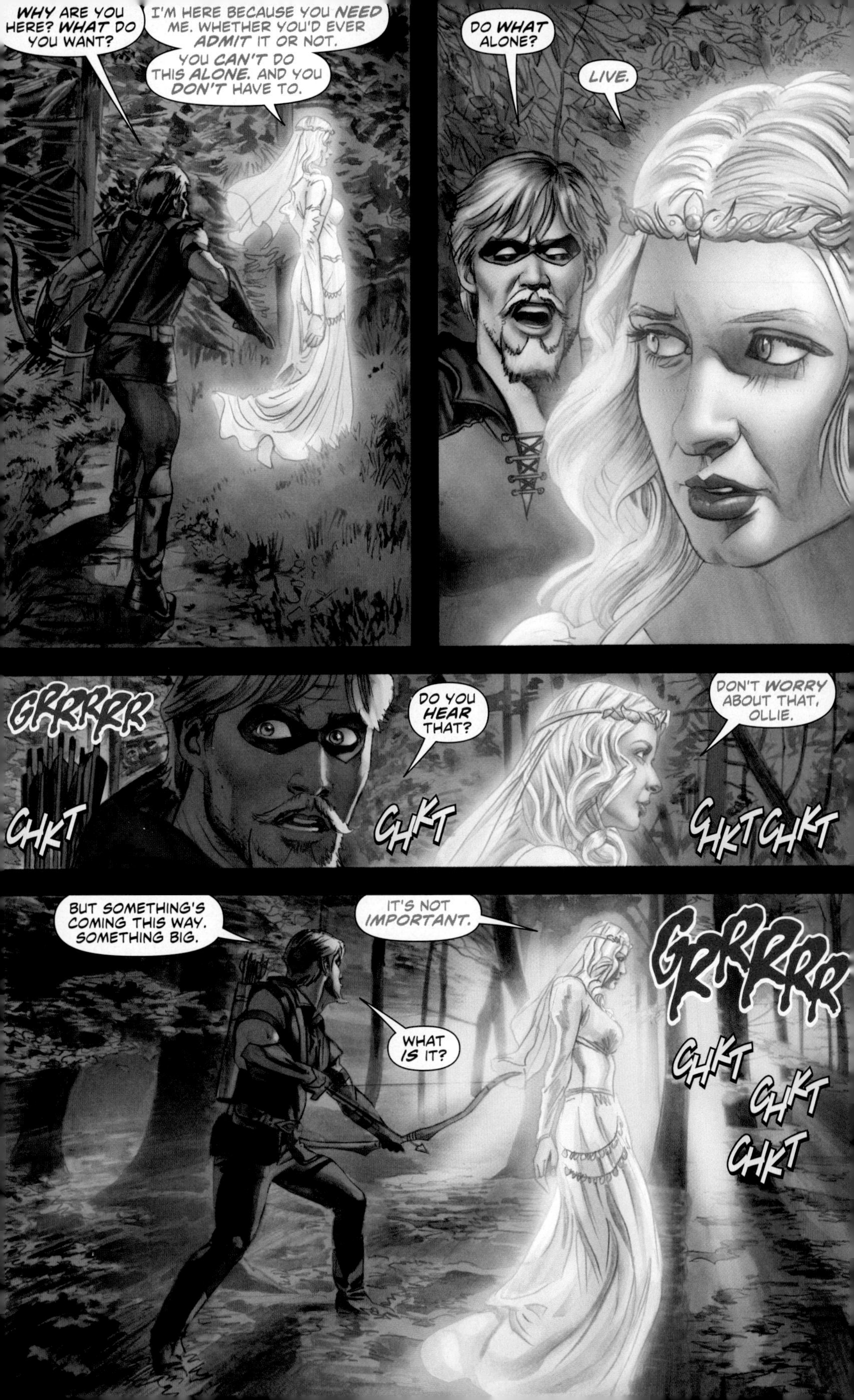
WHY ARE YOU HERE? WHAT DO YOU WANT?
I'M HERE BECAUSE YOU NEED ME. WHETHER YOU'D EVER ADMIT IT OR NOT.
YOU CAN'T DO THIS ALONE. AND YOU DON'T HAVE TO.
DO WHAT ALONE?
LIVE.
GRRRRR
CHKT
DO YOU HEAR THAT?
CHKT
DON'T WORRY ABOUT THAT, OLLIE.
CHKT CHKT
BUT SOMETHING'S COMING THIS WAY. SOMETHING BIG.
IT'S NOT IMPORTANT.
GRRRRR
WHAT IS IT?
CHKT
CHKT
CHKT

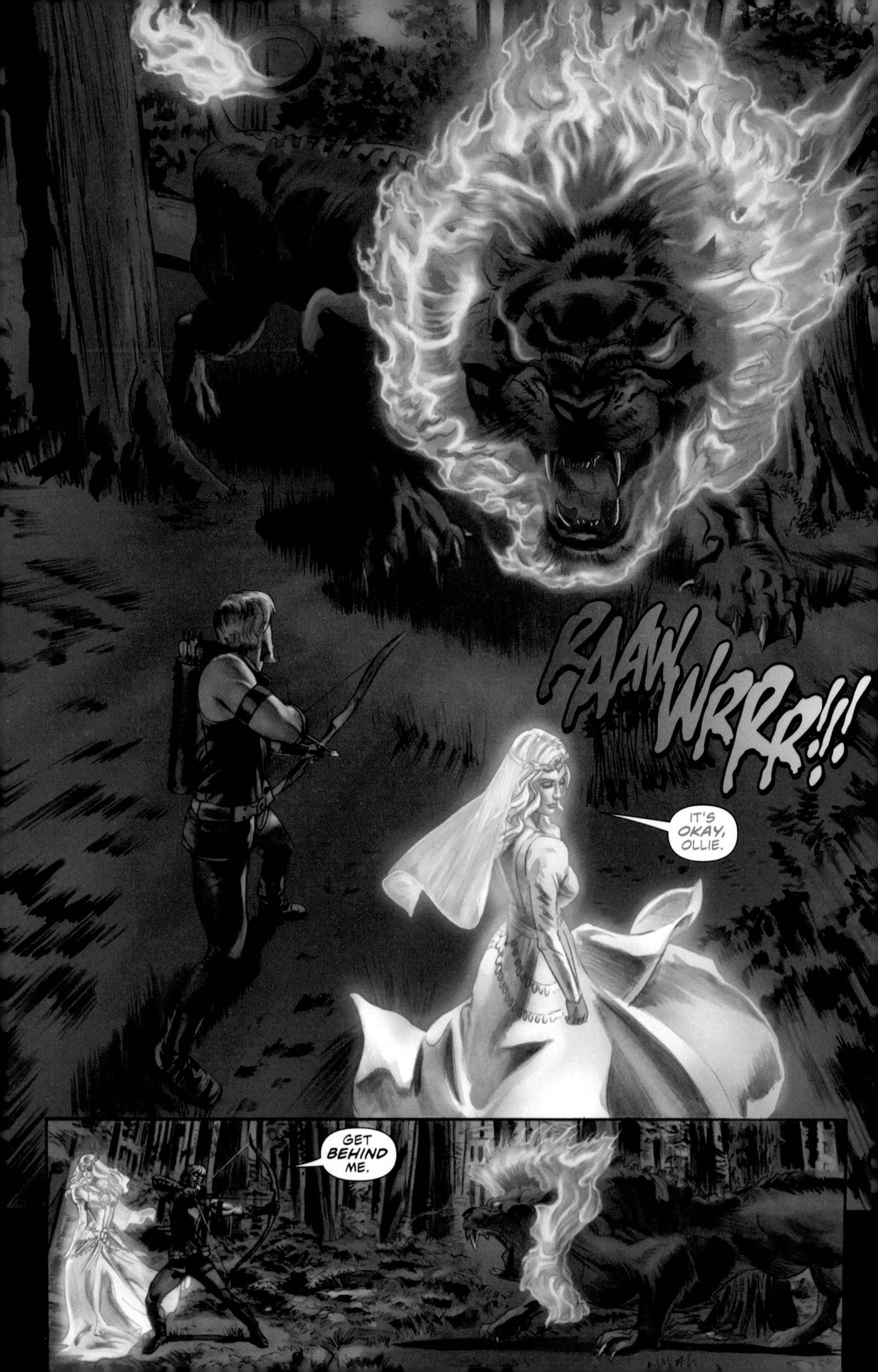
RAAWWRRR!!!
IT'S OKAY, OLLIE.
GET BEHIND ME.

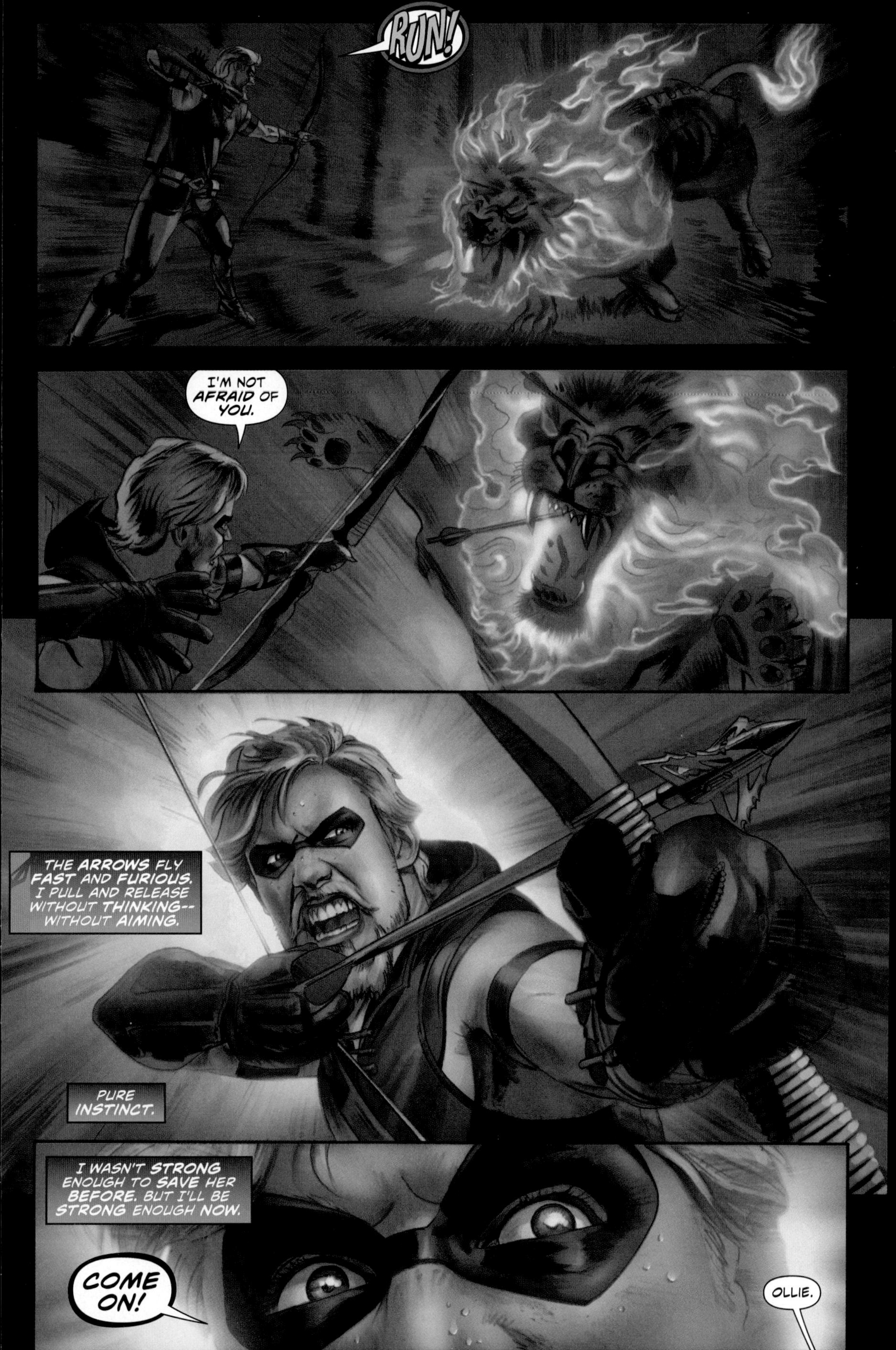
RUN!
I'M NOT AFRAID OF YOU.
THE ARROWS FLY FAST AND FURIOUS. I PULL AND RELEASE WITHOUT THINKING-- WITHOUT AIMING.
PURE INSTINCT.
I WASN'T STRONG ENOUGH TO SAVE HER BEFORE. BUT I'LL BE STRONG ENOUGH NOW.
COME ON!
OLLIE.

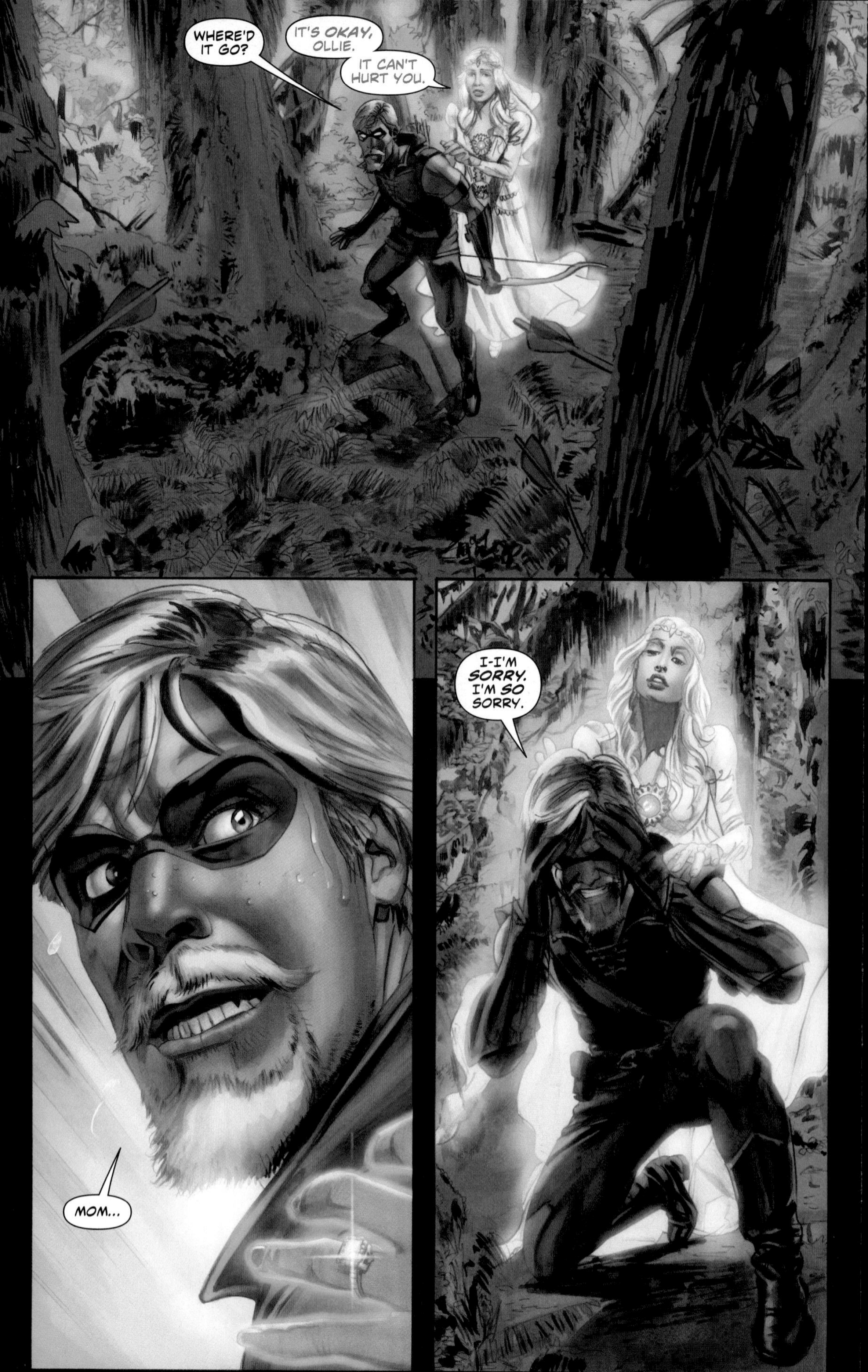

WHERE'D IT GO?
IT'S OKAY, OLLIE.
IT CAN'T HURT YOU.
MOM...
I-I'M SORRY. I'M SO SORRY.

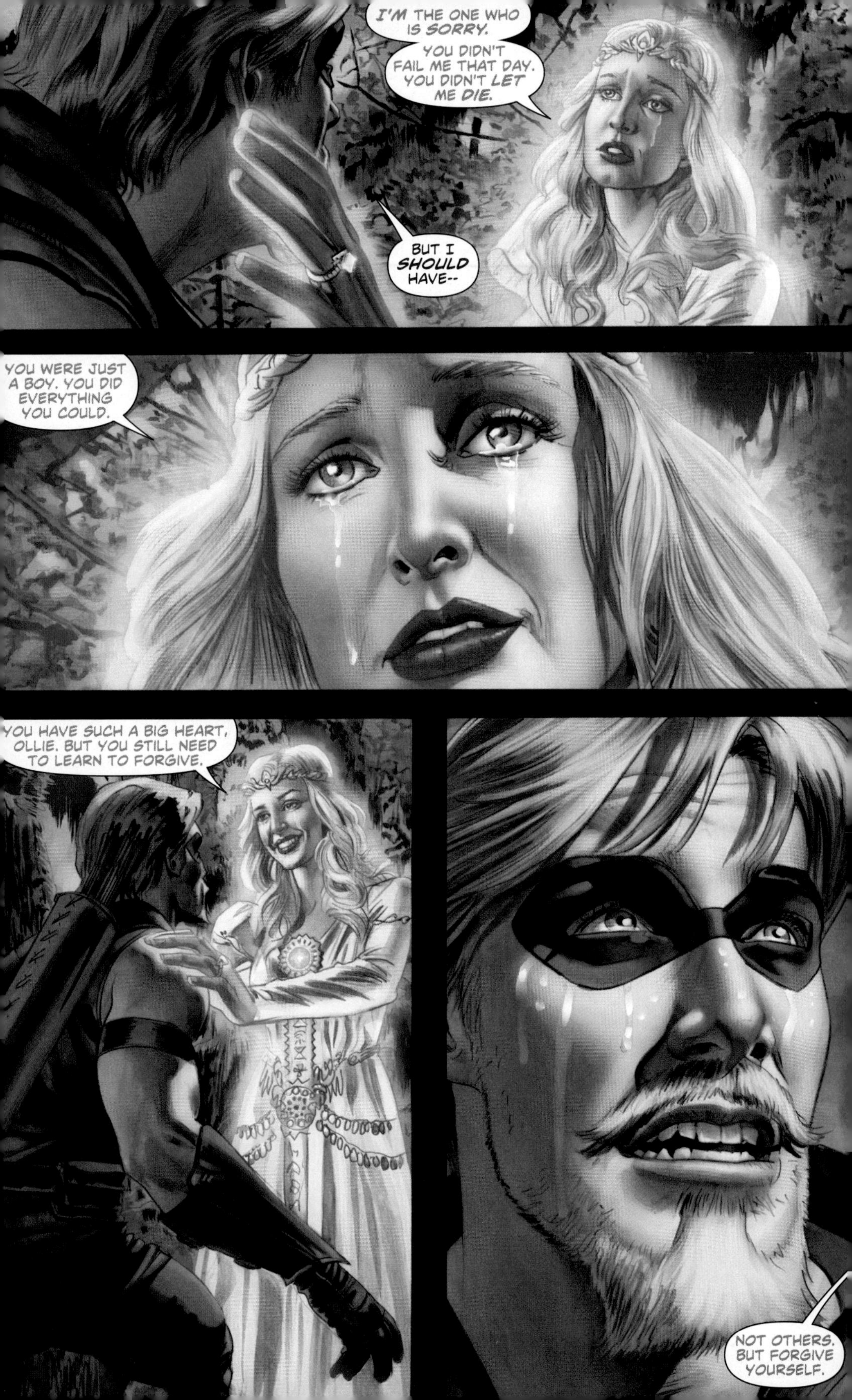
I'M THE ONE WHO IS SORRY.
YOU DIDN'T FAIL ME THAT DAY. YOU DIDN'T LET ME DIE.
BUT I SHOULD HAVE--
YOU WERE JUST A BOY. YOU DID EVERYTHING YOU COULD.
YOU HAVE SUCH A BIG HEART, OLLIE. BUT YOU STILL NEED TO LEARN TO FORGIVE.
NOT OTHERS. BUT FORGIVE YOURSELF.

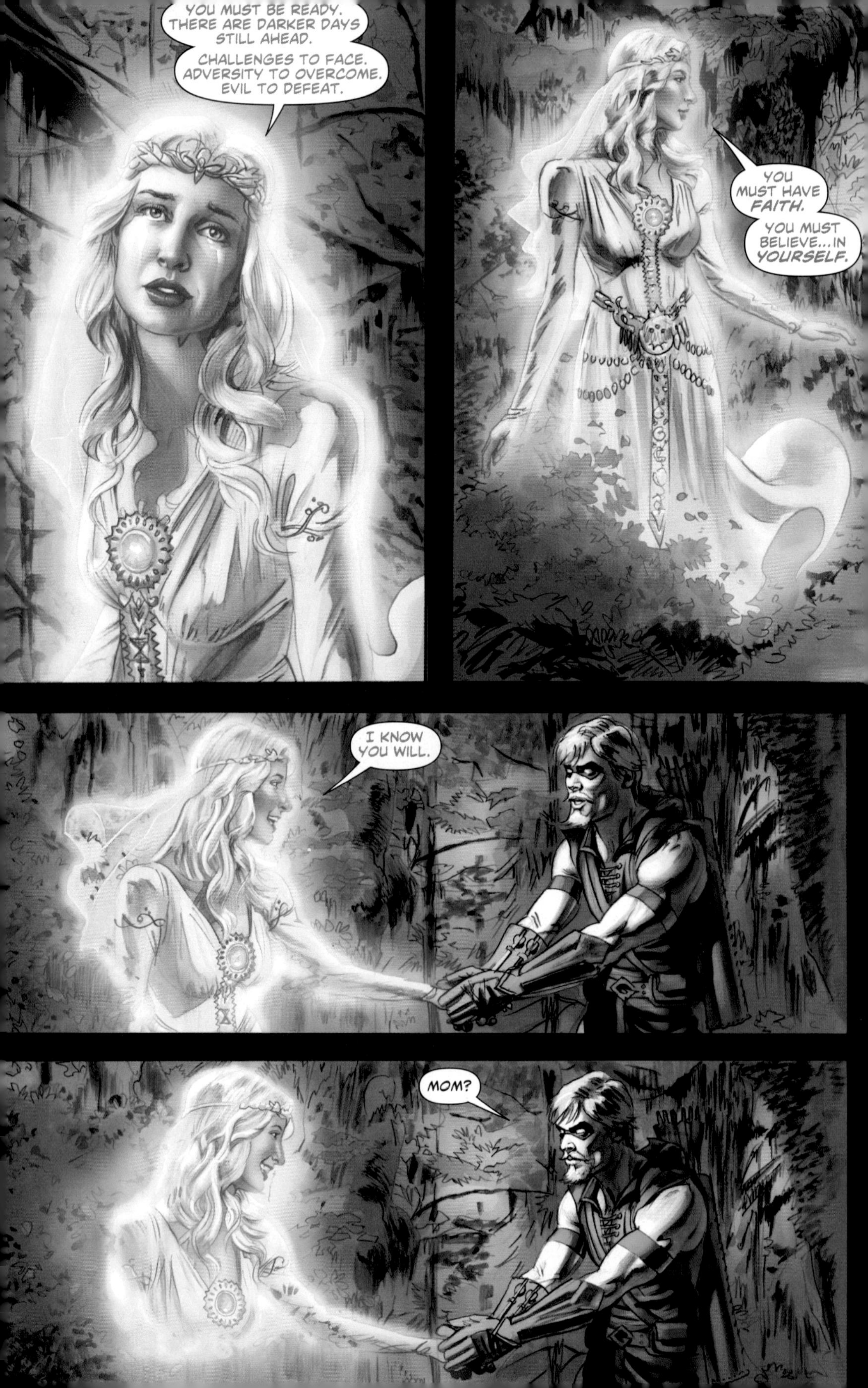
YOU MUST BE READY. THERE ARE DARKER DAYS STILL AHEAD.
CHALLENGES TO FACE. ADVERSITY TO OVERCOME. EVIL TO DEFEAT.
YOU MUST HAVE FAITH.
YOU MUST BELIEVE... IN YOURSELF.
I KNOW YOU WILL.
MOM?

I... I'LL DO MY BEST.

I LOVE YOU, OLIVER.

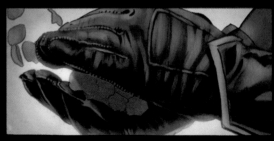

I LOVE YOU, MOM.

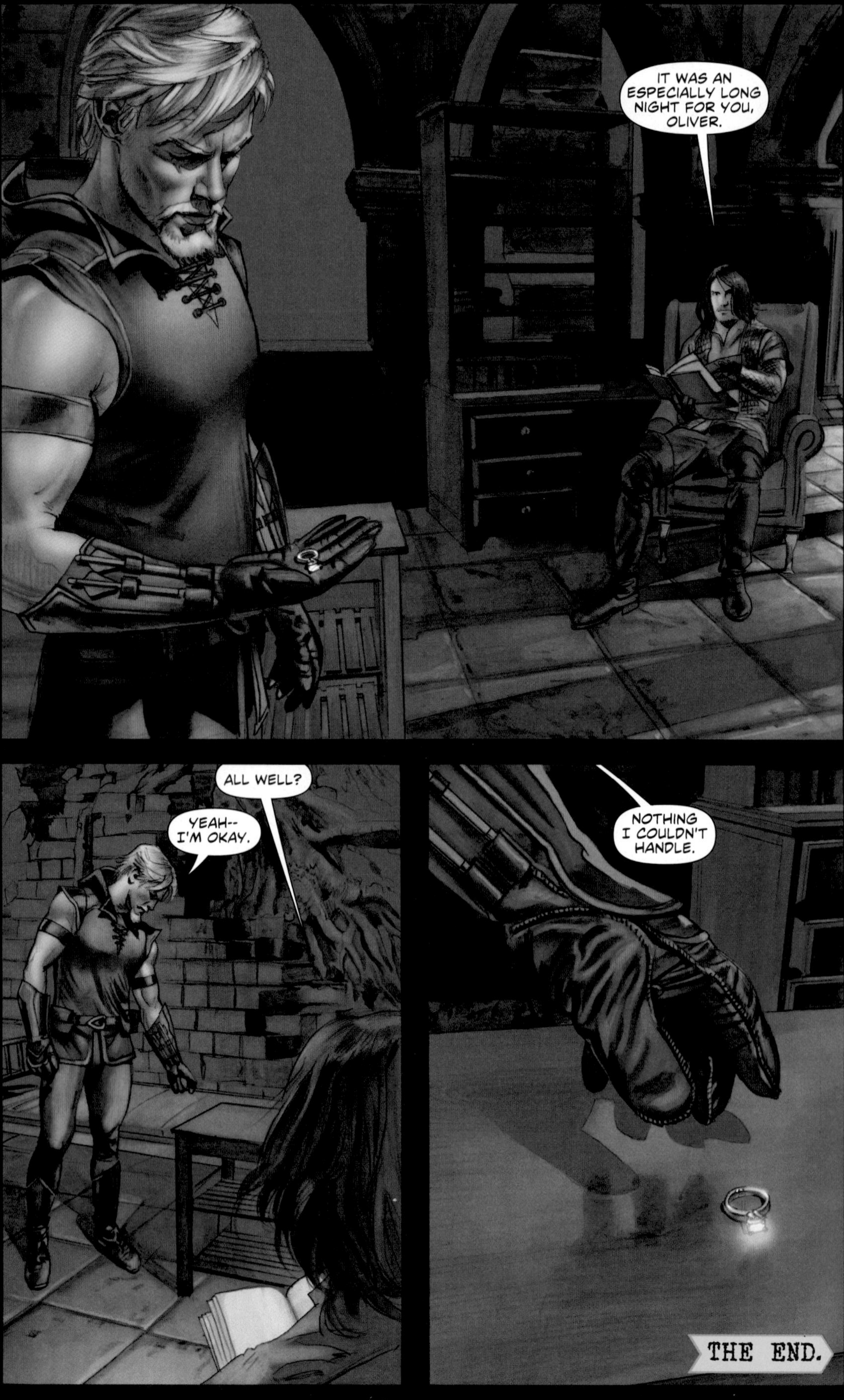
IT WAS AN ESPECIALLY LONG NIGHT FOR YOU, OLIVER.
ALL WELL?
YEAH-- I'M OKAY.
NOTHING I COULDN'T HANDLE.
THE END.

VARIANT COVER GALLERY

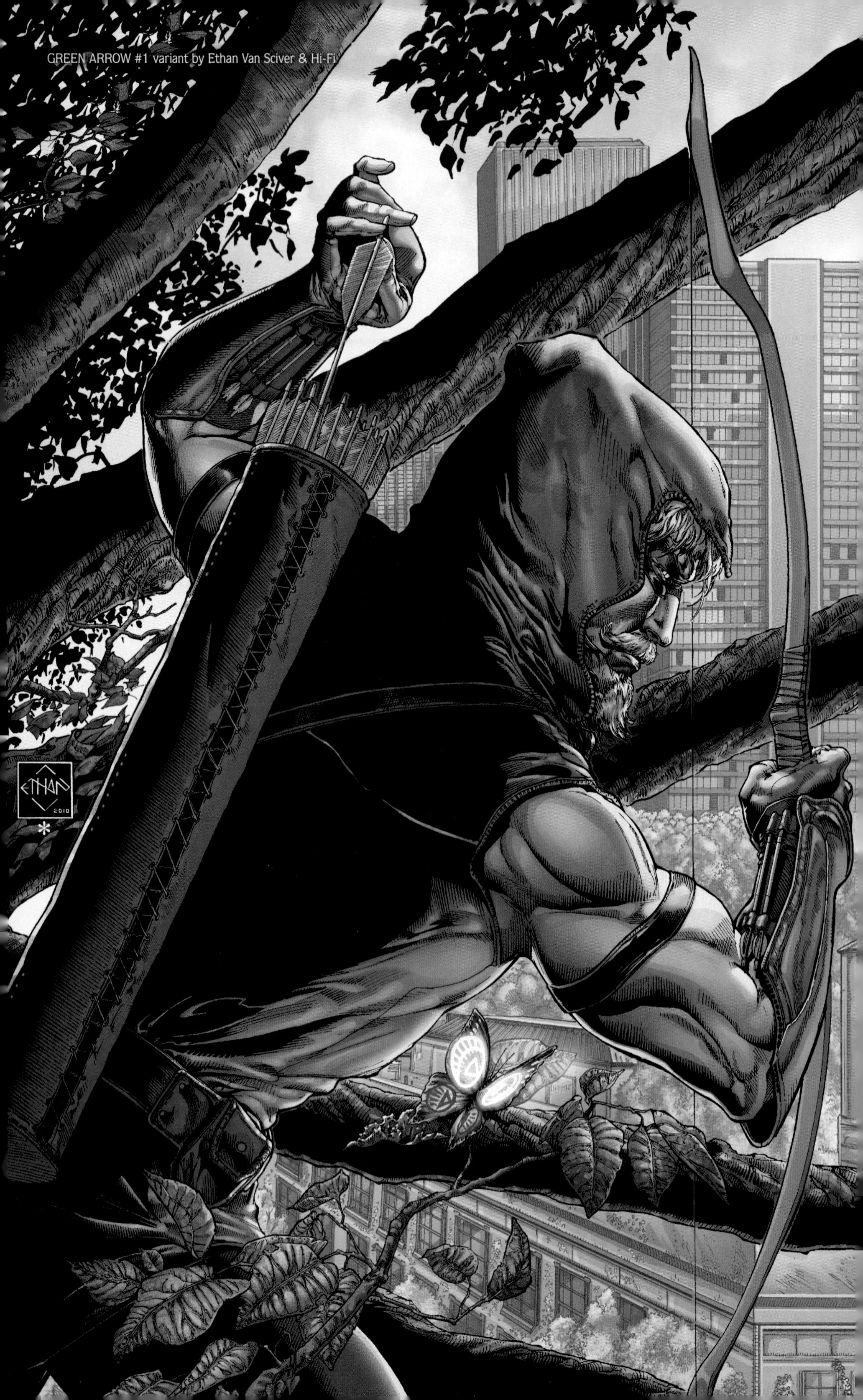
ETHAN
2010

GREEN ARROW #1 variant by Ethan Van Sciver & Hi-Fi

GREEN ARROW #4 variant by Philp Tan & Pete Pantazi

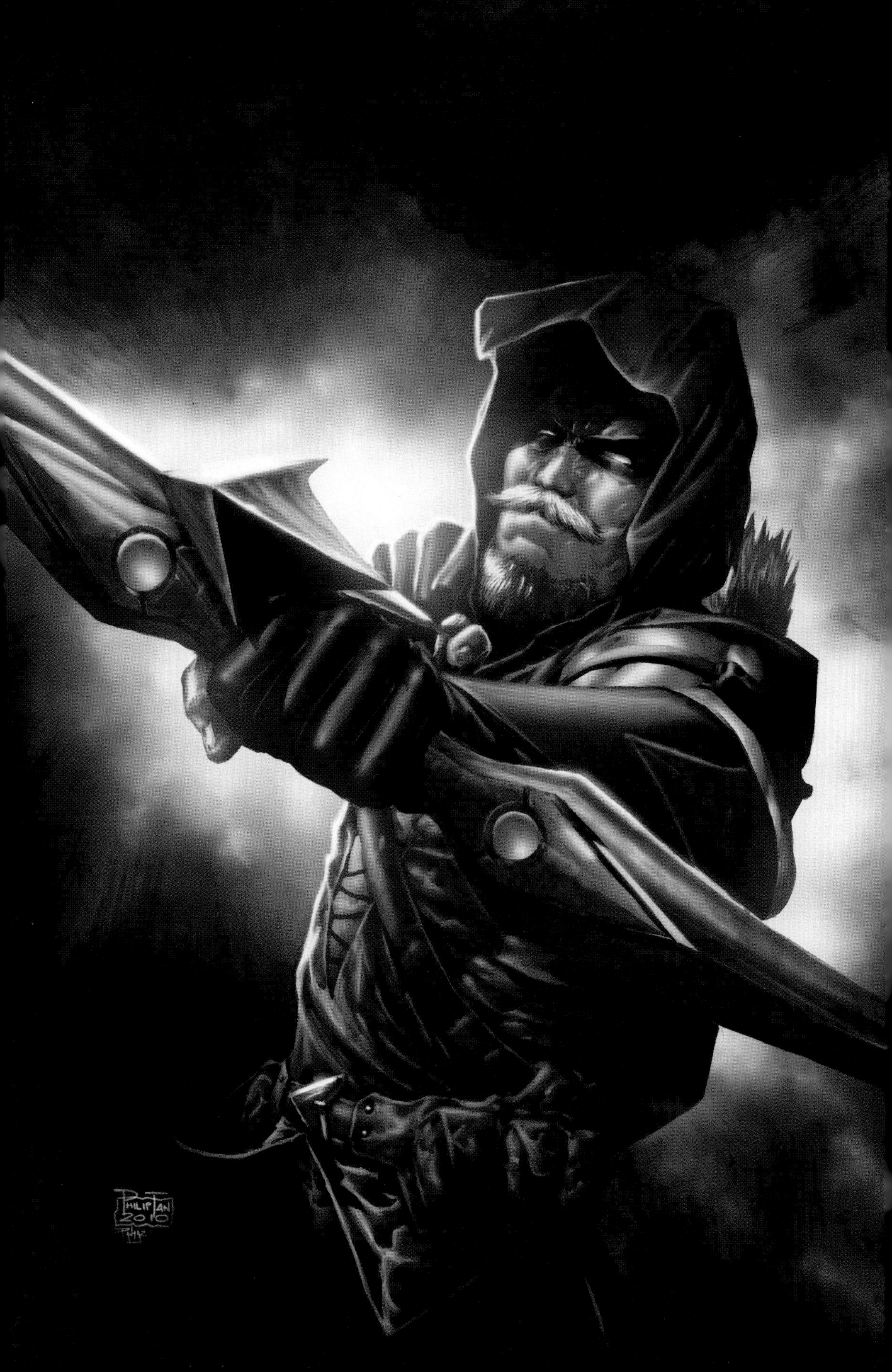

GREEN ARROW #5 variant by Gary Frank & Brad Anderson

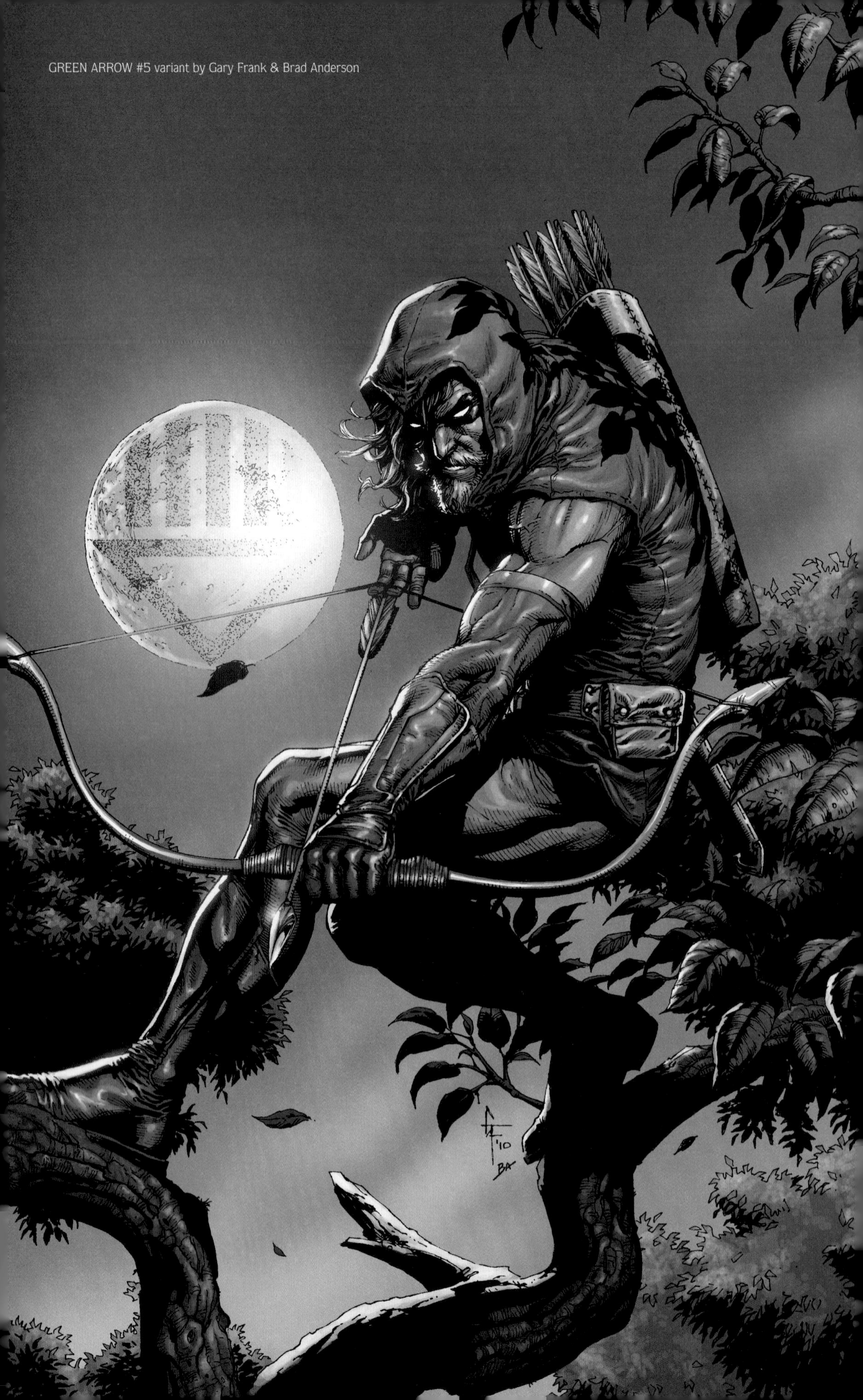

GREEN ARROW #6 variant by Alex Garner

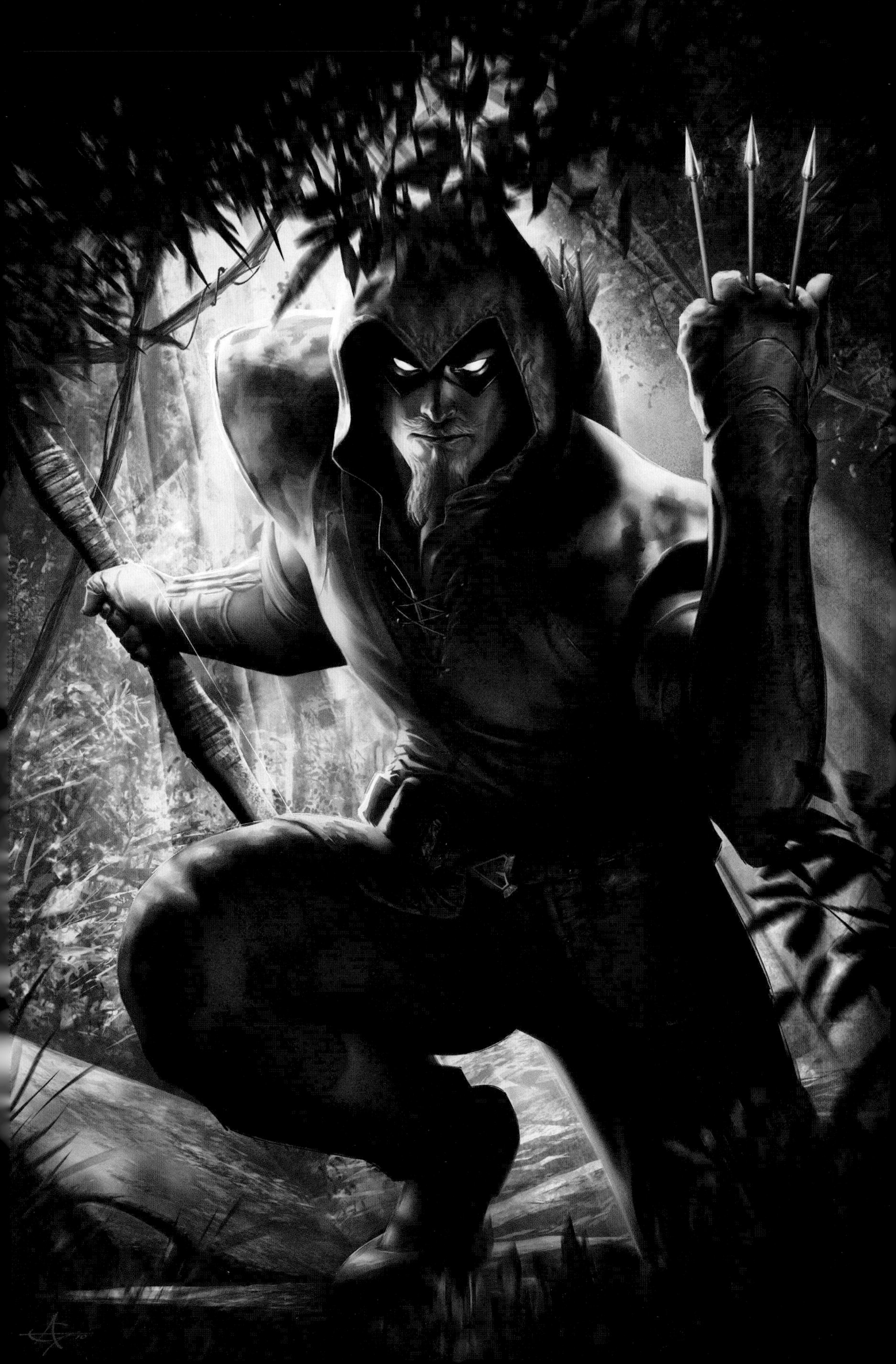

GREEN ARROW #7 variant by Gene Ha

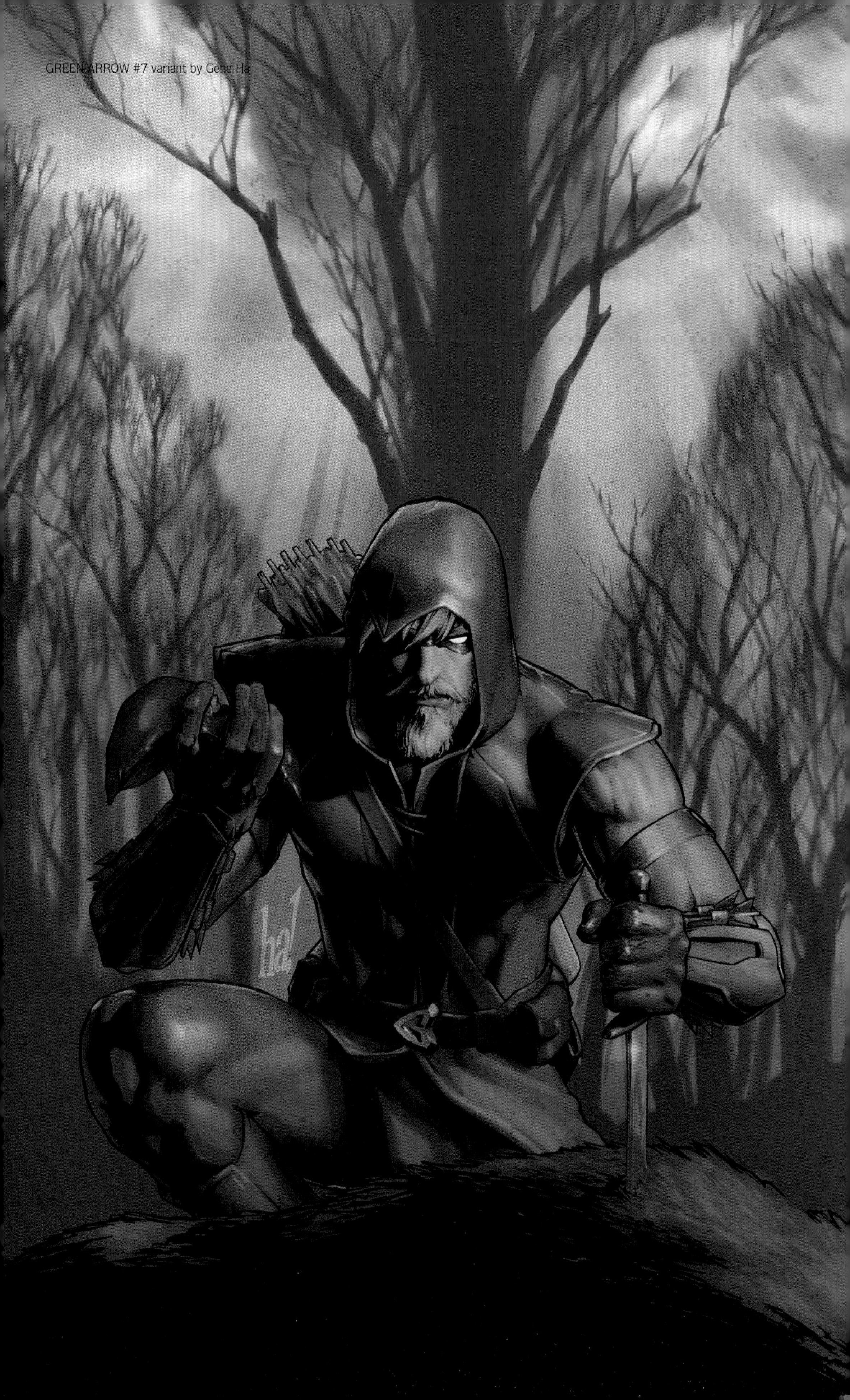

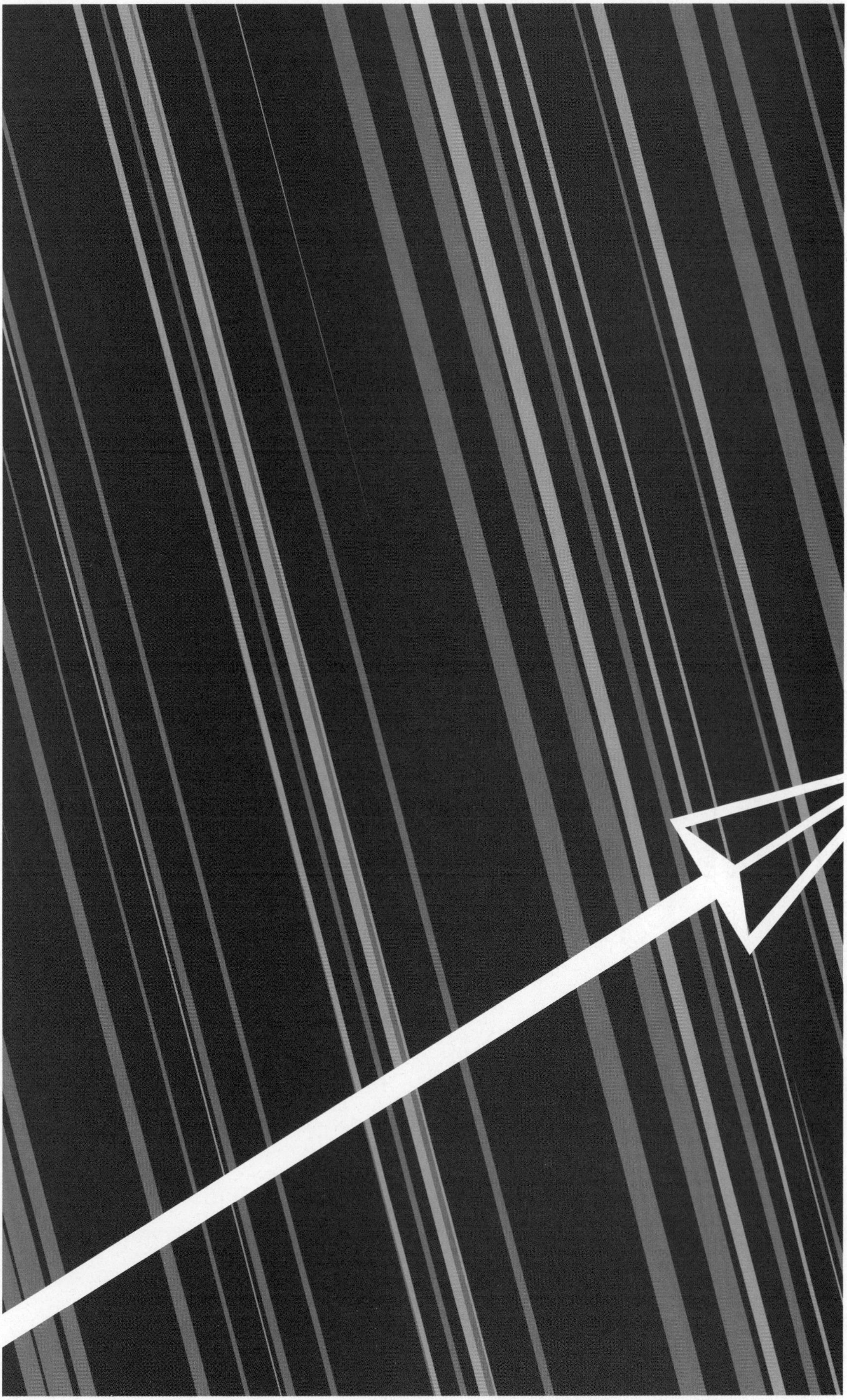

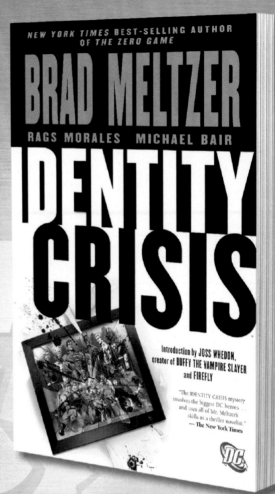

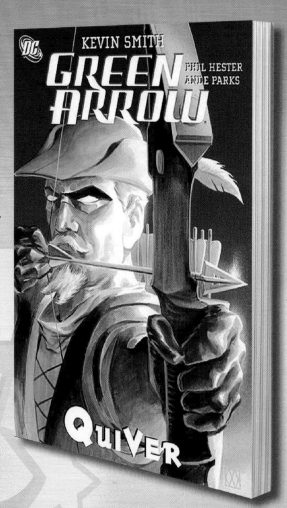